DISPUTED MESSIAHS

DISPUTED MESSIAHS

JEWISH AND CHRISTIAN MESSIANISM IN THE ASHKENAZIC WORLD DURING THE REFORMATION

Rebekka Voß

TRANSLATED BY JOHN CRUTCHFIELD

Wayne State University Press

Detroit

ISBN 978-0-8143-4861-1 (paperback)
ISBN 978-0-8143-4164-3 (hardcover)
ISBN 978-0-8143-4165-0 (e-book)

Library of Congress Control Number: 2021938616

On cover: *The Jews' Entrance with Their Messiah*, undated colored reproduction from Dietrich Schwab, *Jüdischer Deckmantel* (Mainz, 1619). Historical Museum, Frankfurt am Main, C 10154. Cover design by Michel Vrana.

Wayne State University Press rests on Waawiyaataanong, also referred to as Detroit, the ancestral and contemporary homeland of the Three Fires Confederacy. These sovereign lands were granted by the Ojibwe, Odawa, Potawatomi, and Wyandot Nations, in 1807, through the Treaty of Detroit. Wayne State University Press affirms Indigenous sovereignty and honors all tribes with a connection to Detroit. With our Native neighbors, the press works to advance educational equity and promote a better future for the earth and all people.

Wayne State University Press
Leonard N. Simons Building
4809 Woodward Avenue
Detroit, Michigan 48201-1309

Visit us online at wsupress.wayne.edu.

TO MY PARENTS AND GRANDPARENTS

CONTENTS

ILLUSTRATIONS

PREFACE TO THE ENGLISH EDITION

The idea for this book originated a long time ago, during an academic residency when I was a graduate student at Columbia University in the Fulbright Foreign Student Program. It was in the context of a two-semester lecture course taught by Yosef Hayim Yerushalmi, of blessed memory, entitled Messianic Movements and Ideas in Jewish History, that I began to explore this fascinating topic. As we examined the sixteenth century and the messianic revival following the expulsion of the Jews from the Iberian Peninsula (1492–97), we learned about Isaac Abravanel and Abraham ha-Levi, about David Re'uveni and Solomon Molkho; but within this illustrious circle of messianic protagonists and their followers, German Jews were hardly represented at all. I decided to investigate this surprising gap.

The study of Ashkenazic messianism during the Reformation became my dissertation project and eventually resulted in the publication of a book in German with the publisher Vandenhoek & Ruprecht in the series Jüdische Religion, Geschichte und Kultur in 2011. I am excited that a revised and updated English edition now makes my research available to a broader audience. In the ten years that have elapsed since the first edition, scholarship on Jewish messianism in the Ashkenazic world during the sixteenth century has remained as scarce as it was at the inception of my project. Besides the updated bibliography, this English translation in particular features a revised introduction that sharpens my original argument of how to rethink messianic expectation among Ashkenazic Jews in Central Europe, northern Italy, and Poland-Lithuania.

Unfortunately, Yerushalmi was unable to witness the book's original publication; nevertheless, the first thanks go to him—for leading me to this theme, for the careful exploratory conversations we had, and above all for his confidence in my scholarly aptitude. In the end, I did not do my doctoral work at Columbia but rather at Heinrich Heine University in Düsseldorf (Germany) under the supervision of Stefan Rohrbacher. I would like to express my heartfelt thanks to him as well as to Marion Aptroot, who took on the role of second reader, for their invaluable support. I am especially indebted to Elisheva Carlebach, now at Columbia University, who from the very beginning supported me with her expertise. Her groundbreaking study, *Die messianische Haltung der deutschen Juden* (2001), closes with the expectation that "a fresh consideration of these source materials" will produce "a new profile of the Ashkenazic messianic attitude." I have endeavored to begin where she left off; and I thank her for this indispensable foundation and for her critical acumen. The English edition would not have come to fruition without the encouragement of Matt Goldish, who suggested I turn to Wayne State University Press. I wish to thank the anonymous readers for the press for their insightful comments that have further strengthened my manuscript.

For stimulating discussions on various aspects of the project, I would also like to thank Jeremy Dauber, Yaacov Deutsch, Micha Perry, Lucia Raspe, Ursula Reuter, David Ruderman, Anselm Schubert, Wolfgang Treue, and Israel Yuval. For many other useful references and suggestions, thanks go to (among others) Moti Benmelech, Dagmar Börner-Klein, Stephen Burnett, Abraham David, Jonah Fraenkel, Yacov Guggenheim, Elisabeth Hollender, Iris Idelson-Shein, Maoz Kahana, Birgit Klein, Stefan Lang, Tamar Lewinsky, Gianfranco Miletto, Rotraud Ries, Elisheva Schönfeld, Renata Segre, Bernard Septimus, Erika Timm, and Sara Zfatman, as well as to the participants in conferences, symposia, and seminars where I have presented my theses. Furthermore, I would like to thank the staff at the libraries and archives where I have conducted my research.

Various scholarships and stipends made it possible for me to focus for several years exclusively on doing research for my dissertation and on consulting source materials in Israel, the United States, and Europe. Without the financial support of the Studienstiftung des deutschen Volkes, the Gerda Henkel Foundation, and the Rothschild Foundation Europe, this book could not have been written. A Harry Starr Fellowship in Judaica at Harvard University in 2008–9 provided me the necessary time, in scenic Cambridge, to begin to rework the dissertation into a book. Finally, the present translation into English has been made possible by an ARCHES award from the Federal German Ministry for Education and Research (BMBF), administered by the Minerva Foundation.

It was a pleasure to work with John Crutchfield, who completed the translation from German into English. The book's production was capably supervised initially by Kathy Wildfong and then by Annie Martin and their team at Wayne State University Press. I wish to thank my student assistants Mellanie Plewa and Alena Rabenau for their help in the technical preparation of the manuscript. Any remaining errors or inaccuracies in the book are, of course, my own. Throughout this project from dissertation to translated English book, many others, above all my husband, Robert, and my parents, as well as other family, friends, and colleagues, who cannot all be named here, supported me in different ways—and distracted me from it, which was at least as important for shaping this book into what it is.

Frankfurt am Main
January 2021

TRANSCRIPTION RULES AND
OTHER CONVENTIONS

The transcription of Hebrew and Yiddish follows the general principles laid out in the *Encyclopaedia Judaica*, vol. 1 (2nd ed., 2007), 197–98. Technical terms and proper names in Hebrew are generally simplified and rendered in the current English form, while Israeli authors are given in the forms in parallel titles or in foreign language publications. Whenever possible, Hebrew and Yiddish titles are given according to their parallel titles, otherwise in transcription as outlined above.

Biblical quotations in English translation follow the *JPS Hebrew-English Tanakh*. For the New Testament, the *King James Version* is used. Biblical sources are abbreviated in accordance with the *Chicago Manual of Style*; rabbinical literature, in accordance with the *Encyclopaedia Judaica* (177–96). Additional abbreviations are found in the abbreviations list.

INTRODUCTION

Early modern Europe, with its revolutionary events and dramatic political, social, religious, and cultural upheavals, offered fertile ground for apocalyptic expectations. The Reformation, the wars against the Ottoman Turks, European geographical expansion, the anni mirabiles of astrological significance and natural catastrophes—all these were seen as omens of the imminent cataclysm. The doctrine of the Last Days and its contemporary interpretations experienced a surge in popular interest. Classical works in the apocalyptic traditions were copied, commented on, and printed, while new prophetic texts became international bestsellers. Apocalyptic prophets and messianic pretenders enjoyed an eager audience for their message—at once frightful and hopeful—of the approaching end of the world.

Jews and Christians often interpreted these historical events and celestial wonders in similar ways. What is more, each group ascribed to the other a cosmic role in their respective apocalyptic scenarios, the key moment of which was the coming of a redeemer: at last the Messiah would overcome the powers of evil that had for so long oppressed the righteous. Having defeated the Antichrist or Armilus and put an end to the horrors of the eschatological wars of Gog and Magog, the Messiah would finally usher in a golden age on earth, an age of peace and prosperity, of justice and joy. After this cataclysmic final act of history, the order of things would be completely renewed in an unimaginable and sublime reality, such as no human eye had ever beheld. The Last Judgment, presiding over both the living and the resurrected dead, would determine who would be allowed to enjoy this future world, the new Heaven and the new Earth.[1]

For Christianity, presuming as it does the Second Coming of the Messiah, Jesus of Nazareth, the Son of God, this particular atmosphere of the early modern period found its strongest expression in Reformation Germany.[2] Martin Luther's reform activity and the Lutheranism of his followers can hardly be separated from the apocalyptic perspective, in which the pope appeared as the Antichrist and the corrupt Roman Catholic Church as his satanic work.[3] To be sure, the official doctrine across confessional lines denied the literal fulfillment of the chiliastic scriptural prophecy regarding the thousand-year reign of Jesus Christ *in persona*, understanding the millennium instead as a spiritual kingdom that had already begun with his resurrection;[4] nevertheless, the millennial expectation of an earthly kingdom of God continued to flourish, especially in the radical wing of the Reformation. Spectacular indeed was the revolutionary impetus of groups like the Anabaptists, who in 1534 in Münster (Westphalia) established a short-lived kingdom of Zion.[5]

While Christians, in fear and trembling before the Day of the Lord, expected the parousia, or Second Coming, at the latest by the time of the Last Judgment, Jews in Europe longed no less ardently for the arrival of their own Messiah, whom they expected to be a monarch of the line of the biblical King David who would reestablish an independent kingdom of Israel in the messianic age. He was to rebuild the temple and summon exiled Jews from around the world to the land of their ancestors.[6] Two of the largest Jewish messianic phenomena of the early modern period occurred during the time of the Protestant Reformation, episodes of furor that were hardly less intense and widespread than the movement surrounding the self-proclaimed Messiah Shabtai Zvi in the following century. Around the turn of the fifteenth century, the apocalyptic prophet Asher Lemlein and shortly after him the scintillating figures of David Re'uveni and Solomon Molkho held large swaths of Jewish society under their spell.[7]

Although scholars have long considered Germany to have been the epicenter of Christian apocalyptic-chiliastic thought during the Reformation, Jewish messianism in the Ashkenazic world, that is, the German lands, northern Italy, and Poland-Lithuania, has till now scarcely been investigated.[8] There are scientific as well as historical reasons for this deficit in research: in the nineteenth century, representatives of the emerging academic field of *Wissenschaft des Judentums* (science of Judaism) deliberately marginalized the apocalyptic element. On the one hand, this was a consequence of their essentially rational perspective on Judaism; on the other, it was owing to the desire to write Jewish history apolitically, such that in particular the historical impulse of the eschatological hope for a return to the Land of Israel was downplayed.[9] Wherever this messianic enthusiasm could not be ignored, it was explained with reference to a characteristically disadvantaged situation of the Ashkenazic Jews of Germany and Poland. Historian Heinrich Graetz, for instance, condemns Ashkenazic Jews for having been made "receptive to such spasmodic expectations" by "suffering and cabalistic befuddlement,"[10] while the Spanish and Portuguese Jews are portrayed as being less susceptible.[11] Yet Graetz admits that even they, in the face of the catastrophic nationwide deportations of 1492 and 1496–97 from Spain and Portugal, respectively, might have hoped that it all belonged merely to the birth pangs of the Messiah; but according to Graetz, the Sephardic Jews never would have allowed such longing for the speedy advent of the redeemer to be translated into irrational deeds.[12] As exemplary evidence for his thesis that active messianism was the métier of Ashkenazim alone, Isaak Markus Jost adverted to the "German Rabbi" Asher Lemlein, whom the theoretical deliberations of his Sephardic contemporary Isaac Abravanel on the dawn of the messianic age allegedly so convinced that he called for immediate repentance in active preparation for the end. "Without a doubt" his message found willing ears "only among the Ashkenazim."[13] According to this reading of history, even the mysterious David Re'uveni, who claimed to be a prince of the Ten Lost Tribes of Israel, must in reality have been a Jew of German descent.[14]

The twentieth century interpreted the supposed messianic mentalities of Ashkenazim and Sephardim in exactly the opposite way. In his pioneering study of Jewish mysticism, Gershom Scholem strove to set himself apart from his predecessors and to secure a place in modern Jewish historiography for the mystical element in Judaism. With his investigations into Sabbatianism, which according to Scholem is founded in Lurianic Kabbalah, the scholarly study of messianism finally became respectable. At the same time, the central meaning that Scholem, his students, and other historians of the Jerusalem school (among them Yitzhak Baer, Ben-Zion Dinur, Isaiah Tishby, and Haim Hillel Ben-Sasson) attributed to the expulsion of the Jews from the Iberian Peninsula led, in fact, to a recasting of the alleged lead role in early modern messianism: now it belonged to the Sephardic exiles in Italy, in the Land of Israel, and in the broader Ottoman Empire. The year 1492 was deemed a critical turning point; its trauma was believed to have unleashed a powerful messianic response that culminated in the Lurianic kabbalistic revival in Safed and in messianic agitation throughout the period culminating in Shabtai Zvi.[15] The impact of the Jerusalem school on the Jewish historiography of the early modern period was immense. From this perspective, not only the messianic excitement around Lemlein and Re'uveni was subsumed under a postexilic Sephardic messianism characterized by dispossession. For these Israeli historians, messianism emerging from the Sephardic world dominated every aspect of Jewish culture in the post-1492 period.

The banishment of the Ashkenazim to messianic insignificance was effectively set in stone by Gerson Cohen. Writing in the mainstream historiographic tradition, which had long identified medieval Ashkenaz with rabbinical fundamentalism standing in opposition to the supposedly more open Weltanschauung of the Sephardim, Cohen developed an influential typology to characterize the two most significant Jewish cultural groups according to their respective means of expressing the traditional hope for redemption. Relative to Graetz and Jost, however, he did so using an inverted calculus: according to Cohen, the more quietistic, reserved, and passive messianic stance was that of the Ashkenazim, while Sephardic messianism is better described as having been active, explosive, and revolutionary. Cohen postulates that virtually all instances of messianic activity of the medieval and early modern periods, including all self-proclaimed messiahs and prophets as well as their followers, but also public messianic speculation, are to be categorized as Sephardic. Ironically, Cohen's interpretation also must depend for its proof on the familiar documents, since even Lemlein, the only messianic figure he acknowledges who emerged from the ranks of the Ashkenazim, was in his view "an obscure and short-lived affair, which shows traces of Sephardic influence." The messianic passivity of the one group and the flourishing activism of the other are in Cohen's interpretation distinctive elements of the cultural identity formation of medieval Ashkenaz and Sepharad that remained through later historical periods.[16] To these messianic postures Cohen adds a second, related distinction: while Ashkenazim are quietistic with respect to messianism, they uphold an acute religious sensibility regarding what they call the sanctification of God's name (*kiddush ha-shem*) through dying for religious principles. Cohen juxtaposes this religious attitude against that of the Sephardim, who are philosophically inclined, are more rational, and prefer conversion and marranism (the secret practice of Judaism) in the face of social pressure as a pragmatical compromise prior to the messianic coming.[17] The dialectic between passive messianism and martyrdom, on the one hand, and active messianism and forced conversion, on the other, constitutes the core of Cohen's analysis and posits different expressions of specific orientations of religious belief: the Ashkenazic mindset is characterized by an absolute faith in God's providence and ultimate redemption, while Sephardic rationality is committed to the laws of nature and history, resulting in different kinds of resistance and responses to persecution.

To this day, the thesis has generally been accepted that messianic expectation played no significant role in the history of the Ashkenazic world. External circumstances are added to bolster Cohen's typology of the very nature of Ashkenazic (and Sephardic) religious belief. Thus,

Marc Saperstein, for instance, sees confirmation for Cohen's typology in the findings of the sociologist Stephen Sharot, who investigated the shock the Sephardim experienced as a result of their expulsion, a trauma involving the loss of a social and cultural integration that was, compared to that of Ashkenazic Jews, relatively deep.[18] Shlomo Eidelberg, in turn, sees in the social environment of the German Jews the cause of their ostensible messianic passivity. The precarious existential conditions in the empire forced them to adopt a "particularly realistic sobriety." Given their pragmatic efforts to guarantee the greatest possible political and economic stability for the community, the attempt to accelerate the end would have seemed utterly delusional.[19]

Israel Yuval in particular has extended and further clarified Cohen's position. Essentially his starting point is Cohen's observation that Ashkenazim, instead of rising up in messianic revolt like their Sephardic brethren, channeled their apocalyptic hopes into "commemorative ritual and into visionary phantasy. . . . In other words, far from inciting riot, apocalyptic literature actually tranquilized and served as a release" of emotions.[20] For Yuval, the Sephardic scenario for the end-times emphasized the ultimate turn of the nations of the world to the God of Israel, while Ashkenazic Jews upheld a messianic belief grounded in vengeance. In this concept of vengeful redemption, the focus is on God taking out his anger on the Gentiles as vividly painted in messianic literature at the end of time when Jewish suffering is finally repaid. In this, Yuval combines the Ashkenazic focus on sanctification of God's name in the present with a future Messiah of revenge, arguing that this type of messianic consciousness typifies the medieval Ashkenazic position in contradistinction to the Sephardic one.[21] He attributes the inhibited public expression of messianic expectation in Ashkenaz not least to the very real fear of anti-Jewish reprisals and political persecutions that such longing for a vengeful Messiah could provoke.[22]

Elisheva Carlebach has also recognized the anxiety of Jews in Germany about the stigmatization of their messianic hope by Christians. With a gaze sensitized to the historical context, Carlebach, in contrast to Yuval, strongly criticizes Cohen's messianic typology. From the vantage point of Jewish messianism in the early modern period, she disagrees with the thesis of specific attitudes inherent to Ashkenazic or Sephardic culture over time but argues for expressions of messianic hopes determined by the broader social and religious framework. According to Carlebach, the difference lies in the production and transmission of source materials. By examining contemporary reports on the messianic excitement caused by Lemlein, Re'uveni, and Molkho, she demonstrates how German-Jewish expectations of the end-times are in general reflected only indirectly and in distorted form in the sources, thus easily escaping the historian's notice. The same is true for the appearance of Shabtai Zvi and his divergent reception among Ashkenazim and Sephardim.[23] She finds the reason for the careful self-censorship of Jewish authors in German lands in a specific Christian animus in this region toward the hope for the Jewish Messiah. While Christian texts foregrounded in polemical fashion the failure of one or another Jewish messianic pretender or false prophet and, at the same time, emphasized the danger of Jewish messianism for Christendom, Jewish authors, fearing precisely just such Christian polemics, remained silent on these same events or else preserved the memory of them in veiled form.[24] The scholarly perception of messianic quietism throughout Ashkenaz, according to Carlebach's critique, reflects less an actual paucity of apocalyptic speculation and activity than it does the specific conditions of historical preservation and an eclectic selection of apparently unambiguous documents.[25]

Indeed, the place of Ashkenaz in the history of Jewish messianism has thus far been misunderstood. As will be shown in the present work, on the basis of an investigation of messianic thought and activity among Jews in the Ashkenazic world during the Reformation, an acute messianic expectation and enthusiasm was, in fact, as widespread among Ashkenazic Jews as it was among Sephardim of the same period. As put forth by Carlebach and others, a comparative approach linking Jewish phenomena with contemporary Christian thought enables us to challenge the traditional paradigm of Jewish messianism. Situating Jewish apocalyptic expectation within its larger historical context is a relatively recent trend in research. Although Aaron Aescoly concerned himself with the issue as early as the 1930s and 1940s, the tendency nevertheless was to consider Jewish messianism largely without regard to its political, social, and cultural environment. An essay entitled "Hope against Hope," composed in the late 1970s by David Ruderman, was one of the first and tentative criticisms of the Jerusalem school and its dominant interpretation of messianism by deemphasizing the expulsion of Spain and looking more broadly at the larger Christian context. This preliminary attempt to compare Jewish and Christian messianic expectations in Renaissance Italy reveals their entanglements with each other.[26]

A few years later, Moshe Idel began to challenge the primacy of the messianic pattern of the Jerusalem school more forcefully. In a critical dispute with Scholem he especially contradicted the alleged messianism of post-expulsion Safed. In his efforts to qualify the Sephardic community's significance for messianic yearning in the early modern period, Idel draws his conclusions from the case of Lemlein among others. The first messianic prophet after the expulsion from the Iberian Peninsula was not, he points out, a Sephardic Jew but an Ashkenazi, one who found popular reception above all in Central Europe and northern Italy rather than in other areas where the majority of the Iberian exiles had sought asylum.[27] Moreover, Idel's work on Jewish mysticism questions the notion that Jewish messianism was primarily earthly while the Christian one was primarily spiritual by showing that their perspectives were not always so different.[28]

Since the late 1980s, the question of contact with the eschatological traditions of other religious communities has shifted into the foreground. Scholars in various disciplines have shown that Jewish and Christian apocalyptic speculation and activity in the early modern period— an epoch of intense sociocultural contact between Jews and Christians in Europe—cannot be considered separately.[29] Although Jewish and Christian expectations for the end-times were, in principle, mutually exclusive, the hopes that Jews and Christians placed in the eschatological future often corresponded with each other rather precisely due to their common biblical foundation. The promises, fears, and imaginings were, of course, fundamentally self-contained and parallel; yet one can observe a reciprocal cultural transfer.[30] Jews and Christians perceived in the longings of the respective other a confirmation of their own expectations, and they often compared notes. The prophesies and ideas of the other were adopted, adapted, and integrated into one's own conception of the end.[31] There were even attempts aimed at hastening the end through combined effort.[32] In a word, what emerges here is a dense interweaving of a kind that has also been demonstrated with regard to all areas of life and time periods in the history of Jewish-Christian relations, during which certain central elements of Judaism and Christianity have always dialogically informed each other.[33]

The present study of Jewish and Christian messianism takes its place among more recent research that establishes a close, dynamic interaction between Jews and Christians in the Middle Ages and the early modern period, an interaction that involved mundane association as well as religion and ritual.[34] In terms of methodology, this study is framed according to the concept of *histoire croisée* ("entangled history"), which goes beyond comparison and the analysis of an often one-directional cultural transfer from majority to minority to focus on the interaction of distinct cultures, societies, and traditions and to elucidate their mutual influence, processes of reception, and cultural exchange from multiple perspectives. It is therefore an approach well suited to the multilayered interpenetration of end-time visions of the two religious groups.[35] We will see that in sixteenth-century Ashkenaz, Jews and Christians reacted in complex ways to each other's messianic claims, eschatological assumptions, and apocalyptic interpretations. For this reason, an integrative consideration of both sides is essential for a nuanced understanding of Jewish and Christian messianism during the era of the Reformation.

Elisheva Carlebach has highlighted that the meaning of Jewish messianic hope was distinct for Christian- and Muslim-dominant societies. For the Islamic rulers, Jewish messianism—with its potential for sedition and social unrest—was indicative primarily of political insubordination. In Christian Europe, by contrast, this perspective was supplemented by a religious component. That the Jews longed for a redeemer other than Jesus was simple blasphemy, an unacceptable affront to the basic tenets of Christian belief and life. Jewish messianism was thus fundamentally incompatible with the Christian social order. Corresponding to the different reactions and pressures of the respective majority cultures, Carlebach argues, the manner in which Jews expressed their messianic longing differed as well.[36] To understand (or, rather, to refute) the apparent dichotomy of acute apocalyptic expectation and messianic activity between Ashkenazim and Sephardim, we must consider the conditions of Jewish life in the different cultural zones. Many of the Spanish and Portuguese refugees eventually settled in the Ottoman Empire under Muslim rule, whereas the Jews in Europe continued to live in a mainly Christian context.

Admittedly, differences also existed between individual Muslim and Christian countries themselves. That is to say, the experience of Ashkenazim in Italy was not the same as that in Central or Eastern Europe. The special role of Italy as a center of apocalyptic speculation has already been noted. Here, Jews of various cultural backgrounds—Ashkenazic, Sephardic, and Italian—met, and their apocalyptic traditions naturally converged.[37] The enhanced geographic mobility, which is a signature of the early modern period in Jewish history, accelerated the social mixing not only in Italy but also in Poland-Lithuania and other parts of Europe, as well as in the Ottoman Empire. Jews were on the move, due to forced mass migrations and economic hardship, as well as the voluntary wanderings of individuals in their quest to improve their economic and social standing. Besides the unprecedented intensity of physical meeting between Jews from different regions and also with non-Jews, any investigation into early modern messianism must consider the effects of the printing revolution that further propelled the movement of ideas on an international book market across geographical, cultural, and linguistic borders. The messianic experiences among Sephardim and Ashkenazim as well as other Jewish groups in Germany, Italy, and the Ottoman Empire were therefore deeply linked and cannot be neatly regionalized. It is impossible to study Lemlein and certainly Re'uveni and Molkho, who traveled widely between Iberia, the Land of Israel, Italy, and Germany, in an exclusively Ashkenazic or Sephardic orbit. They are obvious examples of how porous the cultural boundaries were with respect to messianism, especially in an age of enhanced mobility, social mixing, and print.[38]

In fact, the messianic excitement that Asher Lemlein caused in the Ashkenazic world was a relative novum in the pre-Reformation and Reformation periods of the sixteenth century. The Lemlein phenomenon is not typical of what preceded the expression of messianic hope in Ashkenaz; rather, it interacted significantly with Jews from other regions, as well as Christians, as we will see. Lemlein's intellectual background, for example, had "Italianized" to some extent. While Cohen acknowledged that Lemlein was an exception to his typology, Carlebach's arguments indeed apply to messianic activity in the sixteenth century and less to the Middle Ages. I argue that to some extent the Cohen/Yuval interpretation of Ashkenazic messianism with its vengeful projections into the messianic future is still relevant in the sixteenth century, but, with an increased mobility of people and ideas, the regional distinctions were more blurred in relation both to the medieval past and to other Jewish communities in the present. At the same time, we see a greater interaction with Christian apocalyptic notions and events. Messianism in the Ashkenazic world in the sixteenth century was both a continuation and a break from the past: a continued adherence to the principle of careful expressions, as foregrounded by Carlebach and Yuval, links sixteenth-century messianism in Ashkenaz to what preceded it, while the disruptions of this era fueled messianic activity among Ashkenazic Jews and are to be seen as discontinuous with the past.

Despite the connected histories of the different epicenters of early modern messianic excitement, each had distinct features accounting for their specific regional frameworks. Within Christian culture in Germany, an especially hostile attitude toward Jewish messianism had been developing since the Middle Ages (chapter 1). Here the Jews were vituperated for their blindness to the Christian truth of the Messiah, having been first deceived through erroneous scriptural exegesis by their own rabbis and by the seductive artifices of false Messiahs. They were accused, furthermore, of combining the expectation of the Messiah's arrival with the long-awaited revenge upon their Christian oppressors. During the Reformation, this view appears to have been adopted generally, regardless of confession. We also witness significant changes in the Christian perception of Jewish messianism during this era, however. Above all, polemical ethnographies about contemporary Jewish beliefs and practices, printed in the German vernacular, reached an ever-wider audience, broadening the public discourse about the alleged danger of Jews to Christian society in messianic matters. While awareness of this negative Christian view naturally continued into the early modern period among German Jews, to some extent, this sensibility surfaced in the Ashkenazic diasporas of Eastern Europe and northern Italy.

The development of Jewish messianism in premodern Ashkenaz can thus only be understood within the context of the dominant Christian society as laid out by Carlebach and Yuval. Because Christians' perception of Jewish messianic hope was fed on the anti-Jewish conceptions inherent in their own eschatology,[39] an investigation of Jewish messianic hope in the Ashkenazic world in the sixteenth century must give particular consideration to contemporary Christian messianism. Herein lies the key to Jewish messianic thinking and behavior at that time—a sphere that had to be kept hidden at all costs from the polemical quills of Christian observers. The critical consideration of Christian apocalypticism—in its chiliastic, reformatory, and Catholic variations—is of great pertinence because, in the dispute with its Jewish counterpart, it reveals the covert vitality of Ashkenazic messianism. The Reformation takes on a central role, since, on the one hand, Jewish-Christian discourse on the Messiah question and the intrareligious conflicts among adversarial Christian confessions overlapped and, on the other, due to the collapse of unity in Christendom, Jewish messianism found itself with different interlocutors and new points of interaction.[40]

An instructive example is the important though to date scarcely researched messianic excitement around Asher Lemlein, which receives for the first time in the present study a comprehensive examination (chapter 2). Jewish and Christian views of Lemlein's call for penance and its representation in the interplay of polemics and apology clearly suggest that eschatological competition more often than not stood in the way of the unhindered expression of Jewish messianic hopes. As I show in chapter 3, each community's eschatology and the necessary preparations for the expected end of the world were adapted to the corresponding hopes and fears of the other, with the result that Jewish and Christian messianism cross-fertilized each other to a remarkable extent. Here I lay out five interrelated case studies that foreground the dynamic contact between Jewish and Christian end-time expectations in the 1520s and 1530s and in various confessional permutations. Jewish expectations that altered Christian apocalyptic concepts, Christian prophecies that influenced Jewish prophets, and popular legends that emerged from interreligious discourse furnish evidence not only of an astonishing exchange of ideas but also of the far-reaching political implications of this encounter between conceptual worlds. Bringing these perspectives together, the epilogue concludes by considering the apparent paradox that repeatedly characterized the relationship between Jewish and Christian messianism: their simultaneous mutual rejection and enrichment.

Insight into the complex, interwoven relationship of Jewish and Christian apocalyptic ideology and politics is furnished by a body of source materials that is still largely unexplored. Few of the sources used here appear at first glance to be messianic. In addition to Hebrew and Yiddish texts, materials of Christian provenance are of particular value, since, due to the specific religious and social context, they not only speak to the Christian side of the discourse but also shed light on Jewish messianic hope. To be sure, these Christian accounts are conventionally hostile and tendentious; nevertheless, beneath a thick veneer of polemic-theological stylization and anti-Jewish commonplaces, they register actual Jewish expectations and betray precisely what Jewish sources, under pressure of self-censorship, typically leave unexpressed—or else seek to minimalize and obscure beyond recognition.

The dispersed and often accidental manner of textual preservation has resulted in a body of sources that is rather diverse, comprising various genres, forms of transmission, and languages. Bits and pieces of information are to be found in familiar Hebrew chronicles by the great Jewish historiographers of the sixteenth century—in Joseph ha-Kohen's *Emek ha-bakhah* (Vale of Tears), in Gedalya ibn Yaḥya's *Shalshelet ha-kabbalah* (Chain of Tradition), and in *Zemaḥ David* (The Scion of David) by David Gans—but they are also found in German pamphlets in which anonymous authors enlighten the public on the appearance of the Ten Lost Tribes of Israel. Correspondence between individuals and diplomats in Damascus and Venice, in Cracow and Frankfurt am Main, contains data of no less value than polemical writings, missionary treatises, and ethnographies of the kind that Victor von Carben, Johannes Pfefferkorn, Antonius Margaritha, and after them Christian Hebraists had been producing on the beliefs and practices of contemporary Jews since the beginning of the sixteenth century. Jewish messianism was even a topic of discussion in the court case against the Augsburg Anabaptist Augustin Bader, which caused a furor throughout the empire in early 1530, as documented in remarkable fashion by the eyewitness accounts that have come down to us. The conversation between Jews and Christians regarding the end of the world was also pursued in ethical literature, in learned commentaries on Scripture, and in vernacular folk legends, and it found expression in visual representations and other realia preserved in museums, archives, and libraries from Prague to Paris.

The aim of the present book is to paint a new picture of Jewish messianic hope in the Ashkenazic world during the Reformation, a portrait that coalesces into a variegated mosaic of the apocalyptic images, ideas, and visions of different communities, their religious and political motives, and, finally, their concrete behavior during a time that was perceived as being the end. Jews, Catholics, Lutherans, and Anabaptists were all involved, across regional, religious, and confessional borders and regardless of social class, age, and gender. Among them were many notable personalities in sixteenth-century politics and society such as Martin Luther, Wolfgang Capito, and Josel of Rosheim, while many others remain anonymous. Priests and rabbis, scholars, political rulers, and other leading figures joined the conversation on the eschatological scenario—in its elaboration, rationalization, and realization—just as much as ordinary folk, peasants, craftspeople, and merchants, did.

1

CHRISTIAN PERCEPTIONS OF JEWISH MESSIANIC HOPE

This imbrication of the religious and the social, of theological and political reflection—which seems so inaccessible to the modern consciousness—characterizes the most general structure of self-understanding.

—Richard van Dülmen, *Reformation as Revolution*, 1977

The Messiah question has been a point of contention between Jews and Christians since the origins of Christianity. The question was not whether the Christians would find their savior earlier or the Jews theirs later or which individuals would play the role of hope bearer. The Jewish concept and the Christian concept of salvation both make an absolute claim that fundamentally excludes any alternative eschatological identity. Just as the Christian recognition of Jesus's messiahship declares all of post-Christian Judaism to be a fossil, the Jewish expectation of a future fulfillment of messianic hope casts a shadow over the very basis of Christianity.

For Christians, the messianic error of the Jews was quite obvious. The refusal to see that the Messiah had already appeared and that, as a consequence, all expectation of another Messiah was futile—this merely proved the Jews' blindness and obduracy. During the Middle Ages, the refutation of this absurd Jewish messianic hope and the demonstration of the truth of the Christian story of salvation were significant theological themes.[1] Especially in Germany, the vernacular polemic against Jewish conceptions of the Messiah exhibited a remarkable dynamism and complexity, undergoing numerous variations that in other European national languages appeared either not at all or in forms that were less explicitly anti-Jewish.[2] Thus, for example, it is only in German sources that the Ten Lost Tribes of Israel, whose return the Jews expected in the end-times, are identified with the so-called Red Jews. The latter were considered to be in reality the servants of the Antichrist, the demonic figure who was to afflict Christendom prior to the Last Judgment. Starting in the late thirteenth century, the legend concerning the Red Jews was transmitted via both religious and literary texts, and it made up an essential element of Christian apocalypticism in Germany.[3] In fact, the Christian perception of Jewish messianism had its mirror image in the Christians' own apocalyptic tradition. This two-sidedness is expressed most clearly in the identification of the Jewish Messiah with the Antichrist, the final adversary of Christ.

The characteristic role of the Jews in the eschatological drama was deeply anchored in popular thinking in the German-speaking lands, due to various medieval folk traditions and to reinforcement by pictorial representations, such as the monumental Antichrist window in St. Mary's Church in Frankfurt an der Oder.[4] Dating from the second half of the fourteenth century, this magnificent stained glass represents the biography of the Jewish Antichrist, and it offers even illiterate viewers an unmistakable portrayal of the Red Jews (fig. 1): on the other side of the river, wild men (marked as Jews by their pointed hats) wait for the Antichrist to fetch them, so that they may begin his work of destruction.[5] Arguably the most effective means of propaganda in the late Middle Ages were public theatrical performances, whose anti-Jewish tendencies also came into play in the representation of apocalyptic fears.[6]

Figure 1. *The Red Jews Waiting beyond the Sambatyon River,* panel in the Antichrist window at St. Mary's Church, Frankfurt an der Oder, ca. 1370. (Brandenburg State Office for the Preservation of Monuments and the State Archaeological Museum, Zossen, photo archives, no. s II 4b, photo: Peter Thieme and Florian Profitlich, 2006)

The themes and motifs of the Middle Ages continued uninterrupted and remained efficacious well into the sixteenth century, and they were often communicated by the same media.[7] Thus the genre of the religious play retained its attraction and its great influence as disseminator of negative stereotypes of Jews.[8] But the sixteenth century also brought changes. Not least of these was the invention of letterpress printing, which revolutionized the media landscape. Printed texts reached an ever-broader audience, and pamphlets in particular enjoyed widening circles of readership.[9] In the first place, they were largely composed in the vernacular. Second, they contained new forms of illustration, such that the message of a text was now often rendered more emphatic through the effective combination with images. This bold and innovative picture language made it possible for the uneducated masses to take part in public discourse.[10]

But above all, Christians of the sixteenth century perceived Jews from a new angle. Instead of a criticism concerned with relevant biblical texts and with the abstract discussion and rebuttal of the doctrines of Jewish belief, a criticism of contemporary Jewish religious and social practices stepped into the foreground.[11] The study of Judaism was now joined by the study of the Jews themselves and of their actual behavior. This change in perspective is closely associated with a new literary genre that arose in Germany in the sixteenth century: the polemical ethnography of Jews and Judaism.[12] These texts claimed to offer a realistic description of the contemporary life, customs, and religion of the Jews. In the first decade of the sixteenth century, the converts Johannes Pfefferkorn and Victor von Carben sought to provide their Christian readers with a detailed picture of contemporary religious practices among their former fellow believers.[13] The subtitle of Pfefferkorn's *Der Juden veindt* (The Jews' Enemy, Augsburg, 1509) announces, "I will not be ashamed to tell of their roguishness that was a long time hid, but will now reveal it to all Christian people, for I am fully versed in their Hebrew scriptures, and will not spare their perverse kind from the truth."[14] In 1530, with his *Der gantz Jüdisch glaub* (The Entire Jewish Faith), Antonius Margaritha offered the first systematic representation of Judaism and of Jewish life, and the book became a model for an entire wave of ethnographies.[15] These writings, almost all composed in the vernacular, were immensely popular in the German-speaking lands, and they fundamentally shaped Christian perceptions of Jews in the early modern period.[16] Information about the Jews and their religion was now no longer based, as in the Middle Ages, on literary stereotypes but instead on first-hand knowledge, however tinted.[17]

DECEIVED DECEIVERS

It was a Christian commonplace that the Jews were deceived in their messianic hopes. During the late Middle Ages, this messianic self-deception became the focus of Christian polemics, since the misery of Jewish existence could be shown there in an exemplary way. Not only the destruction by the Romans of the Second Temple, and the loss of all political power, but also in particular the seemingly endless exile were considered primary evidence that God had cast off his erstwhile chosen people for having failed to recognize Jesus as the long-awaited savior. It seemed obvious that Judaism had been overtaken by Christianity and that the Christians had supplanted the Jews as the chosen people of Israel.[18]

A historical confirmation of this topos was to be found in the recurring appearances of false Jewish Messiahs, something Christian polemicists in Germany increasingly tried to make use of in the early modern period.[19] The Jesuit preacher Georg Scherer interpreted failed messianic movements as divine punishment: "Because they want neither to recognize nor to acknowledge the right and true Messiah, the righteous God hath passed the judgment upon them that they shall be oft and ignominiously deceived by their own false Messiahs and seducers and miserably defrauded of life and limb."[20] As the convert and rector of the University of Vienna, Paul Weidner, preached to his former community of believers in 1561 in Prague, it was widely known that they had always willingly followed "false fictitious Messiahs" (falsche erdichte Messie). In the end, according to Weidner, these supposed saviors all either went mad or died in disgrace. And not one of them arose like Jesus from the dead! The price "if ye wish to have more than one Messiah" is the scorn that the Jews must bear as a consequence. Yet "happy the man who grows clever from other people's disgrace" and who learns from the experiences of deceived predecessors. For he shall realize that the true Messiah must be more "than an impudent human being" (dann nur ein vurlauter Mensch).[21]

After the middle of the sixteenth century, converts and Christian ethnographers began composing lists of false Messiahs, the purpose of which can easily be guessed from the titles, such as *Das ist: Gründliche Außführunge vnd Kräfftige Beweißthume* [...] *daß Jesus Christus* [...] *der rechte versprochene Messias* [...] *sey* (This Is: Complete Demonstration and Irrefutable Evidence [...] That Jesus Christ [...] Is [...] the Rightful and Promised Messiah).[22] The first of these enumerations seems to have been compiled by the aforementioned Paul Weidner.[23] With the turn of the seventeenth century, such lists appeared on the market in ever greater numbers. The polemical and missionary interest in Jewish messianic figures continued to increase especially with the appearance of Shabtai Zvi and a renewed wave of Jewish-Christian expectation of the end-times.[24] It is remarkable how quickly news of the supposed Jewish Messiah, following his appearance in 1665, reached Christian circles and found its way into print. One convert recalls "all manner of oral and written newspapers ... that were gradually found to be utterly false, invented, and untruthful, and our joy therein, engendered in all too great a gullibility, was lost, yea was transformed into general scorn."[25]

The tabulation found in *Der Jüden Thalmud* (The Jews' Talmud, Goslar, 1607) enjoyed seven reprints and appears to have served as an authoritative source for many subsequent writers. Here, the convert Christian Gerson of Recklinghausen numbers the messianic "deceivers" up to and including Asher Lemlein and David Re'uveni.[26] Moreover, to lend these lists an aura of authenticity, Jewish sources are routinely quoted, above all the chronicles *Zemah David* (Prague, 1592) by David Gans and *Shalshelet ha-kabbalah* (Venice, 1587) by Gedalya ibn Yahya.[27] Johann von Lent perfected this procedure in his massive historical-philological survey of the false Messiahs of the Jews, *Schediasma historico-philologicum de Judaeorum Pseudomessiis* (Herborn, 1683), which remained the standard work on the topic into the eighteenth century. The book devotes a hundred pages exclusively to the discussion of false Jewish Messiahs: nineteen persons in total, from Bar Kokhba to Mordechai of Eisenstadt. Roughly half of the text is concerned with what we call the early modern period.[28] Von Lent bases his portrayal on Jewish and Christian sources as well as on the testimony of converts, whose words he quotes, translates, and supplements with his own introduction and commentary.[29]

According to Christian understanding, Jewish messianism led to disillusionment in a double sense. The repeated failure of Jewish messianic hopes ought to open the eyes of the deceived, so that they might finally acknowledge Jesus as the Messiah. In this way, Jewish messianic hopes, though false in their objects, would in the end reveal the way of true salvation: "This new Messiah-Jew-Cry is harmful to the Jews yet for some useful in the end . . . which with all our hearts we Christians too would wish the Jews."[30] And, indeed, converts repeatedly cited disappointed messianic expectations as the most important motivation for their conversion to Christianity.[31] The notion that Judaism would capitulate to Christian salvation and thereby find its messianic culmination in Christianity rests on the traditional Christian eschatology expressed in Paul's Letter to the Romans: the Jews would be converted in the end-times.[32]

The perception of Jewish messianism in Germany was influenced by another aspect of Christian eschatology as well: the Jewish Antichrist. Beginning already in antiquity, Christian theologians had identified the Antichrist with the Jewish Messiah. In other words, they saw in the Antichrist the figure whom the Jews expected as their Messiah. Ultimately, the Jewish Messiah personified the denial of the messiahship of Jesus; he was, in the language of the times, the "Widerchrist" (adversary to Christ) par excellence.[33] It was feared that the Jews would accept the Antichrist as their long-awaited Messiah and become his first and most loyal adherents, servants, and accomplices. Since the late fifteenth century, this fear converged with the discourse on the Jewish deceiver and his beguilement of Christians. The motif of the Jewish deceiver played an increasingly prominent role in the Christian perception of Jews and Judaism in the early modern period and also left its mark on eschatology: the deceived Jews themselves were recast as the deceivers. Not only had the Pseudo-Messiah/Antichrist become master of apocalyptic pretense, but this role was now transferred to the entire Jewish people. The error of the Jews regarding the identity of the Messiah was no longer considered to be an innocent mistake that worked only to their own detriment. On the contrary, Jewish messianism as such was now seen as a great, malicious conspiracy against Christians, since the Jews apparently expected none other than the loathsome Antichrist himself as their savior.[34]

In early modern Germany, this Jewish messianic fraud was a favorite theme of popular literature. We find plentiful stories of Jews who, in their attempt to hoodwink the Christians, end up outsmarting only themselves: the deceived deceivers whom the reader is invited to laugh to scorn.[35] The story of the so-called berry of prophecy, for instance, was familiar in numerous versions throughout the sixteenth century. It appears in both the chapbook about Till Eulenspiegel[36] and a Latin version in Heinrich Bebel's famous *Facetien* (Humor).[37] Hans Folz, one of the best-known German poets of the time, took up the story twice during his career.[38] In this tale, a Christian rolls his excrement into little balls, which he wraps in colorful paper and sells to the Jews as "berries of prophecy." Whoever eats these berries, he claims, will have the power to predict the future. The Jews, hoping to find out when the Messiah is coming, are prepared to pay an exorbitant price for the berries. Only when one of them, after great ceremony and formal preparation, swallows a supposed magic berry do the Jews realize the swindle.[39]

At least equally popular was the topic of the birth of the Jewish Messiah. One story, taken up by Caesarius of Heisterbach in the thirteenth century in his Latin anthology, lost nothing of its appeal over the subsequent five centuries. It concerns a Jewish girl who is impregnated by a Christian. To conceal the affair, the young man, mimicking the voices of angels, whispers at night into the ears of his lover's sleeping parents that God had selected their virginal daughter to bring the Messiah into the world. In reality, the supposed virgin birth is, of course, the result of fornication.[40] The motif of this "maculate conception" is taken from the biography of the Antichrist: according to legend, the parents of the Antichrist are debauched individuals, and in some versions, the mother of the Antichrist is a Jewish whore.[41] In Caesarius's retelling, the news of the birth of the Messiah spreads like wildfire, and the Jews come in droves to greet the savior. But when the baby turns out to be a girl, one of the Jews, out of sheer disappointment, grabs the newborn by the foot and slams it against a wall.[42] The incorrigibility of the Jews and their self-deception in the Messiah question are pursued to their utmost in the droll cycle *Wendunmuth*: here, the rabbis discuss whether the Messiah could not also be born in the body of a woman.[43] In Folz's *Von der Juden Messias* (On the Jews' Messiah), the story ends not only with the disappointment of Jewish messianic hopes but also, simultaneously, with the triumph of Christianity. When the Jews in their rage wish to descend upon the unhappy family, the young Christian lover saves his beloved, she converts to Christianity, and the two marry and live happily for the rest of their lives.[44] The literary representation thus takes up both elements of the Christian apocalyptic tradition that determined the perception of Jewish messianism in Germany: the final conversion as single appropriate response to the messianic fraud and the Antichrist as the true identity of the false Jewish Messiah.

MESSIAH OF VENGEANCE

For Christians, the political nature of Jewish expectation for the Messiah, who would come as an earthly ruler, necessarily made Jewish messianism per se an object of suspicion. Moreover, the identification of the Jewish

Messiah with the Antichrist made Jewish hopes for redemption into a screen onto which the most horrific Christian nightmares could be projected.[45] The anxiety and aggression that were originally directed at the Antichrist and his fearsome reign of terror were now transferred onto the Jewish (Pseudo-)Messiah and, collectively, onto his Jewish adherents. Hans Folz's play *Spil von dem Herzogen von Burgund* (Play about the Duke of Burgundy) illustrates this transference. In this play, a clairvoyant reveals a Jewish conspiracy to Philipp of Burgundy, the son of Emperor Maximilian. The rabbis across the land, she says, are announcing the advent of their Messiah, whose intention is to seize for himself all kingdoms and earthly and spiritual princedoms. As the Messiah appears on the stage, his Jewish attendants turn promptly and impudently upon the presumably Christian audience:

> *Step aside, turn around and depart!*
> *For long enough you've kept for yourselves*
> *Power, authority and force,*
> *All of that is at an end now.*[46]

Now it is the Jews' turn to sit upon the throne.

The author clearly equates Jewish lust for power with the desire to annihilate Christendom. The Messiah, whose true identity as the Antichrist is quickly revealed by the seer, explains his contemporary sobriquet "Endchrist" thus: "That is the simple meaning of it, that I am the end of the Christians."[47] As his own motive for appearing and as the reason why the Jews wait for him with such longing, he proclaims the wish for bloody retribution after centuries of oppression and humiliation under the scepter of the Christians.[48]

For the Protestant reformer Martin Luther, the difference from the Christian concept of salvation lay in the feared eschatological revenge of the Jews. Christians had found the forgiveness of sins and the way to eternal life in Jesus, their nonviolent Messiah. But the Jews, according

to Luther, beseeched God to liberate them by force from Christian bondage. "Through their Messiah, He is to murder and exterminate us heathen,
so that they receive all the Earth's land, goods and power. . . . They wish that
war and the sword, fear and all misfortune would overcome us accursed
gentiles."[49] Here, too, we can recognize the motif of deception, which is
everywhere to be found in Christian discourse about Jews and Judaism:
while the Jews pretended to be loyal underlings, on the inside they harbored an implacable resentment against Christians and Christianity. "They
hate the Christians much more than other nations, however friendly they
may pretend to be toward us, yet it is not from the heart." This is because,
as Johannes Pfefferkorn explains it, "we Christians believe in Jesus Christ
and consider him the true Messiah, which is greatly repellent to them."[50]

The important point is that the horror fantasies of Jewish revenge were
explicitly anchored in Christian representations of Jewish messianism. Significantly, as emblem of the alleged Jewish thirst for blood, the Frankfurt
orientalist Johann Jacob Schudt adduces the prototype of the false Messiah,
Bar Kokhba, known as the messianically minded leader of the Jewish rebellion against Rome in 132–35 CE, a time when the Jews supposedly engaged
in the brutal persecution of Christians. Schudt also mentions in a caution-
ary fashion the other Jewish rebellion against the Romans (115–17 CE)
that had messianic undertones as well: "the Jews in the time of Trajan murdered many thousands of people and ate their flesh, wore their skins, and
girded themselves with the still bleeding entrails."[51]

Although misunderstanding and polemical bias deeply informed the
Christian point of view, the basic fear of retribution by the Jewish Messiah
was not merely a product of Christian delusion. As Israel Yuval has shown,
the horrific experience of persecution under Christian rule had kindled a
real desire, especially among Ashkenazim, to avenge the innocent Jewish
blood that had been spilled. In this sense, the messianic expectation of Ashkenazic Jews did indeed contain within it the physical extinction of their
oppressors. "This [final] Redemption . . . will involve the ruin, destruction,
killing and eradication of all the nations: they, and the angels who watch

over them, and their gods . . . The Holy One blessed be He will destroy all the nations except Israel." Thus, the thirteenth-century *Sefer Nizzaḥon* (Book of the Victory), a collection of polemical arguments for self-assertion against Christendom, portrays the dawn of the messianic age.[52]

The representation of the Christians' downfall is based upon the biblical prophecy of the fall of Edom—according to Jewish tradition a necessary precondition of salvation. In the story of Esau (Edom), who cedes his birthright to his younger brother Jacob (Israel), the text reads: "The older shall serve the younger" (Gen. 25:23). Ever since the final loss of sovereignty through the conquest of Jerusalem and the destruction of the Second Temple by the Romans in the first century CE, this biblical verse had been understood to refer to the messianic future, and "Edom" was reread as Rome. In the end-times, with the advent of the Messiah, God would avenge the sins of Edom against His people. With the Christianization of the Roman Empire, the typology then received a double meaning, one political and one religious: Edom could mean both the political entity of the *Imperium Romanum* and Christendom itself.[53] Thus, the last of the four world empires, which according to the Book of Daniel would precede and eventually give way to the messianic age, was interpreted to mean either Christendom or Rome in the narrower hegemonic sense.[54]

According to the medieval doctrine of *translatio imperii*, the Roman Empire found its continuation in the Holy Roman Empire of the German Nation. This meant that Jews in Germany still lived and suffered directly under the political hegemony of Edom and that "all the hopes and prayers of the Jews are that the scepter of the Christians be removed and come to nothing."[55] The messianic decline of Edom was thus equated in Germany with the end of the Holy Roman Empire. Since Germany was the seat of the empire, German Jews in the sixteenth century apparently expected the Messiah to appear in their midst. Together with the herald Elijah, his warlike precursor Messiah ben Joseph, and the High Priest of the end-times, the Messiah would destroy the last bastion of Edom's power, as foreseen by the biblical prophet Zechariah in his vision of the four blacksmiths and the four horns: "and these men have come to throw them into a panic, to hew down the horns of the nations that raise a horn against the land of Judah, to toss it." According to an interpretation transmitted by Isaac Abravanel, the four horns symbolized the seat of the empire, which had been transferred over the centuries from Rome to Constantinople, then under Charlemagne to France, and finally to the Roman-German Empire.[56] In a parallel tradition based upon the Talmudic legend of the Messiah who sits before the gates of Rome, the Jews of Worms believed the Messiah would be born in that ancient imperial city.[57] According to a Christian source, it was common practice in the city of Worms during the festival of Purim (commemorating the rescue of the Jewish people from imminent danger in the Persian diaspora) to smash dishes; a parallel was drawn thereby to the biblical Book of Esther, in which Haman, adviser to the Persian king, wants to eradicate the Jewish people from his realm: "Just as Haman was shattered and annihilated, so also must the Roman Empire be at once crushed utterly to the ground."[58]

The messianic idea of retribution expressed itself in various ways in Ashkenazic ritual and custom. Thus the *Amidah*, the central prayer of the Jewish liturgy, contains in Pfefferkorn's exegesis the request for "revenge on the entire community of Christian churches, and especially that the Roman Empire be utterly shattered and destroyed."[59] In the canonical version, *Birkat ha-minim*, the "blessing on the heretics," sounds less tendentious: "Let there be no hope for the slanderers, and may all reprobates be destroyed in an instant, may they all be suddenly exterminated, and the defiant be quickly eradicated, shattered, thrown down and humiliated, quickly, in our days. Praise to you, Eternal One, who crushes your enemies and humiliates the defiant!"[60] While it is to be assumed that not every supplicant harbored violent intentions toward Christians, sources like Pfefferkorn demonstrate that liturgy was open to a polemical interpretation and was understood by some Jews to be thoroughly anti-Christian. Haim b. Bezalel of Friedberg, the elder brother of Judah Löw, the Maharal of Prague, may have had something similar in mind when he declared every utterance of "amen" at the end of a prayer to be an expression of the deepest hope "soon to behold your glorious power . . . that atrocities vanish from the Earth."[61]

In a peculiar way, the Passover Feast, which both commemorates the Exodus from Egypt and points toward the future redemption, was associated with the request for apocalyptic retribution. According to Margaritha's testimony, the Haggadah that is read in the family at the seder table execrates the Christians and explicitly beseeches God to visit catastrophe upon their "capitals" (hauptstett) and "their highest regiment and rulers" (jr oberst regiment vnnd regierer).[62] During the Middle Ages, the curse Shefokh ("Pour out your fury on the nations")[63] found its way into the Ashkenazic Haggadah. Its recitation is accompanied by a heavily symbolic gesture: immediately before the curse is uttered, a door is opened in order to admit Elijah, harbinger of the Messiah. Traditionally, in communities in Germany, a member of the family took on the role of the prophet and entered through the open door. Afterward, in the hope that the desired revenge would soon be carried out upon the non-Jews, the fourth and last glass of wine—the glass of salvation—was drunk.[64]

An additional Ashkenazic custom at Passover is described toward the end of the sixteenth century by Jacob Kitzingen of Lithuania in his book on the seder. He considers it a prefiguration of the inverted relations of power in the messianic age: the leader of the seder was dressed in a white kitl (Yid., robe), the garment of the dead, "as is the way of authority and freedom. Thus did our teachers of blessed memory in the Great Sanhedrin explicate the verse, 'let your clothing always be white': R. Yohanan b. Zakkai said, wherever is written 'with white clothing,' that means the white garments that the nations of the world have, etc. From this is to be deduced that the white garments are the way of authority worn by the nations of the world."[65]

The white death garment possibly also functioned as a memorial for the countless Jewish martyrs under Christian oppression and was intended to awaken God's wrath and move Him to his apocalyptic revenge.[66] Pfefferkorn's description of the Last Judgment tends to support such an interpretation: after the resurrection of the dead, Jews and non-Jews will gather together on the Day of the Lord, so that Elijah (!) may pass judgment on them.[67] Thereafter, the Jews will enter the paradise of the world to come, since they have obeyed the laws of the God of Israel. As symbolized by the white clothes they wear, they bear no blemishes. The non-Jews, by contrast, who have transgressed the religious laws, who have not practiced circumcision, and who have made graven images and eaten unclean meat, are damned to eternal torment in Hell. Moreover, Jewish blood stains their hands, since "you have also grievously tormented and persecuted the chosen people of God, and therefore you are not dressed in white garments."[68]

In illuminated Haggadah manuscripts from the German-speaking area in the fifteenth century, the text of the *Shefokh* is illustrated with representations of the Messiah of retribution. Occasionally, he is represented as a warrior or as God's wrath pouring from a vessel in the form of fire or blood over a group of Christians.[69] In numerous illustrations, the Messiah rides upon a donkey, the animal hero of a popular Jewish folk legend about eschatological revenge. As related by Antonius Margaritha, the legend is based upon the typological model of the biblical Exodus from Egypt: the Messiah brings the Jews safely on the back of his mount through the sea into the promised land, while the Christians sit upon the donkey's tail. In the middle of the roaring flood, the donkey drops his tail, so that the Christians fall off and drown, just as the ancient Israelites' Egyptian pursuers were drowned in the Red Sea.[70]

As the ethnographic publications of converts like Margaritha and Pfefferkorn make clear, it was commonly believed among German Christians in the early modern period that Jews saw in the messianic annihilation of the Christians the flip side of their own salvation. *Der Juden Einritt mit jhrem Messia* (The Jews' Entrance with Their Messiah, fig. 2) testifies to Christian familiarity with and distortion of Jewish messianism. The colored etching that reproduces a copper engraving from Dietrich Schwab's *Jüdischer Deckmantel* (The Jewish Disguise, Mainz 1619)[71] portrays a Jew at the head of a procession: he carries the cup of salvation in his hands as he rides upon the

Figure 2. *The Jews' Entrance with Their Messiah*, undated reproduction from Dietrich Schwab, *Jüdischer Deckmantel* (Mainz, 1619). (Historical Museum, Frankfurt am Main, C 10154)

so-called *Judensau* (Jews' sow).[72] He is followed by Elijah blowing a shofar (ram's horn) to announce the advent of the redeemer; then comes the Messiah, and after him is the donkey with the Jews seated safely on its back. On its tail sit the condemned Christians. In the upper left of the image, representing the crimes it was feared the Jews would commit against Christians in the end-times, the corpse of a boy is pictured upon the rocks: Simon of Trent, who in 1475 supposedly fell victim to a Jewish ritual murder.[73]

Because of its political dimension, Jewish messianism presented Christian society with a problem that was more than merely theological. It could not simply be derided and dismissed as foolishness. Instead, it was seen rather as a clear and present danger, as a tangible attack upon the divinely ordained world order. The revolutionary tendency of apocalypticism, whether Jewish or Christian, was sufficiently clear to contemporary observers. Every attempt to bring about a messianic age necessarily threatened the reigning social order and contained the potential for social unrest.[74] We can see this in the example of Hans Böhm, a sheepherder and gleeman from Niklashausen in the Franconian Tauber Valley near Würzburg, who toward the end of the fifteenth century announced the dawn of the thousand-year reign of universal equality. In light of Jesus's imminent return, the so-called Piper of Niklashausen preached against both the clergy and the civil authorities. He condemned their greed and profligacy and encouraged his hearers to refuse to pay their taxes and rents. For a short time, he inspired tens of thousands from across southern and central Germany, from the Alps to the Rhine and even from Thuringia, to journey to the Franconian village to hear his subversive teaching.[75] Similarly, one of the leading figures of the Peasant War, the preacher Thomas Müntzer, who was appropriately dubbed the "theologian of the revolution," was also led by millennial expectations.[76] The most famous episode in the history of political chiliasm is certainly the Münster Rebellion of 1534–35.[77]

The complicating factor in the case of Jewish messianism was revenge. How was one to view the Jews not as enemies but rather as "citizens" of the Holy Roman Empire when their constant prayer was "that God send them a Messiah who shall come in great power and force and overthrow Christianity"?[78] As early as the High Middle Ages, the Jews were considered the enemies of Christianity precisely on the grounds of their messianic expectations.[79] In the sixteenth century, the ethnographies of converts provided detailed firsthand exposures of Jewish messianic revenge fantasies. This information was highly effective in shaping public opinion. Victor von Carben, Johannes Pfefferkorn, Antonius Margaritha, and many others emphasized the idea that Jewish hate for Christians was concentrated in the eschatological concept of the annihilation of the Holy Roman Empire and of Christianity itself. By revealing the alleged truth about the empire's Jewish subjects, Margaritha intended to give Christian authorities a basis for a harsher politics regarding the Jews. His explicit advice was to place them under greater social and economic restriction.[80]

Such writings posed a threat to Jewish communities precisely because of the evident proximity to real attitudes and practices among Ashkenazic Jews. Catholics and Protestants alike ascribed special authority to the words of Margaritha, in part because he was known to be the scholarly son of a rabbi. In decisive ways, he inspired Luther's own anti-Jewish agitation, the severity of which exceeded even the demands of the convert himself. Although Luther expressed an awareness of Jewish "blasphemies" as early as 1514, this awareness seems at that point not yet to have exerted an undue influence on his attitude. This can be seen first and foremost in *Daß Jesus Christus ein geborener Jude sei* (That Jesus Christ Was Born a Jew, Wittenberg, 1523), in which Luther shows himself to be favorably disposed toward the Jews. But Margaritha's book, as well as the characterization of the Jew as obdurate and inimical in Sebastian Münster's *Messias Christianorum et Iudaeorum* (Messiah of the Christians and the Jews, Basel, 1539), contributed to an about-face on the reformer's part. The writings of contemporary experts like Margaritha, a learned convert, and Münster, a renowned Hebraist, seemed to confirm and to place on a broad "scientific" basis what Luther had till that point only indirectly gathered from the Bible and the history of the church. The henceforth incontrovertible knowledge about Jewish contempt for Christians and Christianity caused Luther to reevaluate the question of the treatment of Jews in favor of protecting Christian society.[81] Margaritha's accusations drew the notice even of the emperor, who summoned him in 1530 to the imperial diet in Augsburg for a disputation with Josel of Rosheim, the well-known advocate and public representative of Jewish interests. One of the points of contention was the vilification of non-Jews. Although Margaritha was defeated in the debate and expelled from the city, the fact that his accusations found resonance at the highest political levels shows that the Christian perception of Jewish apocalyptical revenge could have quite dangerous consequences. High treason was a serious crime; the accusation alone could suffice to threaten the Jewish communities' already precarious existence in the empire.[82]

And, indeed, the Christian fear of Jewish messianic expectation, a fear that often fueled existential anxieties of a more general kind, did have practical consequences. It legitimized harsh anti-Jewish measures designed to protect Christian lives.[83] The poet Folz of Nuremberg intentionally composed his plays, especially *Herzogen von Burgund*, as support for the city's long campaign to expel the Jews, a policy that finally succeeded in 1499.[84] In his anti-Jewish tract *Von den Juden und ihren Lügen* (About the Jews and Their Lies, Wittenberg, 1543), in which he considers the Jewish expectation that the Messiah would destroy the non-Jews, Luther even takes up the horror story of Jews poisoning wells and practicing ritual murder: every day at home and on Saturdays in the synagogue, the "thirsty blood hounds and murderers" (dürstige blut Hunde und Mörder) would curse the hated Christians. But, writes Luther, since God had not yet heard their cries for vengeance, and since they didn't want to wait in passivity any longer for the arrival of the savior, they had poisoned the Christians' drinking water, kidnapped their children, and stabbed them to death with bodkins or mangled them with flax combs, "so that they might secretly vent their wrath on the blood of Christians." The accused Jews had therefore justly been punished without mercy.[85] In fact, during the plague of 1348–49 and the pogroms associated with it, the rumor circulated that the Red Jews had sent their European brothers the toxic substance used to poison the wells.[86]

During times of actual Jewish messianic agitation, the fear among Christians was correspondingly intense. A Bavarian chronicle reports for the year 1337 that the Jews in Germany interpreted the dispute between Emperor Louis IV and the pope as a sign of the collapse of the empire and the end of Christendom. Since they expected their Messiah to appear, the Jews allegedly formed a pact against the Christians, and, according to the chronicler, they "dared to destroy them with poison, stole our sacrament of the body and blood of Christ, threw it in the ovens, smeared it on their anvils and practiced all manner of mockery with it."[87]

In Yuval's reading, the events around 1240 indicate a similarly close connection between Jewish messianic hopes and Christian fear. The year 1240 marked the end of the fifth millennium in the Jewish calendar, and many Jews expected the dawn of redemption. Their hopes were strengthened by the advance of the Mongols, who were understood to be the Ten Lost Tribes of Israel on their way to Europe to free their brethren from the hand of Edom. The rise in Jewish messianic expectation caused fear and alarm among Christians in Germany, who for their part identified the Mongolian nomads as the bloodthirsty Jewish agents of apocalyptic annihilation. This Christian fear evidently contributed to the general mood of an anti-Jewish pogrom, which culminated in 1235 in blood libel accusations in various places, among them the town of Fulda in Hesse. Emperor Fredrick II saw no alternative but to take the Jews under his protection against the enmity of the Christian majority. He effected this through the privilege of 1236, a law that for the first time designated the Jews "servants of the royal chamber" (servi camerae regis). Furthermore, the defeat of the Christian armies by the Mongols at Liegnitz may have been connected with the pogrom in the Judengasse, the Jewish quarter of Frankfurt am Main, in the spring of 1241, which resulted in the murder of 180 Jews.[88]

The influential stereotypes of Jewish messianism were intensified and elaborated into a powerful, self-sustaining dynamic within Christian polemics. In this way, Jewish messianism became a metaphor for Jewish perfidy as such and served to draw attention to the threat that the Jews represented for Christian society.[89] Eschatological anxieties that, in fact, pertained to the figure of the Antichrist/Messiah were displaced onto contemporary Jewish communities or, in particular political situations, onto single individuals who were seen to represent them.

An extraordinary example of the use of such motifs in a non-apocalyptic context is a pamphlet that purports to elucidate the circumstances of the death of the Margrave of Brandenburg's court agent, Michel von Derenburg, in 1549.[90] Here, Michel is equated with the figure of the ultimate evil Jew, that is, the Jewish Messiah or Antichrist. To set the stage for this portrayal, the anonymous author takes up the familiar motif of extramarital conception.[91] He goes on to designate Michel as the "Kochab" of the Jews,[92] a name derived from Bar Kokhba. Luther employs the same image, by the way, when he cites Michel as the epitome of the rich Jewish usurer who travels about the country with a large entourage: "I hear tell that a rich Jew rides about the land with twelve horses (he wishes to become a Kochab) and profiteers princes, lords, land and people, such that great lords grow suspicious."[93]

As becomes clear through the further characterization of Michel in the pamphlet, "Kochab," as a synonym for the Jewish Messiah, designates a ringleader who rises up against the rightful Christian authority. The financier appears less as a servant of the prince than as a master at whose feet the Christian rulers must grovel, since, as is well known, money rules the world. "For this reason the impoverished princes have called upon this rich Jew as their patron and helper in need, whom they regard more highly than our Lord Christ."[94] Just as, in the end-times, the Jewish Messiah as the Antichrist is to obtain for a short period the world domination the Jews have so long dreamed of, so too the Jewish usurer Michel succeeds in dominating his Christian clients by bringing them into financial dependence.[95] The stylization of Michel as the Antichrist is strengthened further by imputing to his princely debtors a proximity to the Antichrist. The

author of the pamphlet, a Protestant from Magdeburg in Saxony, characterizes the Catholics in Brandenburg in accordance with the familiar Lutheran
denunciation of the pope as "the Roman Antichrist's . . . predatory and
bloodthirsty mob" and "our Lord Christ's enemies and the friends of the
Jews, . . . Judaists, papists . . . and false Christians."[96]

Framing these events, which in the pamphlet's portrayal eventually cost Michel his life, are the feud-like disputes between the two rival
Christian confessions, the Catholics of Brandenburg and the Protestants
of Magdeburg. In the course of these conflicts, a group of Saxonians near
Frankfurt an der Oder take several of their adversaries from Brandenburg
prisoner, among them Michel von Derenburg. The Saxonian authorities
capture the group along with their prisoners, and thanks to the intervention of his employer, the Margrave of Brandenburg, Michel is soon set free.
The Magdeburgians who had seized him, meanwhile, are all put to death
by hanging—"all pious honest people," as the author laments.[97] As they
wait for their execution, Michel sends emissaries to all Jewish communities throughout the empire—in Frankfurt am Main, Mainz, Worms, and
elsewhere—to announce his triumph over the Christians. The Jews celebrate a feast of jubilation in honor of his power, during which they curse
the Christians and blaspheme their savior: "The Christians would have to
live in their graces, . . . fie on you, rogue Christ, you have lost, we have won;
your gentiles have come to wrack."[98]

In the end, however, God's righteous judgment asserts itself: Michel
falls down a staircase and breaks his neck. In spite of all their smugness, the
Jews are once again the losers. Michel von Derenberg fails, as Bar Kokhba
before him had failed and as the Jewish Messiah-Antichrist, according to
the Christian view, must also fail. And as the pamphlet's author proclaims
at the end of his report, drawing on the destruction of the ungodly
described in Psalm 73, all the Jews will similarly lose their lives.[99] Thus evil
can triumph only temporarily over good, the obligatory happy ending sets
the Christian world spinning back on its rightful axis.

JEWISH REACTIONS

The Jews were well aware of the unfavorable reception that their messianism was met with in Christian society. Hence, the Christian perception of Jewish messianic expectation also had a significant reverse effect on the way Jews expressed their longing for redemption. Moreover, the Talmud itself takes cognizance of the morally destructive power of disappointed messianic hopes among believers and, in order to preserve social stability, rejects both the calculation of the end of the world and all political-revolutionary attempts to bring about the Messiah's appearance.[100] The adoption of this traditional attitude, with one eye on the Christian observer, was urgent in Europe, especially in Germany, during the Middle Ages and early modern period in light of the dominance of Christianity.[101]

The concern about causing alarm among Christians and the desire for damage control were easily recognizable in moments of messianic jubilation anywhere in Europe. During the zenith of the Sabbatian movement, for instance, the Venetian rabbi Samuel Aboab called for a more prudent attitude, citing a sense of responsibility for the welfare of the community. Despite one's own enthusiasm, it was necessary to practice discretion and reserve, since the news of the advent of the redeemer could provoke anti-Jewish agitation. The community leadership in Venice codified these appropriate standards of behavior in a formal resolution.[102] Following the apostasy of Shabtai Zvi and his conversion to Islam, documents and writings containing the name of the renegade Messiah were burned in Germany, Holland, Poland, and Russia in an attempt to erase all memory of his deception. The destruction of the damning material appears to have stood in immediate relation to the publication of a Christian book that listed approximately twenty false Messiahs, including the Messiah of Smyrna.[103]

As Elisheva Carlebach has shown, the extraordinarily inimical attitude that prevailed in the Christian environment led in general to greater caution and reserve in public expressions of messianic hope, especially among German Jews. The recognizable subtext here is the discrepancy between an inner belief in imminent redemption and a form of public behavior that attempts to be as unremarkable as possible.[104] We can see this clearly when we compare the reactions of the two Jewish communities in Hamburg to the appearance of Shabtai Zvi: on the one hand, the oldest of the Sephardic communities issued a decree to the effect that one should remain outwardly reticent in order to conceal the messianic movement from non-Jews. This endeavor was supplemented by the further action of confiscating all copies of the book *Fin de los dios*, which contained the collected Sabbatian sermons of Moses Abudiente, because the book was likely "to endanger our position among the Christians."[105] On the other hand, the community members openly celebrated their enthusiasm for the Messiah in the synagogue. By contrast, the Ashkenazim in Hamburg, who over the course of generations had internalized the inimical attitude of Christians toward Jewish messianism, appear to have put their convictions much less on display. They celebrated the alleged Messiah not out loud with drums and dancing as the Sephardim did but rather by preparing themselves in secret for the redemption. The father-in-law of Glikl of Hameln, for instance, packed two kegs with necessities for the coming journey into the Holy Land. His luggage, containing among other things nonperishable comestibles, stood for three years untouched in the port city of Hamburg.[106] We can observe this sort of mentality already in the Middle Ages. Among the many European Jews who, inspired by messianic omens, immigrated to the Land of Israel over the course of the first half of the thirteenth century, there were apparently no German Jews. While groups of Jewish scholars from France wished to prepare for the advent of the Messiah by resettling in the Holy Land, the rabbis in the Rhineland rejected all such attempts to intervene publicly in messianic events, even under penalty of death.[107]

The stance of the German rabbis is explained by the warnings of *Ḥasidei Ashkenaz* (the German Pietists) against apocalyptic speculation. The primary ethical work of this pietistic current in Judaism, which established itself in the thirteenth century in Germany, is *Sefer Ḥasidim* (The Book of the Pious). Here, the reader is urged to be cautious whenever someone prophesies about the Messiah: not only will he himself "come to ruin and ignominy . . . but also this place will suffer misfortune because of the sorcerer."[108] Judah he-Ḥasid (Judah the Pious) of Regensburg did not forbid messianic calculation as such, however, nor did he deny its reliability. In fact, he himself appears to have expected the imminent redemption and determined its precise date. But this was to remain an esoteric secret kept carefully guarded within a narrow circle and was by no means to be made public.[109] Accordingly, Judah he-Ḥasid shows up in the travel report of Petaḥya of Regensburg as an apocalyptic censor. Petaḥya relates that, in Nineveh, the astrologer Solomon informed Judah of when the Messiah would come. "But Rabbi Judah the Pious would not write it down lest he should be suspected of being a believer in the words of Rabbi Solomon."[110] Why did the scholar attempt to conceal the date of the end? Judah he-Ḥasid himself gives the answer in a homily on Isaiah 63:4 ("For I had planned a day of vengeance, and My year of redemption arrived").[111] Under the immediate rule of those whose destruction would be brought about by the messianic upheaval, that is, the Christians, the open expression of Jewish messianic expectations and activities was simply too dangerous.

Thus, if the dominant Christian society felt threatened by the destructive wrath of Jewish messianism, the Jewish minority was anxious in turn about the possible consequences of this same Christian fear. One response was the self-censorship of the written record of messianic traditions.[112] It is no coincidence that the apocalyptic dimension in a miracle story passed on from generation to generation is revealed only in a work composed by a convert.[113] In a small, handwritten Hebrew anthology that appeared in the late fifteenth century in Italy, we find the following narrative: During the plague of 1349, the citizens of Worms rose up against the Jews and persecuted them. Suddenly there appeared a marble column in the Jewish cemetery. Much to the horror of the Christian persecutors, the column grew toward the sky until it was higher than the cathedral and leaned threateningly toward the city. The Christians withdrew in fear and left the Jews alone. As a warning, however, the column remained a few days more and began to shrink only after the civil unrest had completely ceased. The writer closes out his story by reporting that the column remains to this day in the Jewish cemetery of Worms, standing now about two cubits tall.[114] The convert Johannes Pfefferkorn, who relates the same story at the beginning of the sixteenth century, reveals to the Christian reader what was passed on among German Jews only orally and in secret: the legendary stele measures the time remaining till the advent of the Messiah. Every day, it sinks a bit more, until finally, on the day of redemption from the willfulness of the Christians, it will have disappeared entirely into the earth.[115]

This stone without inscription, which is said to have stood between the graves of two famous Jews of Worms—the renowned synagogue poet Meir Shatz and Eleazar of Worms, a prominent representative of *Ḥasidei Ashkenaz*—was apparently a destination for religious processions in the sixteenth century; Jews from all of Germany and beyond made pilgrimages to the Holy Sands cemetery on its account.[116] Presumably the pilgrims prayed there for help and protection in times of acute danger, as was also the custom at the "graves of the righteous" throughout Ashkenaz. After all, the column had saved the Jews once before.[117] As Pfefferkorn derisively adds, the pilgrims even took to sitting upon the stone in the hopes of pressing it farther into the earth and thus accelerating the Messiah's arrival. This polemical remark suggests that visiting the miraculous stele had an apocalyptic component and that the pilgrims undertook the journey to Worms not merely for immediate rescue from a given threat but also for the definitive future redemption of the people of Israel. Furthermore, it was believed that whoever damaged the holy stone or attempted to excavate it would die on the spot. Extrapolating from this, one might speculate that behind the destruction of Jewish gravestones during the Fettmilch Rebellion of 1615 there lurked a similarly anti-messianic politics, an attempt to annihilate all Jewish messianic hopes along with the feared consequences for the Christian oppressors. If in the time of the Black Death the column had merely menaced the persecutors of Worms, at the end of time they could expect horrific revenge.[118]

The caution of German Jews in messianic matters can be seen also in the reports that Carlebach has analyzed, which were composed in retrospective reflection upon periods of messianic activism. In contrast to their colleagues in Muslim countries or in the comparatively open atmosphere of Italy, the Jewish chroniclers who lived within the larger Christian society of the Holy Roman Empire were mostly concerned with supplying a purified version of events. Their laconic reports tend to veil and minimize the apocalyptic element or else to omit it altogether.[119]

Numerous Sephardic chronicles from the sixteenth and seventeenth centuries, for example, report in detail on the messianic movement of David Re'uveni and Solomon Molkho. In the seventeenth century in Egypt, Joseph Sambari combined the older reports of Joseph ha-Kohen and Gedalya ibn Yaḥya of Italy in order to relate in detail the history of Molkho, who was seen by many contemporary Jews as the Messiah, and of his prophet Re'uveni, who wished to lead the armies of God in the apocalyptic wars.[120] Ashkenazic chroniclers are by comparison rather tight-lipped. As Josel of Rosheim and David Gans portray them, the activities of Molkho and Re'uveni are completely devoid of apocalyptic character. Josel suppresses the fact that their visit with the emperor in Regensburg was in pursuit of a clear messianic goal and that it occasioned a sustained messianic enthusiasm among the Jews in Germany: "At that time the man from Italy, the righteous convert named Rabbi Solomon Molkho, may his soul rest in Eden, came with his alien ideas to stir up the Emperor by telling him that he had come to gather all the Jews to wage war against the Turks."[121] For his part, Gans describes Molkho as a learned mystic and portrays his meetings with European rulers as missionary actions.[122] Precisely because the apocalyptic program of Molkho and Re'uveni was well known to Jewish contemporaries and later generations, Josel and Gans deliberately omit it in order to avoid setting down in writing the messianic imagination and expectations of their people.

Given the ever-present Christian polemic, the Jews in Germany also sought to avoid explicitly acknowledging a messianic movement's failure. Neither a failed prophet nor a failed Messiah was as a rule publicly denounced as charlatan; nor did one mention the negative consequences of disappointed hopes for redemption. For this reason, in the testimony of Ashkenazic Jews in the German lands, there is to be found no mention at all of the conversion of the failed prophet Asher Lemlein's disappointed followers, who had become a kind of myth in both the Jewish and the Christian collective memory. Christian polemicists, by contrast, continued well into the eighteenth century to obsess on this particular detail. To be sure, there were Jewish authors who adverted to Lemlein's call for repentance as an admonition about the spiritual dangers of messianic movements: believers could be thrown into despair by the acute disappointment of their apocalyptic expectations and, as a consequence, lose their trust in the God of Israel. Yet these authors were either Sephardim or Ashkenazim who lived in Italy or Poland-Lithuania.[123]

The reticence of German Jews, however, does not mean that an ineffectual repentance, an unfulfilled prophecy, or a failed Messiah affected them less than their brothers and sisters in other parts of the predominantly Christian or the Islamic world. The Jews in Germany followed the news of David Re'uveni's and Solomon Molkho's travels no less breathlessly, and they were equally convinced that the prophet Asher Lemlein would lead them on the right path to imminent salvation. On the contrary, the manifestation of acute apocalyptic expectation or of active messianism must be given a particular weight, since Jewish messianic hopes were faced with an extremely negative and inimical Christian perception, a perception that carried with it a host of clear and present dangers for the lives of Jews in the Holy Roman Empire.

ASHER LEMLEIN BETWEEN
APOLOGY AND POLEMICS

They wield the sharpness of their tongue like sword and lance to mar
what is sacred, so that they can say of a lamb without blemish, "it is
an offensive thing, it will not be acceptable."

—Joseph b. Asher, [*Defense of Lemlein*], circa 1502

At the turn of the sixteenth century, messianic expectations among European Jews and Christians reached a zenith.[1] Just as the apocalyptically tinged peasant rebellions of the Bundschuh Movement were erupting in the southwestern part of the Holy Roman Empire,[2] a wave of messianic enthusiasm was sweeping through Spanish society.[3] The millennial mood found expression in Albrecht Dürer's woodcut series, *Apocalypse* (1498). Based upon the Book of Revelation, these dramatic images make the biblical vision of the end of the world powerfully concrete. In *Die vier apokalyptischen Reiter*, the Four Horsemen of the Apocalypse—harbingers of the approaching end of the world—brandish their swords and bows menacingly at the Christians (fig. 3). It is no accident that the horsemen wear Turkish hats: having conquered Constantinople, the center of the Eastern Church, in 1453, the Ottoman Turks now appeared to be marching

Figure 3. Albrecht Dürer, *Die vier apokalyptischen Reiter*, in *Die heimlich Offenbarung Iohannis* [Nuremberg, 1498], fol. 3. (Houghton Library, Harvard University, Cambridge, MA, Typ Inc 2121B PF)

inexorably toward Central Europe. They had become, in European consciousness, a *terror Christianorum*.[4] In 1521, Belgrade fell; the following year the Turks took Rhodes, a key position in the eastern Mediterranean. Soon the ancestral lands of the Habsburgs and the Holy Roman Empire itself came under direct threat. In 1526, at the Battle of Mohács, the Turks defeated the Hungarian army, and three years later they stood with a force of 120,000 soldiers before the gates of Vienna, the residential city of the emperor. Although they withdrew again temporarily in 1529, by the time the great conqueror Sultan Suleiman the Magnificent died in 1566, the area of Muslim rule extended from Persia across Asia Minor and the Balkans to Hungary and from the Middle East over the entire coast of North Africa to Morocco. The Islamic world thus reached uncomfortably close to the borders of the Holy Roman Empire, and as the Turks were also the dominant sea power in the eastern Mediterranean, they posed a threat to Italy and the Vatican—and thus to the heart of Catholic Christendom.

This confrontation was about more than territorial hegemony. It was also about the collision of two absolute religious claims, and it appeared to many contemporaries to forebode the catastrophes that were expected to descend upon the world prior to the Day of Judgment. The Ottoman danger was frequently associated either with the Antichrist or with the apocalyptic destroyers identified in the Bible as Gog and Magog.[5] But whereas Christians, especially of the Protestant confessions, perceived in the Turks the rod of the Lord with which He punishes sinful Christendom, the Jews saw in them the divine instrument that was finally to bring down the Christian rule of Edom.[6] For the crowd of people on the bottom of Dürer's picture, any attempt to escape the horrors of the end-times—the wars, the shortages, the famine and plague—is utterly in vain. All will be trampled without mercy beneath the rickety old mare of death.

Jewish and Christian scholars alike, such as Johannes Lichtenberger and Sebastian Brant in Germany and Isaac Abravanel and Abraham Farissol in northern Italy, made apocalyptic calculations that all revolved around the first years of the new century.[7] The encyclopedic opus *Prognosticatio*, by Lichtenberger, who served as imperial astrologer, enjoyed over fifty additional printings after its initial publication in 1488; beside the Latin original, it also appeared in German, English, French, Italian, and Dutch.[8] Especially well regarded in Jewish circles was the eschatological schedule compiled by Abravanel and included in his famous messianic trilogy, which was printed in 1496/97 in *Ma'ayenei ha-yeshu'ah* (Wells of Salvation), his commentary on the Book of Daniel. As the Italian kabbalist Mordechai Dato retrospectively remarked of Abravanel's computations, "his words accumulate themselves in the heart more strongly than do the words of others. And still more, because they are better known since being printed."[9]

Abravanel ascribes great eschatological significance to the year 5263 (1503 in the Christian calendar). Other contemporaries shared this understanding, among them the otherwise unknown Moses Vibne ha-Levi, who in the summer of 1500 composed a celebratory poem in Hebrew, in which he declares, "the end-time of salvation has come for the seed of Abraham! Sing praises to the Lord for his grace!"[10] The poet expected the advent of the Messiah during the year 1503, corresponding to the numerical values of the Hebrew letters in the phrase "*his crown* shall sparkle on us."[11] The date is also revealed by summation of the first and last letters of the individual stanzas that compose an artfully designed and calligraphically embellished acrostic pattern.[12]

For the years 1503 and 1504, the astronomers calculated a conjunction of the superior planets Mars, Saturn, and Jupiter, an event that was awaited with great excitement. In an illustrated broadside, Sebastian Brant sings of "der planeten trölich zeichen" (the true signs of the planets) and the "streiche" (tricks) that their meeting in the constellation Cancer would cause upon earth (fig. 4):

> Cancer will soon shake off many
> Who have long ridden in comfort
> Much turmoil will he cause
> Great confusions of war.[13]

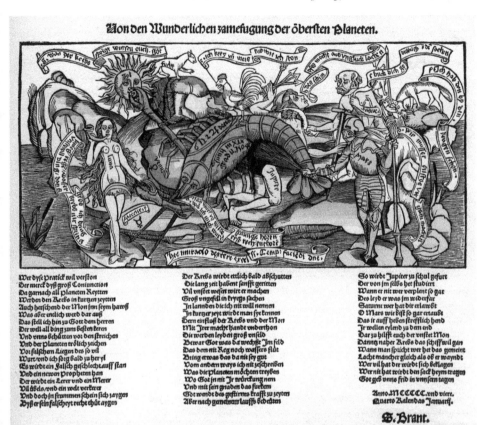

Figure 4. Sebastian Brant, *Von den Wunderlichen zamefugung der öbersten Planeten* ([Pforzheim], 1504). (BSB, Munich, Einbl. I, 44)

Abetted by the position of the moon—visible as Lady Luna on the left-hand side of the picture—the imminent miseries and confusions of war are personified in Brant's illustration by the violent collision of the sickle-bearing Saturn and Jupiter with his bow and arrow. In the foreground stands the warlike figure of Mars, armed like a knight with lance and rod. The situation appears dire indeed.

The unusual astronomical event was considered among both Christians and Jews to be the harbinger of a new prophet, whose appearance Lichtenberger had already announced for the year 1503:

He will be a teacher and a sower
Of much evil, and a world-inverter
And yet show himself in pious appearance
Till he does justice to his own falsity.[14]

Von der zukunft eins newen propheten (Of the Future of a New Prophet), who will seduce multitudes over the course of many years with his false teachings: this is also the subject of a *Practica* by the celebrated astrologer Johannes Virdung of Hassfurt.[15] His Jewish colleague Jacob b. Immanuel Provenzale (aka Bonet de Lattes), who was active in the papal court in Rome, likewise submitted "much evidence to prove how this conjunction indicates that a prophet will arise among the people of Israel."[16] And, indeed, around 1500, numerous prophets appeared, whose predictions enjoyed great authority among both Jews and Christians.[17] Especially in Italy, these charismatic emissaries bringing God's message to the people were to be met with at all levels of society. The most famous among them was Girolamo Savonarola. As prior of the Dominican Cloister of San Marco in Florence, until his execution in 1498, Savonarola gave fiery sermons on the fearsome wrath of God that would descend upon sinners on the Day of the Lord, and in vivid colors he illustrated for his listeners the splendor of the millennium that would follow for the righteous. His critique of the degenerate moral conduct of the times and of the abuses in the church found a receptive audience, who readily embraced his call for repentance.[18] In such soteriologically overdetermined times, the news of repentance was also heard among the Jews. Chief among these charismatic voices was Asher Lemlein of Istria, who through his activities sought to bring about the advent of the Messiah. Looking back from the middle of the sixteenth century, Mordechai Dato saw in Lemlein the fulfillment of the astrological prognostication for 1503/4: "And it happened thus, that in these days a Jewish man arose who prophesied from his heart, and many turned away from sin in repentance and fasting, and this was his name: Lemlen Ashkenazi."[19]

The unmistakable traces that Lemlein's activity left among both Jewish and Christian sources leave no doubt as to his remarkable performance. While the Jewish chroniclers of the sixteenth and seventeenth centuries remain silent about other messianic movements and have but little to say about influential apocalyptic thinkers such as Isaac Abravanel, nearly all of them report on Asher Lemlein. This episode was not inscribed merely out of a special interest in apocalypticism; rather, as one of the most significant events of Jewish history in the sixteenth century, no chronicle could omit it—neither in a tale of woe among the Bohemian Jews[20] nor in the representation of Jewish history in the Islamic East.[21] Just how wide a swath Lemlein's enterprise cut even outside the Jewish world is attested by various Christian sources. Thus, the French Orientalist and Hebraist at the Collège Royal in Paris, Gilbert Génebrard, devotes a terse entry in his world chronicle to the prophet.[22] By contrast, he makes no mention at all of other Jewish messianic movements, not even the widespread uproar surrounding David Re'uveni and Solomon Molkho, which occurred during his own lifetime. While Génebrard's interest appears to have been primarily historiographic, other Christian authors and converts writing of Lemlein did so with largely polemical intentions, as we will see.

The messianic excitement sparked by Asher Lemlein, who in the first years of the sixteenth century attracted great numbers of followers, above all in northern Italy and Germany, provides an excellent illustration of Jewish and Christian perceptions and representations of Jewish messianic activity per se. Testimony by both followers and opponents of the prophet offers insight into the polemical-apologetic discourse pursued by Jews and Christians in an environment that had traditionally judged Jewish messianic expectation with extreme censure. The Jewish and Christian interpretations of this episode—no less during the zenith of Lemlein's activity than after the prophet's ultimate failure—make clear how important it was for each side to come to terms with the antagonistic eschatological identity of the other and to take proper account of it when expressing their own convictions.[23]

FROM ISTRIA TO ALEXANDRIA: THE PROPHET ASHER LEMLEIN

Asher b. Meir Lemlein Ashkenazi announced his message of the Messiah's imminent advent on the Istrian peninsula, the border zone in the northern Adriatic where the Venetian territory abutted the lands of the Habsburgs. Little is known of the life and person of the self-proclaimed prophet. When he first appeared around 1500, he was already an older man.[24] His sobriquet "Reutlingen" indicates the origins of his family, that is, in the imperial city of the same name, from which the Jewish community had been definitively expelled in 1495. In all likelihood, however, Lemlein lived for many years in Italy and was perhaps even born there, given that the marks of the Italian-Jewish intellectual world are unmistakable in his thinking. Jews from Germany were at that time settled in the entire region that today belongs partly to Italy and partly to Slovenia. Increasingly motivated by the persecutions during the plague years in the mid-fourteenth century and the expulsions from the imperial cities of the Holy Roman Empire in the late Middle Ages, they had immigrated to Istria, Venetia, Friuli, and Carniola.[25] German Jews had settled in the early fifteenth century in the Venetian coastal city of Isola, several kilometers south of the port of Trieste, where Lemlein lived.[26]

Lemlein was highly regarded in Italy as a kabbalist. His colleagues, even those who were not in agreement with his teachings, treated him with respect.[27] He was in fact best known for views that caused outrage and indignation, in particular his conception of the transmigration of souls and of the resurrection of the dead. Already in an early, handwritten draft of ibn Yaḥya's *Shalshelet ha-kabbalah* from the 1560s, Lemlein is characterized as someone whose scholarly opinions were often sharply criticized.[28] Joseph ibn Shraga objected so vehemently to Lemlein's teachings that his own name has remained indissolubly associated with his opponent's: In a copy of his works, he is presented as the author who raised objections to "Asher, the prophet."[29]

Above and beyond his kabbalistic teachings, prophecy was the gift for which Asher Lemlein was to go down in history.[30] At the turn of the century, Lemlein proclaimed himself a prophet to a sizable group of students at his residence in Isola.[31] Having led an ascetic life, he could enter self-induced ecstatic states in order to obtain visions. It was allegedly through such visions that he communicated with God.[32] Moreover, he professed the ability to produce signs and wonders with the help of angelic and divine names, certainly not least of all as a means of legitimizing his claim to prophethood.[33]

While Lemlein appeared to many as either insane or possessed by a demon,[34] even so critical an eyewitness as Abraham Farissol of Ferrara had to admit that Lemlein's spectacular performance caused his following to grow rapidly.[35] Lemlein's fame spread beyond Istria, and "almost all synagogues in Italy and in the adjacent regions sent their most learned men to see him."[36] The most important Jewish chronicler of the sixteenth century, Joseph ha-Kohen, remarks that "the Jews went to him in droves and said: Yes, he is a prophet, for the Lord has sent him as a leader to his people Israel, and he will gather the dispersed of Judah from the four corners of the earth."[37] Lemlein's good news spread rapidly over the entire "exile of Edom"[38] and caused tumult and disquiet[39] in all Christian countries of Europe in which Jews still lived after the late medieval expulsions.

Apart from Italy, this meant in particular the German-speaking lands, where both Jewish and Christian sources testify to the messianic turmoil stirred up by Lemlein's activity. While reports from Italy emphasize Lemlein's influence in "Italian exile,"[40] for authors beyond the Alps, the horizon of perception shifts along with the geographical center of life. Jacob Kitzingen places Germany first as a center of the messianic turmoil, followed by Italy and "the other nations of Edom," including Poland-Lithuania, where Kitzingen's hometown of Szrem was located.[41] The French scholar Génebrard is aware only of Lemlein's reception in the neighboring empire.[42] In the German countries, authors could assume a familiarity with events on the part of their readers, regardless of religion. Thus, Pfefferkorn begins the corresponding section of the Latin edition of his *Juden Spiegel* (The

Jews' Mirror, Cologne, 1507) with the phrase "memini ego vna vobiscum": I remember together with you all.[43]

Pfefferkorn tells of numerous Jews "who have waited for the fifteen hundredth year, in which certainly the Messiah shall come."[44] His contemporary in Cologne, Victor von Carben, quotes the statement of "the Jewish rabbis here" (iuden Rabi alhie) that in that year, the faith of Christians throughout the world would fall into confusion, so that the Messiah might gather the Jews without impediment in Jerusalem. "Then everyone will in that time be so concerned with himself that none shall pay attention to them."[45] The chronicler David Gans describes vividly the sustained effect of Lemlein's message. His grandfather Seligmann, who at that time presumably lived in Lippstadt in Westphalia, "destroyed and shattered the special oven for the matzot in his complete certainty that in the coming year he would be baking matzot in the Holy Land."[46] Not only did Lemlein's prognostication of the imminent appearance of the Messiah grip Jewish men, women, and children in all of Europe and across ages and social classes, but "also among the non-Jews, the voice grew ever louder, and many of them likewise believed his words."[47] Some Christians were unsure what to make of such joyful anticipation among the Jews. In particular because of the prophecy that "much war, turmoil and other tribulations would arise," many anxious Christians sought out Victor von Carben as an expert in order to question him. After all, it was evident that "the strife grows from day to day." Moreover, a new comet had appeared to announce the coming of a new age. Were the Jews perhaps so learned that they could predict the course of the heavens? Victor was at great pains to pacify these troubled souls with the suggestion that all ages had seen deprivations, war, and pestilence. One should therefore lay no special value on the gossip of the Jews, who have always been led by such catastrophes to hope in vain for the advent of their redeemer.[48] Other Christians met Lemlein with curiosity. The Christian kabbalist Agostino Giustiniani reports that even Christians had numbered among the prophet's visitors in Isola. In his commentary on a Hebrew psalmody that includes the seventy-two names of

God, Giustiniani mentions the well-known humanist Paride da Ceresara of Mantua, who, out of an esoteric interest in magic and exotic alphabets, had traveled to Istria to take part in Lemlein's lessons on the holy names. It was Lemlein's practice, according to Giustiniani, to purify his body seven times before dawn with cold water and then, before the sun rose, to teach his disciples how to read out loud with perfect pronunciation the holy names that he had previously written on golden plates.[49]

While the "the simple-minded among the common people" saw in Lemlein's miraculous deeds clear evidence for his messiahship and cele-brated the prophet accordingly as the expected redeemer,[50] Lemlein seems to have understood himself to be merely the harbinger.[51] He was convinced that the time of redemption had come; yet the actual beginning, he warned, still depended on the moral conduct of the Jews. The end could be fur-ther delayed due to their sins. The idea that the chosen people were obli-gated to contribute actively to the realization of their own messianic hopes gained immediate currency. Lemlein preached collective repentance in the promise of redemption, and in 1501/2 called for a half year of penance. Afterward, "a fiery column with a dark cloud shall surround all Jews, in the same way as happened in the times of the Pharoah, and drive them again to Jerusalem, where the temple shall be rebuilt and offerings made."[52] In Lemlein's messianic vision, even the dead can repent, since the point of the resurrection of the dead in the end-times is "that the sinners better them-selves." In contrast to the traditional understanding, according to which resurrection and a place in the world to come are the reward for a pious life, Lemlein refers this event of the Last Days solely to the repentant sinners. The righteous have no need of resurrection, of course, since they are even "in death called living, while the sinners are in life already dead."[53] Lemlein finds justification for his controversial view in the original plan of creation. God created man for eternal life; but when Adam ate of the forbidden tree in paradise, God punished him with death. Since then, the sinner must die, while he whose soul is unspoiled has, like the prophet Elijah, risen into the heavenly spheres and gained eternal life. In his infinite grace, however,

God gives a last chance to those who, due to their sinful behavior during life, were unable to achieve purity of soul but who have the will to better themselves: in the end-times, he awakens them to new life.[54]

Lemlein's call to bring about the end through pious behavior was answered by widespread penance. An anti-Jewish polemic, *Liber fidei* (Hebr. *Sefer emunah*, The Book of Faith), probably written by a German convert in the 1520s, reports that "several times the Jews did great penance, with the whole heart, a full soul and with all their strength, in order to manifest the end for themselves."[55] Yet nothing compares, so the author continues, with what followed Lemlein's call. The enthusiasm for repentance did not let up even after the half year of penance that Lemlein originally called for had passed without result. In fact, this seems only to have spurred the Jews on to greater efforts, such that they did penance "for the advent of the Messiah almost an entire year, young and old, children and women. There had never been such penance done as they did in those days."[56] Ibn Yaḥya compares this "miraculous affair" with the biblical penance of the residents of Nineveh, after the prophet Jonah had prophesied the destruction of the city. The events earned the year 5262 in the Jewish calendar a special name in Jewish memory: "the year of penance."[57]

As the year passed, however, and still the Messiah failed to appear, the broader public penance ground to a halt. From rabbinical circles the demand grew louder for Lemlein to finally give evidence of his exceptional abilities. Giustiniani reports that the prophet then boarded a ship and fled to Alexandria.[58] Lemlein's presence in the eastern Mediterranean between 1505 and 1509 is, in fact, attested by his own manuscripts. Until May 1509 he appears to have settled in Safed in Upper Galilee, where a new center for Kabbalah was in the process of forming.[59]

In Safed, Lemlein attempted to find an explanation for the failure of the great penance. Why, despite everything, had the Messiah not appeared? In August 1509, the answer was revealed in a vision:[60] one night in the synagogue, a woman clad in black appears to him. She is at once extremely beautiful and horrifying to behold, and she introduces herself as the princess

Tefillah ("prayer"), the daughter of God and the Torah.[61] She complains of changes to the prayer texts. *Ḥasidei Ashkenaz*, she says, still stood in the chain of tradition reaching from Moses and the forefathers through King David and the men of the Great Sanhedrin and had passed on the mystery of the prayers, "neither adding anything to these words nor taking anything away."[62] The present generation, however, lacks decency and has no respect for earlier authorities. Thus, "they shorten what is long and lengthen what is short. Not even the least among them is hindered from adding things. Each individual dreams up numerous words every day in order to set them up as he thinks best." Through these arbitrary expansions and contractions of the texts, however, the inner harmony of the prayers was lost, since the numerical value of their words was altered, thereby destroying the alphanumeric mysticism. In this deformed form, Tefillah warns, the prayers can no longer ascend into the heavenly spheres, and the human being's communication with God is disrupted.[63]

For Lemlein, this vision was a clear call to lead his contemporaries back to the original form of the prayers.[64] His message is similar to the concept of *tikkun*, the repair of the world, soon thereafter popularized by Lurianic Kabbalah: cosmic significance attends upon the correct recitation of the prayer, because language plays a role in repairing the incongruities in the universe and restoring its original order. This in turn creates the right circumstances for the Messiah.[65] In this sense, the holy vision closes with the plea: "Because you shall mend the break . . . your profit shall be that the redeemer shall come for us and for all of Israel."[66] Here, Lemlein situates himself in the prayer mysticism of the German Pietists, a tradition that places great importance on the power of the letters of the holy language and that seeks a mystical solution to the problem of exile. As representative of a pietistic messianism, he emphasizes the importance of every sentence, every word, and every individual letter of the Hebrew alphabet—in both written form and pronunciation—for the dawn of the messianic age.[67]

To the high priority afforded the unalterability of the prayers Lemlein adds the determination that the Ashkenazic rite itself constitutes the single original and legitimate version, thereby in effect denying the other major line of tradition in Judaism its existential justification. Lemlein's criticism is directed, moreover, against the very use of the Hebrew language by Sephardic Jews. In a short treatise on the form of the letters, he finds fault with the fact that, as he sees it, the knowledge of the kabbalistic meaning of the Hebrew alphabet and its written form, which was given to Moses together with the Torah on Mount Sinai, had largely been forgotten.[68] First of all, he argues, everyone these days writes the letters however they see fit, without regard for the damage done thereby in the heavenly spheres. Lemlein has, above all, the Sephardic script in mind.[69] Second, he denotes Sephardim as "stutterers" in their pronunciation of the divine language. Here Lemlein deploys the writings of Sephardic scholars themselves to undergird his argument, using the expression of lingual titubation (stammering), with which Maimonides and others designate those who in their pronunciation make no distinction between *alef* and *ayin*, between *heh* and *ḥet*.[70] Thus the polemic weapon originally directed at Ashkenazic Hebrew is now turned against the Sephardic pronunciation and, by extension, against the Sephardic Jews themselves. The gutterals, according to Lemlein, have at least a common origin; much more serious is the identical sound of the sibilants *samekh* and *ẓadeh* in the Sephardic mouth![71] Moreover, Sephardim cannot correctly distinguish between the lengths of the individual vowels, which Nahmanides himself considered "the head and foot of the letters."[72]

The alleged linguistic confusion of Sephardic Jews is for Lemlein a consequence of their openness vis-à-vis the non-Jewish environment, thus giving Psalm 106:35 a new currency: "but mingled with the nations, and learned their ways." As a matter of historical fact, the Jews on the Iberian Peninsula had indeed been more integrated in the culture, economy, and politics of their surroundings than had Jews in any other European country. Their arrogance, according to Lemlein, had even led them into the courts of kings. Out of their need to be accepted, they had learned the science of astrology and the philosophy of the "uncircumcised"—to say nothing of their language and writing, with which the Sephardim sought to distinguish themselves before the powerful and in disputations with priests. Their efforts at assimilation had finally even driven them, in the inherited language of their fathers, to use only the five vowels of the Christian languages; and, thus, the various lengths and pronunciation of the Hebrew vowels had with time sunk into forgetfulness.[73]

Lemlein's harsh criticism of the Sephardim thus related not only to their religious rite but also to their entire mode of life. The numerous conversions in Spain and Portugal were easily explained: "Because of the study of philosophy, the number of heretics among the people of Israel has risen." As a consequence of their intellectual stance, Sephardic Jews could not have withstood the divine test in the form of Christian persecution. "They all became apostate . . . , because they did not believe in God and had no faith in his redemption, saying belief is but an invention of the masses. And all of this is merely the fruits of philosophy."[74] This view was widespread in Italy in the early sixteenth century. Kabbalists were especially inclined to see in the study of philosophy a decisive factor that led in 1492–97 to their expulsion from the Iberian Peninsula. They warned, in a fashion similar to Lemlein in his later writings, that only a renunciation of philosophy and a return to Jewish praxis through repentance, prayer, and good deeds—all of it bound up with the correct mystical intention—offered the way to redemption.[75]

Lemlein's vision assimilates tensions between the various Jewish cultures that, as a consequence of expulsions and migrations, encountered each other in the sixteenth century with previously unknown intensity. Particularly in northern Italy, Lemlein's homeland, the different religious rites and forms of cultural life came into marked conflict. Moreover, the Sephardic refugees streaming into the region were proud of their origins and their cultural inheritance and were often viewed as comporting themselves arrogantly toward the long-established Ashkenazim, to whom they felt superior in worldview, way of life, and education.[76] Lemlein's later writings, however, are not unique in their apology for Ashkenazic Judaism in the face of the immigrants' self-important attitude. Nor is Lemlein alone in the absoluteness of his condemnation of the entire Sephardic lifestyle, going even so far as to accuse them of godlessness. Rather, what makes Lemlein's anti-Sephardic stance singular is its eschatological framework. His new radicalness as defender of Ashkenazic traditions and values arises from a messianic logic.[77] One implication of his later writings is that the power of redemption lies exclusively with the Ashkenazim, in particular in their prayers and in the Ashkenazic use of the Hebrew language. In the end, Israel could only be redeemed, according to Lemlein, when the Sephardim gave up their religious rites. Lemlein thus linked the delay of the Messiah's appearance with a concrete attribution of guilt and found the scapegoats in the Sephardim and their way of life. The dawn of redemption, which had been within arm's reach in 1502, was hindered by Sephardic misconduct.

REPENTANCE, REVENGE, CONVERSION

The messianic awakening of 1502, which encompassed the entire Central European diaspora, was unique not merely due to its sheer size. It was, above all, the quality of penitent enthusiasm that impressed both contemporaries and later generations. The southern German convert Paulus Aemilius compares its intensity to the annual ten days of repentance that begin on Rosh Hashanah, the Jewish New Year, and culminate on the Day of Atonement, Yom Kippur. During this time, according to tradition, an individual can alter his personal destiny through contrition and repentance. While the question here is of the individual soul's salvation after death, in 1501/2 the goal was the collective forgiveness of sins.[78] As on the ten days of repentance, everyone acknowledged his lapses, turned back from his evil ways, and strove henceforth to act with righteousness and to live in a manner pleasing to God.[79] In a special sense, one also obligated oneself to practice charity, such that numerous people "gave all their goods to the poor."[80] This had obvious practical reasons as well, since possessions could not easily be brought along for the imminent journey to the Land of Israel. Like the grandfather of the chronicler David Gans, the repenters wished to be prepared for the day when the Messiah would lead them to Jerusalem, where they expected, as Paul Weidner notes with a polemical edge, that they "would be rich again and made into great lords."[81]

The great repentance found its characteristic expression in the radical practices of asceticism and self-flagellation, such as had already been typical of *Ḥasidei Ashkenaz*.[82] The sources report that the penitents put on special garments of repentance and refused to wear adornments of any kind. One girded oneself in sackcloth or else (in accordance with the usage of the high holy days) in a white robe, the color of which symbolized not only righteousness but also, in a second interpretation, dominion over the non-Jewish nations in messianic times; it was even supposed to summon God's apocalyptic vengeance.[83] One contemporary speaks also of flagellation using a whip.[84] Above all, however, Lemlein called for fasting, and the rabbis who were favorably inclined to him appear to have implemented this concretely in the form of ordinances for the regulation of fasting times.[85] Some declared two days a week as days of fasting, while others set the number at three.[86]

But Lemlein's activity also provoked opposition in Jewish society.[87] From a fervent apology written during the time of the repentance by one of his disciples (possibly his son, Joseph b. Asher), we learn of a "cry of war, a voice of upheaval" that arose like "a whirlwind out of the North" (beyond the Alps?).[88] The anonymous critic had evidently questioned Lemlein's prophethood and demanded an unambiguous sign from him.[89] Since Joseph was well aware of the difficulty of producing clear evidence, he answers the objections evasively, saying that his master, the personification of humility, had never boasted of the gift of prophecy.[90] Nor had he ever raised himself up in the name of God "in order to command in any matter or to warn against it."[91] But this was precisely the suspicion harbored by Lemlein's critics. In the massive and enthusiastic reaction to the call for repentance, the prophet's power over his followers had become clear. Therein lay a considerable danger: were Lemlein to command these people, who now fasted two and three days a week for redemption, to "go and fight the fight X in the name of Y!" the simple-minded among them would blindly obey him.[92] This was by no means merely a metaphor for Lemlein's enormous influence. Behind it stood a real concern about the socially explosive power his activity carried with it.

Joseph counters Lemlein's detractors with the positive effects of his deeds. How could one hold Lemlein's call for repentance against him, since it obviously contributes to moral improvement? One could hardly accuse him on these grounds. Moreover, Joseph argues, "envy, contention, pride and conflict, deceit, profanity, calumny, false witness, fornication, [the enjoyment of] impure meat," and much more have been the order of the day for more than twenty years in those districts of Italy.[93] Now that someone has finally arisen who has set himself against these sins and already turned many people aside from their godless ways, one would seek to muzzle him with the specious argument that he is a false prophet.[94] The motivation of "this quarrelsome person" in denouncing Lemlein as a charlatan thus arises from "ambition and self-righteousness."[95] "The reason behind this obvious lie is none other than the love of domination, of contention and of polemic."[96] Finally, the opposition to the prophet serves the maintenance of power by the elite, which sees itself threatened by Lemlein's influence. Although Lemlein's call for fasting had been without communal authority and without issue of any ordinances for repentance, the masses repented, "even almost against the will of the community leaders. But they listen to the words of the perfect one, and to his speeches alone."[97]

That the widespread appeal of Lemlein's prophetic activity was, in fact, perceived by the governing class of the Jewish communities as a threat to the status quo can be seen in Sambari's remark on the elites, the community leaders, and the sages. His chronicle reports that, although these groups tended to lend credence to Lemlein's words about the end of time and many members of the Jewish upper class themselves expected the imminent advent of the Messiah, they did not heed his call to fast,[98] likely because they viewed it as a presumptuous and disagreeable encroachment into their own areas of competence. In the end, then, it was a question of authority: who had the right and the certified halachic knowledge to issue religious and moral ordinances that intervened so massively into daily life? If everyone were to start writing his own rules, the gates would be thrown wide open to toppling the authority of rabbis and community leaders.[99] Even in the Last Days, the order of this world ought not to be invalidated. With sarcastic irony, Joseph b. Asher prophesies that legal scholars, too, out of self-interest, would soon close ranks with the critics of Lemlein's call for repentance, since if peace and friendship ruled the world and strife and hate no longer existed, then there would also no longer be any need for legal judgments. "But the disappearance of the need for a judge reduces his honor and his high position among the people."[100]

After revealing the actual motivating reasons behind the polemic against his master, Joseph goes on the attack: According to Maimonides, here quoting Alexander of Aphrodisias, it is precisely "ambition and self-righteousness" that prevent human beings from recognizing the truth. The complexity and obscurity of prophecy make it difficult for human ratiocination to distinguish a true prophet from a soothsayer, sorcerer, or dream interpreter, to say nothing of a false prophet. Add to this, as in the case of Lemlein's nameless detractor, the deficiency of one's own power of reasoning, and it becomes utterly inappropriate to allow oneself to judge of prophethood at all. Thus, Joseph completely denies the doubter's capacity to pass judgment on Lemlein's prophetic competencies[101]—and thereby relieves himself of the burden of furnishing positive evidence.[102]

The revolutionary tendencies within Jewish society were presumably not the only source of fear among the community leaders and rabbis who were ambivalent about messianic repentance. The image of conflict and soldierly obedience that Lemlein's anonymous critic conjures up points to another very real danger: That messianic hopes could provoke acts of violence against Christians. After all, revenge on the Christian oppressors represented an important part of the Ashkenazic hope for redemption. Moreover, as emblem of the Messiah, Lemlein had predicted the collapse of Christian churches, something that could easily be construed as their actual destruction.[103] Although no known physical assaults occurred, the apocalyptic mass excitement certainly ran the risk of being seen by Christians as a threat. And the Christians, one could only assume, would defend themselves accordingly.[104]

In the absence of significant source materials, it is impossible to say to what extent Christians actually felt threatened by Jewish repentance. In the surviving texts of Christian observers, an entirely different effect of the repentance unleashed by Lemlein stands at the center of attention. Nearly all Christian (and convert) polemics circulating in Germany that report on Asher Lemlein associate his failure to bring the Messiah with conversion to the Christian faith. For these writers, the ineffectual repentance exemplifies the triumph of Christianity over Judaism. "Not even a single sign or a single intimation, much less the reality," of redemption was revealed to the Jews.[105] The anonymous author of *Liber fidei*, and later the Hebraist Sebastian Münster of Basel, put any causal relation between repentance and redemption fundamentally in question. Although the ancient Israelites knew nothing at all of many of the religious strictures followed by Jews in Europe in the sixteenth century, they had nevertheless been redeemed from captivity in Babylon. Then, by contrast, one kept the Sabbath and adhered to all other laws, one prayed and gave alms, and still the Messiah did not come.[106] From this it could clearly be seen that the most virtuous mode of life and the most perfect deeds could not rescue the Jews from their misery. As to the agonizing question of why the prayers of the people of Israel went unanswered by God, the author of *Liber fidei* suggests the reason lies in the rejection of the Jews. The only way to regain divine grace is to acknowledge Jesus as the Messiah. Because in the Christian concept of redemption, in contrast to the concept of justification by works, Jesus vicariously took the sins of humankind upon himself and paid for them with his death, human beings are now justified before God. To stand again in a correct relation to God, the Jews would therefore only have to accept the redemptive act of Jesus for their own lives.[107]

As a historically grounded argument for the gullibility of Jewish messianic hopes and for God's rejection of the erstwhile chosen people, the story of ineffectual repentance lost nothing of its appeal over the subsequent two centuries. Lemlein appears together with the best-known messianic pretender of Jewish history, Shabtai Zvi, in every messianic list from the sixteenth through the eighteenth centuries.[108] In 1650, in his "Vermahnung an die Juden" (Admonition to the Jews) of the landgraviate Hesse-Kassel, the preacher Justus Soldan refers to the Lemlein episode as the nadir of the Jewish people's suffering. Was it not promised to them that the Messiah would come if they did but one day of penance? At that time it was an entire year, and still, as Soldan remarks with a parodic wordplay on the name Lemlein, "ging die sache auff ein La-mi auß" (the matter piffled out in a *la-mi*) and came to a miserable end.[109]

Soldan may be alluding here to an oft-quoted passage from ibn Yaḥya's *Shalshelet ha-kabbalah*, according to which many of the prophet's followers converted to Christianity out of disappointment when his prophecies failed to come true.[110] Nevertheless, the historical value of this quote ought to be taken with a grain of salt.[111] One cannot fail to notice that the motif of conversion functions in ibn Yaḥya's chronicle like a literary topos.[112] The author makes conversion the rule, whereas, in fact, it was the exception, and he posits it even where other historians either know nothing of it or directly contradict it. Thus, ibn Yaḥya closes his report on the Shepherds' Crusade in Spain and France in 1320 with the summary, "many were killed, but the majority converted," despite the fact that the chronicles upon which he relies mention conversions merely as a fringe phenomenon, something that occurred exclusively in Toulouse.[113] For the year 1163, the chronicler Samuel Usque, one of the central sources for ibn Yaḥya, reports in detail how a mass conversion in Toledo was interrupted at the last moment by divine intervention.[114] In ibn Yaḥya's telling, by contrast, God does not intervene, with the result that here once again, "many Jews were killed . . . and the rest of the Jews converted."[115] Even in connection with the crusade persecutions of 1096, idealized in Ashkenazic memory as the epitome of

Jewish martyrdom, ibn Yaḥya reports of conversions. More than five thousand souls chose the death of martyrdom, "but the apostates were numberless."[116] Ibn Yaḥya's brief reports appear thus as variations on a single topos, that is, as schematic formulas that could be filled with concrete contents and specifications of time and place as needed. For ibn Yaḥya, himself a descendent of Sephardic exiles, conversion is symptomatic for the suffering of the people of Israel. Corresponding to the alternatives that the Jews in Spain were confronted with in 1492, the defection from Judaism belongs for ibn Yaḥya alongside violent death and expulsion as obvious parts of the history of the Jewish diaspora.

Viewed against this background, ibn Yaḥya's statements about conversions resulting from Lemlein's failed prophecies are simply too cliché to be credible without further evidence, especially when one considers their larger context. Ibn Yaḥya handles Asher Lemlein as part of a long series of false Messiahs, messianic prophets, and apocalyptic calculations, and it is the author's expressed intention to put before the reader's eyes the dangers of messianic speculation and activity. He warns of the "many sufferings of Israel" that resulted from them in the past.[117] Once, a "high fine was imposed upon the Jews."[118] Messianic pretenders and prophets were executed, and their followers suffered the same fate. One ruler "sent an emissary after them to kill them, and he was brought the head of the agitator."[119] In another instance, "several communities were annihilated."[120] In this roundup, Asher Lemlein serves as an example of the spiritual threat to belief that a messianic movement represented: "When the simple-minded saw that the Messiah did not come, they converted."[121]

Significantly, the list of Messiahs is missing from the earlier manuscript version of ibn Yaḥya's chronicle mentioned above.[122] Here, Lemlein's activity constitutes merely one historical event among many, a sober entry in the world-historical part of the chronicle. Around 1500, ibn Yaḥya writes, there lived an Ashkenazic Jew in Istria, a scholar by the name of Asher Lemlein, who was involved in a doctrinal argument about the transmigration of souls. Furthermore, he was active as a prophet and caused widespread messianic repentance. When he died, his generation had not yet succeeded in bringing about the redemption. Nothing at all is said of conversions.[123] For the first printing, ibn Yaḥya deliberately changed the passage. As part of a pedagogical tabulation of false Messiahs, only the messianic preacher Lemlein still interested him. To be convincing as an admonition about the danger of accelerating the end, his activity had to be fatal. What could lie closer at hand than for the ineffectual repentance to end just the same as so many other catastrophes in Israel's long history of suffering, with apostasy?

The myth of conversions that ibn Yaḥya created became a hot item on the polemical market. Although several Jewish authors adopted this tenuous detail,[124] no mention of it is to be found in any of the testimonies originating in the German-speaking countries. This is no surprise. Given the concern for the perception among Christians here, conversions following failed messianic hope—whether or not they occurred—would have had no place in Jewish collective memory. In the end, such reports were merely grist for the mill of Christian polemics.[125] Most Christian authors, in fact, all too eagerly took up the episode's sad finale as alleged by ibn Yaḥya.[126] Paulus Aemilius, in a master stroke of hyperbole, even has Asher Lemlein himself convert. When his prophesies turn out to be false, he realizes the reason for it: the Messiah has already come, and long ago.[127] Thus his followers were doubly deceived by the charlatan. First he seduces them with false prophecies about the advent of the Messiah and then abandons them to their error while he himself acknowledges the Christian truth.

Ibn Yaḥya's portrayal, however, possesses more historical facticity than even he himself could have known. Evidently out of disappointment at the failed messianic expectation, Johannes Pfefferkorn and his entire family in Cologne crossed over to Christianity in 1504/5.[128] "Since the year has turned . . . and it is no different now than before,"[129] he asked himself why the Messiah had failed to appear despite the general repentance. Why hadn't God at least given some indication that he had seen the strict fasting of his people and heard their prayers? Continuing the penance seemed pointless; after all, it had already been extended half a year without any recognizable effect. Despite "hard, heavy penitence of a kind you have neither lived nor read about before," the messianic time had not begun. In the end, Pfefferkorn felt he had been led into error by his Jewish messianic faith, exactly in the way descried in Christian polemics. His deep despair can be heard in his exclamation, "Ah, how miserably we have been deceived!"[130]

Far from giving up his messianic expectation, however, Pfefferkorn merely carried it over into his new religion. He continued to interpret the signs of the times and the strife in the world, the threat to the Christian West through external enemies such as the Turks, and the internal crisis of the church itself as indications of the imminent revolutionary transformations before the end of the world. He now combined the universal interpretive framework with the conversion of the Jews as part of the traditional Christian eschatology, understanding his own baptism as an exemplary act in the run-up to Judgment Day and justifying at the same time the urgency of his own sense of evangelical mission.[131] On the basis of his personal experience, Pfefferkorn devoted himself actively to a missionary program aimed at bringing about the long-awaited general conversion of the Jews. None knew better than he how a well-aimed argument could hit a sensitive nerve. He saw in the situation following Asher Lemlein's fall a promising opportunity for Christian evangelism, an opportunity that he did not want to let pass unexploited. The Jews in their despair over the disappointing outcome of the great repentance would certainly now be ready finally to accept Jesus as the Messiah.[132] For a decade after his baptism, Pfefferkorn traveled widely as an itinerant preacher,[133] and he published numerous polemical-propagandistic writings with the explicit aim of converting his former fellow believers.[134]

In his first publication, *Juden Spiegel*, he addresses himself to the Jewish reader: "My most dearly beloved brothers! . . . consider that you are deceived, where is your Messiah?!"[135] To make the alleged messianic error of the Jews comprehensible to them, he adverts to the recent events: Despite precisely calculated messianic dates and energetic attempts to bring about the redemption, nothing had happened. What is the use of your penance and martyrdom? he mocks.[136] Any further waiting for the Messiah is quite obviously pointless. The only correct conclusion to be drawn from these disappointed hopes is the necessity of conversion to Christianity, in which the Jewish religion had long ago found its eschatological fulfillment.

If Pfefferkorn still oscillates in *Juden Spiegel* between brotherly admonition and criticism, his tone thereafter becomes ever sharper. More and more it is the supposedly demonic essence of the Jews that comes to the fore, a danger against which Christian society must defend itself by all means necessary in order not to be corrupted. With *Der Juden veindt* (The Jews' Enemy) in 1509, Pfefferkorn openly propagandized for the massive repression of the Jews. One must forbid them the lending of money with interest, he argued, and instead assign them to menial labor such as sweeping the streets.[137] But, above all, what Pfefferkorn calls for is the confiscation and incineration of the Talmud and other postbiblical writings, which he considers a primary reason for the Jews' blindness. The empty promises of their own rabbis prevented them from recognizing and acknowledging Christ.[138] At the instigation of the Dominicans of Cologne, who made use of the convert in their fight against Judaism,[139] Pfefferkorn, in fact, received a mandate from Emperor Maximilian I to seize Jewish writings, which he immediately began executing in Frankfurt and other cities of the Rhineland. This stirred up such fierce resistance among the local authorities, however, that in the end the emperor ordered the books restored.[140]

Pfefferkorn's efforts take their place in the long tradition of the Dominican order, which sought the exclusion of Jews and Judaism from Christian society. The confiscation of books was intended to facilitate their isolation and, finally, to prepare their complete expulsion, were they to persist in cleaving to their religion.[141] The use of force appeared to Pfefferkorn himself as an appropriate means of converting the Jews. The abuse they endured was ultimately for their own good. "Doubtless after such treatment they would be of a different heart and mind, and they would surely emerge to leave their falsehood and follow the truth of our belief."[142] In 1510, Pfefferkorn boasted of the success of his missionary efforts: "Others too had at his urging abandoned the Jewish error and adopted the Christian faith."[143]

For other Jews, however, the failure of the Messiah to appear did not lead to the radical conclusion of a fundamentally false religious conviction. They were more likely to attribute the inefficacy of repentance to the fact that they had been taken in by a charlatan. Farissol describes Lemlein as a power-hungry seducer who led the whole region into error. "And in the end it was futile and a pursuit of wind."[144] Ibn Yaḥya condemns him without further ado as a false prophet, accusing him of arbitrarily appointing himself divine messenger.[145] The majority, however, appears to have taken the typical path of silence and to have refrained from announcing their disappointment publicly.

But the fact that Lemlein's prognostications went unrealized did not necessarily discredit him with all of his followers, nor was the repentance in the wake of his prophecies invariably written off as a meaningless error. There were also voices emphasizing that redemption could indeed have begun in 1502. On the pattern of the traditional formula "It is the fault of our great sins," the delay was attributed to human failure alone.[146] Exemplary here is the expression of Eliezer Treves, as told by David Gans, who was his student in Frankfurt am Main. Decades after Lemlein's prophecy, Treves was heard to say "that it was no empty word and that he had produced signs and wonders. And he said that perhaps our sins led to it and delayed him [the Messiah]."[147] Whenever a positive—or at least not decidedly negative—memory of Lemlein was preserved in Germany, the aggressive stance of the Christian environment certainly stands in the background. This is because the view that redemption might have been possible defied the standard Christian argument of fraudulence. If the failure of repentance could be explained without putting Lemlein's prophetic authority in question, then the final word as to the fulfillment (or nonfulfillment) of his prophesies had yet to be spoken.

This reaction ought not to be dismissed as merely apologetic. At the same time, it is an expression of the strong apocalyptic hope stirred up by Lemlein's activity. His messianism appears, in fact, to have been an important precursor to the apocalyptic awakening of the later sixteenth century.[148] Thus Eliezer Treves, who as a child in Germany likely lived through the failed attempt to realize the advent of the Messiah through repentance,[149] felt as a grown man that the fulfillment of his messianic longing was still within reach. In 1531 he wrote enthusiastically from Cracow to his father, Naphtali Hirtz, in Frankfurt, saying that he had learned from certain "holy writings," which had reached him via Budapest from the port city of Caffa (today Feodossija) in the Crimea (or Capua in Italy?), that the time of redemption had now begun. In Jewish communities from Jerusalem to Salonika, the Monday and Thursday of every week had already been designated as days of repentance and fasting,[150] and "even the women pour out their hearts while they fast." Moreover, every community had organized at least one special prayer association.[151] Nevertheless, Treves was clearly worried that this time, too, the penance might not suffice to summon the Messiah. He therefore asks his father, the great kabbalist who was at that time cantor in Frankfurt, to set his *kavanah* (mindfulness in prayer) in Psalm 6 of the daily *taḥanun* (supplication) on the success of the movement.[152]

Many years later, when he was chief justice in Frankfurt, Eliezer Treves was himself involved in a similar messianic prayer cycle. In 1552, the imperial city suffered for many weeks when it was besieged by rebellious Protestant princes under the leadership of Margrave Albrecht II Alcibiades of Brandenburg-Kulmbach and Elector Moritz of Saxony. During this time, ten heads of household fasted daily together with their dependents over the age of eighteen years, with the exception of pregnant and nursing women. And on Mondays and Thursdays they ate no meat and drank no wine. Moreover, each day they said selihot (prayers of repentance) as well as psalms, and they arranged daily vigils shortly before daybreak. After the prayer, they also spoke the liturgical poem *Shir ha-yiḥud* (The Hymn of Unity) every day and accompanied it with additional beautiful songs.

In each instance, R. Eliezer read the first verse of the psalm and of *Shir ha-yihud* and the community read the second.[153]

In the German-speaking territories, a special apocalyptic significance seems to have been attributed to the hymn *Shir ha-yihud*, which praises God. As late as the eighteenth century, Isaac Wetzlar, an educated merchant from Celle whose business trips had taken him far across Europe, considered it fatal that in his time the song of unity was no longer sung by the majority of scholars and in many places was not sung at all. He considered this negligence to be a decisive reason for the Messiah's delay.[154] In many communities that during the Middle Ages had used the German-Polish rite, the mystical song of unity was recited daily at the close of the divine service. Owing to a controversy about its place in the liturgy, however, geographically distinct uses developed in the mid-sixteenth century. While some communities maintained the recitation every day of the week, others restricted *Shir ha-yihud* to the Sabbath and to festival days or else reserved it exclusively for the evening prayer on Yom Kippur.[155] In his hometown of Celle, Wetzlar advocated for speaking the song of unity scrupulously every day.[156] Accordingly, it was to be spoken everywhere "better and more easily, word for word," so that it would "be a significant aid to our redemption."[157]

During the Second Schmalkaldic War, the Princes' Revolt of 1552, the leaders of the Jewish community in Frankfurt am Main, upon the recommendation of R. Feidel zum Esel,[158] also adopted a certain practice of Gaon Mannes of Worms, one stemming from the time early in the same year when the city on the Rhine was menaced by a French army.[159] Feidel had witnessed how the Worms community walked in procession around the *bimah*, the lectern in the synagogue from which the Torah is recited, while speaking together a part of the liturgy of the weekly Sabbath service. After the example of Worms, the community of Frankfurt then every Tuesday after the evening prayer circled the lectern three times, led by Treves, who carried the Torah scroll in his arms and sang, in alternation with the group, the piyyut *Adonai elohei Yisra'el* (Lord, God of Israel). The text pleads with God for salvation in the face of sufferings and persecutions, and in the

Ashkenazic tradition, it is added to the *taḥanun* every Monday and Thursday as part of the morning prayer.[160] Feidel also led in this procession children under ten years of age, who in contrast to the adults were considered to be free from sin. Together with the children, he sang a further selection from the liturgy of the morning worship service, *Shirat ha-yam* (Song of the Sea). In this song of victory, Moses and the children of Israel praise God after crossing the Red Sea unharmed. The song describes in detail the demise of the Egyptian pursuers, and, noting the fear that gripped Edom and the other nations in the face of the powerful God of the Israelites, it points in the messianic context toward apocalyptic revenge on the Christians. At the end stands the confidence that the people of Israel will retake their land and rebuild the temple there.[161]

The penitential exercises that the communities in Frankfurt and Worms performed were intended to dispose God toward mercy. But this was conceived not merely in the short term, that is, that God might rescue his people from the immediate dangers of the siege, such as plundering, expulsion, and corporeal abuse by soldiers. The exercises also had a long-term eschatological significance and were aimed at influencing the course of the war between the emperor and the French-allied Protestants in such a way that at its conclusion the Messiah would appear. The Princes' Revolt, like the First Schmalkaldic War, was for the Jews in Germany an event of apocalyptic dimensions. Like Catholic Christians, they hoped the victor would be Emperor Charles V, who appears in various sources as a quasi-messianic figure of salvation. The triumph over his enemies, the Protestant adversary within and the French enemy without, was understood—with reference to contemporary Christian prophecies of the Last World Emperor—as a precondition for the beginning of the messianic age.[162] "Thus may he [God] set us free from servitude to salvation."[163]

Also, the great messianic uproar surrounding David Re'uveni and Solomon Molkho in the 1520s and early 1530s seems to have been carried to a large extent by the same milieu as in the repentance call of Asher Lemlein. In both cases, the Venetian territories were an important zone of intersection for the flow of messianic news. From the Holy Land, Damascus, and Egypt came ominous rumors concerning the return of the Ten Lost Tribes of Israel. These rumors circulated in Venice and spread from there across Italy and into Central Europe.[164] In 1523, Trieste in Istria, the region of Lemlein's activity, was an important distribution center for these novelties.[165] Illustrative in this context is the transmission history of Lemlein's later writings, written between 1506 and 1509, after he had apparently turned his back on Europe in flight. The surviving manuscript was prepared in 1537 for the library of the Venetian doctor and kabbalist Elijah Menahem b. Abba Mari Ḥalfan, a friend and benefactor of Solomon Molkho.[166] The scribe Judah (Laudadio) b. Solomon de Blanis had several years earlier copied letters from the eastern Mediterranean that reported on the Ten Tribes. On the way, he became one of the first Europeans to learn of the appearance of the alleged Prince of Ruben, one of the Lost Tribes of Israel, half a year before this very David Re'uveni (David, the Rubenite) reached Italy. When Re'uveni finally arrived in Rome in February 1524, de Blanis journeyed there to determine with his own eyes the man's identity.[167]

Thus, Johannes Isaac, a convert and professor of Hebrew at the University of Cologne, linked the histories of the two great messianic episodes of the sixteenth century with good reason. In 1555, he announced a forthcoming treatise on the events surrounding Asher Lemlein "together with the matter of R. David [Re'uveni]."[168] Contemporaries like Isaac and Treves and like Ḥalfan and de Blanis demonstrate that the strong hopes for redemption that had gripped Jews in northern Italy and Germany in the first years of the sixteenth century did not quietly subside when the appointed time went by uneventfully. Rather, Asher Lemlein's urgent message of the near arrival of the Messiah was revived during later episodes of messianic excitement.

3

JEWISH AND CHRISTIAN MESSIANISMS

CULTURAL TRANSFER AND REALPOLITIK

The turn of the sixteenth century saw a resurgence of Jewish-Christian end-time expectation. Once again, particularly in the 1520s and 1530s, there were increased efforts to calculate the apocalyptic schedule; and because of a planetary conjunction, the year 1524 was considered especially rich in significance. The woodcut adorning the title page of a calendar by the south German astrologer Leonhard Reynmann vividly illustrates the expectations that were in the air at the time (fig. 5). The conjunction of the planets Saturn, Jupiter, and Mars, which was to take place at the beginning of the year in the constellation Pisces, was for Reynmann the unambiguous sign of a deluge that would destroy villages and cities. Images of drummers and pipers hint at a military confrontation that Reynmann predicted would also occur under the planetary influence. The result would be social revolution: In the lower half of the picture, a menacing army of peasants stands opposite the rulers, the worldly and spiritual authorities.[1] Beginning in 1524, local peasant revolts did, in fact, become more frequent in southern and central Germany as well as in the adjacent regions of the Alps. The

Practica vber die grossen vnd ma-

nigfeltigen Coniunction der Planeten/die im
jar M. D. XXiiij. erscheinen/vñ vnge-
zweiffelt vil wunderparlicher
ding geperen werden.

Auß Rö.Kay.May.Gnaden vnd Freihaiten/hüt sich menigklich/diese meine Practica in zwayen Jaren nach zütrucken bey verliehrung. 4.Marck lötigs Golts.

Figure 5. Leonhard Reynmann, *Practica vber die grossen vnd manigfeltigen Coniunction der Planeten, die im jar M.D.XXiiij. erscheinen* (Nuremberg, 1523), title page. (HAB, Wolfenbüttel, A: 171.21 Quod. [5]1)

Jewish astronomer Abraham Zakuto interpreted the constellation of the stars analogously: "It points toward great hardships in the western lands of Edom, namely that the sea will break through and overwhelm a part of their lands." For Zakuto, however, the catastrophes were at the same time an occasion for joy, since "in the very same year redemption will come as well as salvation for Israel, although there will also be wars and confusion. . . . Mars in conjunction with Saturn and Jupiter indicates great wars, like the wars of Gog and Magog. . . . But because Venus stands nearby, on that day the salvation of Israel will sprout and Messiah ben David will come."[2]

A Christian pamphlet from the beginning of 1524 bears witness to acute messianic expectations among the Jews of Germany.[3] It concerns an encounter between two travelers, Vivus (Haim) and Johannes, at an inn outside the city gates of Nuremberg. In the course of their conversation, the Jew declines the Christian's attempts at proselytizing, because the advent of the Messiah is, after all, just around the corner: "Our Messiah will come, as the rumbling among you means something."[4] He is referring here to the unrest within Christian society as a result of the Protestant Reformation, which strengthened the feeling among both Jews and Christians that they were living in the end-times. Thus, Johannes shares the Jew's apocalyptic expectation, although in a somewhat different sense: "Yes, we hope for the last coming of our Christ so that he may set the world right and establish the heavenly eternal temple."[5]

The apocalypticism of the 1520s and 1530s was indeed strongly influenced by the Reformation. Martin Luther and other reformers understood their own activities in the millennial framework, according to which the pope in Rome had revealed himself to all the world as the Antichrist. Many Jews likewise interpreted the conflict within the Christian Church as a sign of the approaching end. The appearance of Luther seemed to portend imminent redemption, and the great reformer was seen as the precursor to the Messiah. On the one hand, the Reformation destroyed the unity of Christendom—the insidious dissolution of Edom?[6] On the other hand, Christianity seemed, in the first years of the Reformation, to draw closer to Judaism, since through Luther's teachings Christians were learning to distance themselves from their "idolatrous" usages. Thus, the reformatory efforts at returning to the roots of Christianity, the emphasis on the authority of the Hebrew Bible, and Reformation iconoclasm were interpreted as the gradual dissolution of belief in Jesus, which would finally lead to the longed-for eschatological return of Christians to the God of Israel.[7]

Moreover, early Reformation discourse reveals a stance toward the Jews that was relatively tolerant compared to the usual view. Above all, Luther's *Daß Jesus Christus ein geborener Jude sei* (That Jesus Christ Was Born a Jew, 1523), an admittedly proselytizing text calling for the friendly treatment of the Jews, found a positive response in contemporary German Jewry.[8] Luther speaks out sharply here against the practice of the "Papists," saying that "they have treated the Jews as if they were dogs and not human beings, and done nothing but curse them and take their possessions."[9] Against this, he avers that the Jews are "blood brothers, cousins and brothers of our lord. . . . If one wants to help them, then one must do not as the pope decrees but practice the precept of Christian love and accept them as friends."[10] From the Jewish perspective, such words seemed full of promise, as if announcing a fundamental change in the relation between Jews and Christians.

The convert Antonius Margaritha, however, explicitly warned against this new intercourse with Jews, saying he considered it ineffective as a means of convincing them of the truth of Christian belief. On the contrary, the Jews, according to Margaritha, saw even in the mere fact that the Christians tolerated them a confirmation of their status as the chosen people. "They take great comfort now that many Christians have for some time shown themselves to be friendly to them and more [open to] fellowship with them, also that they now may openly trade and sojourn in many places where they previously might not go at all, and such things bring them at present much advantage that had been strange to them before, but from this follows only that they all the more curse and despise Christ and all who adhere to him."[11]

This interpretation of the Reformation as a positive force, formulated as it was in the context of Jewish messianic expectation, nevertheless quickly dissipated in the face of cold reality. Luther's positive stance toward the Jews was short-lived, and he soon pivoted to Margaritha's line. As early as 1538, with *Wider die Sabbather* (Against the Sabbatarians), he began to espouse radically anti-Jewish views, calling for the Jews to be persecuted and driven out. The polemical zenith was reached in 1543 with the publication of *Von den Juden und ihren Lügen* (On the Jews and Their Lies) and *Vom Schem Hamiphorasch und vom Geschlecht Christi* (On *Shem ha-meforash* and the House of Christ).[12]

Although Luther himself recoiled from millennial upheaval (despite his apocalyptic worldview), radical reformatory circles in the 1520s and 1530s adhered to chiliasm with its revolutionary attempts to erect the kingdom of God on earth.[13] Thus, the Thuringian theologian Thomas Müntzer became one of the most influential leaders in the German Peasant Rebellion, which sought to eradicate the godless political elites and to reorder the world for social justice in accordance with God's will. In Anabaptist circles among others, numerous millennial thinkers and activists appeared during this time. In 1528, the Anabaptist leader in Augsburg, Hans Hut, expected the Day of Judgment on Pentecost,[14] while in Erfurt, Hans Römer, a companion of Müntzer, planned to plunge his home city into Anabaptist violence in hopes of inspiring a renewed revolt of the lower classes. Before Römer was able to realize his millennial Anabaptist kingdom of equality, however, the conspiracy's cover was blown, and he was arrested along with his followers.[15] More successful, at least temporarily, were similar efforts in Münster in Westphalia. Beginning around 1530 in Strasbourg, Melchior Hoffmann proclaimed a theocratic kingdom in preparation for the Second Coming of Jesus. When he was arrested three years later by the city council, some of his followers managed to seize power in Münster and to realize the promised "New Jerusalem" there. In 1534, the year Hoffmann had calculated for the end of the world, they proclaimed the kingdom of Zion.[16]

At the same time, David Re'uveni and Solomon Molkho were causing a furor in the Jewish world. Re'uveni first appeared in 1523 in the Middle

East and then in Europe, claiming to be an emissary from the Lost Tribes of Israel sent to help liberate the Holy Land from the Turks. His mission, in which he was eventually supported by Molkho, a former converso from Portugal, caused a resurgence of Jewish hopes for an imminent return to Jerusalem, and for a short time, he received encouragement even from the most powerful European authorities. The pope praised the plan, as did the king of Portugal, who promised military aid; Charles V, king of Spain and emperor of the Holy Roman Empire of German Nations, granted Re'uveni and Molkho an audience in Regensburg in 1532.[17]

The apocalyptic landscape in the Germany of those years reveals how tightly interwoven Jewish and Christian messianism actually were. For both Jews and Christians, the encounter between their end-time imaginations had far-reaching ideological and political consequences. The intensive interreligious discourse concerning the events of the Last Days played out in diverse social strata and religious groupings, and it took the form of indirect cultural exchange as well as personal dialogue. Paired with considerations of realpolitik and practical measures, since ultimately the end was expected in the concrete here and now, this discourse reveals a reciprocal influence of apocalyptic expectations, concepts, and ideas. Through a cultural transfer that, given the nature of the situation, necessarily had polemical undertones, new variations on traditional patterns of thought and argumentation arose. Ultimately, this led to a profound entanglement of each group in the messianic activity of the other.

I. THE RED JEWS: CHRISTIAN AND JEWISH COLORING

> *These Red Jews shall come and redeem them.*
>
> —Antonius Margaritha, *The Entire Jewish Faith*, 1530

In the sixteenth century, numerous "little Hebrew and German [i.e., Yiddish] booklets" were in circulation concerning the so-called Ten Lost Tribes of Israel—or "Red Jews," as they were known in the contemporary

Jewish-Christian vernacular idiom in Germany.[18] After part of the Israelite population that had inhabited ancient Israel's Northern Kingdom was led into exile by the conquering Assyrians, the Jewish myth arose about a return of these "lost" tribes. The myth established itself firmly within the apocalyptic literature during the period following the destruction of the Second Temple by the Romans in 70 CE. According to the legend, the Ten Lost Tribes were cut off from the rest of the world by the Sambatyon River. During the six days of the week, the raging waters and tumbling debris make the Sambatyon impassable, while on the Sabbath the waters rest. But the strictures of the Sabbath forbid the Jews from crossing then. Thus they remain trapped until the messianic age, when God will quell the roaring of the Sambatyon, so that the Ten Tribes may cross over unharmed.[19]

In the political situation after the destruction of the Second Temple, the Jewish expectation began to take root that Edom would fall by the hand of the Messiah of the tribe of Ephraim (Joseph), who would come leading the Lost Tribes.[20] Decisive for the consolidation of the military hero image of the Ten Tribes was the travelogue of Eldad ha-Dani, who reached the Jewish community in Qairawān (today's Tunisia) at the end of the ninth century, claiming to be a member of the lost tribe of Dan.[21] Eldad describes the situation of the settlements of the individual Lost Tribes, praises their righteous king, and reports on their religious traditions as well as on the ceaseless wars against their neighbors.

In the early modern period, this image of the Red Jews figured prominently in the eschatological scenario for both Jewish and Christian writers. According to the Jewish conception, the Red Jews represented the powerful warriors who were to finally liberate the people of Israel from domination under Edom. In addition to describing *Mancherley Abergläubischen Ceremonien/ vnnd seltzamen Sitten/ so die zerstreweten Jüden haben* (Various Superstitious Ceremonies and Strange Customs of the Scattered Jews, Erfurt, 1624), the Protestant theologian Hermann Fabronius also lays out the Jewish scenario of the messianic wars: prior to the actual Messiah

(Messiah ben David), his precursor Messiah ben Joseph would appear, "a powerful man of war" from one of the Lost Tribes, who would

> come from the land beyond the River Sambatyon . . . with the tribe Ephraim, Manasseh, Benjamin, and a part of the children of Gad, . . . enter the field, attack the King of Edom, Gog and Magog, that is the Roman Empire, and vanquish and annihilate the Emperor and the Turks.[22]

Although Messiah ben Joseph would fall in battle, his victorious campaign would prepare for the reign of the redeemer from the dynasty of David. From time to time among European Jews in the medieval and early modern periods, it was rumored that the messianic army, in light of the oppression of their brothers in the diaspora, was already arming itself for the fight.[23] And were it not for the unbridgeable Sambatyon, "the Red Jews [would have] come long ago and redeemed us."[24]

Given the centrality of the motif of eschatological revenge on Christians in Ashkenazic thought, the Red Jews were seen no less as apocalyptic avengers than as messianic saviors. The seriousness of the threat to Christians posed by the kingdom beyond the Sambatyon can be clearly heard in Victor von Carben:

> These same Jews are the Red Jews and [they are] strong. They are as many more than all Christians in all of Christendom as you Christians are now more than us, as you will then realize. . . . And here, it should well be noted how great the number of the Ten Tribes must be . . . who can yet help us. And [who] will free us from our imprisonment.[25]

The intra-Jewish discourse on messianic revenge was known to Christians; it therefore comes as no surprise that in Christian images of the millennial scenario, the Red Jews had a nearly identical function. Here, too, the assumption was that this fearsome horde would descend upon Christian Europe in the end-times.[26] According to the Christian view, however, the Red Jews would hardly bring redemption to the Jewish people. Indeed, since the Red Jews were seen as accomplices of the Antichrist, the false Messiah allegedly awaited by the Jews, their triumph would be illusory and short-lived. Together with their demonic leader, they would ultimately be destroyed at the advent of the kingdom of Christ. The apocalyptic construct of this imaginary people, who were to bring wrack and ruin to Christianity, began to develop toward the end of the twelfth century in Europe, and it arose from the combination of Jewish hopes for the return of the Lost Tribes with two other, originally independent, traditions. On the one hand, the Ten Tribes were identified with the barbaric nations whom Alexander the Great, according to a legend from late antiquity, had sealed up in the Caucasus Mountains in order to protect the civilized world. On the other hand was the Jewish-Christian tradition of the apocalyptic wars of Gog and Magog, who in the Latin West were commonly equated with the enclosed nations of the Alexander story.[27] Thus, the Ten Tribes finally became, in the twelfth century, the Jewish destroyers of the Apocalypse.

While Christians in all of Europe were familiar with the Ten Tribes and their role in the end-times, the legend had a particular coloring in Germany that was without parallel in other areas. Here more than elsewhere it was indelibly marked as anti-Jewish. This is expressed already in the specific name given toward the end of the thirteenth century to the Jewish destroyers of the Apocalypse wherever German was spoken: the Red Jews. In the other European languages, this or similar expressions were unknown, a fact that caused the French scholar Guillaume Postel, for example, some confusion. While reading the Latin translation of Victor von Carben's ethnography of Jewish life and ritual, which was originally written in German, Postel came across the expression "Judaei rubri" (Red Jews); he asked himself if it were not perhaps a "figmentum," a thing of Victor's own invention. As he was unable to find further textual evidence, Postel wrote in the margin of his copy of the book (preserved in the National Library of France): "Ubi est regestum?"—Where is this written?[28]

Apart from German, the only other language in which the expression "Red Jews" existed was Yiddish. By the early modern times, the moniker

"Red Jews" was the standard designation for the Ten Tribes in the Yiddish vernacular of Central and Eastern Europe. While it is true that use of the term among Jews in the German-speaking lands prior to the early sixteenth century has thus far not been documented, nevertheless it was at that time already sufficiently current for its origins to have been forgotten. Thus, Antonius Margaritha notes in 1530, "It makes me greatly wonder why one calls these Ten Tribes the Red Jews."[29] It is therefore to be assumed that the term "Red Jews" likely became part of Yiddish linguistic usage around the same time it appeared in German in the late thirteenth century.[30]

Moreover, there is reason to believe that the legend of the Red Jews could already be found in several early Ashkenazic prayer books for the festival days. These first versions, which unfortunately have not survived, were written in Hebrew and very likely arose in the context of a piyyut commentary.[31] In 1630, a new Hebrew translation of the story was justified by noting that the text survived only in Yiddish versions, excepting a few rare older *maḥzorim*.[32] Conversely, the first known Yiddish printing of the story (*Megiles Reb Meyer*, Cremona, circa 1560, also lost) is described as a translation from the Hebrew.[33] But before the story of the Red Jews found its way into writing, it was certainly first transmitted orally, that is, in Yiddish.[34] The earliest surviving Yiddish documents, which we will examine below, date from the end of the sixteenth century.

For both Jews and Christians in Germany, then, the Red Jews were an actual political-military power. The fact of their existence went uncontested up to the Reformation, and their supposed territory in eastern or northern Asia was marked on maps until into the sixteenth century. Only with the increasing knowledge of geography did the Red Jews' territory ultimately disappear from the maps. On the *mappa mundi* of the Salzburg Benedictine monk Andreas Walsperger (Constance, 1448), for instance, "the land of the Red Jews, who are closed up in the Caspian Mountains," is indicated far in the northeast, immediately adjacent to the (likewise illustrated) land of the Cannibals (fig. 6).[35] Their cartographical moniker *iudei inclusi* (or *iudei clausi*), "enclosed Jews," is paralleled in Hebrew literature, where the

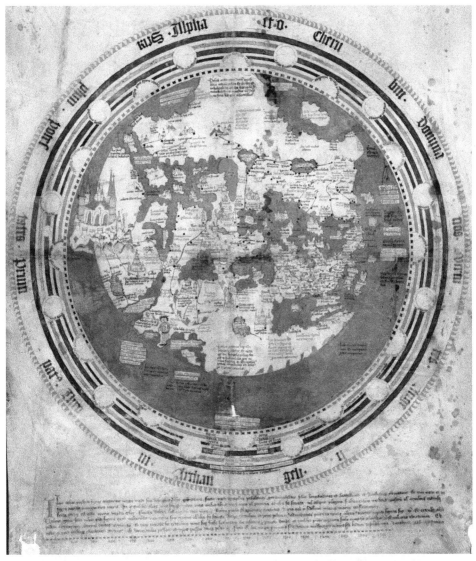

Figure 6. Andreas Walsperger, *Mappa mundi* (Constance, 1448). (Biblioteca Apostolica Vaticana, Cod. Pal. lat. 1362 b)

Ten Tribes are at times described as "enclosed (or hidden) Jews."[36] Jewish sources also often locate them beyond the Mountains of Darkness, such as in the Hebrew legend of Alexander (*Ma'aseh Alexandros*).[37] A map by Hans Rüst, written in the German vernacular and intended for a wider audience (circulated as a pamphlet in three printings around 1480), envisions the Jewish tribes in more than one site. Here, a figure wearing a Jewish hat marks the location of the kingdom of Gog and Magog in the southeast, behind a chain of mountains. In addition to this traditional position, Rüst's *mappa mundi* also labels an island in the Red Sea as the home of the Red Jews (fig. 7).[38]

Since the Red Jews were believed to be living in the land where pepper grows, and thus to have access, as in the other spice countries of Asia, to large sources of the "black gold" as well as to "ginger and cinnamon and all kinds of spices,"[39] one could easily imagine them also as trading partners. "On Friday the Red Jews place many sacks of pepper at the port of the water [the Sambatyon River], then come the heathens on the Sabbath and bring as much grain to the city."[40] By means of such trade, involving luxury goods very much in demand in Europe, the Red Jews were thought to provide themselves with necessary staples, despite being cut off from the rest of the world by the raging river: "On the Sabbath, [the river] is completely calm and the neighboring Christians and heathens deliver the enclosed Jews, as they are called, victuals to sell them, for the Jews are not allowed to travel on the Sabbath."[41] According to the legend, the Red Jews also imported iron from the Ottoman Empire for the manufacture of weapons.[42] This raw material was said to be so valuable to the warlike Jews beyond the Sambatyon that they weighed it out in gold. In 1631, out of curiosity about the river and its inhabitants, the traveler Gerson ha-Levi Yidls of Prague joined up in the hinterlands of Thessaloniki with a trade caravan bound for the Indian subcontinent, which was to make a delivery of the sought-after metal to the Red Jews. He claims to have observed that "for a hundredweight of iron, they pay a hundredweight in gold."[43]

Figure 7. Hans Rüst, *Mappa mundi* [Augsburg, ca. 1480]. (Pierpont Morgan Library, New York, PML 19921)

In addition to spices, the traders brought another product from the Sambatyon River to Europe: small amounts of its water and sands. In the seventeenth century, Samuel Sanvil Treves reports that a market crier in Linz offered a small flask of it for sale.[44] Individuals and synagogues alike prided themselves on the possession of this souvenir.[45] The water samples were especially desirable, since they retained the mysterious quality of the river itself—for six days of the week roiling in agitated motion and then resting on the Sabbath. Thus, every Friday these practical hourglasses indicated the beginning of the Sabbath.[46] Nor was this all, for were they finally to cease their movement altogether, it would mean the beginning of the redemption. In Europe, the supposed waters of the Sambatyon were apparently used for medicinal purposes as well. Gerson Yidls reports that the Christians living in the vicinity of the river firmly believed in its healing powers. They

> do not drink of it nor do they give their animals to drink. For they say the stream is holy; it is God's envoy and does ever his commandment to rest on the Sabbath. Therefore no man is worthy to drink of it. But whoever is scabrous and bathes in it the water heals. Also whoever is afflicted with shingles and washes with it is healed.[47]

Travelers regularly set out on the way to the Ten Tribes. Their fantastical descriptions of the distant kingdom and of the lifestyle of its Jewish inhabitants were beloved by European readers in both the medieval and the early modern periods. Thus the well-known twelfth-century Hebrew travel narratives of Benjamin of Tudela and Petahya of Regensburg, as well as the earlier report of Eldad ha-Dani, were among the first texts printed after the invention of the printing press, appearing throughout the fifteenth and sixteenth centuries in multiple editions and in Latin translation.[48]

The Ten Tribes also figure in the popular group of legends surrounding Prester John, the mythological ruler of a utopian kingdom of Christian fantasy. Beginning in the thirteenth or fourteenth century, after the news of a Christian community in East Africa had reached the West, the kingdom was imagined in what is present-day Ethiopia. Parallel to the Jewish representation of the rescuers beyond the Sambatyon, the figure of Prester John kept alive the hope during the time of the Crusades that beyond the Arabian lands a potential ally against the infidels was to be found. In the twelfth century, an alleged letter from the priest-king to the Byzantine emperor Manuel I. Komnenos caused a great stir. The text, originally composed in Latin, existed in various versions and was translated into nearly all European languages as well as into Hebrew. Leaning on the Eldad ha-Dani tradition, the author also counts the ten Jewish tribes, who live behind a "river of stones," among the numerous nations that are subject to Prester John's authority.[49]

Because any information concerning the Red Jews carried with it an apocalyptic significance, both Jews and Christians—albeit for different reasons—followed the developments beyond the Sambatyon with great interest. This did not change in the early modern period. On the contrary: the age of expanding European sea travel, with its pioneering geographical discoveries, meant an enormous widening of the borders of the known world. The European reader was overwhelmed with astonishing novelties about distant lands and peoples. These were taken up on the horizon of established thinking, however, and far from being undermined, the old legends—about populous nations and powerful rulers who had a precisely defined task to fulfill at the end of time—were seen as being bolstered by the new knowledge. The interest in the lost Jewish tribes also gained a lively currency in this way, and one located their supposed homeland in the newly opened regions of Asia, Africa, and the New World beyond the ocean.[50]

In 1523, a year of intense apocalyptic speculation, it was widely rumored that "news of saviors from beyond the Sambatyon River spread among all the lands."[51] In Germany in the second half of the year, various pamphlets circulated "concerning a great multitude and host of Jews, long enclosed and hidden by uninhabitable deserts, who have now broken out and appeared."[52] The illustration on one of the title pages shows the Red Jews as a great military force, heavily equipped with armor and lances (fig. 8). They emerge from the Mountains of Darkness in order to cross the Sambatyon, which lies placid before them. They are marked as Jews by the pointed Jewish hat, which also is shown emblazoned on their standards.

The sensational news of the march of the Ten Tribes was a theme of heated discussion between Jews and Christians, since ultimately it affected both groups. For the Jews, the alleged advance toward Jerusalem, with its deeply internalized messianic consequences, was an occasion for joy; for the Christians, it was grounds rather for concern. The Jewish messianic expectation was thus further strengthened by Christian interest, as Christian Gerson well knew: "Many Christians also have much to say about the Red Jews, although they have never seen them, wherefore the false delusion is spread that the Messiah could indeed be born from the tribe Judah of the Red Jews."[53]

The information disseminated by the 1523 pamphlets supposedly came first—by "letters and genuine accounts sent from Jerusalem and Damascus and elsewhere"—to a certain Jew in the area of Romance languages.[54] This individual's cousin passed the news on to a high-ranking official in Trieste, where it was overheard by one of the man's servants, who in turn was the means by which the news finally came to the pamphleteer's ear.[55] The contents of the letters from Damascus arrived by other channels in Italy, as reported by Lorenzo Orio, the Venetian ambassador to the king of Hungary, who tells of similar rumors that the Jews in Hungary had received from Syria. Orio himself was, of course, reluctant to believe that a massive number of Jews, after having been sealed up for two thousand years in the inaccessible mountain regions of India, had now set out en masse for the Holy Land. Nevertheless, on October 5, 1523, he conveyed the information to the Venetian historiographer Marino Sanuto the younger. The matter was politically and militarily explosive. Prior to the invasion of Hungary by the Turks in mid-August of that year, many had been wondering what had caused the sultan to hesitate for so long. Although this had generally been attributed to the outbreak of the plague in the Ottoman Empire,

Von ainer grosse meng

vnnd gewalt der Juden die lange zeyt
mit vnwonhafftigen Wüsten beschlossen vnd verborgen
gewesen/ Yetzunder auß gebrochen vñ an tag kommen seyn/ Dreyssig tag rayß von Jherusalem
sich nyder geschlagen/ Was sy fürgenõ-
men haben findt man nach laut dises
Sendbrieffs zum tayl glaubliche vnderricht.

1523.

Figure 8. *Von ainer grosse meng vnnd gewalt der Juden* ([Augsburg], 1523), title page. (HAB, Wolfenbüttel, A 131.1 Theol. [27])

the conjecture now spread from Jewish circles that the military power of the Turks had been tied down by the advance of the Jewish armies from East Asia.[56]

It is no surprise that the Jewish-Christian obsession with the Red Jews had polemical undertones. At the beginning of December 1523, Michael Kramer, a pastor in Kunitz near Jena (who belonged to the broader Wittenberg circle around Luther), met the Jewish merchant Jacob of Brucks. The woodcut on the title page of the pamphlet in which Kramer describes the encounter shows the two interlocutors in the midst of their conversation (fig. 9).[57] They spoke, writes Kramer, about this and that, "of the country's customs" and "out of the old testament."[58] Soon, however, they touched upon the contentious Messiah question. In his efforts to convince Jacob of the fulfillment of biblical prophecy in Jesus, Kramer deploys a tried-and-true weapon of Christian polemics: Genesis 49:10, "The sceptre shall not depart from Judah, nor the ruler's staff from between his feet; until Shiloh come and the homage of peoples be his." Evidence for the messiahhood of Jesus is seen in the standard Christian interpretation of Shiloh as the Messiah, since Israel had lost its political sovereignty in the time of Jesus and thus far had failed to regain it, such that the Jewish people had lived in dispersed exile for some fifteen hundred years.[59] Against the Christian interpretation, Jacob counters, "We have never yet lost our scepter completely, but have always had kings, princes and prophets." To the snide response of the pastor, "where then?," Jacob slyly asks whether it is possible that Kramer has never heard of the independent Jewish kingdom beyond the Sambatyon. In the mercantile world, it is after all common knowledge, says Jacob.[60]

With this, Jacob adverts to the discussion surrounding the Christological significance of Genesis 49:10, which is the basis for the contending legends of the Red Jews and of Prester John. Scholars agree that the Christian description of the realm of the priest-king was intended to refute the Jewish claim to political independence through Eldad ha-Dani. On the one hand, the Jewish legend is confirmed in the famous letter of Prester John,

Eyn vnderredūg vom
glawben/durch herr Micheln kromer/
Pfarherr zu Cunitz/ vnd eynem Judischen Rabien/ mit
namen Jacob vonn Brucks/ geschehenn ynß
Richters hauße do selbst zu Cunitz.
Mitwoch nach Andree
M. D. xxiij.

Pfarherr.   Jacob Jud.

Figure 9. Michael Kramer, *Eyn vnderredung vom glawben* (Erfurt, 1523), title page. (HAB, Wolfenbüttel, H: Yv 2272.8° Helmst)

for indeed, "ten Jewish tribes live beyond the river of stones." On the other hand, however, "although they claim to have kings, they are nevertheless our servants and pay our Excellency tribute."[61] In marked contrast to this, the Jewish interpretation presented the image of a powerful kingdom, in which the Ten Tribes lived under their own sovereign king, in effect refuting the Christological exegesis. The popularity of this legend is easily understood in light of the misery in much of the Jewish diaspora. The existence of the Ten Tribes offered psychological support to Jews living in an inimical Christian environment, and it seemed to guarantee, in spite of that environment, Jewish messianic hopes.

The convert Paul Joseph, who had been rabbi at Poznań before having himself baptized in 1611, explains the Ten Tribes' peculiar designation in Yiddish by referring to their red garments. "Whence the Jews of that same land are called the Red Jews," he concludes.[62] Crimson was considered the color of dominion; thus, in a certain sense the existence of the Red Jews was in itself vivid proof of an uninterrupted Jewish monarchy. A booklet from the mid-eighteenth century explains in a similar way why the German Jews referred to the Ten Tribes as the Red Jews. Here the convert Friedrich Albrecht Augusti, pastor at Eschenbergen in the region of Gotha, explains:

> Under the term Red Jews they certainly understand the dwellers beyond the River Sambatyon, whom they give this name that is so magnificent and highly regarded among them, as much because of the vivid red color of their countenances as of the precious crimson garments in which they go about as a free people in order to distinguish themselves from all others living in misery. [Note:] The European and Asian Jews are not allowed to wear red garments, because they are still in mourning for the temple and the city of Jerusalem; the red color is considered among them a sign of freedom as well as of the greatest joyfulness. The royal children have always been distinguished from others by this color, but they say the Red Jews have never suffered *galut* or *ḥorban*, i.e., neither enslavement nor

destruction; these Jews dress themselves in the most beautiful crimson, and none can forbid it them.[63]

The use of the term "Red Jews" in Yiddish reflects a hidden polemical dialogue with the rival concept of the Red Jews in Christian apocalypticism. This aspect of the genealogy has thus far gone unrecognized by scholars of Yiddish language and literature, the majority of whom know the *royte yidlekh* only from classical Yiddish literature. It has generally been assumed that the concept is an autonomous invention of East European Jews in the modern period, the much older use in western Yiddish having simply been forgotten. Consequently, why the Lost Tribes were humorously referred to as Red Jews could not be further explained in terms of etymology.[64] The Red Jews became popular above all through *Kitser masoes Binyomin hashlishi* (The Brief Travels of Benjamin the Third), one of the most famous novellas of Sholem Yankev Abramovich alias Mendele Moykher Sforim. This quixotic travel narrative, first published in 1878, is the earliest documentation of the Red Jews in modern Yiddish literature. Here they refer to the Ten Lost Tribes of Israel, whom Benjamin, a Jewish Don Quixote, sets out to find.[65]

The Red Jews turn out to be a prime example of the polemical genre of counter-history. As formulated by Amos Funkenstein, counter-history is defined as "the systematic exploitation of the adversary's most trusted sources against their grain."[66] By adopting an adversary's central motifs and reinterpreting them against their original intention, counter-history stages an attack on that adversary's collective narrative and thus strikes a blow to his self-image. Ultimately, what is achieved is the negation of the adversary's identity. The case of the Red Jews is remarkable in this regard, for they appear in a double sense as counter-historical protagonists: while the Christian legend of the Red Jews presents an alternative reading of the Jewish hopes for the return of the Ten Lost Tribes, the Old Yiddish concept is for its part an answer to the challenge of the Christian interpretation. The Red Jews thus were absorbed in a Christian anti-Jewish counter-history, which was then reinscribed in a Jewish polemical-apologetic variation: in effect a counter-counter-history.

The Jewish counter-history of the Red Jews takes up the concept itself, that is, the association of Jews with the color red. There have been numerous attempts to explain the genesis of this attribution. Most derive the name from an ethnic group that historically has been identified in one way or another with the Ten Lost Tribes: from the Arab tribe *Ḥimir* (red); from red-complected peoples in China or North America; from the Mongols, who invaded Europe in the thirteenth century and wore red clothing and head-dress;[67] or from the Khazars, who are described in medieval Arabic texts as being red.[68] None of these conjectures are supported by the source material.

David Biale has refined Funkenstein's definition of counter-history and extended it beyond the realm of simple contradiction. Counter-history, according to Biale, does not exhaust itself in the mere pejorative inversion of intention. Because it is also motivated by other narrative impulses, the counter-historical construction can be significantly more complex. We see this, for example, when an adversarial narrative is supplemented through the adhesion of alternative folkloric traditions.[69] The use of the color red in the image of the Ten Tribes is a case in point. According to the admittedly ambiguous and frequently subjective moral logic of color symbolism, the Christian coloration of the Jews beyond the Sambatyon was in itself a polemical move:[70] red was considered a color of warning, and it had a strongly negative connotation in Christian Europe. Thus, in medieval iconography the enemies of Christ are often both singled out and stigmatized through the color red. (The color yellow was used similarly to emphasize certain characteristics.)[71] Often this took the concrete form of red hair. Because of its deviation from the norm, red hair, a rarity in all ethnic groups, was generally held to be an outward sign of a furtive and malicious character. In religious art, Christ's enemies were therefore portrayed with red hair and beard; this was particularly true of the betrayer of Christ, Judas Iscariot, who in the late Middle Ages in Germany was often also given a reddish complexion as a badge of his treachery.[72]

The Red Jews thus embodied the negative message that the color red already communicated. In the final analysis, they personified the ultimate Jewish evildoers, the last and greatest adversaries of Christ, plotting together with the Antichrist, their leader and Christ's archenemy. The famous Antichrist window in Frankfurt an der Oder portrays them with red garments and red faces to underline their enmity and violence (fig. 1, fig. 10).[73] In an illustrated historiated Bible from the fifteenth century, portraying the Red Jews' incarceration by Alexander, they are shown with red hair and beards, in stark contrast to the blond Macedonian king (fig. 11).[74]

Although a mutual influence of image and text may certainly be assumed, it seems unlikely that the negative meaning of the color red constituted the single generative background for the name of the imaginary apocalyptic nation. Other traditions almost certainly came into play as well. Annette Weber has drawn attention to Eldad ha-Dani's description of the beautiful linen garments worn by the Sons of Moses (*Bnei Moshe*), who he claims lived in the vicinity of his own tribe, Dan, though divided from them by the Sambatyon. The Sons of Moses are the Levites, who after the destruction of Solomon's Temple are said to have been carried across the mythical river on a cloud.[75] According to Eldad, the descendants of the lost temple servants dyed their garments scarlet red using cochineal, similar to the historical robes of the biblical high priests.[76] At the time when the term "Red Jews" was coined, Eldad's narrative was evidently known in Christian circles, as its reception in the legend of Prester John makes clear.[77]

By the sixteenth century, the polemic concerning the Red Jews was also linked to the Jewish-Christian typological interpretations of the biblical pair Jacob/Israel and Esau/Edom.[78] Even before the twin brothers' birth, God had announced to their mother, Rebecca: "Two nations are in your womb, two separate peoples shall issue from your body; One people shall be mightier than the other, and the older shall serve the younger."[79] The elder son is Esau, the younger Jacob, who defrauds his brother of his birthright as the firstborn and thus becomes progenitor of the people of Israel. The Bible transfers the enmity between the two brothers onto the rivalry

Figure 10. *The Antichrist with the Red Jews beside the Sambatyon River,* panel in the Antichrist window at St. Mary's Church, Frankfurt an der Oder, ca. 1370. (Brandenburg State Office for the Preservation of Monuments and the State Archaeological Museum, Zossen, photo archives, no. s II 4c, photo: Peter Thieme and Florian Profitlich, 2006)

Figure 11. Historiated Bible, fifteenth century, fol. 531v. (Berlin State Library, Prussian Cultural Heritage, manuscript collection, Ms. Germ. 2° 565)

between the two nations, the Israelites and the Edomites, and resolves it, according to Genesis 25, with the Edomites's submission to King David. In the year 70 CE, however, when the Roman legions under Titus destroyed the Second Temple and the Jewish state permanently lost its sovereignty to Rome, the typology received a new cast: Edom became a synonym for Rome, whose demise was postponed to the messianic future. With the Christianization of the Roman Empire in the fourth century, a religious meaning was added to the political meaning: the enemy Edom was from now on also identified with the Christian Church.[80] In the Christian narrative, the roles were cast inversely: the Christians themselves were Jacob/Israel, while the Jews were Esau/Edom. After all, the Jews had lost their status as God's people to their younger brothers, the Christians, and thus the Christian Church was the new, true Israel (verus Israel). Proceeding from Paul's distinction in the Letter to the Romans between the rejection of the corporeal Israel (the Jews) and the election of the spiritual Israel (the Christians), the church fathers raised the implicit equation of Esau with Judaism and Jacob with the Christian Church to the level of doctrine.[81]

Both sides thus laid claim to the identity of the chosen and finally victorious Israel, and each assigned to the other the role of the defeated and rejected Edom. The name Edom, moreover, is derived in the Bible from the term for red (Hebr. *adom*), whose consonant stem suggests the same root. Edom is therefore "the red one."[82] In the metaphorical sense, this means that the loser in the drama of salvific history is in either case "red"; and, in fact, Esau is described in the Bible as having been "red" even at his birth.[83] The biblical etymology of the name was used by both Jews and Christians as a means of characterizing the other, whom they each equated with Edom. Thus, in the early modern period, the Ashkenazic piyyut *Ma'oz ẓur* (Stronghold of Rock) refers to Christians as "the red ones in the shadow of the cross."[84] A later Midrash paraphrases Esau's redness as "bloody," since "he hates the blood of circumcision."[85] Against this, Meliton of Sardes declares that the Jews are called Edom because they are red with the blood of Christ, which still clings to their hands.[86]

In the sixteenth century, the German characterization of the Ten Tribes as "Rote Juden" (Red Jews) was thus derived from the equation of the Jews with Edom. Justus Jonas, known as the translator of Luther's works, suspects as much: "Yet it seems to me that by the term Red Jews it is made known that they are Edom, for Edom means red."[87] A further source several decades later supports this explanation. The pastor Georg Nigrinus (Schwarz) of Giessen speculates that the name comes

> perhaps from Edom or from their bloodthirst.[88] For this reason the Jews in Europe secretly favor them and hope they will be set free by [the Red Jews] and come again into their land. They are happy too when the Turk rises up against Christianity and hope the scepter of the Christians will thus be taken away. For all of their scribes say as long as the Edomites have the scepter they cannot regain their kingdom. Thus do they refer to us Christians.[89]

In this passage, the author not only explains the term "Red Jews" by means of the biblical typology, but he also uses a classical rhetorical technique of counter-history: he takes the Jewish concept, according to which Edom will be overthrown at the end of days, and turns it on its head. In the Christian representation of the Red Jews, it is not the Christians who play the role of the red losers at the end, but the Ten Tribes—those whom the Jews expected to bring about the destruction of Edom.[90]

The Yiddish answer to the Christian legend created a new field of associations for the Red Jews. In the Yiddish counter-history, the redness of the Jews beyond the Sambatyon is traced back not to Edom but to the biblical King David, whom the Bible likewise describes as "red."[91] With this deft device arose a polemical-apologetic satire that negated the Christian definition of the Red Jews. The key is the second of the two passages in the First Book of Samuel that describe David in this way. It is the famous story of the combat between David and the Philistine giant Goliath, from which David famously emerges victorious.[92] The Yiddish counter-history tells anew the story of the Red Jews according to the model of "David versus Goliath," thus restoring to the main protagonists the aura of victory.

The Jewish legend of the Red Jews was transmitted in various versions in Old Yiddish literature. The oldest known and at the same time the best loved of these is the version designated in modern scholarship as *Ma'aseh Akdamut* (The Story of Akdamut).[93] It survives as the only Yiddish narrative in the small, otherwise Hebrew-language circle narrative about the synagogue poet R. Meir b. Isaac Shatz. Meir Shatz was cantor in the Jewish community of Worms during the second half of the eleventh century. (This is also the source of the acronym "*Shaz*": *sheliah zibbur* is "emissary of the congregation," i.e., cantor). He is best known as the author of the Aramaic piyyut *Akdamut millin* (Introduction to the Words), which paints the future salvation of Israel during the messianic age in brilliant colors and is recited in the Ashkenazic liturgy before the Torah reading on the first day of Shavuot, the Feast of Weeks.[94] The origin legend of the hymn is a specific instantiation of the myth of the Red Jews.

By virtue of its attachment to a beloved piyyut, the richly detailed and dramatic narrative of Rabbi Meir and the Red Jews became very popular in the sixteenth century.[95] Just how well known it became is evidenced by the censor's lists of books possessed by the Jewish citizens of Mantua in 1595: they register eight copies of the first printing of the narrative, which had been published circa 1560 in Cremona under the title *Megiles Reb Meyer*.[96] Since this edition has apparently been completely lost, the earliest preserved version of *Ma'aseh Akdamut*, and at the same time the oldest known text of the Yiddish legend of the Red Jews at all, dates to the late sixteenth century. The text is preserved in the Yiddish manuscript of a historical-folkloric anthology of edifying narratives (ca. 1580–1600) in which also a second version of the legend of the Red Jews appears in a letter from Safed, dated 1579.[97] Both texts underwent numerous editions under various headings in the early modern period and thereafter. At least four additional Yiddish printings of *Ma'aseh Akdamut* followed in the seventeenth through early nineteenth centuries in Fürth and Amsterdam,[98] while the letter from Safed, together with a miracle story about Isaac Luria, appeared in Prague in the 1660s.[99]

The Old Yiddish legend of the Red Jews tells of a Jewish community under duress from an evil Christian. In *Ma'aseh Akdamut*, which sets the scene in the traditional and storied community of Worms, a Christian magician, master of black magic, and notorious hater of Jews murders many thousands with the help of his satanic arts. When the Jews ask the authorities for protection, the sorcerer agrees to leave them unmolested in the future under one condition: within a year the Jews must present to him a Jewish magician of equal power. Should they fail, however, he will destroy them all. The Jews have no choice but to agree, and in despair they go in search of a Jewish miracle worker capable of standing up to the fearsome black sorcerer in a contest of magic. The emissary Meir Shatz is entrusted with this apparently impossible task, and his search finally leads him to the Sambatyon, behind which the Red Jews dwell. The Red Jews, for their part, are known for their learning in the magical uses of the names of God, which are frequently part of Jewish magic formulas. Meir Shatz must wait till the beginning of the Sabbath, however, before he can ford the river that still divides him from the land of the Red Jews, since during the week the river roars so mightily that it is impossible to cross. Only on the Sabbath do the waters grant passage to travelers, since on that day, in adherence to the general law of the Sabbath, they lie quiet. As the Sabbath finally begins, Meir Shatz does not hesitate to break its law and cross over to the Red Jews, since the success of his mission is ultimately a matter of life and death. Having arrived at the other side, he explains the unhappy situation to the locals, who immediately come to the aid of their fellow believers and select one of their own for the contest with the evil sorcerer. The climax of the narrative describes the subsequent battle between the black magician and this Red Jew, from which in the end the Jew emerges victorious and thus frees his brethren from the deadly menace. *Ma'aseh Akdamut* adds: since the contest took place on the evening before Shavuot, Meir Shatz composed a piyyut with an acrostic of his own name for the festival, *Akdamut millin*, which he then gave to the Red Jew before his departure for Worms, with the request that it be taken up in his hometown's liturgy in memory of him.[100]

The analogy of motifs between the Yiddish legend of the Red Jews and the biblical story of David and Goliath is obvious. The Christian oppressor slips easily into the role of Goliath. His adversary, the Red Jew, corresponds to David. Now it becomes clear why the Old Yiddish version describes only this single Red Jew, the savior from the land beyond the Sambatyon, as *rot yudlayn*: "little Red Jew." By contrast, in the collective, the Trans-Sambatyonians are called *rote yudn* (Red Jews), without the diminutive (not *royte yidlekh*, as in modern Yiddish). Insofar as the narrative assigns the little Red Jew further attributes, such as "old," "shaking," "lame and limping," it presents the reader from the beginning with a hero who is apparently weak.[101] He is neither the supernaturally strong, universally feared prototype of a Red "muscle-Jew," as described in the Christian tradition, nor a proud hero and brave warrior, as Eldad ha-Dani characterizes the members of the Ten Tribes. He is a fellow who, like David against Goliath, stands up to an enemy power that is in every way and by any human measure hopelessly superior to him. Thus, in the version of the Red Jews' story featured in the letter from Safed, the rescuers from afar are two seven-year-old children, a girl and a boy.[102]

It is precisely David's redness that reveals his supposed weakness. When Saul sends him forth as an equal opponent into battle, Goliath can hardly believe his eyes: "for he was but a boy, ruddy and handsome."[103] Jewish commentators in the Middle Ages, for example, David Kimhi, understood this ruddy quality or redness as "rosiness" in the sense of young, tender, and pretty.[104] Two passages in Rashi likewise interpret a redness of the face as a sign of beauty and good health.[105] One would ascribe none of these attributes to the dangerous, malevolent, and barbaric folk of the Christian apocalypse. Thus, the Christian imagination of the Red Jews is already held up to ridicule in the fact that, although they are—at least measured in terms of bodily strength—weak, pretty, and essentially innocent as children, they triumph in the end.

The biblical model is traceable through the entire narrative thread. Just as Goliath challenges the armies of the Israelites to decide the war through a duel, the evil Christian in *Ma'aseh Akdamut* forces the Jews to send their candidate into a life-and-death contest of sorcery.[106] His words are similar to those of Goliath, who calls out to the Israelites, "Choose one of your men and let him come down against me. If he bests me in combat and kills me, we will become your slaves; but if I best him and kill him, you shall be our slaves and serve us."[107] The magician declares likewise that he will leave the Jews in peace, under the condition that "they must present to me in one year's time a Jew that can compete with my magic. If not, I will kill them and leave not one of them alive."[108] In the above-mentioned later Hebrew translation of the Yiddish story from 1630, the malevolence of the Christian challenger is explicitly equated with that of "Goliath, the Philistine."[109]

In the biblical story, King Saul is at first reluctant to send the shepherd boy David into the field against Goliath. Similarly, in the Yiddish narrative, the chosen dueler's outward appearance inspires more anxiety and doubt than confidence among the Jews of Worms. How should this puny, lame, limping figure stand up to a powerful sorcerer who is backed by the devil himself? As expected, the evil Christian is incensed when the little Red Jew steps forth to accept the challenge: "The Jews are making a mockery of me, allowing me to do magic against a small, limping, shaking little man."[110] The words recall Goliath's astonishment, mixed with rage and scorn, when he first sees David—a reaction that is even quoted word for word in the Hebrew translation of *Ma'aseh Akdamut*: "Come here, and I will give your flesh to the birds of the sky and the beasts of the field."[111] In the same version, the brave Jew counters with words similar to David's: "This day will not pass before the Lord has delivered you as a conquered carcass before the eyes of this assembly of people."[112]

And, in fact, the little Red Jew achieves the impossible. With the help of the divine names, and in clear imitation of David, who, armed only with a sling, defeated the giant warrior Goliath, the little Red Jew overcomes the black magic of the sorcerer and slays him.[113] The happy ending of *Ma'aseh Akdamut* also has its model in the biblical story, in which Saul promises his daughter in marriage to whoever can defeat Goliath.[114] The little Red Jew in *Ma'aseh Akdamut* marries the daughter of Meir Shatz and remains with her in Worms, the scene of his triumph. For his part, Meir Shatz, who must remain beyond the Sambatyon in the land of the Red Jews in order not to violate the Sabbath again—and this time without sufficient reason—marries the daughter of his son-in-law, henceforth also his father-in-law.[115]

The Yiddish legend switches the casting of good and evil from the Christian template. The original association of the Red Jews with Edom, whose wickedness was a matter of agreement in both Jewish and Christian traditions, is dissolved and replaced by a connection with David, such that they now represent the good. Aggadic lore had shown a previous concern with the different meanings of redness in Esau and in David: when Samuel sees David, he is taken aback, thinking the future king of Israel to be a second Esau, since he interprets David's redness as a bodily sign of his disposition to spill blood. God nevertheless reassures Samuel: in contrast to Esau, David will only slay those who have already, by their misdeeds, forfeited their lives.[116]

On the metaphorical level, then, it is the evil Christian magician who now represents Edom, since the biblical Edomites were subjugated by David.[117] One further level of meaning arises in *Ma'aseh Akdamut* through naming the Red Jews "sons of saviors." The prophet Obadiah is quoted as a source: "And saviors shall come up on Mount Zion."[118] The context of this prophecy was familiar from the daily liturgy. It refers to the final destruction of Esau/Edom and the simultaneous exaltation of Jacob/Israel, as celebrated in the morning prayer following the "Song of the Sea": "And saviors shall come up on Mount Zion to wreak judgment on Mount Esau; and dominion shall be the Lord's."[119] Finally, according to the Midrash, the avengers in the struggle against Edom, the red one, will also be red, namely, "dressed in red."[120] At the end of the commentary on the parashah *Va-yishlaḥ*, Midrash *Lekaḥ tov* makes the executor of messianic revenge explicit with reference to David's own redness: it happens "through the Messiah ben David, who is called 'ruddy, and withal of a beautiful countenance.'"[121]

The Yiddish legend of the Red Jews is, therefore, to be understood as an allegory for the Jewish hope for redemption. This reading is further supported by an implicit inversion of motifs surrounding the color red. According to the Aggadah, David's brothers wanted to kill him and his mother, since they considered his ruddiness a sign that he was conceived out of wedlock. But David's father prevailed: his youngest son was instead henceforth to be considered a slave, who would for many years tend his family's herds—until finally being anointed king.[122] David's biography can for this reason be seen as a typological model for the redemption of the Jewish people from oppression in the diaspora, a redemption to be effected through the advent of the Davidian king and Messiah. Finally, David's redness is twice thematized in the biblical narrative: in addition to his fight with Goliath, there is also his selection as king of Israel. When David comes before Samuel, "he was ruddy-cheeked. . . . And the Lord said, 'Rise and anoint him, for this is the one.'"[123] The redemption is also clearly symbolized by the double wedding with which Ma'aseh Akdamut ends. It prefigures in miniature the expected gathering of the people of Israel at the end of time: The Ten Lost Tribes of Israel are to be reunited with their brothers and sisters in the diaspora.

At this point, we can begin to delineate two complementary functions of the Yiddish myth of the Red Jews. First, in the polemic directed against the Christian other, it rescinds the validity of the theological interpretation casting the Red Jews as accomplices of the Antichrist. Thus, it undermines not only a central aspect of Christian apocalypticism, but also the Christian eschatological identity per se. In its second function, the Yiddish narrative constitutes an apologetic affirmation of the validity of Jewish messianic doctrine, including the fall of Edom. Especially in Germany, this involved the image of the Ten Tribes as rescuers, avengers, and harbingers of the Messiah. The little Red Jew becomes in a certain sense the agent of God's apocalyptic revenge on the Christian oppressors, the executor of a tradition of redemption through revenge: "So Israel was saved."[124]

In this way, the multilayered counter-historical construction gives old symbols and elements a new meaning. It explains as well the overdetermined symbolism of the little Red Jew's name in *Ma'aseh Akdamut*: Dan.[125] In Jewish tradition, not only is Dan the tribe of the Messiah's mother,[126] but the tribe's members are also considered to be especially warlike, and for this reason the tribe plays a central role in the drama of redemption.[127] Here too, then, the Red Jews confirm the Jewish interpretation. At the same time, the Christian interpretation of Dan as the tribe from which the Antichrist would emerge[128] is undercut by assigning the identity of the redeemer's last adversary to the evil magician. Like the Antichrist, he too is a master of black magic.[129] Of course, his defeat implies not the return of Jesus, as in the Christian version, but rather the advent of the true (i.e., Jewish) Messiah. In the Jewish counter-history to the Antichrist vita, *Toldot Yeshu* (The Life of Jesus), in which many characteristics of the Antichrist are transferred to Yeshu as a false Messiah, Yeshu also appears as a magician. Like that of the sorcerer in the Yiddish narrative, Yeshu's demise is brought about by a magical contest, in this case against Judas Iscariot, whose powers, like those of the little Red Jew, draw their strength from the holy names. It stands to reason that *Toldot Yeshu*, which was widely known in the German-speaking regions during the Middle Ages and the early modern period, may have provided a model for the contest of magic in which the Yiddish story of the Red Jews culminates.[130]

As we have seen, the concept and legend of the Red Jews, as expressed in both Middle High German and Early New High German texts, as well as in Old Yiddish literature, developed from a close and intensive dialogue with the religious and cultural other. In the myth of the Red Jews, Christians and Jews in Germany spoke the same apocalyptic language. The respective messages, however, stood in direct contradiction to each other, such that the conflict between the two religions was precisely reflected in the conceptual congruences and substantive parallels. The ideas associated on either side with the Red Jews were essentially mirror images. They were constructed from the same elements yet pointed in opposite directions. The logic of the other was in both cases adopted, yet its meaning was inverted and undercut.

In the final analysis, the legend of the Red Jews is an expression of the old Jewish-Christian argument about the identity of Edom. In the narrative of redemption, each cast the other in the role of the great loser, Edom, while identifying itself with the victorious counterpart, Israel. The Jewish legend is thus constituted not merely as counter-history to the Christian millennial scenario. At the same time, it positions itself fundamentally in contrast to the church's self-understanding as the new, true Israel, and it bolsters the contrary Jewish self-understanding as the people of Israel with whom God has an indissoluble bond.

The myth of the Red Jews staged what we might call a subliminal theological resistance to the Christian domination of cultural meaning making. Such strategies were necessary to ensure the Jewish minority's survival in an inimical environment, one in which they were seemingly powerless. The Red Jews directly addressed the doubts that must have arisen in the face of such oppression and suffering that had defined the Jewish experience for centuries, doubts about the unconditional reliance upon the God of Israel—in other words, doubts about the bedrock of Jewish belief. The story of the Ten Tribes reminded Jews that, all appearances to the contrary, God had not forgotten his people and that, despite everything, one day the page would turn. The time would come when the small would triumph over the great.

Naturally, such subversive convictions were kept out of public discourse. During the early modern period in Central Europe, they found uncensored expression in particular in the concealed form of a Jewish popular culture that remained largely obscure to outsiders and that was typically propagated via the Yiddish language.[131] Analogous to the Christian world, in which the Red Jews are known—with the exception of translations—only in the vernacular tradition,[132] the Jewish version is found only in Yiddish literature. The Hebrew translation of *Ma'aseh Akdamut*, which appeared in northern Italy around 1630, makes no use at all of the term "Red Jews."[133] While the myth of the red saviors, as a further variation on the tradition of the Ten Lost Tribes, ultimately spread also among Sephardic and Mizrahi Jews, the expression "Red Jews" was confined to the Yiddish language. The surviving Hebrew versions replace the term with neutral expressions such as "the Ten Tribes of Israel," "the Sons of Moses," or simply "the Jews beyond the Sambatyon."[134] Not even Menasseh b. Israel, who in his *Sefer mikveh Yisra'el* (The Hope of Israel, Amsterdam, 1650) gathers copious material on the Ten Tribes, makes mention of the Red Jews.[135]

As a medium of transmission, the Yiddish text was less problematic than the Hebrew, since in their hunt for incriminating anti-Christian utterances, the Argus eyes of Christians had long been focused on the canonical texts of Jewish teaching. These are written primarily in Hebrew (and Aramaic). Here the Christians found normative Judaism. Only beginning with the convert ethnographies of the sixteenth century was the Christian public offered an insight into Jewish tradition outside the Talmud and the prayer book. For their polemical studies on Jews and Judaism, Christian Hebraists began drawing on Yiddish literature not before the late seventeenth century and increasingly into the eighteenth century.[136] It is perhaps illustrative that, even in the waning years of the fifteenth century, Peter Schwarz (Petrus Nigri), a Dominican and professor at the University of Ingolstadt, still did not know of the Jews "across the Red Sea" in their anti-Christian function. For him, they were nothing more than the false guarantors of an autonomous reign whose continuity was postulated, wishfully, by the Jews.[137]

The resistance to Christianity embodied by the story of the Red Jews was firmly anchored in the Yiddish language and in Yiddish legend, as well as in ritual and prayer. Among Ashkenazim, *Ma'aseh Akdamut* was apparently read out loud annually during Shavuot, the feast associated with the legendary rescue of the community in Worms. The Italian Jewish scholar Abraham Yagel reports that several Ashkenazic communities possessed an actual scroll of the text. He himself claimed to have seen a copy of this scroll in Mantua, namely, in the possession of Gerson b. Abraham of Porto.[138] Yagel likely meant the lost Cremona first printing of *Megiles Reb Meyer*.[139]

In Jewish circles it was not unusual, when memorializing the escape from a specific danger or persecution, to take as a model the festival of Purim, commemorating the rescue of the Persian Jews by Queen Esther, and thus to integrate a second Purim into the annual cycle. As a rule, for this sort of local or regional holiday, a special megillah was composed to narrate the events in the style of the biblical Book of Esther.[140] The Jews of Frankfurt am Main, for example, celebrated their return to the city after their expulsion during the Fettmilch Rebellion (1614–16) by reciting *Megillat Vinz*. A Hebrew version was recited in the synagogue, like the Book of Esther at Purim, while an additional Yiddish version was used domestically.[141] In a similar way, *Megiles Reb Meyer* may have been recited in private circles as part of Shavuot.

In contrast to other megillot, *Megiles Reb Meyer* does not refer exclusively to a (supposed) historical event lying in the past.[142] The representation is oriented just as much toward the future. Specifically, *Megiles Reb Meyer* inscribes the eschatological hope for the apocalyptic destruction of Edom, which was anchored in the annual liturgy through the constructed commemoration of a miraculous rescue. Noting that the Book of Esther and, accordingly, *Megillat Vinz* were both recited at the transition from fasting to feast day, Lucia Raspe has posed the question of what relation the liturgical use of *Ma'aseh Akdamut* may have had to the local fasting days before Shavuot, with which the communities of the Rhine commemorated the crusade persecutions of 1096.[143] According to Israel Yuval, these fasting days, with their remembrance of the martyrs of the crusade pogroms, were intended to implore God to finally make good on his promise to destroy Edom, so that the way would be made free for the advent of the Messiah.[144] Through the celebration on Shavuot of the triumph of the Red Jews as apocalyptic destroyers, this plea was evoked and, typologically, already anticipated.

A suggestion of the great apocalyptic meaning of the recitation of *Akdamut millin* on the first day of Shavuot can be found in the complaint of Isaac Wetzlar of Celle in the eighteenth century: *Akdamut* may be spoken for the redemption, but the Messiah will hardly come as long as another mystical piece, *Shir ha-yihud*, continues to be neglected or no longer prayed as prescribed.[145] Although *Akdamut millin* was recited on the first day of Shavuot in virtually all of Ashkenaz, in Worms (the home community of its author) this piyyut was no longer part of the liturgy by the early modern period. In the famous, richly decorated, and beautifully illustrated 1272 Worms Mahzor (which, although it did not originate in the city after which it was named, was nevertheless in the possession of the Worms community a generation later), the poem is still preserved. Here, too, one finds no marginalia to indicate that *Akdamut* was not recited in Worms.[146] When exactly its recitation was discontinued cannot be said with any certainty, but it would have been sometime prior to the seventeenth century, since the two minhag books originating in Worms in the seventeenth century already confirm the absence of the piyyut in the Worms liturgy.[147]

And yet the piece was certainly well known in the city. It was even taught in the Jewish elementary school;[148] and apparently there was an awareness that, by not reciting it on Shavuot, one was adopting a peculiar stance within the Ashkenazic rite. In his 1625 compilation of customs and practices, Judah Löw (Liva) Kirchheim felt compelled to cite a rather threadbare reason for the absence of the well-known poem in Worms synagogues: At one time there had been a prayer leader in the community who had recited *Akdamut* with such a beautiful voice and such great fervency that God took him to himself at the end of the prayer. For this reason, according to Kirchheim, *Akdamut* was no longer recited in Worms. Needless to say, this explanation is far from convincing; Kirchheim himself seems not entirely to have believed it, suspecting instead that the true reason had been forgotten.[149]

Similarly mysterious is the situation with regard to the transmission of *Ma'aseh Akdamut* in Worms. There can be little doubt that the story of the origins of the piyyut was familiar to the Jews of the city. We find evidence for this in *Mayse nissim*, the magnificent collection of narrative traditions from Worms, which the synagogue servant Yuspa Shammes redacted in the mid-seventeenth century and which his son, Eliezer Lieberman, expanded after his father's death and brought to print in Yiddish (Amsterdam, 1696). The book contains mention of the printed version of the story of *Akdamut* but without further reference to its contents. Such was the degree of familiarity among readers that this information would have been unnecessary. The story itself, however, is not included in the otherwise comprehensive collection.[150]

It is remarkable that although *Akdamut millin* was taught to Jewish children in Worms, the work of their own poet was not recited in synagogue, and while *Ma'aseh Akdamut* was well known and of the utmost significance, it found no place in Yuspa's canon of legends from Worms. These omissions may be explained, however, when one considers the fear of Christian eyes and the concern to keep potentially incriminating poetry from being in any way officially associated with the city of Worms and its Jewish residents. After all, the story of the cantor and religious poet Meir Shatz and the Red Jews took explicit aim at the Christian authorities and at Christianity itself. *Ma'aseh Akdamut* at once celebrated and summoned the Red Jews' eschatological victory over Edom.[151]

Even as late as the mid-eighteenth century, the legend of the Red Jews appears to have remained part of Jewish popular culture in Germany.[152] Although with the advance of the modern age, Yiddish began to lose its importance as a medium of cultural creativity in the West, the motif of the Red Jews continued to be preserved among Yiddish-speaking Jews in Eastern Europe. This geographical displacement is registered in the printing history of *Ma'aseh Akdamut*. The first of many editions of the story printed in Lviv (Ukraine) in the nineteenth and twentieth centuries dates from 1805, the same year *Ma'aseh Akdamut* was printed for the last time—as far as we know—in Central Europe.[153]

Although the Red Jews have withdrawn from the field of anti-Christian counter-history in modern Yiddish belles lettres, their roots in the Jewish-Christian argument of earlier periods remain clearly visible. Mendele, for instance, knew of the *Akdamut* story in a form adopted from the older Western Yiddish version, and the hero Benjamin explains to his companion the preparations for the trip they have planned across the Sambatyon with reference to *Akdamut millin*:

> Sendrel, . . . And by the way, do you know what I was humming? It was the Akdomus for Shavuos, and don't think I didn't have my reasons. You see, once we arrive, God willing, in the land of the ten tribes, we're going to have a great deal to talk about, and the language spoken there is the very same Chaldean that the Akdomus is written in. In fact, it was composed by Eldad the Danite and I'm brushing up on it right now.[154]

In fact, *Akdamut millin* is not mentioned in the tradition of Eldad ha-Dani. What we are dealing with here is much more Mendele's own treatment of the old origin story of the piyyut.[155]

2. THE RESTITUTION OF ISRAEL AS CHILIASTIC LEGITIMATION OF WORLD AFFAIRS

> [T]hat blindness in part is happened to Israel, until the fulness of the Gentiles be come in. And so all Israel shall be saved.
>
> —Romans 11:25–26

While the Red Jews proved long-lived in the Yiddish-speaking world, over the course of the early modern period they disappeared from Christian apocalypticism. This was due in no small part to the fact that the Christian image of the Red Jews had been reinterpreted during the sixteenth century, as different concepts arose of Jewish participation in the millennium. To some degree, these concepts were more in accord with the changing historical circumstances. Under pressure from the Turkish threat, the Red Jews came to be seen less as the archenemies of Christianity and more as potential allies in the struggle against the Muslim unbelievers. In a pamphlet from 1562, for instance, they appear as a danger not to the Christians but rather to the Turks.[156] Finally, by 1596, the Red Jews were explicitly seen as instruments of God's apocalyptic punishment of the Ottomans and therefore as allies of Christendom.[157] By virtue of this changed image, the Red Jews necessarily lost not only their ancestral function as eschatological nemesis and henchmen of the Antichrist but even their basic relevance in the Christian millennial scenario. Emptied of its traditional meaning, the term "Red Jews" became a mere lexical shell and eventually disappeared altogether.[158]

The beginnings of this change in the Red Jews' role can be felt in 1523 with the appearance of David Re'uveni. In Michael Kramer's pamphlet of the same year, the Jewish interlocutor's remarks about the geographical situation of the Sambatyon and about the dwellers beyond it offer an interesting variation on the legend of the Red Jews. Jacob understands the Sambatyon as a sea, not as a river, and identifies it with the Red Sea. He associates the origins of the residents of the land beyond it with the story of Exodus: "There were twelve tribes beyond the sea in Egypt, but not more than eleven and a half came across [it] in the exodus."[159] The Jews beyond the Sambatyon are, therefore, not the descendants of the Ten Tribes of the Northern Kingdom who were led into exile by the Assyrians but rather a half tribe that remained behind during the Exodus from Egypt. This "forgotten remnant," Jacob continues, has been waiting patiently since then for a sign from God that he will redeem them. In the summer of 1523, the time had finally come.

> This past summer God showed them his grace, for the water . . . this summer stood still on the Sabbath and eight days [following]. The prophets, therefore, exhorted the Jews to make them understand that God wanted to liberate them, and thus that they ought to set out for the Holy Land that God promised them.[160]

To be sure, the Sambatyon legend already alludes to the crossing of the Red Sea. This is in accordance with the widespread typological recourse to the Exodus from Egypt as prototype for future messianic redemption. Nevertheless, in Jacob's portrayal, the expected messianic Exodus is given a new twist: It is to transpire not only in parallel to the events represented in the Second Book of Moses but in literal repetition of them.

This explanation for the existence of an independent Jewish kingdom beyond the Sambatyon does more than simply enrich the body of legends about the Ten Lost Tribes. It seems rather to reflect a synchronization of the legend with contemporary events. At precisely this time, a certain David Re'uveni appeared on the scene, claiming to have come from the Lost Tribes. He was, he said, the brother of the king who ruled over a part of these tribes, namely, his own tribe of Ruben as well as Gad and half the tribe of Manasseh. Their kingdom lay east of the Red Sea, in the heart of the Arabian Peninsula. Writing of his travels, Re'uveni tells of crossing the Red Sea to Nubia and Egypt and finally arriving in the Land of Israel. He had been sent, he claimed, to lead the Jews back from exile.[161]

What has till now gone unrecognized by scholars is the context linking David Re'uveni to widespread reports in German-language pamphlets on the military advance of the Ten Tribes. These same pamphlets contain some of the earliest news of Re'uveni's activities, which fascinated the world for a decade. It is here that, for the first time, the Red Jews do not appear in their traditional role as the enemies of Christendom. We thus have strong evidence for the existence of an actual link between Re'uveni's appearance and the changing Christian narrative of the Red Jews. In fact, so radical a shift from the conventional image of the fearsome Red Jews is to be attributed, with great certainty, to Re'uveni's own early activities prior to his arrival in Europe in 1523.[162] Hebrew correspondence confirms and supplements the information of the German pamphlets regarding the impact that this first, less well-known part of Re'uveni's travels had upon his contemporaries.[163]

According to his own testimony, Re'uveni came first to Cairo in 1523. Immediately upon arrival, he sought out the Egyptian mintmaster Abraham de Castro to "reveal a mystery" to him.[164] In all likelihood this revelation involved details about the coming redemption and the role that the Lost Tribes were to play. De Castro, however, firmly rejected the self-proclaimed emissary. The failure of his mission in Egypt may be the reason Re'uveni passes over this episode with relative brusqueness in his travelogue. Concerning his further adventures in the Middle East, we learn next to nothing from Re'uveni himself. After he left Egypt, he traveled through the region as a pilgrim to visit the graves of the patriarchs in Hebron and the holy sites in Jerusalem.[165]

Re'uveni claims to have used the power of prayer at the Western Wall to cause the half-moon atop the Dome of the Rock to bow toward the east, much to the horror of the Muslims.[166] This claim is confirmed indirectly by a letter from Safed, in which R. Raphael Trabot reports that the man from the tribe of Ruben had been sent to Jerusalem by his king to perform a mysterious act of magic that would make it possible for the Jews to return from exile to the land of their fathers. The army of the Lost Tribes, he writes, had already crossed the Sambatyon; they waited now only for the last two signs of the Messiah before they could continue their advance and "accelerate the end."[167] One of the two remaining omens was presumably the bowing of the sickle moon, the emblem of Islam, which would signal the fall of the Ottoman Empire and the end to its occupation of the Holy Land.

From Galilee, Re'uveni traveled on to Damascus, another center of the Ottoman province of Syria, to which Jerusalem also belonged. A second Hebrew letter reports of his stay there.[168] The letter's anonymous author informs his fellow believers in Italy that on that very day in Damascus he had met an emissary by the name of David from the Tribe of Ruben. Let the glass of wine they drank together be evidence enough that he speaks the truth, says the author, before he reports in more detail upon the mysterious man and the circumstances of his journey. This man, he writes, was sent by a king who recently crossed the Sambatyon with an army of six hundred thousand. Such was only possible because the river was as dry now as if water had never flowed there.

The correspondent from Syria also confirms Re'uveni's own claim that his endeavors in Egypt had come to naught:

> The people in Egypt made a mockery of him and his words. And as he perceived this, he directed his words only to the few, and had nothing more to do with the masses. And then he left Egypt and went to Jerusalem, and from Jerusalem into Samaria, and from Samaria he arrived here in Damascus.[169]

Shortly after Re'uveni had left Egypt, the writer continues, one must have realized that the mockery and scorn had been ill-placed: no sooner had the alleged prince departed than the Egyptian Jews received a missive signed by the king of Ruben himself and twelve of his princes, which confirmed the identity of his royal emissary. In great haste, then, the Egyptian Jews had written to Damascus, Re'uveni's next station, and urged the community there to support him. The Syrian Jews did not long hesitate, according to the writer, and sent a delegation of twelve men to the sultan.[170]

Whether, in fact, a Jewish delegation ever reached the court in Istanbul and was received by the sultan cannot be known with any certainty. Nevertheless, two German pamphlets relay the rumors surrounding the appearance of such a commission at the court of Suleiman the Magnificent. The editor of the pamphlet *Von ainer grosse meng*, which explicitly cites the same letters from Damascus, relates that the twelve delegates demanded the return of the land of their fathers from the Turkish occupiers and admonished the sultan "to return to them their ancient and ancestral homeland, that is the promised land. If he should not do so, the Jews were prepared to conquer this land by force of arms."[171] At the date of the pamphlet's printing, the sultan's answer had not yet been given.[172]

In the meantime, according to the pamphlet's testimony, "a great multitude and host of Jews, more precisely as many as five or six hundred thousand, have arrived in the land of Egypt and made camp thirty days' march from Jerusalem."[173] The anonymous correspondent from Damascus knows further details concerning their movements and reports to his readers that the royal army of the tribes stood already in the Negev at Mount Hor. And yet this powerful force was only a vanguard—it would be followed by warriors without number. One heard "that now the tribes like the sand of the sea and stars of the sky are making ready to come"; it was expected that the armies would join in battle in only a few days.[174] Such was the supposed situation on the apocalyptic front in the summer of 1523, after Re'uveni had made his peregrination about the Middle East announcing the imminent fall of Islam. By December at the latest, however, it was clear that the Turks would not willingly withdraw from the Land of Israel. As Jacob of Brucks allegedly informed Michael Kramer, "since it had been their fathers' and was given to them by God, he was willing to sell it to them. To which the Jews retorted: God gave it to them, they would not buy it, but would win it back by the sword."[175]

Toward the end of that same year, Re'uveni found himself on the way to Europe in hopes of persuading the Christians into an alliance against the Muslims and, with their help, of reconquering Jerusalem. To be sure, a Jewish-Christian military alliance would also be of interest to the Europeans, menaced as they were and had been—repeatedly—by the Turks. At the beginning of December, in Alexandria, Re'uveni embarked on a ship bound for Venice to begin his tour diplomatique. And, in fact, with his offer to lead the army of his brothers along with the soldiers of Christ against the Turks, he at first found a receptive audience among the powerful of Europe. As early as February 1524, he was received by Pope Clement VII.[176] The audience of a representative of the Red Jews with the leader of Christendom was doubtless a sensation in the Jewish world, since according to Nahmanides, the Messiah—already connected with Rome in the Talmud and the Midrashim—would journey to the pope to proclaim his messiahship.[177] Just as Moses sought out Pharaoh prior to the Exodus from Egypt, at the end of time, the Messiah, under God's command, would step before the pope and demand of him, "Let my people go!"[178]

Re'uveni appears to have performed a second curious sign in Rome. According to his own rather cryptic remarks, before entering the city, he purchased an ox and proceeded as instructed by the seventy elders of his people.[179] Presumably, as he had done before at a central sacred site of Islam in Jerusalem, in the Christian capital he prophesied the fall of Christianity, the second archetypal enemy of Israel. After all, in rabbinical literature the eschatological ox Behemoth is already identified typologically with Christendom.[180] Perhaps this was to be the final sign of the Messiah, the sign for which the Ten Tribes were waiting before continuing their advance. Re'uveni apparently wished to bring about the quick destruction of both Edom and Ishmael by entangling Christians and Muslims in a war of mutual annihilation. His diplomatic efforts had in this sense a clear ulterior motive and apocalyptic intention: by provoking the eschatological wars between Gog and Magog, embodied in Christianity and Islam respectively, he sought to fulfill the prerequisite for the restitution of Israel.[181] While Re'uveni was still making his way to Europe, the rumor had already begun to spread in Germany that "the emperor of the Turks [the sultan] and the Red Jews have now resorted to arms to fight for the promised land."[182]

In Christian polemics, the duration of exile had long been a central piece of evidence for the Jews' rejection by God. How was this assumption to be squared, however, with the news that a powerful Jewish army was on the verge of taking Jerusalem from the Turks? All at once, it appeared no longer entirely far-fetched that the Jewish messianic expectation of a return to the Holy Land would be fulfilled. The news was particularly explosive given the fact that many Christians likewise expected the end of the world at precisely this time. Traditional Christian eschatology did not, however, foresee the restitution of Israel in the form of an actual, renewed political existence in the Holy Land.[183] Apart from their function as the first followers of the Antichrist, the Jews' role in the millennial drama was limited to their conversion to Christianity, and in this way they would finally experience the fulfillment of their promise of salvation in Jesus. The expected return to the Land of Israel and the establishment of a Jewish kingdom were thus from the Christian point of view only thinkable metaphorically, in terms of the acceptance of the true religion. And at that point, the Jews would cease to be Jews and would enter into the kingdom of Christ.

In the Christian world, one was aware of the painful contradiction presented to church doctrine by the imminent fulfillment of biblical prophecy in literal form (i.e., an actual Jewish state), no matter whether one assumed the millennial conversion of the Jews or their eternal damnation. Since the historical phenomenon of the Red Jews could not be ignored, however, Christian theologians felt obliged to grapple with it. This is documented in the lively debate that took place in the 1520s among both the lower clergy and the scholarly elites.

An awareness of the problem is noticeable by the end of 1523. When Jacob of Brucks informs Michael Kramer of the fight for Jerusalem already underway between the army of the Red Jews and the Turks, Kramer asks whether the Jews could possibly be so numerous as to dare to take on the Turks. With reference to the pamphlet *Von ainer grosse meng,* Jacob declares his confidence: "yes, there are six hundred thousand of them. I am certain of that."[184] Kramer believes the information, since his interlocutor appears learned and expressed himself eloquently. Moreover, for contemporaries who believed in this formidable army of Red Jews, the conquest of Israel by strength of arms cannot have appeared entirely implausible. The alleged reality of a powerful Jewish army marching toward Jerusalem forces Kramer to admit the basic possibility that the Jews might indeed return to the Holy Land:

> Jacob, it is possible that you might well take Jerusalem once again. But it is impossible for you to regain the scepter of kingship. Authority will remain with the Turks or the Christians. For the heathen have never wanted or tolerated a Jewish king, but have always opposed this by force. But it is written of this Shiloh or Messiah that the nations and the heathens will recognize him as king.[185]

While the pastor of Kunitz is unable to exclude the possibility, in light of recent events, that the Jews may reconquer Jerusalem, he remains steadfast in his denial of the messianic expectations linked to such an event. Even if the city should fall, it would never again come under Jewish rule. For all eternity, the Land of Israel would remain under Turkish—or Christian—rule, for (of this Kramer is certain) the Ottomans would hardly accept a Jewish sultan. The Jewish expectation of the king Messiah, who is to be acknowledged by all nations of the world, will thus find fulfillment neither now nor later. And then, in a move that is typical for the Jewish-Christian disputation, Kramer transitions to an attempt to convince the "stubborn" Jew of the Christian truth on the basis of his own holy Scripture. If he wanted a king Messiah, then he should accept Jesus. For "which king on earth has ever been so powerful and so mild in whom the heathens have believed so passionately as in the Jewish king Christ, for whose sake many thousands of them have been martyred."[186] Interestingly, despite Kramer's literary editing, the episode ends without the conventional enlightenment and conversion of the Jew: "Jacob's servant prepares the saddles and Jacob takes his leave from the pastor and rides."[187]

A similar argumentation on the return of the Jews to the Land of Israel and its messianic implications appears in *Liber fidei* and thus also in Sebastian Münster's fictive dialogue based on it, in which a Jew and a Christian discuss the Messiah question. In the context of the polemical discussion of Asher Lemlein's failed call for penance, the authors add the following reference to the events of 1523/24: "Even if the penance should bring about a gathering from your exile, you will never be redeemed, because you have ever been an obdurate and rebellious people."[188]

In the years that followed, a sophisticated theological solution was worked out for the contradiction between Christian doctrine and a return of the Jews to the Land of Israel, a solution that went beyond pure polemic. This was the controversial doctrine of the restitution of Israel, propounded by the reformer Wolfgang Capito of Strasbourg and Martin Cellarius (Borrhaus), a young man who was known for his tendency toward radical opinions. The latter had begun by 1525 to espouse chiliastic views that two years later, in 1527, he published in Strasbourg under the title *De operibus Dei* (Of the Works of God). The book deals primarily with the doctrine of predestination, but in the third part, Cellarius considers the imminent return of Christ, which in his unorthodox view is connected with the restitution of Israel. He presumes not only a thousand-year reign of Christ on earth; more radically, he refers the restitution of Israel to the Jews.[189]

In accordance with the *interpretatio christiana*, which sees in the history of the Jews an anticipation of the Christian story of redemption, Cellarius understands the true Israel to be those elected by God for salvation. For him this means not only Christians but also, according to God's inscrutable will, selected Jews and even heathens. This true Israel finds the model for its spiritual destiny, according to the contemporary exegetic method of typology, in the Israel of the old covenant, that is, the Israel of the flesh: the Jews. "What happened to [the fleshly] Israel according to the Apostles by means of the Romans was like a shadow [of the truth], but it will happen in truth to the Israel of promise."[190] From a consistent deployment of these hermeneutic premises, the radical conclusion emerges for Cellarius that the new heaven and the new earth also require a prefiguration. Before the Christian salvific narrative can arrive at its expected end, the promises of the prophets concerning the redemption of the people of Israel must also be fulfilled to the letter. Cellarius thus makes the liberation of the Jewish people a necessary prerequisite within the framework of Christian salvation, essentially functioning as a typological prefiguration of the Second Coming of Christ and the redemption of the elect in the kingdom of God. The Day of Judgment must therefore be preceded by an actual gathering and return of the Jews from exile into the Land of Israel and the reestablishment there of an independent kingdom of David.[191]

In this way, Cellarius goes from a typological scriptural exegesis to a typological interpretation of history. The biblical prophesies regarding the people of Israel are for him not merely a symbolic model for the destiny of the true Israel. The actual historical destiny of the Jews prefigures the present and future of the elect. Cellarius thus understands the restitution of Israel quite literally and adopts it as an essential and imminent part of his own millennial expectations. The otherwise mutually exclusive expectations of the reign of Jesus on earth, among Christians, and of a messianic age, among Jews, are thus made to overlap. As a necessary precondition for the perfection of Christian salvation, the fulfillment of Jewish hope is written into the Christian millennial scenario.[192]

The reformer Wolfgang Capito of Strasbourg took notice of Cellarius's doctrine of restitution toward the end of 1526. At that time, Cellarius was a guest in Capito's house while preparing the manuscript for publication. When the book appeared the following year, Capito contributed a rather euphoric preface[193] and, what is more, himself adopted the theory together with the doctrine of predestination and the theology of history espoused by his house guest. While Cellarius stayed in Strasbourg, Capito worked at expanding a lecture on the prophet Hosea into a comprehensive commentary.[194] He incorporates Cellarius's ideas from the very start and deploys them particularly in his explication of Hosea 1:9–2:2, in which Israel is first rejected and then immediately accepted again. Like Cellarius, Capito distinguishes between the "Israel according to the flesh" that God repudiates and the "true Israel" mentioned in the positive part of the biblical verse. Capito postulates that, just as God's rejection of the external Israel serves as emblem of the true Israel under the rule of the Antichrist, so too the glorious redemption of the elect must also have a typological model:[195]

> Because, in the image, Israel has suffered and continues to suffer every-
> thing that, in truth, was done and will be done with the believers, it follows
> that the magnificent promises that have been made to this nation must
> be fulfilled, so that the true images—according to the unshakeable order
> of God's works—here, too, present a prefiguration of the certain truth, as
> they have not yet been fulfilled. For in this special nation is an image that
> presents, so to speak, a shadow of the truth. For this reason, Israel, after its

long-lasting captivity, will increase, and this allegorical nation will, together
with the heathens, after the fullness of the nations have entered, cross over
into the kingdom of Christ, in enormous numbers, uncountable as the
sands of the sea.[196]

On the basis of the typological premises he adopted from Cellarius,
Capito maintains that entry into the kingdom of Christ cannot be fulfilled
by means of the traditionally expected millennial conversion of the Jews.
As laid out by Cellarius, the messianic prophesies for Israel must come
true literally and externally.[197] Thus Capito, too, proceeds from the assumption that in the very near future the Jews would reconquer Canaan and
"be allowed to return into the land in great numbers."[198] Soon, indeed, the
Jewish nation would "take free possession of its land in great glory."[199]

Although the theoretical basis of the chiliastic doctrine of the restitution comprises a classically Christian, strictly typological exegetic tradition, one cannot help suspecting that Martin Cellarius and Wolfgang
Capito considered the possibility of a return of the Jews into the promised
land in a specifically contemporary light. That very possibility had after all
been a topic of concrete general discussion just a few years earlier in connection with the supposed military advance of the Red Jews. Thus Capito
assures his reader that the Jews "will occupy the Land of Canaan in great
peace"—as if wishing to dispel his contemporaries' deep-seated fear of the
apocalyptic revenge of the Red Jews upon the Christians.[200] After all, their
role as menace chiefly to the Turks, from whom they were preparing to take
the Holy Land, was still quite new.

The doctrine of restitution gained renewed currency a few years
later, when it was discussed around the imperial diet of 1530 in Augsburg. Reformed theologians considered Cellarius to be sympathetic to
Anabaptism and were alarmed at his growing influence over the reformer
Capito.[201] Thus, while the criticism of Capito and Cellarius by Lutheran
colleagues took place largely in the context of the argument about Anabaptism, they impugned the doctrine of restitution on the basis of the sharp

rejection of all forms of chiliasm. The line of demarcation found its most emphatic expression in the primary confession of faith of the Lutheran Church, which the Lutheran imperial estates presented on June 25, 1530, at the imperial diet in Augsburg. Article 17 of the Augsburg Confession (*Confessio Augustana*) explicitly condemns as "Jewish doctrines" (*judische Lehren*) the millenarian belief in an earthly thousand-year messianic reign in which "before the resurrection of the dead, vain saints and pious ones have a worldly reign."[202] In fact, the doctrine of a return of the Jews as Jews into a terrestrial kingdom of Israel resembles a Jewish messianic understanding of scripture, such that it was in later times adduced by Christians for missionary purposes among Jews.[203]

At the end of May of that year, an earlier version of the confessional document had appeared that went even further. In this earlier version, the authors also rejected anyone who explicitly claimed that "the conquest of the promised land must be understood in the flesh."[204] That this clause appears in neither the Latin nor the German version of the final *Confessio Augustana* is evidently due to the actual historical events of the time. In particular, during the early summer months of 1530, the rumor circulated once again of the advance of the Red Jews. The theologian Adam Weiß, who accompanied the Margrave of Brandenburg-Ansbach to the imperial diet, noted in his journal for June 5 that many thousands of Jews had gathered out of Egypt to reconquer the promised land.[205] Similar information about the Red Jews is also found in the correspondence of the reformer Philipp Melanchthon, the author of the Augsburg Confession. On June 15, he notes, "It is written from Ferrar that the Red Jews have come out, Gog and Magog, and draw in a great host toward the holy land."[206] Four days later, he informed his friend, the scholar Joachim Camerarius the elder, calling the news "rather like a fable, yet a certain and true story concerning the Jews, who have gathered an innumerable host in order to invade Palestine."[207]

Melanchthon received this news shortly before submitting the final draft of the confession document to the emperor. That this news had great significance for him can be deduced from the curious fact that, in his complete correspondence for the years 1530–32, no single additional mention of contemporary Jews is to be found.[208] Lutheranism had, of course, to distance itself from the unorthodox restitution theory of Cellarius and Capito, since they assumed a terrestrial millennium. During the Peasant War, Melanchthon himself had impugned the rebels' millennial dreams of the Messiah as worldly ruler. Such dreams had to be vigorously condemned, especially now, since the renewed advance of the Red Jews meant that the theory might find new adherents. And still the current situation would not allow one to completely deny the possibility of a conquest of the promised land. As of yet, the outcome remained uncertain. For Melanchthon, it was precisely the Jewish longing for the Land of Israel, and especially the repeated failure of any attempt thus far to reconquer and retain it, that confirmed the spiritual interpretation of the millennium: the punishment of the people of Israel with eternal exile was proof that God had not sent the Messiah to establish a political kingdom.[209]

World events and the alleged advance of the Red Jews on Jerusalem appeared to bring within reach what had for so long been the object of Jewish hopes: the reestablishment of Israel. For Christians, this meant the challenge of thinking the unthinkable and referring the restitution of Israel to the actual Jewish people. Between 1523 and 1530, because of the shared apocalyptic image of the Red Jews, European Jews and Christians arrived at similar conclusions. This happened to a large extent independently in the two religious groups, although the interpretation of Cellarius and Capito corresponded in fundamental ways (up to a certain point) to the Jewish stance on what was to be expected in the messianic age. The knowledge of the military might of the Red Jews brought the Jewish conquest of the Land of Israel into the realm of actual political possibility and made necessary its theological discussion. Nevertheless, as far as its eschatological implications and the interpretation of salvific history were concerned, the differences of opinion could hardly have been greater.

3. AUGUSTIN BADER: THE JEWISH MESSIAH, A SWABIAN ANABAPTIST?

To all appearances the greatest practices of these horrifying deeds
proceed from the Jews and may be directed by them.

—Report of the Vice Governor and the Regents of

Further Austria to King Ferdinand, 1530

In the same year in which the Lutheran authorities presented their confessional document to the imperial diet at Augsburg, a leader of the Anabaptists from the same city was arrested in the small village of Lautern near Ulm. The young journeyman weaver Augustin Bader had ensconced himself there with a small group of followers and their families to await the end of the world. Bader embodies the paradoxical phenomenon of a Christian messianic pretender—the only known case from the Reformation period who represented, as it were, a kind of Jewish messianism. Here, too, the Red Jews played a role.[210]

Although the persecution of the Anabaptists was initially justified by accusing them of heresy, after 1529 an imperial decree changed Anabaptism from a religious error to a political crime. With this, the political unrest stepped into the foreground; Anabaptists were charged with inciting the common people to rebellion against the lords.[211] This accusation seemed to meet with clear evidence when the regional government of Further Austria (which comprised Habsburg possessions in Swabia in southwestern Germany, among others) arrested Bader and his followers in 1530. During the subsequent trial, the prisoners apparently used the courtroom as a forum for making public their expectation of the messianic *"verenderung"* (change) that same year. Their astonishingly forthright pronouncements convinced the Habsburg authorities that they had uncovered a massive conspiracy.[212] The political dimension of the case was immediately clear to the government in Stuttgart by virtue of Bader's own claim that he was called to messianic kingship. Moreover, a crown, a scepter, a sword, and a dagger had all been found in Bader's possession: the unmistakable appurtenances of a future king. The small group from Lautern obviously intended to depose Archduke Ferdinand I of Austria, the emperor's brother, and set the crown on Bader's own head.

What made the Bader case a political event of extreme explosiveness throughout the empire, however, was in effect a historical coincidence.[213] At precisely the same time, a confederation of Protestant princes was holding secret negotiations to reinstate Ulrich, the former Duke of Württemberg, as territorial prince after his territory had been appropriated by Ferdinand when Ulrich was exiled in 1520.[214] In the same month as Bader's arrest, the Habsburgs learned from their spies that John the Elector of Saxony, Landgrave Philipp of Hesse, and Margrave George of Brandenburg, along with several cities, had sworn allegiance in support of Ulrich and were preparing for war. The alleged plan was to provoke peasant rebellions simultaneously in Allgäu and at Lake Constance, thereby opening an additional front against the emperor. When the intentions of the radical Anabaptist sect, whose members had been arrested in Württemberg territory, came to light, the suspicion was strong that the two efforts were related. The apparent connection presented the emperor and the Catholic authorities with a welcome opportunity to discredit the Protestant lords by association with the dangerous Anabaptists and to prove their alleged desire to usurp the imperial throne. Against this background, Bader was portrayed as a political exemplum, and his case became for the whole empire a public event. The unmasking of the alleged conspiracy was announced through publication of the court confessions (*Urgichten*), even before Bader's spectacular execution in Stuttgart.[215]

The authorities also reacted in alarm to the apparent involvement of Turks and Jews in the planned revolt. The Jews were even suspected of being the driving force behind the rebellious Anabaptists, "from whom they have had much help and consolation."[216] And in point of fact, Bader and his followers had cultivated Jewish contacts, who were decisive not only for the formulation of their messianic doctrine but also for the concrete realization of their plans. An important connection in this regard was Oswald

Leber, Bader's teacher and most important henchman, who was also largely responsible for Bader's messianic program. Oswald, a pastor from the village of Herbolzheim near Wimpfen an der Jagst (north of Heilbronn), had been a preacher during the Peasant War. After the rebellion was crushed, he fled to Worms out of fear of being arrested. There, during 1525 and 1526, he studied Hebrew and the Kabbalah.[217] Christian students of Hebrew were at that time no unusual figures. The revival of the humanistic study of classical antiquity during the Renaissance had also awakened a Christian interest in the language of the Hebrew Bible. Alongside the Old Testament, Christian Hebraists studied the postbiblical Jewish corpus, albeit only in the service of Christian religion and culture.[218] In this endeavor, they were, of course, largely dependent upon Jews and converts: above all as language teachers but also in the acquisition and printing of Hebrew books. Despite the injunction against teaching the Torah to non-Jews, a number of Jews were willing to assist Christians interested in the Hebrew language and in the rabbinical and kabbalistic traditions.[219]

Examples of a remarkable cooperation between Jewish and Christian scholars in the first half of the sixteenth century are known in particular from southern Germany. It was apparently the regional rabbi (*Landes-rabbiner*) of Swabia, Isaac b. Joseph Segal, who mediated a relationship between the itinerant Jewish printer Haim Schwarz and the convert Paulus Aemilius. The latter, for his part, was well connected in Christian humanist circles. In 1542, likely in the presence of the regional rabbi, Aemilius and Schwarz formed a business agreement to explore the market for the printing and sale of Hebrew books in Ferrara. Soon after the Italian trip, however, the partnership was dissolved.[220] Two decades earlier there had been a case of Jewish-Christian collaboration for the provision of Hebrew books in Günzburg. Upon inquiry, the provincial of the Augustinians, Caspar Amman, who had taken up residence in nearby Lauingen, received an answer from a certain Isaac Kohen promising the delivery of a book within eight days. The desired text was the classical lexicon of the Talmud and the Midrash, *Sefer arukh* (first printing in abridged form in Constantinople,

1511), penned by the Italian scholar Nathan b. Yeḥiel.[221] Caspar Amman also corresponded with a certain Elhanan Bacharach in Burgau.[222]

The contacts of the Swabian Hebraists were not restricted to their own region. Next to Günzburg, Worms also played an important role as a center of Jewish-Christian bibliographic exchange. Amman likely corresponded at the beginning of the 1520s with the famous kabbalist Naphtali Hirtz Treves, who at that time still lived in Worms before transferring to Frankfurt as cantor. Treves lent Amman numerous Hebrew—above all kabbalistic—books. He had them sent to Günzburg, where in at least one case the Jewish physician Lazarus (Leizer) received them and delivered them to Amman in Lauingen.[223] Another Jewish scholar in Worms, a certain R. Liva, answered the request of the Christian Hebraist Johann Reinhardt, also of Swabia, by providing him with certain books. On the occasion of the upcoming imperial diet in Worms, he even invited Reinhardt to his home.[224]

Treves also may well have discussed kabbalistic biblical exegesis with representatives of the local clergy.[225] Anselm Schubert postulates that Treves is also the teacher in Worms who gave Oswald Leber lessons in Hebrew and initiated him into the world of Kabbalah.[226] Moreover, during his course of study in Worms, Leber even became acquainted with current messianic calculations. This was highly unusual. Normally, Jews hesitated to pass on eschatological secrets to non-Jews. The kabbalist Abraham ha-Levi of Jerusalem, although he attributed apocalyptic significance to the spread of Hebrew among Christians,[227] took great pains to ensure that his messianic writings did not fall into Christian hands. He thus declined the request of a Jewish correspondent in Italy to be sent a copy of his "Treatise on the Mystery of the Redemption," for the sole reason that Italy was then the center of Christian Kabbalah.[228]

Why, then, was the injunction against revealing eschatological secrets to Christians overruled in Worms? It is hardly less than astonishing that Jewish scholars were prepared to place sensitive information at the disposal of Christians, who all too easily could have turned it against Judaism itself. And yet, these Jews were willing not only to sell the desired books but also, though they constituted valuable personal property, to lend them temporarily without remuneration or even (as in the case of the regional rabbi of Swabia) to associate thereby with an apostate. This all but enthusiastic willingness of Jewish scholars in southern Germany to assist Christian humanists—both in learning the Hebrew language and in gaining access to Jewish literature—may have been motivated, as Eric Zimmer first suggested, by acute messianic expectation. The hope that the Christian study of Jewish (and especially kabbalist) writings might bring them closer to Judaism, and thus also accelerate the end of history, appears to have eclipsed more pragmatic concerns.[229]

The Jewish willingness to teach and the Christian desire to learn went hand in hand with the shared expectation of the imminent end. Indeed, a considerable number of Christian kabbalists believed that they could prepare the way for the Second Coming of Christ through the study of hidden aspects of the divine creation, which lay encoded in Jewish mysticism. Very much like their Jewish counterparts in such cooperation, they often associated this task with an acute eschatological perspective vis-à-vis the other—in their case, the hope of finding, with the help of the Kabbalah, a new way toward the millennial conversion of the Jews.[230]

In Worms in the years 1525–26, the apocalyptic collaboration went so far as to involve mutual speculation on the exact date of the end. Among the Jewish community of Worms, the Messiah was apparently expected to make his appearance in 1530, as had been calculated by numerous scholars.[231] Oswald Leber at least heard it thus from a Jew in Worms: "He showed Oswald the change in all detail and the Jew said that such a change was to happen in the year [1530]."[232] The Jew in question, whose name is withheld in the sources, was so certain of his messianic expectations that he planned to immigrate to the Land of Israel. But at first, "in Worms they did not permit it for a long time, until he was allowed [to leave]."[233] Soon after having entrusted Leber with the date of the Messiah's advent, he departed—but not before offering his interlocutor a friendly invitation to visit him in Jerusalem during the time of the redemption, even "show[ing] him in which house and in which lane he would find him there."[234] It would appear that Naphtali Hirtz Treves shared this expectation regarding the year 1530, since his son wrote to him cheerfully the following year that the redemption had now indeed begun.[235]

With this valuable information among his effects, Oswald Leber left the city at the end of 1527 and made his way to Strasbourg. There, in the empire's second-largest Anabaptist community after Augsburg, he would have found scholarly circles that were occupied, like himself, with Kabbalah and that had arrived at a certain synthesis of Jewish mystical traditions and Anabaptist theology.[236] In Strasbourg, Leber soon began to proclaim the end of the world in 1530—a date that is otherwise completely unremarked in Christian apocalyptic literature.[237] He had attained certainty regarding the Day of Judgment, he explained, by means of a secret revelation: "Rejoice with your whole hearts, and with your whole strength, thanking and praising God, for the Lord has revealed to us brothers the time in which he will punish those who have persecuted and scattered you."[238]

Leber's date for the millennial Day of Judgment stood in competition with the accredited prediction of the late Hans Hut, one of the founding fathers of the Anabaptist community in Augsburg, who had put the beginning of the Last Judgment at Pentecost 1528.[239] For this reason Hut's followers in Augsburg sent their new community leader, Augustin Bader, to Alsace that April to learn more details from Leber about his revelation. Leber initiated Bader into his doctrine, yet the latter at first remained committed to Hut's calculation and returned to Augsburg to await the appointed time at Pentecost. Only when Bader saw with his own eyes that Hut's prophecy went unfulfilled did he adopt the Jewish date he had learned from Leber. After numerous visions, which he understood to mean that Hut's predictions had not been false but merely that the Second Coming of Jesus had been postponed, Bader finally began in the autumn of 1528 to preach his own doctrine of the great change that was to dawn in the year 1530, with Easter as the new Judgment Day.[240]

Bader's chiliasm is rooted in Hut's *Christliche Unterrichtung* (Christian Teaching). In his initial dispute with Leber, whom he later considered his most important teacher and most loyal follower, Bader connected Hut's work with kabbalistic traditions. Bader later stated that "Oswald the pastor taught him much and strengthened him in the change."[241] Despite his studies in Worms, Leber drew his knowledge of Jewish mysticism primarily, as Anselm Schubert has shown, from the writings of Christian Hebraists, especially Johannes Reuchlin's *De arte cabalistica* (On the Art of Kabbalah, Hagenau, 1517). Moreover, Leber familiarized Bader with the Jewish conception of a messianic kingdom, which Maimonides details in his introduction to the tenth chapter of the tractate Sanhedrin in his Mishna commentary. It is possible that Leber appropriated this aspect of Jewish tradition only indirectly via Christian-Hebraic literature, since in his discussion of the Messiah in *Vikku'aḥ* (Disputation, Basel, 1529), Sebastian Münster also includes Maimonides's notions of the messianic time.[242]

With respect to Hut's teachings, Bader at first understood his own role as that of a prophet, whose task was to prepare the believers for redemption by proclaiming the divine message and thus to save them from judgment. In the following years, however, he derived from Leber's teachings certain more extensive messianic claims for himself and for his male descendants as heirs. Building on the salvific doctrine of Reuchlin, whereby the human being obtains salvation through progress in the knowledge of God, Bader's prophetic pronouncements were fundamentally messianic. Bader assumed as well, however, that as God's elected prophet of judgment he would effectively reign as messianic king in the subsequent thousand-year empire. His task was not merely to proclaim the change but also, by the power of this prophetic word itself, to rule the kingdom as terrestrial representative of Jesus. For within his teachings, so he claimed, dwelled the spirit of Christ. Thus, despite Bader's royal aspirations, Jesus would remain the true spiritual authority in this terrestrial millennium. Bader thought of himself as a spiritual-prophetic Messiah.

No less unique in Bader's apocalyptic conception is the role imagined for the Jews. A certain number of them were to be admitted to the millennial reign. They would belong to the survivors of the Lord's judgment, while the godless and the unbelievers, according to Bader, would be destroyed. The composition of this chosen group of the righteous is remarkable. Alongside Christians, Jews and even Turks and pagans could be included: He "will not have excluded anyone from the change, neither Jews, heathens, Turks, since he did not know whom God has called to it, for Paul has written: if he has not protected the noble branch but cut it off, how much less will he save the wild [branch]."[243] The Jews had not only Paul's Letter to the Romans to thank for their place in the coming kingdom of Christ but also the apocryphal Fourth Book of Ezra, of which Bader possessed a partial transcription in German translation. In a vision, the prophet Ezra sees the Messiah. After destroying the enemies of the Lord, the Messiah gathers the peaceful nations about him, which Ezra identifies as the Ten Lost Tribes of Israel.[244] From this, Bader concluded that he could hardly exclude the Jews from the millennium.[245]

Indeed, with his doctrine of the change, as he called it, Bader hoped to expand his following to include many of the Jews themselves.[246] In the summer of 1529, chiefly because of its proximity to Jewish settlements, Bader chose the village of Westerstetten near Ulm as his headquarters. This rural region in Further Austria, situated between Ulm and Augsburg and bounded by the Lech and the Danube Rivers, had become for Jews an important settlement area after their expulsion during the late Middle Ages from nearly all German imperial cities, including most recently Regensburg in 1519. In *medinat Schwaben*, the "land of the Swabia" in Jewish geographical understanding, many Jews lived scattered in smaller communities or singly in villages and market and country towns. The de facto capital was Günzburg, with its small but significant Jewish community: here the Swabian regional rabbi had for a time his official residence.[247] But personal relationships also quite possibly played a role in Bader's choice, since Naphtali Hirtz Treves, whom Oswald Leber very likely knew from Worms, had close ties to Günzburg.[248]

In November 1529, the Anabaptist community once again changed its residence, removing to the solitude of the nearby village of Lautern, reachable from Westerstetten by foot, in order to prepare for the judgment they expected in the coming spring. Bader now began to cultivate targeted contacts with Jews in the surrounding area. In their court testimony, Bader and one of his followers reported of two direct encounters. Together with Oswald Leber and Gastl Miller, his other most important devotee, Bader apparently sought out the Jew Süßlin (Dulcius) of Leipheim in the latter's place of residence and presented Süßlin and another Jew with his doctrine.[249] Süßlin, according to Bader, was extremely interested and supported him in his mission, saying he ought to continue in this direction, as it was the right one. Bader went on to declare that, on a different day, he and Leber encountered another Jew from Günzburg on the post road to Augsburg, "whose name [they] did not know."[250] They informed this man, too, "how their altar and sacrifice had not lasted, and usury was also of no use, for a change would come, which was already here. The Jew answered that he would like to know it and be with him."[251] This Jew was, in Bader's words, so enthusiastic that he immediately wanted to join the Anabaptist group; he "wished to know where he and his associates stayed, so he could join them. But he [Bader] did not want to show it to them at that time."[252] The Jews of Günzburg allegedly even provided financial support for Bader's plans.[253]

Bader's wife, Sabina, moreover, was alleged to have spoken of a great messianic excitement caused by her husband among the Swabian Jews: "They ran after him and honored him greatly, and they welcomed him, [saying] he was the right one and should speak more with them."[254] Although Sabina Bader may well have exaggerated the effect of the Anabaptist messiah on the Jews, it is nevertheless entirely plausible that Bader's message gave fresh impetus to contemporary Jewish messianic hope.[255] The Jews' willingness to engage in dialogue is itself remarkable here. What is more, the proximity of Bader's teachings to Jewish messianism points to the possibility that the Jews may very well have desired, as Bader alleged, to "learn more about it." Of course, Bader would hardly have been acknowledged by the Jews according to his self-perception as the Messiah. But the fact that a Christian group shared the Jewish expectation of the year 1530 as the dawn of the end-times ought not to be underestimated in terms of its effects. Whenever the time frames of Jewish and Christian apocalyptic expectations coincided, the discourse typically tended to strengthen the respective conceptions.[256]

Moreover, essential elements of Bader's millennial scenario seemed to be in accord with Jewish hopes, such as, for example, the participation of the Jews in the messianic time. Among noninitiates, therefore, the impression could easily arise that Bader "thought nothing of neither the old faith, Anabaptism, the Lutheran nor of the new doctrine,"[257] but rather "more of the Jews than of our faith."[258] Similarly, Bader's expectation of the annihilation of the pope and the emperor in the Last Judgment aligned well with the Jewish hope of messianic revenge on Edom/Rome. Bader appears to have been strengthened in this belief by a second vision of Fourth Ezra, in which the prophet sees in the disappearance of a four-headed eagle the destruction of the fourth and final world empire.[259] This prophetic vision attained urgent relevance in the time of the Reformation, because the image of the raptor was referred to the reign of the Habsburgs, whose coat of arms is adorned with a double-headed eagle.[260]

Bader's hopes for a positive reception among the Jews of Swabia, however, were based not only on the fact that his doctrine appeared in many parts to be Jewish but also on the connection he assumed between them and the Turks. At that time, the Turkish forces stood at the gates of Vienna, and Bader viewed them as the tool of the Lord's revenge against the corrupt spiritual and terrestrial authorities.[261] Since many Jews lived under comparatively favorable circumstances in the Ottoman Empire,[262] the fall of Constantinople in 1453 meant that they were increasingly accused of being in league with the Turks and of promoting the Ottoman expansion at Europe's expense.[263] Such an alliance of the enemies of Christendom was attributed, among other things, to the Jewish hope for the messianic annihilation of the Christians.[264] A Jewish-Turkish alliance was presumed by Bader as well, although more in the sense of a family relation. Proceeding from the contemporary identification of the Red Jews with the Turks, Bader concluded that the European Jews must be their cousins.[265] While he saw in the advance of the Turks the fulfillment of the prophecy from the Fourth Book of Ezra about the return of the Ten Lost Tribes of Israel, he also assumed that the European Jews, as their relatives, must have no less interest than he himself did in a Turkish victory. He and Leber, therefore, made this an important theme of conversation in their efforts to recruit Jewish followers: "Oswald said to the Jew from Ginzburg that the Turk is their cousin and of their kind."[266] The Jew countered, however, that he did not share the apocalyptic expectation that Bader linked to the Turk, "for he [the Turk] had murdered the Jews in Kronweissenburg, but had he not done so, they would have held and accepted him as the one who was to initiate the change and abolish and destroy Christendom."[267] Whether the answer is to be understood ironically as a precaution against revealing one's own messianic hope to a Christian or in fact indicates a change in Jewish messianic expectation of the time is impossible to determine on the basis of the extant sources.

In any event, the Jewish-Anabaptist friendliness toward the Turks, whether real or imagined, would have had serious consequences for the Jewish communities in the empire. The case against Bader and his people gave the impression that "to all appearances the greatest practices of these horrifying deeds proceed from the Jews and may be directed by them."[268] Through the defendants' testimony, age-old and general suspicions crystallized, at the beginning of 1530, into a list of specific accusations supported by witnesses: the Jews were enemies of Christianity (precisely in the light of their subversive messianism), they were allies of the Turks, and they were in league via secret agreements with the Anabaptists.[269] Already in the court proceedings, which went to press in Augsburg on March 19 and 20, that is, immediately after the interrogation, we find the beginnings of a Jewish conspiracy theory that was taken up again and again in various political contexts.[270]

In Antonius Margaritha's influential text *Der gantz Jüdisch glaub*, which appeared at virtually the same time in Augsburg in two editions within a single month (first on March 16 and then, as a consequence of the great demand, again on April 7), there is also a clear reaction to the revelations of the Bader case. Margaritha, who lived in Augsburg and had very likely heard rumors of the trial, makes use of the occasion to connect the general accusation that the Jews pray for the demise of the Christians with the Jewish hopes for a victory of the Turks over Edom: "Just as they now take an excessive joy in the Turkish war, so they hope the scepter of the Christians will be taken away."[271] Elisheva Carlebach has suggested that Margaritha purposefully scheduled the publication of his anti-Jewish work with a view to the coming imperial diet in Augsburg, which was to begin on June 15.[272] Was he perhaps counting on the great political explosiveness of the Bader case? It is certainly plausible that the immense success and rapid reprinting of the defamatory work (which portrays the Jewish danger in the starkest black-and-white terms) were due to current political events and that, precisely for this reason, Margaritha's accusations were explicitly taken up at the imperial diet. Significantly, the discussion there was concerned above all with the anti-Christian position of the Jews and with their desire to see the authorities destroyed, while the theme of Jewish usury, which also stood on the diet's agenda and which Margaritha also assigns an important place in his book, was barely touched upon. Nevertheless, in a public disputation, Josel of Rosheim succeeded in refuting all of these allegations.[273]

Josel had already successfully turned aside the threat of repressions immediately following the Bader case. The government of Further Austria in Stuttgart had informed King Ferdinand I, who at that time was in Prague, of the alleged Jewish backers of the conspiracy and recommended a brutal crackdown.[274] In its written reply, the royal chancellery instructed that Bader be interrogated by both "amicable and painful treatment" (gutliche vnd peinlich Handlung), especially regarding his Jewish contacts, "so that the same Jews may be brought to prison and the truth of their actual intentions may be learned." The Jews of Günzburg, Leipheim, and Pfühl were warranted for arrest so that they could be compelled to confess their intentions and "so that such evil action, as an example to others, be grievously punished whereby none shall be spared."[275]

The Swabian League, a federation of Swabian imperial cities and territorial princes, reacted similarly to the alleged schemes of the Jews. Here, too, the supposed collaboration with the Turks was the aspect of the case that caused the greatest furor. The Augsburg town clerk and humanist Konrad Peutinger found in the testimony clear confirmation of the accusations that had arisen the previous year, when the Turks had laid siege to Vienna, namely, of collusion with infidels and of spying and financial support for the enemy.[276] A report by Peutinger to the city council of Nördlingen mentions a plan to drive the Jews from the cities of the Swabian League or at least to complicate the terms of settlement.[277] Although this project was openly discussed at a meeting, it was eventually not taken up in the Swabian League's legislative record; nor did the memorandum against the Jews presented by the Swabian League at the imperial diet make mention of Jewish-Turkish collusion, although it was based on Peutinger's report.[278]

There is no evidence that, as a consequence of the Bader episode, the Swabian League or the royal chancellery undertook corresponding measures against the Jews. Admittedly, the Jewish history of Upper Swabia for the decade 1525–35 is poorly documented overall; but there is nothing to suggest either imprisonments or a break in continuity for the history of Jewish settlements. This is confirmed by an anonymous Hebrew chronicle from Prague:

> In all the lands there was a new accusation against the Jews, one not found in the Pentateuch, impugning that they spy on the emperor, may he be exalted, for the Ottoman sultan. In consequence, there was a plot to deny the Jews their rights, leaving them unprotected and liable to massacre and extermination, Heaven forbid! All the governors of the lands intended

to issue an edict of expulsion, Heaven forbid, with the king's approval, may
he be exalted. But God, Blessed be He, nullified their evil intent.[279]

That the Bader episode remained in the end virtually without consequence for the Jews appears to be largely due to the activity of Josel of
Rosheim. In his chronicle for the year 1530, Josel reports on the calumny regarding the Jews' alleged spying for the Turks, which supposedly
even reached the ears of Emperor Charles and his brother, Ferdinand:
"Whereupon we were outlawed and were not permitted to set foot in
several lands."[280] "With the consent of the communities," Josel therefore
composed a vindicating document that he submitted to both Habsburg
rulers in Innsbruck.[281] Although this document does not survive, it is
abundantly clear that he succeeded in convincing them of the baselessness of the allegations, since on May 18, 1530, Charles affirmed the Jews'
privileges in the empire.[282]

In his efforts against the consequences of Bader's activity for the Jews,
Josel appears to have been successful in a third arena as well. In the summer of 1529, Ferdinand, as Württemberg's new territorial ruler, had issued
a mandate that granted Jews passage through the territory despite their
previous expulsion in 1521. (At the same time, the mandate denied them
many other rights.) On the basis of Josel's remarks in the chronicle, it seems
that the king wished to revoke even this mild concession in light of the
revelations in the Bader case. But after Josel had submitted his petition in
Innsbruck, Ferdinand slightly altered his mandate to the advantage of the
Jews.[283]

For Augustin Bader and his followers, the episode ended less favorably. In various places on March 30, 1530, they were all executed. The final
moments of their leader, the king Messiah, were particularly spectacular: a
burning crown was set upon Bader's head, and after he had been quartered
with red-hot tongs and decapitated using his own golden sword, his body
was incinerated and the ashes strewn in the Neckar River.[284]

4. THE LAST EMPEROR OF EDOM: JEWISH PROPHECY AND EMPEROR CHARLES V

But God saw the suffering of his people; he sent an emissary, a king
of mercy, and laid strength and power in the hands of the lord, His
Majesty, the emperor Charles.

—Josel of Rosheim, *Sefer ha-miknah*, 1546

Josel of Rosheim's priorities in the year 1530 were clear. His greatest concern was the welfare of the Jewish communities that had been endangered
by their association with Augustin Bader. Whenever the basis of Jewish
existence in the empire had been at stake, as it seemed to be once again
in the aftermath of the Bader case, Josel had (often successfully) intervened with the ruling powers to mitigate the threat.[285] Is it possible that, in
1530, Josel simultaneously practiced a messianic politics out of Christian
view? Hidden behind the effort to distance himself from the Anabaptists'
plan of deposing the emperor with help from the Turks, did he not have
an apocalyptic schema of his own? Although till now Josel has appeared
in the relevant scholarship only as a practitioner of realpolitik and a rational opponent of messianic movements, the truth is that he harbored his
own acute apocalyptic expectations. As we will see, he placed faith in the
emperor not only as the centralized power and guarantor of the rights
granted in the imperial privileges for the Jews[286] but also as an actor in
the eschatological drama. In Josel's apocalyptic interpretation of history,
Charles V appeared as a kind of messianic savior: he is the last Roman
emperor before the advent of the Messiah. Thus, his untimely fall would
hardly have lain in Josel's interests.

The concept of the Last Emperor evolved during late antiquity and the
Middle Ages into a central figure of Christian apocalypticism in the West.[287]
With the Christianization of the Roman Empire in the fourth century, the
image arose of an ideal ruler who would reign as the last Roman emperor
shortly before the end of the world.[288] According to the prophecy, the Last

Emperor destroys or converts all enemies of Christianity and establishes a Christian kingdom of peace. At the end of his reign, with the symbolic surrender of his imperial insignia in Jerusalem, he gives all power back to God, thus making room for the Antichrist, whose reign of terror is finally abolished by the Second Coming of Jesus and the Last Judgment. Under pressure from the Islamic expansion in the late seventh century, however, the prophecy of the Last Emperor experienced a revision of wide-ranging significance, namely, in the *Revelationes* (Revelations) of Pseudo-Methodius: the Last Emperor's victory was from that point on linked to the annihilation of Muslim power.[289]

The image of the Last Emperor mutated further under the influence of the conception of history espoused by the Calabrian abbot Joachim of Fiore. Although the Last Emperor idea does not appear in Joachim's doctrine, over the course of time the two concepts underwent a partial fusion. According to Joachim, world history is divided into three phases corresponding to the Trinity. Following the Age of the Father, which covers the time frame of the Old Testament, there comes the Age of the Son, beginning with Jesus and covering the time of the New Testament. Following the reign of the Antichrist, the last phase arrives, the Age of the Holy Spirit. This, according to Joachim, will be a time of religious revival and new spirituality through enlightenment by the Most High. During the transition between the second and third phases, after the persecution of Christendom and the affliction of the Roman Empire by the Muslims but before the arrival of the Antichrist, Joachim presages a brief period of peace, in which a *novus dux* appears to renew Christendom. Although Joachim's "new leader" is likely a pope rather than an emperor, his concept of ecclesiastical revival had an effect upon the image of the Last Emperor of Rome: it became a figure of reformation. The precondition of the golden age now appeared to be a fundamental reform of the church and of Christian society, since their deficiencies were considered the source of all evil.[290]

Over the course of the medieval and early modern periods, Christian political prophecy cast various contemporary rulers in the role of the Last

Emperor, such that at some time or other nearly every powerful king in Europe was seen in this light. Corresponding to the Christian concept and influenced by the ways that concept was actualized in contemporary politics, Jewish prophecies of the Last Emperor can be traced back to at least the late Middle Ages and possibly (in the case of Frederick Barbarossa) even earlier.[291] Until now, this particular genre of eschatological speculation has not been clearly identified within the framework of Jewish messianism, despite the fact that a group of Hebrew prophecies survives from the seventh century, which resemble quite strongly the pre-Joachim conception of the Last Emperor.[292] One of them is the apocalyptic text *Otot ha-mashi'aḥ* (Signs of the Messiah), which predicts a final Roman ruler, the king of Edom, who will rule the entire world.[293] Having arisen, like Pseudo-Methodius, under pressure of the growing power of Islam, another text of this group has the last king of Edom marching into Jerusalem to drive out the Ishmaelites. In Jerusalem, according to the prophecy, he then lays down his crown before God.[294] In bloody succession, the reigns of Messiah ben Joseph, Armilus the Son of Satan, and Messiah ben David follow. It is unclear whether we are dealing here with an independent Jewish tradition or with a version of what was originally Christian material.[295] To be sure, the expectation per se of a Last Emperor of the Romans is ultimately based on the Jewish image of the final earthly kingdom that is to precede the advent of the messianic age. Moreover, specific elements of the Last Emperor prophecy are already found in older Jewish traditions, by which the Christian image in turn was presumably influenced.[296] In the late Middle Ages and early modern period, however, the Jewish tradition of the Last Emperor, though continuing to develop indigenous ideas, was nevertheless clearly shaped by its Christian counterpart. This explains why Hebrew prophecies celebrate, somewhat surprisingly, the Last Emperor of Edom as the ideal ruler who, prior to the end of the world, is to destroy all enemies of (Catholic) Christendom.

In the sixteenth century, as the Ottoman menace to Europe reached its zenith and the Reformation had already for some time been causing volatile grievances to erupt within the church, there was no more appropriate casting for the role of Rome's last ruler than the Habsburg emperor Charles V, whose sphere of influence had expanded massively within Europe and reached even as far as the New World. What is more, he bore the mythical name capable of reawakening the old expectation of the Last Emperor as a return of Charlemagne. By 1519, the prophecy of the Last Emperor, which circulated throughout Europe in both Latin treatises and vernacular versions, had reached a high-water mark; the election of Charles as Holy Roman Emperor was seen as a mandate for global empire and for the gathering of the entire Christian flock under one shepherd. After the imperial coronation in 1530, these hopes intensified throughout the realm.[297]

From this second phase, two Hebrew prophetic texts are known that stand in close relation to contemporary Christian prophecy regarding Charles. The first was written in 1530 and survives in multiple versions from Italy and Muslim areas. Where precisely it originated cannot be determined with any certainty.[298] The prophecy's connection, in an older version, with important scholars of medieval Ashkenaz implies at the very least an earlier dissemination of the Last Emperor tradition within the German lands. Accordingly, the brief text appears, among other places, as a later addition in the margins of a manuscript containing a work by Abraham of Rothenburg. A messianic prophecy that is nearly identical in form and content to the 1530 version is here attributed to Abraham's brother, Meir of Rothenburg, the Maharam, and is possibly a direct precursor to the later text.[299]

In this version, the Maharam beseeches heaven to reveal to him the secret of the end. Instead of an answer, he receives a mysterious acronym, which he cannot interpret. He requests clarification, and the acronym is deciphered for him: the end of the world is connected with the reign of a certain Emperor Frederick. In thirteenth-century Christian circles, parallel prophecies circulated relating to the person of Frederick II of Hohenstaufen, after whose death in 1250 either his return or a third Frederick was expected.[300] Viewed from this perspective, it seems likely that more than mere polemics was behind the label hung upon the deceiver Tile Kolup: "king of the Jews." Tile Kolup (or Dietrich Holzschuh) appeared in 1285 in the Rhenish city of Neuss, claiming to be Emperor Frederick II, who had died thirty-five years earlier. This false Frederick, who in fact possessed a certain physical resemblance to the deceased Hohenstaufen emperor, was immediately hailed and acknowledged as emperor by the local authorities. Moreover, he was offered financial support by the city and members of the ruling class. The Jews of the city were among his most enthusiastic followers and creditors, and they acted on his behalf in such a way that soon earned him the moniker "king of the Jews." Presumably, behind the great success that Tile Kolup enjoyed equally among Jews and Christians lay a shared set of expectations regarding the Last Emperor.[301]

The propagation of Maharam's prophecies into the sixteenth century corresponds to the way Christians updated their predictions regarding Frederick, and the next public figure who became the focus of Christian expectation, the Habsburg emperor Frederick III, appears also in the Jewish tradition. The "Frederick" familiar from the prophecy attributed to Meir of Rothenburg was in the fifteenth century identified with Frederick III.[302] In the following century, both Christians and Jews reinterpreted the unfulfilled Frederick prophecies for a new candidate and replaced Frederick with Charles—just as occurs in the Hebrew dream vision of 1530.[303] Here, too, the questioner interested in the end does not know at first what to make of the answer from above, but he receives an elucidation that leads him on:

> I shall humiliate Sama'el, I shall bring him low. And King Francis shall make war with Charles in order to restrain his power. During the wars of his enemies, I shall raise Charles's crown to the imperial crown in the year 1530. I shall destroy both Rome and Turkey.[304]

This scenario of redemption brings the apocalypse into immediate proximity with the contemporary Christian prophecy of the Last Emperor, at the center of which stands Charles V's rise to imperial honors. The Hebrew *vaticinium ex eventu*, too, refers to the Habsburg ruler's rapid ascent. After he was named successor to his grandfather, the king of Spain, and three years later made Holy Roman King by the electors, he obtained through his coronation by the pope in Bologna the ultimate promotion to emperor. Significantly, the Jewish prophecy sets the date of redemption at 1530. In terms of syntax, the phrase "in the year 1530" can refer as readily to Charles's coronation as to the expected destruction of Rome and the Ottoman Empire and thus the end of times.[305]

According to this prophecy, the time during which Charles becomes emperor would be one of wars and upheaval. As in the Christian prophetic literature, he would have to assert his power as Last Emperor on three different fronts. He must not only triumph over the unbelieving Ottoman Turks but also face the difficult task of reforming the church. The third threat, however, and perhaps the greatest one, would arise from the French king Francis I, who appears here in his role not only as ally of the pope and the Turks[306] but, above all (in a reworking of a prominent motif of pro-Habsburg prophecy), as archenemy. Neither sultan nor pope is called by name; that is an honor reserved for Francis alone as active contender against the emperor, and Charles must go to war to reduce his influence.[307]

By the critical year 1530, Charles could already boast of successes against his three enemies. In 1525 in Pavia, he had won a decisive victory against Francis in the Italian wars for hegemony in Europe, where he even succeeded in taking the French king prisoner.[308] In 1527 there followed the sack of Rome (*sacco di Roma*) and the siege of the pope, who had allied himself with the French. From the point of view of the emperor's adherents, this was confirmation of Charles's central role in the reform of the church, for it appeared that the corrupt church would finally be put on God's trial at the hands of the emperor.[309] Two years later, the conflict with France was resolved for the time being; in the same year, the Turks were beaten back from the gates of Vienna. Although Charles had largely left the waging of this defensive war to his brother, Ferdinand, and could lay claim to a large victory of his own against the Ottomans only with the conquest of Tunis in 1535, nevertheless he enjoyed an early reputation as the chief defender of Christendom. He had lent dramatic expression to his crusading spirit when, immediately following his coronation, he marched at the head of the procession through Bologna carrying the banner of the cross.[310]

In the final drama upon the world stage, the Hebrew apocalypse imagines the leading role of Charles V in an unusual way. The emperor functions not simply negatively as God's proverbial scourge who brings about Edom's downfall—an image we also find applied, for example, to the Turks or to Martin Luther. Instead, the image of the emperor also has a decidedly positive aspect, which suggests the influence of Christian conceptions. The difference from the older Jewish tradition as expressed in *Otot ha-mashi'aḥ* is obvious: there the Roman ruler also appears as a victor, yet he merely fulfills a necessary function in the eschatological scenario. He is not the brave hero who captures the reader's sympathy. Just as little are the Ishmaelites defined in the seventeenth-century prophecy as the representatives of evil. On the contrary: what is placed—for good reason—in the foreground are, above all, the failures and humiliations of the king of Edom. According to *Otot ha-mashi'aḥ*, the Edomites suffer severe losses from the army of the Ishmaelites, and the king is compelled at first to retreat. When he finally enters Jerusalem, he does so not after a glorious victory but only after the death of the Muslim commander.[311] By contrast, the sixteenth-century text foregrounds the triumphs of Charles V and explicitly assigns the emperor the role of the hero in the apocalyptic drama. He is the subduer of evil. To fill out the dramatis personae, the satanic force, "Sama'el," whose abasement is foreseen at the beginning of the prophecy, is personified threefold by Charles's nemesis, the French king Francis I; by the Holy See in Rome; and by the Turks.

The end-time scenario is given a Jewish turn only with the final sentence of the prophecy: "The Ten Tribes [and] their heads shall I gather to their Messiah Joseph, a friend of David."[312] Thus despite the adoption of a Christian leitmotif, it should be clear by now that the reign of the Last Emperor does not lead, as in the Christian tradition, to the reign of the Antichrist and then to the Second Coming of Jesus. Corresponding to the sequence of apocalyptic figures as *Otot ha-mashi'aḥ* presents them, the Last Emperor of Edom makes way directly for Messiah ben Joseph as chief of the Ten Tribes, who is ultimately followed by Messiah ben David.[313]

The second Jewish prophecy regarding Charles V as the Last Emperor originates from none other than Josel of Rosheim himself. His *Sefer ha miknah* (The Book of Acquisition, 1546), which survives only in part, contains a brief passage on God's mercy and grace as seen in history. At the same time, Josel writes, "There lies in some forms of the good, which he has given us to know in every epoch and time, a deep and hidden significance."[314] Josel discovers one such proof of grace with transcendental meaning in the bellicose debates between Protestants and Catholics that were convulsing the empire during his lifetime. After Lutheran Frankfurt am Main surrendered in December 1546 to the imperial army in the Schmalkaldic War, Josel wrote of the signs that could now be recognized

in the case of a nation that has created a new belief for itself with certain alleviations in order to cast off the yoke.[315] They intend to destroy us and to root out the people of Israel by means of various harsh laws and persecutions. But God saw the suffering of his people; he sent an emissary, a king of mercy, and laid strength and power in the hands of the lord, His Majesty, the emperor Charles, so that he might overcome them many times, destroy their [Schmalkaldic] league, thwart their conspiratory plans, bring them low, and without effort conquer and possess [their] territories and cities. By a miracle he was victorious and rescued the people of Israel from the hand of this new belief that the priest by the name of Martin Luther, an impure man,[316] had created. This man wanted to destroy and murder all Jews, from boys to old men. Blessed be God, who has baffled his intention and reduced his plan to nothing. And he let us see vengeance and many rescues, till now on the 23rd of December, His Majesty, the emperor has sent a prince, a general [Count Maximilian von Büren] with his army before the city of Frankfurt.[317]

From these events, Josel concludes:

> Perhaps it is granted us to be near the time as he promised us in the entire
> Torah: "Then the Lord your God will restore your fortunes and take you
> back in love. He will bring you together again from all the peoples where
> the Lord your God has scattered you."[318] ... May it soon become reality![319]

The episode is a rare historical interjection in the second half of *Sefer ha-miknah*, the argumentation of which is otherwise largely dependent upon Abraham Bibago's philosophical work *Derekh emunah* (Path of Faith, Constantinople, 1521).[320] Josel, as if suddenly aware of an indiscretion, all but begs his readers' forgiveness for interrupting the flow of the narrative with this excursus: "Out of joy at the miracle, which took place as described above, I could not resist and close my eyes and not write it as a memorial to the last generation, that they may gain insight therein."[321] To include this theme that is so important to him and to share with his readers his certainty regarding the imminent advent of the Messiah, Josel had, in fact, inserted an additional page in the middle of the book, although the manuscript had actually been completed half a year earlier.[322]

A second text by Josel from the year 1552, which is preserved in the same autographic manuscript collection, makes clear that the characterization of Charles V as the miraculous savior sent by God has its basis in the Christian expectation of the Last Emperor.[323] At first glance, Josel appears to summarize political events in the empire out of a purely historiographic interest and without especial reference to Jewish history.[324] In reality, however, the events he narrates are for the author signs of divine providence. We see this in his prefatory remarks: "Who is wise and discerning will recall to memory the miracles and wondrous acts that the God of Mercy, in His kindness and compassion, has marvelously performed and increased for the people of Israel, day by day, which our eyes have seen."[325]

For Josel, these historical events, on the surface having nothing at all to do with the fate of the Jews, nevertheless foreshadowed imminent salvation. Their significance for Josel was so great, in fact, that they even eclipsed another group of events that are traditionally and more immediately recognizable as signs of God's omnipresent and protecting hand held over the people of Israel: the innumerable instances of the Jews' deliverance from various existential dangers. Josel's chronicle quotes these at length as "favours He has bestowed in every generation."[326] The eschatological particularity of his own time lies for Josel precisely in those miraculous events, which he summarizes as "confusion and panic, which have prevailed and increased from the day that our lord the Emperor Charles, may he be exalted, was appointed [king] in the year 1519, and to this day."[327]

Just as in the Hebrew prophecies of the Last Emperor from 1530, the French king Francis I appears in Josel's account as the emperor's chief adversary. Josel pursues their competitive struggle as if it were a dualism of apocalyptic significance, beginning with Francis's defeat in the vote for king of the Romans, after which "the land was not at peace" due to the Frenchman's envy of the imperial crown. With this premise, the guilt for the subsequent French-Habsburgian war lies unambiguously and solely with the French king himself. Francis thus appears here in the role of the tyrant who harries the hero of the messianic drama. Accordingly, since the Last Emperor prophecy foresees the ultimate triumph of the good, Josel's report on the war reads as the story of Charles's victories. Defeats and setbacks at the hands of the enemy are simply elided. Again and again, until his death in 1547, Francis rose up against Charles, although he never, according to Josel, succeeded in gaining the upper hand. In this long and bitter war, which flared up in various places and in which fortune was in fact sometimes with one side and sometimes with the other, the only battle Josel mentions is, not surprisingly, the Battle of Pavia in February 1525, in which Charles took his rival captive.[328]

In this text as well, the two additional fronts on which Charles V had to assert himself as Last Emperor are the reform of the church and the defense against the Turkish threat. Josel discusses both at length. On the one hand, as he had already done in *Sefer ha-miknah*, he describes Charles's conflicts with the Protestant princes and imperial cities that had formed the Schmalkaldic League. Josel's interpretation of history reaps no small benefit from the fact that the outcome of the Schmalkaldic War had already been decided in 1547 at the Battle of Mühlberg on the Elbe in favor of the emperor's party.[329] In the context of church reform, Josel draws attention to Charles's initiative in convening the Council of Trent in 1545. The emperor, according to Josel, "came to an agreement with all the princes of the realm, and with the Pope and bishops, that a ruling should be given in the city of Trent in respect of their religious differences, at what is known as a council."[330] The Concilium Tridentinum, which is considered the beginning of the Counter-Reformation, convened intermittently until 1563. Its explicit goal was the detailed definition of Catholic doctrine and the implementation of necessary reforms within the church. So that Charles, as Last Emperor, might also shine in his role as crusader, Josel also emphasizes his successes against the unbelievers in the Mediterranean; and for a short time in 1532, the Turks were in fact driven from Koron and Patras in the Peloponnese. Although the admiral Andrea Doria was chiefly responsible for these small victories, Josel ascribes them to the emperor personally. It was three years later that Charles himself led his troops into Tunis.[331]

Up to this point, Josel's historical observations resemble contemporary Christian views in such striking ways that a direct transfer is likely. He seems to adopt analogous prophecies that must have been familiar to him regarding Charles V. Of particular note in this regard is the *Fragmentum vaticinii cuiusdam Methodii* (Fragment of the Prophecies of a Certain Methodius). This work establishes Charles's calling as Last Emperor on the basis of precisely the same events Josel himself selects from imperial history, and it matches Josel's representation in nearly every detail. First appearing in 1547 in Vienna, the book comprises a group of prophecies collected by the physician and university lecturer Wolfgang Lazius, who was also court historiographer for Ferdinand I.[332]

As important evidence for Charles's role as Last Emperor, Lazius adduces the same military victories over Islam and Protestantism that Josel does. The resurgence of unbelievers and heretics he even finds predicted in the Apocalypse of John, where the biblical author writes of seeing "a beast rise up out of the sea" (Apoc. 13:1) and "another beast coming up out of the earth" (Apoc. 13:11). Corresponding to their elements—water and earth—Lazius equates the beasts of the biblical apocalypse respectively with the Muslims beyond the Mediterranean Sea and with the Schmalkaldic League of Protestants in the middle of the empire.[333] Lazius makes consistent use of this New Testament typology, and—like Josel—he emphasizes the maritime war against the Turks. Again, like Josel, he gives the emperor full credit for the reform of the Catholic Church, noting that the Council of Trent ultimately came to fruition due to Charles's efforts. The pope and the recalcitrant curia are degraded to the status of extras. And, finally, Lazius, too, opens a third front in the millennial wars of the Last Emperor, pointing to the Battle of Pavia and the capture of the French king.[334]

Josel's representation of the apocalyptic conflict continues with the rebellion of the Protestant princes against the emperor in 1551/52. At that time, he writes, "an evil wind blew in from the north"—an allusion to the Book of Daniel, in which the terrible king of the north makes war on the king of the south, bringing death and destruction at the end of time.[335] Indeed, the violent conflicts narrated in the Book of Daniel, interrupted now and again by treaties and times of peace between the rulers of the north and the south, read very much like an allegory for the religious wars that convulsed the Holy Roman Empire in the early modern period. The king of the south, according to Josel's interpretation, is none other than the emperor himself, along with the loyal Catholic cities and territories, which largely lay in the southern part of the empire. The king of the north is embodied in the secret federation of the Protestant princes of the northern lands. Josel mentions by name the Elector Maurice of Saxony and the Margrave Albrecht of Brandenburg-Kulmbach.[336] He describes how they aligned themselves with the new French king and imperial archenemy, Henry II, who eventually declared war on Charles in the autumn of 1551 and advanced as far as the Rhine. In doing so, the French army left a swath of death and destruction across much of Alsace.[337] The French king remains in the role of tyrant even when he commands his soldiers to spare the Jews.[338] For Josel, this belongs simply to the mercy that God bestows upon each generation, and it pales in the messianic interpretation of imperial politics. There, Josel leans heavily on the starkly good-versus-evil casting of Christian Last Emperor prophecy. The great conflict before the end of the world occurs, for Josel as for his Catholic contemporaries, between Charles V and the triumvirate of evil: the Ottoman Turks, the heretics within the Christian Church, and the French archenemy.

In accordance with Daniel's prophecy, the king of the north—the Protestants in this view—will be defeated in the end. "[A]nd he will meet his doom with no one to help him."[339] On this point, Josel breaks with the strict parallelism to the Christian expectation and prognosticates a Jewish end: during the wars between the northern and southern kings, as portrayed in Daniel, the fourth empire they inherit will also be destroyed.[340] While, for his Christian contemporaries, the golden reign of Charles V stood at the center, Josel turns his gaze further into the future, to the downfall of the divided Holy Roman Empire amid the confusions of the Reformation.

Josel's apocalyptic interpretation of the Reformation is singular. Whereas in the known Jewish sources, a messianic view of events is invariably combined with a certain welcoming view of Martin Luther and the Protestants,[341] Josel's portrayal leaves no shadow of a doubt that he sides with the Catholics. Josel is unambiguously pro-Habsburg and thus also anti-Protestant.[342] This corresponds to his expressly inimical stance to Protestantism in general—which is perhaps understandable in the context of the grave practical consequences of Luther's strategical about-face with respect to the treatment of the Jews. Since Luther and his powerful followers impugned the very existence of the Jews in the empire, Josel remained—even on the threshold of the eschatological era—strongly pro-Habsburg in his allegiance. Significantly, Josel's messianic expectation affords a prominent place to the chastisement of the corrupt church, which, according to Joachim of Fiore's idea of the *reformatio ecclesiae* (reformation of the church), is to proceed renewal and revitalization. In this perspective, even the inner-ecclesiastical reforms of the Council of Trent could become, from a Jew's perspective, a sign of the Messiah.

Hebrew prophecies about the Last Emperor present a further variation on the Jewish-messianic perception of the Turkish menace. Once again, the roles of good and evil are switched, since the Turks no longer are the divine rod employed to punish the Christians but instead must be defeated by the Last Emperor to make way for the Messiah. That the Holy Roman Emperor should, in this variation of Jewish apocalypticism, himself take on a quasi-messianic function is rather surprising. After all, he is first and foremost the loathed last ruler of Edom, upon whose ultimate destruction the fulfillment of Jewish messianic hope depends. Here, paradoxically, he has become a positive figure of salvation. But this transformation takes place without entirely suppressing the older interpretation: in Jewish prophecy, the Last Emperor can only appear as a shining prelude to Edom's fall.[343]

5. THE FATE OF DAVID RE'UVENI AND SOLOMON MOLKHO IN REGENSBURG

The imperial diet was just good enough to lay out our matter
before the eyes of all.

—Max Brod, *Reubeni, Prince of the Jews*, 1925

In his messianic war against the Turks, David Re'uveni hoped for a confederation with the powerful Charles V, king of Spain and emperor of the Holy Roman Empire of German Nations. After all, the empire stood at that time under immediate threat by the Turks, and thus Charles would have good reason to lend a favorable ear to Re'uveni's offer of Jewish military aid. It seems likely, moreover, that Re'uveni found support for his plan in the prophecies of the apocalyptic role of Charles V, which at that time were circulating in Venice and Rome, two cities where the self-proclaimed emissary of the Lost Tribes sojourned at length after his arrival in Europe. Re'uveni's host in Rome, the Christian Hebraist and kabbalist Egidio da Viterbo, for example, saw in Charles the final earthly ruler before the end of the world, the Last Emperor whose role necessarily included triumph over the unbelieving Turks.[344]

By the time he visited the pope in 1524, Re'uveni had come to see it as a matter of great importance that the two traditional nations of the crusades, Germany and France, set aside their differences regarding the domination of Europe and take action instead against the common Turkish enemy.[345] Because a reconciliation between Charles V and Francis I did not stand in his own interests, however, the pope referred Re'uveni to the Portuguese king John III, whose fleet was at that time the dominant sea power in Arabia.[346] John III received Re'uveni in the autumn of the following year and promised him the military support he desired.[347] It was during this time, according to Re'uveni's own testimony, that the emperor heard of his mission. When in early 1526 Charles sent an entourage to the Portuguese court to fetch his future bride Isabella (John's sister) for the nuptial ceremonies, he also had the Jewish emissary informed through an ambassador that he approved of Re'uveni's plan and wished to see him.[348]

Years were to pass, however, before a meeting could take place. In Portugal, Re'uveni found himself for the first time in difficulties that earned him John's disfavor. The cause was messianic unrest among the conversos (Iberian Jews, or their descendants, who were forced to convert). In a country that since 1497 had tolerated no Jews within its borders, the appearance of the alleged Jewish nobleman and emissary of the Lost Tribes, not to mention his formal reception by the king, had occasioned a certain amount of civil commotion.[349] Very quickly, accusations began to circulate that the emissary was seeking to call the conversos back to the Jewish faith. A fatal moment in this context was the open declaration by a young converso at the royal court, a scribe by the name of Diogo Pires, that he had returned to the Judaism of his parents. Re'uveni denied that he had had anything to do with the matter or that he was even interested in the fate of the conversos. Nevertheless, John revoked his offer of military aid and, toward the end of 1526, banished Re'uveni from the kingdom. From that moment on, an evil star seemed to rule over Re'uveni's destiny. The ship that was to bring him back to Italy was instead forced by unfavorable winds to drop anchor on the east coast of Spain, where Re'uveni and his entire retinue were placed under arrest, since Jews were forbidden to set foot in any of the territories of the Spanish crown. Although Charles, as territorial ruler, ultimately granted him free passage, Re'uveni did not manage to see the emperor face to face.[350]

Once again in Italy, and after various other setbacks large and small, Re'uveni began to concentrate his efforts on the possibility of a meeting with the emperor. In February 1530, he traveled to Bologna to take part in the coronation festivities. His hopes for an audience with the emperor were baffled yet again, however, as he had just been found guilty of having falsified certain documents, including a letter from his supposed brother among the Ten Tribes. As a consequence, he was publicly denounced as a baro et ribaldo, a "deceiver and scoundrel."[351] Despite this, Re'uveni refused to give up his ambitions, and some two and a half years later, toward the end of July 1532, he journeyed north to Regensburg, where the emperor had recently held the imperial diet.[352] He was accompanied on this journey by the erstwhile scribe Diogo Pires, who since his reconversion to Judaism had renamed himself Solomon Molkho. Having initially fled to the Ottoman Empire to avoid the Portuguese inquisition, Molkho had by the time of his reunion with Re'uveni in Venice (at the end of 1530) become a prominent mystic and had even earned messianic notoriety through a series of apocalyptic sermons.[353]

Although Re'uveni must be considered the initiator of the expedition to Regensburg,[354] at some point during the sojourn in Germany he stepped into a secondary role and handed the active diplomacy over to Molkho.[355] One can only speculate as to the reasons for this. Perhaps after his cover had been blown in Bologna, Re'uveni feared that he would yet again be denied an audience with the emperor. That Charles at the time was informed at all concerning the unmasked charlatan is doubtful. If he was, it apparently did not work greatly to Re'uveni's and Molkho's particular disadvantage in Regensburg.[356] Moreover, it would not have been unusual for the emperor to knowingly meet with a notorious swindler. In the early modern period, one can observe a relatively unconstrained—by contemporary standards—interaction with persons suspected of imposture and fraud, even if they had already been exposed.[357] In an age without identity cards and birth certificates, one was keenly aware of the limitations on any possibility of obtaining reliable information as to a person's identity. For this reason, the benefit of the doubt was typically given to the accused, especially when they were such charismatic personalities as Molkho and Re'uveni. Ultimately, one could never be entirely certain that someone was not exactly who he said he was, however damning the evidence against him appeared to be.

This is illustrated in Re'uveni's case by the following event: less than a year after he had been unmasked as an imposter, his story was once again subject to investigation. In November 1530, the Venetian senate appointed a special examiner, Giovanni Battista Ramusio, a well-traveled linguist familiar with eastern languages, who was at that time considered Europe's leading authority in the fields of geography and exploration. His assessment of Re'uveni is characteristic. After a personal interview with the suspect, he submitted a sober report to his superiors. The report concludes that

> the man is so convinced in this matter of leading the Hebrew people back to the promised land . . . that nothing more can be said about it. And I am in doubt as to whether he will turn aside from this way. The Jews do indeed honor him like a Messiah. I know nothing more to say.[358]

Although this was precisely the point of the personal examination, Ramusio withheld judgment as to Re'uveni's credibility; nor did the historiographer Sanuto, who copied Ramusio's report verbatim in his diary, append any words of doubt as to the identity of the self-proclaimed Jewish prince.

In any event, the Jewish world resisted calling Re'uveni an impostor. The banker Daniel da Pisa, who had been one of Re'uveni's hosts and interpreters in Rome, closed a letter very much in the same vein as Ramusio: he leaves it to the addressee himself to decide whether or not to believe Re'uveni.[359] Abraham Farissol similarly refuses to call Re'uveni's words lies plain and simple, and he justifies his decision by pointing out, interestingly, that the Christians also assumed the Ten Tribes of Israel still existed somewhere:

> Let his words be true or not—it suffices us today in this our exile and in our lands, that it is considered a matter of fact for kings and princes and for many in the countries of Rome, that the Tribes of Israel still exist, which are numerous and which have many kings. And the Jew who has come, let him be who he is. If the existence of the Jews and kings is true, then it is perhaps possible that he has indeed come in this manner and along this path from the desert of Habor.[360]

Even the pope, Clement VII, received Re'uveni, despite being less than completely certain of the man's credibility. This can be gleaned from the formulation of the letters of introduction he composed for Re'uveni to the Portuguese king and to the Ethiopian negus. He introduces Re'uveni as a prince of a great Jewish nation from the Habor desert—adding, "or so he would maintain."[361] Clement even asked John of Portugal to have his seamen investigate Re'uveni's claims as to his alleged people in the Arabian desert. In the absence of absolute certainty in the case, however, the pope did not wish simply to dismiss Re'uveni's claims as mere fabrications.[362] Despite substantial doubts, Clement finally could not ignore the possibility of help—which was desperately needed—against the Ottoman Turks. The worst-case scenario was that one would have dealt with the wrong person.

One eyewitness report on the sojourn of the two Jewish emissaries in the imperial city of Regensburg stems from Girolamo Aleander, the special papal envoy to Germany, who in 1532 accompanied the permanent nuncio Lorenzo Campeggio. On August 21, Aleander wrote a dispatch to Rome in which he informed the papal counselor and private secretary, Giovanni

Battista Sanga, that "the heretical (*perfidus*) Portuguese Jew" who had sought an audience with the pope in 1529 was now at the imperial court.[363] He had arrived "together with the other from Arabia," who several years earlier had likewise been at the Vatican.[364] The delegation, according to the report, was accompanied by the imperial general Antonio de Leyva, under whose protection (and perhaps even observation, since after all, the Jews had been driven from the city in 1519) they resided in quarters assigned to them by the emperor.[365]

Molkho we know received an imperial audience. Whether Re'uveni was also present remains unclear. As Aleander describes the encounter in his report to Rome, Molkho placed before the emperor the prospect of Jewish support in his war against the Ottomans: "He makes grand promises [to do battle] against the Turks, and says that he must be one of the leaders. He promises certain victory through himself and his sacred objects, and that he will kill or capture the Sultan."[366] Assuming Aleander has left nothing out, Molkho made no reference to the armies of Re'uveni's royal brother, whereas Re'uveni himself in his negotiations with the pope and the Portuguese king had made constant mention of them. This is in line with the role reversal that seems to have occurred between the two men; Re'uveni's identity now remained in the background. Whence the Jewish soldiers were to come, if not from the Lost Tribes, can be gleaned from Josel of Rosheim, who was in Regensburg at precisely the same time in order to advocate for Jewish interests at the imperial diet. In his chronicle, Josel notes that Molkho's intention was "to stir up the Emperor by telling him that he had come to gather all the Jews to wage war against the Turks."[367] As Molkho himself claimed afterward to the envoy Aleander, the emperor had listened to his plans for two hours with great interest and had asked many questions.[368]

In a situation in which the old prophecy seemed in danger of being fulfilled—that is, the Turks would advance as far as Cologne before they could be defeated[369]—it was perhaps understandable that the emperor would welcome any even remotely plausible support. Moreover, Charles was first and foremost a politician and not especially scrupulous about the partners in his alliances.[370] Indeed, since 1524 he had endeavored to form an alliance with the Persian Shah, archenemy of the Ottomans and supposed friend to the Christians. The attempt to coordinate their military maneuvers against the Turks had proven impractical, however, due to the great distance separating Persia and the Holy Roman Empire.[371]

Molkho's proposal of a second front against the Muslims, in fact, offered an attractive prospect in August 1532. Although the emperor's brother, Ferdinand I, had succeeded in driving the Turks from Austria in 1529, parts of Hungary, including the city of Buda, had remained in their possession. Even as Re'uveni and Molkho were arriving in Regensburg, the Turks were busy preparing for a renewed assault on the empire. On April 25, Suleiman had departed from Istanbul at the head of an army of 130,000 men, and they were joined in Belgrade and Osijek by 300,000 more. Gradually, a two-pronged attack began to take shape: the foot soldiers under the sultan's leadership marched on Hungary and the empire, while the Turkish fleet would attack southern Italy.[372] In response, the imperial diet, which had opened but a few days before the Turkish army decamped, placed the Turkish threat and the preparation of a counterattack at the top of its agenda. As the diet was officially concluded on July 27, the Turks under the sultan and his grand vizier Ibrahim Pasha were already on the march northward along the Drava River through Croatia and western Hungary. On August 7, the vanguard reached Köszeg (Güns), and three days later Suleiman followed. The Hungarian fortress successfully defended itself against the superior enemy forces, but the final outcome remained uncertain. Moreover, the Turks threatened to renew their siege of Vienna in September. If the city would not capitulate and they were forced to withdraw, they vowed to pillage and burn all of Hungary on the way.[373]

Under these precarious circumstances, the military help offered by the supposed Jewish delegation was urgently needed, and it is no surprise that the suggestion of a Jewish-Christian military alliance was taken into serious consideration. This is underscored by Aleander's repeated emphasis on the connection to General Antonio de Leyva, one of the greatest military commanders of the time, who appears to have played a decisive role in the planning for the Turkish war. In the same letter in which Aleander informs his superiors concerning Molkho and Re'uveni, he also writes of an emergency meeting between the emperor and de Leyva, occasioned by the Turkish threat to conquer Vienna. The military staff could not afford to brush off such threats as mere rhetoric, especially in light of the disconcerting strength of the Ottoman forces: at 450,000 men, it was a truly massive army.[374] One can speculate as to whether de Leyva might not have been present as adviser during Molkho's audience with the emperor or whether he might not perhaps even have arranged the meeting to begin with.[375] Certainly he would have had reason for doing so.

The proposed mutual Christian-Jewish campaign against the Turks did not materialize. Instead, only a day after the audience, Molkho and Re'uveni were arrested and led before the justice of the peace.[376] The reasons for their failure as messianic activists have been comprehensively laid out by Chava Fraenkel-Goldschmidt.[377] On the basis of current knowledge, however, certain connections that were merely suspected before can now be given concrete form. As Fraenkel-Goldschmidt has shown through an analysis of the papal envoy's letters, Aleander himself played a significant role in the arrest of Molkho and Re'uveni.[378] From the very beginning, he left no room for doubt as to his own stance toward Molkho, whom he viewed as a backsliding converso and a heretic. Already years before, he had advocated in Rome for Molkho's execution, as provided in the laws of the Inquisition for anyone who fell away from the Catholic faith.[379] The judgment failed to be enforced at the time, however, due to the pope's personal intervention.[380] As a consequence, Aleander now expressed himself forcefully against any support of Molkho's intention:

> I hope that the Emperor, who is well acquainted with this man, will not want to hear his empty talk. It does not please me that this heretic brings with him his Jewish emblems; instead of that, we should have brought the

cross, since Christians should place all their faith in the cross, and these delusions of the Jew will cause only harm and dishonour.[381]

Apart from the fact that, for Aleander, any form of traffic with a heretic was simply out of the question to begin with, he also considered the prospect of a Christian-Jewish crusade to be an indelible disgrace for the church. Regardless of the outcome of such an undertaking, it could redound only to the disadvantage of both the church and Christendom itself: "Then, if we are victorious, the world will be scandalized by the fact that the victory is credited to him [Molkho] and to his being a Jew. And if we are defeated in battle . . . this will be credited to His Majesty and to all the Christians."[382]

To be sure, given the charges of heresy bought against new converts in Charles's dominions during the 1520s and 1530s, the fact of Molkho's Catholic past was particularly explosive. At precisely the same time as Molkho was at court in Regensburg, for example, the notorious case against the merchant Diogo Mendez was underway in Antwerp. Noteworthy here is that the persecution of heretics proceeded from the same pragmatic reasoning that moved the emperor to grant Molkho an audience in the first place. Just as Charles hoped to obtain support from Molkho against the Turks, he was proceeding relentlessly against other conversos, often under the accusation of Judaizing, in an attempt to hinder them from aiding the sultan either financially or through weapons trafficking.[383]

Fraenkel-Goldschmidt has pointed toward another factor that likely contributed to the sudden change of fortune for the two emissaries: the fear of stirring up messianic furor among Jews and conversos as well as in Christian chiliastic circles.[384] Like many others, Aleander feared the sort of turmoil that had broken out only a few years earlier in Mantua as Molkho had been preaching there;[385] and, in fact, the 1520s and 1530s saw the high-water mark of messianic expectation among the conversos. As mentioned above, Re'uveni's appearance in Portugal had led to an open rebellion among them.[386] Perhaps this lay nearer to the Spaniard Charles's heart than all other developments within the empire. Yet for his German advisers in Regensburg, the mood among the imperial populace was doubtless the crucial factor.

Josel of Rosheim hints at a significant messianic penitence movement in the German-speaking lands when he reports that Molkho's activities had inspired many sinners to repentance.[387] The source materials suggest that, for contemporaries as well as for subsequent generations in Germany, Molkho's activities commanded more attention than those of Re'uveni—or at least that they remained more deeply inscribed in collective memory.[388] Significantly, in his chronicle, Josel mentions only Molkho as a messianic figure who was significant for German Jews in the sixteenth century, while Asher Lemlein and Re'uveni receive no mention at all. In a similar manner, the chronicler David Gans assigns Re'uveni a merely supporting role, while he is full of praise for Molkho's unusual erudition in the Torah.[389] (This from a writer who is normally rather sober in his adherence to the facts.) Gans also reports having looked into a copy of one of Molkho's works, which was in the possession of his cousin, Nathan Horodna.[390] It is possible that Molkho's kabbalistic doctrine reached Worms in this manner, since Nathan's son later became chief justice there and head of the yeshiva, the Talmudic academy.[391] Molkho's writings were in any event well known in Ashkenaz.[392]

One is tempted to ascribe the discrepancy between the testimonies regarding Molkho and Re'uveni to the mechanisms of internal censorship. As we have seen, these mechanisms owe their existence to the special situation of German Jews. It was possible to write "non-messianically," and hence innocuously, about Molkho, to honor him as a kabbalist and scholar. Re'uveni presented a more difficult subject, since one could hardly avoid mentioning his supposed origin among the Lost Tribes. This does not fully explain, however, why Christian observers also considered Molkho's relation to the Jews in the empire more important than Re'uveni's. Thus in his missionary epistle of 1535 to the Jews in the Duchy of Brunswick-Lüneburg, the reformer Urbanus Rhegius, who was at that time active in Celle, makes reference to the activities of Molkho alone.[393] Twenty years later, Johannes Isaac mentions David Re'uveni but, in speaking of his performance of miracles and his death by burning at the stake, obviously confuses him with Molkho.[394] It would appear that both authors knew nothing at all of Re'uveni's visit to Regensburg.[395] Everything seems to suggest, then, that Molkho's leading role in the meeting with the emperor influenced his reception among both Jews and Christians in the empire. Added to this is the circumstance that, from the Christian point of view, he died the death of a heretic at the stake in Mantua, while for Jews he was a martyr. This certainly also contributed to the interest surrounding him.[396]

The sudden arrest of Molkho and Re'uveni in Regensburg comes as no surprise when one considers that Christians in the empire feared Jewish messianism as a threat to life and limb. One had to protect oneself from this very real and present danger by any means available. Without a doubt, the idea of arming Jews and training them as soldiers, as Molkho proposed in Regensburg, would have been deeply unsettling for many Christian contemporaries.[397] Even though Molkho assured his Christian interlocutors that he wanted only to support them in their struggle against the Ottomans, such protestations could hardly assuage the chronic fear of apocalyptic Jewish revenge. After all, that same fear had been shaping Christian perception for centuries. Johann Albrecht Widmannstetter, who in his function as counsel to the Duke of Bavaria was employed in Regensburg at the time and hence whose business it was to be well informed concerning political events, confirms that Molkho's activities came to an end in Regensburg "from fear of a Jewish rebellion."[398]

Nor did the self-confident and dramatic entrance of Molkho and Re'uveni into Regensburg do much to dispel the Christian nightmare of the apocalypse. For one thing, the delegation itself seems to have been rather numerous: the emissaries were apparently accompanied by an entourage including various persons, servants, and other Jews who had spontaneously joined the group.[399] Perhaps more alarming still was the appearance of the two emissaries themselves. Molkho and Re'uveni bore provocative emblems of Jewish sovereignty. According to Aleander's report, they were armed with swords and shields that had been "sanctified with names of God in Hebrew."[400] The shield reported by one source to have been in Re'uveni's possession was alleged to have belonged to King David, who used it to fight the battles of the Lord.[401] Above all, however, what lent the delegation the appearance of official diplomatic status and enhanced dignity were the banners they carried with them as signs of the Tribes of Israel,[402] icons that had already caused a sensation in Italy and Portugal.[403] According to Re'uveni, the Jewish troops would bear the same colors in the future war.[404]

Several of the large banners had been sewn at David Re'uveni's personal behest; others he had received in Italy as gifts from Benvenida Abravanel, a daughter-in-law of Isaac Abravanel, as well as from the pope himself. They were stitched of white, gold, and silver silks and elaborately embroidered with images and Bible verses.[405] It is not known which of these Re'uveni brought with him to Regensburg.[406] One of the flags that Molkho carried with him in Regensburg, however, is preserved in the Jewish Museum in Prague. Shaped like a divided triangle and fashioned from yellow silk bordered by a tricolored silk fringe, it bears quotes in Hebrew on both sides, mostly from the Psalms, embroidered in silk thread in two different shades of red (fig. 12).[407]

If one had wished to have Molkho and Re'uveni condemned to death for sedition, it would have sufficed merely to translate the Bible verses adorning these flags. A messianic-military program is expressed there without ambiguity, linking the hope for imminent salvation to the downfall of the non-Jewish nations. The God of vengeance is entreated, using the familiar oath *shefokh* from the liturgy of the seder, to destroy the enemies of Israel:

> Pour out Your fury on the nations that do not know You, upon the kingdoms that do not evoke Your name. . . . Oh, pursue them in wrath and destroy them from under the heavens of the Lord! O God of retribution, Lord, God of retribution, appear! He subjects peoples to us, sets nations at our feet.[408]

Finally, now the suffering of Israel under Christian rule is to be avenged: "Strike fear into them, O Lord; let the nations know they are only men. . . . Give

Figure 12. Solomon Molkho's flag, front. (Jewish Museum, Prague, registration no. 32.755)

us joy for as long as You have afflicted us, for the years we have suffered misfortune."[409] Appropriately, the one quote that does not come from the Bible but rather from the liturgy of Rosh Hashanah (which was approaching as Re'uveni and Molkho were in Regensburg) proclaims the God of Israel king over the entire world: "The Eternal One is King, was King and shall always be King and eternal! God reigns over the nations; God is seated on His holy throne."[410]

Under the guise of esoteric insinuation, the arrangement of the quotes informs us as to God's means of preparing for his reign and of casting down the other nations. On the reverse side of the flag, all verses embroidered in dark thread begin with the letter *shin*, the three in the middle even with *shin* and *mem*, Solomon Molkho's initials. Thus, the two closing verses likely refer to Molkho himself and to his divine calling as military commander on the model of King David. The two final verses are selected from David's song of thanksgiving after a victorious battle against his enemies: "Who trained my hands for battle, so that my arms can bend a bow of bronze! I pursued my enemies and wiped them out, I did not turn back till I destroyed them."[411] A banner belonging to Molkho that is now lost apparently expressed a similarly warlike spirit. Widmanstetter, who claims to have seen it in Regensburg in 1541, reports that its Hebrew inscription read "Maccabi."[412] Read as an acrostic for Exodus 15:11, what we find here is, on the one hand, trust in salvation: "Who is like You, O Lord, among the celestials?" On the other hand, it refers to the heroic figure of Judah Maccabi, the famous insurrectionist in the rebellion of the Hasmoneans against the rule of the Seleucids, which finally led to the renewed independence of Judea in the second century BCE. Judah Maccabi appears here as Molkho's role model.

The expectation that the nations would soon be overthrown and their kings brought low but that God would have mercy upon Israel—this idea also found expression in Molkho's *tallit katan*. Although the fringed religious garment has not survived, witnesses describe it as having been divided into three quadrants using red, yellow, and white silk embroidery, of which each contained an inscription of a different name for God in a symbolic color scheme. In red, with respect to Edom, it was written that the Almighty would judge the nations; in yellow, it was declared that he would compel the kings; and the script in the white color of innocence, as symbol of Israel, was reserved for the redemption.[413]

The context of perceived danger, in which the arrest of Re'uveni and Molkho played out, presumably included the Bader trail. As we have seen, the Bader case deeply marked the public imagination in the early 1530s throughout the empire. The authorities could scarcely have forgotten how, a mere two years earlier, the supposed Jewish-Turkish conspiracy to overthrow the Habsburgs had been exposed. Against this background, how could one be expected to lend credence to Molkho and Re'uveni, to subscribe to their plan to lead the Jews into battle against their own proven confederates?[414] Even the mere mention of Jews and Turks in the same context must have awakened unpleasant associations.

In 1532, the allegation that the Jews were in league with the Turks could hardly be entirely defanged by a dubious offer of Jewish military support. The same accusation was to be made again and again in the following years, for example, in 1541 and again in 1545.[415] Moreover, the image makeover of the Red Jews from destroyers of good Christians into a menace to the Turks or even, in the sense of Re'uveni's plan, into allies of the former against the latter—this had not yet taken hold in 1532 but remained only in its first beginnings.[416] In the sixteenth century, the image of the dangerous Red Jews still overshadowed their newer reputation as potentially useful allies. In fact, throughout the century, the outright identification of the Red Jews with the Turks is not difficult to trace.[417] As late as 1570, in his rhyming preface to *Jüden Feind,* Georg Nigrinus warns his readers of the great danger that the Jews, and above all Jewish messianism, presented for Christian society:

They are and remain enemies of Christ. / How do you think they are disposed to us? / If they had rule of the world / They would hoard our money / And if they had people and the strength of an army / As they lust for day

and night / They would strangle us all like rabid dogs. / No Christian
would survive an hour. / Such a Messiah desires / The Jewish mob on
earth / Who would murder and bayonet us all / So that no one would
contradict him. / If a Turk came of a Jewish tribe / They would take him
for the Messiah / Since they are secretly their friends.[418]

Nigrinus proves the supposed Jewish friendship with the Turks not only on
the basis of certain ritualistic commonalities between Islam and Judaism,
such as circumcision and the proscription against eating pork; the decisive
reason, according to Nirginus, is

> the blood relation because they are brothers and cousins. For one calls the
> Turks the Red Jews. . . . Therefore the Jews in Europe secretly favor them
> and hope to be liberated by them and to come again into their land. They
> rejoice as well when the Turk advances against Christendom.[419]

The temporal proximity to the Bader case also played a role in Josel of
Rosheim's choice to distance himself from Molkho and Re'uveni.[420] For
Josel, who was in Regensburg in 1532 for the occasion of the imperial diet,
it was completely unacceptable to submit such a proposal to the emperor.
The idea of recruiting Jews to serve in the war against the Turks was for
Josel simply "alien," contradicting the traditional messianic stance of Jews
in Germany and not appropriate to their special situation.[421] According to
his own testimony, he asked Molkho in a letter to stand down from this
plan; and as Molkho entered the city, Josel himself hastily departed, "so
that the Emperor should not say that I had a hand in his strange plans."[422]
Josel rightly feared that the systematic arming of Jews could only appear
suspicious to the authorities and, hence, could have direful consequences
for the Jewish communities whose situation in the empire was difficult
enough already. After all, Josel had only shortly before been forced to intervene against the threat of reprisals in the wake of the Bader case.[423] Thus,
Josel had immediate knowledge of the potential consequences of acute

Jewish messianic hopes and activity in the face of their negative perception within the Christian environment. Therefore, in his political activities, he was guided by the practical imperative of avoiding danger—regardless of his own personal belief that the advent of the Messiah was indeed close at hand.[424]

Such is the irony of history that the tireless contender against the effects of active messianism was himself accused of reaching for the messianic crown. Three years later, presumed Jewish heresies were also made responsible for the Münster Rebellion,[425] and a connection was alleged to Josel of Rosheim.[426] Eleven days after the fall of Münster, the imperial treasury brought charges against Josel, who, in the course of his activities as Jewish advocate, had for many years and in various documents spoken of himself as "Befehlshaber gemeiner Jüdischeit deutscher Nation" (commander of the entire Jewry of the German nation) and "regierer gemeiner judischait im reich" (ruler of the entire Jewry in the empire) and had been called thus by others as well.[427] The prosecutor brought the accusation of unlawful assumption of public authority and slander against the emperor in connection with the Münster Anabaptist king Jan van Leiden:

> Albeit should you have described improperly . . . as a commander of the entire Jewry in the empire, especially now during these very difficult times (when an artisan of low birth has claimed for himself a royal title), you lessen by no small means our Majesty as the only rightly ruler of this Jewry, setting an insurgent example of derision and mockery for other evil people.[428]

When later in the proceeding Josel was accused of base motives—the perfidious nature of the Jews being, of course, well known—the sound of the Christian fear of apocalyptic Jewish revenge is clearly audible. One suspected, namely, that the defendant

> would certainly rather see the ruin, decline and entire destruction of all Christians with his own eyes . . . , and desires it; also wherever fear of the

violence and power of the authorities doth not dissuade him, he will without a doubt with other Jews dare and act to their advantage and to our complete destruction.[429]

As far as we know, the Jews in the empire suffered no serious consequences from the visit by Solomon Molkho and David Re'uveni to Regensburg. Such consequences were reserved only for the two emissaries themselves. Shortly after their arrest, the papal envoy Aleander feared that they might be set free again through the intervention of a powerful lobby and above all in the emperor's own interest. Therefore, Aleander considered it necessary to write a letter to the responsible parties, urging

> that there should be no hurry about freeing them, for I hear that he [Molkho] is receiving much support (*favori*) from many quarters and that, with this performance of theirs and the promises of this impertinent heretic, there is considerable danger that His Majesty will be disposed to trust him. . . . Extreme vigilance must now be exercised to ensure that they do not escape, on account of the support they are receiving (*per favori*), but what justice and God's honour demands, and the general good of Christianity requires shall be done.[430]

Aleander's concern was to prove unfounded, however: when on September 2, 1532, the emperor and his military escort departed for the south, he took the prisoners with him. The decisive reason why Charles in the end did not set the two free may well once again have been purely pragmatic and with an eye to the course of the war in Hungary. On August 29, the sultan had given up the siege of Köszeg and withdrawn without success; in the end, he returned with his army through Styria to Istanbul. Moreover, the imperial fleet under Andrea Doria's command had in the meantime defeated the Turks by sea at Patras and Castelnuovo. With this, Molkho's offer of Jewish support against the common foe had lost its urgency, and the reasons for rendering him and his companions harmless could now unfold to their full effect. Such an interpretation finds support in the portrayal by the historiographer Joseph ha-Kohen. After the Jewish emissaries had already been in detention for several days, "the emperor saw, when the Turk withdrew, that the situation had relaxed, and he departed from the city. He returned to Italy and led them chained to wagons to Mantua with him."[431] There, in the same year—the imperial entourage arrived in November—Molkho was burned at the stake as a heretic. Re'uveni was led in chains to Spain and cast into the dungeons of the Inquisition in Llerena in the province of Badajoz. Although he apparently converted in the eleventh hour to Christianity in order to save his life, he, too, met his end at the stake.[432]

During their arrest, Re'uveni and Molkho were relieved of their belongings. While the shield that Re'uveni carried with him likely ended up in Bologna and was apparently preserved there in a synagogue till the end of the seventeenth century,[433] Molkho's effects seem to have come into the possession of the Jewish community in Prague in the 1540s,[434] where they were acquired by the influential family Horowitz, builders of the Pinkas Synagogue.[435] Yom Tov Lipmann Heller, who had been rabbi of Prague since 1627, remembered that

> here in the holy community of Prague in the Pinkas Synagogue, to which I
> came regularly even before my appointment as head of the rabbinic court,
> there is a silken *tallit katan* of a greenish color like an egg yolk. And also
> the ritual fringes are silk and of the same color. It was brought here from
> Regensburg and belonged to the holy R. Solomon Molkho, may the Lord
> avenge his blood. Moreover, two banners from him and also his *sargenes*,
> which one calls a *kitl*.[436]

In addition to Molkho's *kitl* and *tallit katan*, his valuable coat, fashioned of fine, sand-colored linen and adorned with embroideries, also ended up in Prague.[437] Beside the flag described above, this coat is the second item that survives and is likewise preserved in the Jewish Museum in Prague.[438]

Of the fate of the remaining objects nothing is known.[439] In the year 1666, however, all three garments appear still to have existed, since they are tallied up in a letter from that year: coat, *kitl*, and fringed garment.[440] The author Max Brod claims to have seen firsthand the silken *kitl* in 1925. An early twentieth-century photograph of it still survives.[441] By contrast, the second flag seems to have already been lost by the first half of the nineteenth century, since a Prague *pinkas* (community record) from that period dealing with times of year and ritual utensils speaks only of one flag.[442]

For at least 150 years, a regular messianic martyr cult bearing all the characteristics of Christian saint worship existed in Prague around Molkho.[443] A letter by an anonymous writer from Vienna to his father-in-law, sent amid the messianic enthusiasm surrounding Shabtai Zvi, reports on the handling of the relics.[444] The author describes how Molkho's possessions were preserved in the immediate vicinity of the holiest place in the Pinkas Synagogue, "within the walled-off area by the Torah cabinet." Every year on Simchat Torah, celebrating the end of the annual cycle of Torah readings, the custom was to present not only the Torah scrolls but also the garments of the martyr for adoration by the community. They were "laid upon the table in the synagogue and children and women went to look at the garments. Only the *tallit katan* was not exhibited, because holy names were embroidered upon it in silk; these names were scattered and disjointed and were not connected with each other."

Moreover, the magical power of the divine names on this garment could harm those who used them in the wrong way:

> Namely when the community beadle once attempted to copy out these names, he was struck blind. Also, the *ga'on* of the holy community of Prague, our teacher, the master R. Lipman, author of *Tosfot Yom Tov*, who during the time in which he was chief justice in the holy community of Prague, relying upon his own piousness, sought to copy out the names. His piousness saved him from being injured, but nevertheless his scribes' paper and inkwell were consumed and vanished from sight in such

a manner that no one knows to this day where they went. Therefore, the chief justice determined that, upon threat of banishment, no one should ever again be allowed to approach and attempt to read[445] the names or to copy them out.

Since that time, no one dared come near enough to examine the holy names on Molkho's prayer robe. It was also expressly forbidden to copy the names and above all to attempt to put them together in order to make sense out of them. But, in the year 1666, however, something "completely and utterly astonishing" had happened in Prague, as the writer of the letter claims to have learned. He quotes a missive that the Prague community in its enthusiasm over the miracle had sent to the community in Vienna:

> Our beloved brothers, members of the yeshiva, know, so that everyone upon [every] island of the earth may know the matter of R. Solomon Molkho. Therefore, we inform you, that here in the holy community of Prague, letters have arrived from the holy community in Aleppo, saying that one is to go to the holy place at which the aforementioned *tallit* lies, and that the holy names are to be copied.

In a mysterious way, the names had combined themselves in 1666 into a kabbalistic formula, according to which redemption was to begin that very year, with Shabtai Zvi as the Messiah: "And the names were combined that previously had been disconnected."

As the letter demonstrates, long after the demise of Solomon Molkho and David Re'uveni, the unique cult surrounding Molkho's relics was known well beyond the region of Prague and could be renewed and reactivated with messianic significance. From Austria to Syria, one knew of the messianic relics in the possession of the Prague community. One knew as well of the legends connected to the magic *tallit katan*. By the 1920s, however, the relics were all but forgotten, and even among those who regularly visited the Pinkas Synagogue, they were known only to a very few.[446]

EPILOGUE

THE ENTANGLEMENT OF JEWISH AND CHRISTIAN MESSIANISM IN THE ASHKENAZIC WORLD DURING THE REFORMATION

The article on the future of the Messiah is by no means either fundamental or necessary to Judaism, which yet the German Jews . . . earnestly contradict.

—Johann Jacob Schudt, *Jewish Notabilia*, 1714

As we have seen, *medinot Ashkenaz*, the German lands, were hardly a messianic dead zone in the sixteenth century. Just as little can one speak of a rigid Ashkenazic-Sephardic border in the topography of Jewish messianic expectation, neither in the general sense endemic to the *Wissenschaft des Judentums* nor in the specific sense of Gerson Cohen. The vitality of Jewish messianic expectation in the Ashkenazic world during the Reformation clearly refutes the common claim as to the inner disposition of Ashkenazic Jews—namely, their alleged predilection to messianic passivity. Apocalyptic prophecies and messianic activity are traceable among German Jews no less than, for example, in Italy and among Sephardic Jews who lived in the Holy Land and other parts of the Ottoman Empire. Indeed, we often encounter the very same themes and dates, and the same individuals are often involved: Asher Lemlein, David Re'uveni, and Solomon Molkho lent wings to the messianic hopes of both Ashkenazic and Sephardic Jews in the Christian lands of Europe as well as in the Muslim East. Despite differences in the development and expressive forms of apocalyptic expectation and activity, which depended both on the respective environments, whether Christian or Muslim, and on the respective minority Jewish cultures, the distinction between cultural spaces by no means implies an impermeable barrier between cultural and geographical entities. Among the individual countries of Christian Europe and the various Islamic realms, there were numerous economic, social, political, and cultural connections, both in general and at the specific level of the Jewish population. The flow of ideas, including apocalyptic ideas, did not stop at political borders.[1] Through an integrative study of Jewish end-time expectation in the Ashkenazic world of the sixteenth-century, the present study seeks to fill this gap in our understanding of messianism. We have seen how important it is to place apocalyptic expectation in its broadest historical, cultural, and religious context. In the final analysis, the expression of Jewish messianic expectation in the German-speaking countries (and among Ashkenazim elsewhere in Europe) was shaped by the inimical Christian perspective on precisely such hopes, a perspective embodied in theological concepts, anti-Jewish polemics, popular horror fantasies, and political persecutions. Furthermore, because the end-times were a topic of substantive debate at various levels between Christians and Jews, Christian apocalypticism itself represented an important part of Jewish messianic discourse.

The simultaneity of acute eschatological moods among Jews and Christians in the sixteenth century prepared the ground for an intensified mutual interest. Each was keenly aware of the other's expectations and hopes. The other's view was seen as being intimately bound up with one's own, whether accepted or rejected, and the two sides debated in particular the advance of the apocalyptic armies and the advent of the redeemer. Although each side made use of what was essentially the same information, they did so in the expectation of quite different outcomes. Thus, the expected Messiah of the one was the other's Antichrist, while the arrival of the Red Jews meant, for the one, rescue and, for the other, destruction. In this way, the divided end-time expectations mutually confirmed and strengthened each other, and yet the hopes and fears of one side functioned simultaneously to constrain the other's expressions of messianic longing. The parallel apocalyptic expectations thus awakened and intensified old frictions. Precisely because of the often overlapping interpretations of the signs of the times, it was necessary to unmask the other's point of view as false and to highlight the advantages of one's own exegesis of history. Thus, the polemic surrounding the question of the Messiah acquired, in the sixteenth century, an even greater explosiveness.

The dynamics of this Jewish-Christian discourse, with its characteristic interplay of polemic and apology, can be recognized in an exemplary fashion in the figure of the prophet Asher Lemlein and in the messianic repentance he inspired. As Elisheva Carlebach was first to demonstrate, the processes of mutual perception and representation operated with particular vigor with regard to Lemlein's activity.[2] While the fruitlessness of Jewish penitence became, predictably, a favorite theme of Christian polemic, with Christian writers declaring the alleged mass conversions of disappointed penitents to Christianity to be an example worthy of imitation, Jewish society acted from the very beginning with extreme caution. Even in 1502, at the high-water mark of the penitence, Christians were to be given no reason for concern that Lemlein might lead his adherents into the apocalyptic battle against Edom. After Lemlein's evident failure and his supposed flight into the Land of Israel, and as the arguments began to run dry that might have continued to uphold the credibility of his message, Ashkenazic authors themselves finally fled into the concealment of self-censorship. That the oral tradition of collective remembrance nevertheless retained a positive memory of Asher Lemlein is indicated in statements such as that of Eliezer Treves, who, decades later, found the responsibility for the prophet's failure not in the prophet himself but in the sinfulness of the people.

The characteristic synchronicity of Jewish hope and Christian fear, which Israel Yuval has pointed out in similar form with respect to the Middle Ages,[3] is particularly evident in two cases from around 1530 that we have analyzed. The first has to do with the Christian reaction to the Jewish contacts of the Anabaptist leader Augustin Bader; the second, with the appearance of David Re'uveni and Solomon Molkho in Regensburg. In both cases, what Jews feared most was Christian fear, that is, that Christians would take proactive measures against Jews out of a sense of terror at the coming vengeance of the Jewish Messiah. Thus, in the aftermath of the revelations in the Bader case in 1530, several Jewish communities in the empire were threatened with persecutions that were averted only through the vigorous intercession of Josel of Rosheim. Two years later, the suspicion of a Jewish-Turkish alliance against the Christian authorities appears to have continued to reverberate, strengthening the arguments in favor of arresting Re'uveni and Molkho. The Christian framework of perception also determined Josel's options for action in Regensburg. Knowing full well the potentially fatal consequences of the negative Christian stance toward Jewish messianic hope—something the Bader episode had made abundantly clear—Josel chose explicitly to distance himself from Molkho.

Josel of Rosheim, whom one encounters again and again in the history of messianism in the first half of the sixteenth century, personifies a tension that is characteristic for the relationship between Jewish messianism and its Christian environment. Josel was both a pragmatic politician and—a facet of his personality that has till now gone unrecognized—an apocalyptic thinker. His efforts at political damage control in the years 1530 and 1532, on the one hand, and his messianic reflections on the Last Emperor, on the other, exemplify the tense juxtaposition of acute messianic expectation with pragmatic action in the here and now that the Christian environment made urgently necessary. Overall, one must conclude that for Jewish messianism in sixteenth-century Germany, apocalyptic expectation and realpolitik went hand in hand—for the simple reason that the apocalypse and messianic time were no mere utopian thought experiments but rather concrete historical events situated in the very near future. Apocalyptic images could determine real action. Thus, Re'uveni and Molkho's proposal of a Jewish-Christian alliance against the sultan, which was made palatable to Christians by presenting it as desperately needed support against the Turkish menace, was in reality about the double aim of both driving the Ottomans out of the Holy Land and plunging the Christians into the self-annihilating apocalyptic wars of Gog and Magog. Lead by pragmatic considerations, their negotiating partners—Emperor Charles V among them—lent credence, at least for time, to suggestions that appear utterly fantastical only to us latter-day observers.

Unlike Re'uveni and Molkho, Josel subordinated his private expectation of the imminent redemption to his public concern for the welfare of German Jewry. Precisely at the center of his surviving Last Emperor prophecy stands the struggle of the final Roman ruler against the unbelievers, a figure he along with many Christians identified as Charles V. In harmony with his apocalyptic worldview, Josel was therefore deeply invested in a Habsburg victory in the Turkish wars. Nevertheless, for practical reasons, he opposed the eschatologically tempting plan of a Jewish-Christian alliance against the Ottomans. It may be no accident, then, that in his autographical miscellany Josel placed Maimonides's famous letter to Yemen, *Iggeret Teiman*, beside his own prophecy.[4] In this letter, Maimonides answers an inquiry by the Jews in Yemen as to how they ought to comport themselves vis-à-vis a messianic pretender. Maimonides's advice is clear: the criticism of Islam and Christianity, which is at the heart of the message of the messianic age, is more perilous than either the sword or the endangerment of religious tradition by Hellenism. The supposed Messiah is, therefore, to be rejected.[5] At the same time, the letter contains Maimonides's own calculation of the Messiah's advent—suggesting that possibly he himself also pursued an actively messianic program.[6] The question arises whether Josel of Rosheim, who as a politician relied upon the central authority of the emperor, could even imagine an apocalyptic constellation that was not in essence pro-Habsburg, with the Holy Roman Emperor cast as central hero in the eschatological scenario until the very moment of Edom's ultimate demise. It should be noted that Josel's Christian contemporary, Martin Luther, harbored millennial expectations of his own and acted in a similarly pragmatic way. His rejection of the rebels in the apocalyptically tinged Peasant War is well known.[7] Both Josel and Luther resisted any intervention into global apocalyptic events, not least of all out of concern for the maintenance of social order.[8]

The relationship between Jewish and Christian messianism thus oscillated between considerations of realpolitik and cultural transfer. This is amply documented in the 1520s, when the end-time expectations of Jews and Christians in Germany collided and interacted with each other in various ways. Examples such as the way the Red Jews were imagined, the theory of the restitution of Israel, and the prophecies surrounding the figure of the Last Emperor attest to the interdependent formation of influential traditions as well as to the emergence of new concepts on both sides. The Jewish tradition of the Last Emperor turns out to have been directly influenced in the Middle Ages and the early modern period by Christian prophecies. Likewise, the chiliastic doctrines of Martin Cellarius and Wolfgang Capito postulating an actual return of the Jews to the Land of Israel were inspired by current geopolitical events, namely, the rumors of a war waged by the Red Jews to retake the promised land from the Ottoman Turks. Whether positively or negatively, these rumors fascinated both Jews and Christians. The Christian exegesis arrived independently at the same conclusion as the contemporary Jewish exegesis: The Jews were at least theoretically capable of driving the Turks out of Jerusalem.

Yet, despite the mutual influence, in terms of content, of Jewish and Christian apocalypticism, the exchange of ideas generally served to reinforce the respective theological conceptions of each group. After all, the advent of the Jewish Messiah stood in opposition to the Second Coming of Jesus—and vice versa. The Last Emperor prophecy and the doctrine of restitution make this abundantly clear: The reign of the Last Emperor is followed, in the Jewish version of the prophecy, by the destruction of Edom, while according to the Christian doctrine, the restitution of Israel is merely the precondition for the Christian version of the end and prefigures the Second Coming and final triumph of Christ.

Naturally the Jewish-Christian dialogue concerning the Messiah question bore polemical overtones, marked by mutual rejection and the desire to distinguish one's own point of view from that of the cultural other. By definition, the expectations that Jews and Christians held regarding the end of the world were finally unreconcilable. Despite all this, however, eschatological expectations were oriented toward essentially the same problem, and one resorted to the same reserves of biblical ideas in order to solve it. Paradoxically, Jewish and Christian end-time expectations—precisely because of their mutual exclusivity—operated in an intimate exchange. In fact, these rival interpretations of ideas drawn from the same texts and events were what constituted the point of contact for a dialogue and thus opened the field for cultural transfer. The question was, How could the other's conceptions best be integrated into one's own messianic agenda, while at the same time undermining the eschatological identity of the other? Understood as counter-history, the task was to confirm one's own apocalyptic truth while at the same time refuting the competing truth. Thus, Jewish messianism adopted Christian conceptions of the millennium in an anti-Christian reinterpretation, while the Christians did the same, only in reverse. In this way, the rivals spoke a common language, through which their respective messages were rendered comprehensible to the other side.

The imaginary nation of the Red Jews presents an excellent example of this polemical interdependence of Jewish and Christian messianic thought in the German-speaking lands. Each version of the story is constructed as a precise counter-historical paraphrase of the other. In the typical manner of counter-history, the Red Jews in Yiddish literature, developing in answer to the Christian perception of vengeful Jewish messianic hope, reinforced the Jews' own eschatological identity using the same conceptual framework. Jews and Christians struggled with each other in the interpretation of numerous central motifs of the eschatological scenario; these motifs were adopted and reinterpreted until they could be organically connected to established parts of one's own tradition. The atmosphere of acute apocalyptic expectation made it necessary to adapt ideology and politics to the actual situation in conflict with the other. Thus, the interreligious debate that took place between 1523 and 1530 concerning the possibility of a Jewish return to the Holy Land sheds light on the processes of reception in what was a lively and, in essence, polemically motivated Jewish-Christian disagreement.

The exchange of ideas between Jewish and Christian milieux was both far-reaching and complex. We can see this complexity in the activities of the Anabaptists Oswald Leber and Augustin Bader, viewed here for the first time in the context of Jewish history. On the basis of the millennial prophecies of the Anabaptist leader Hans Hut, Bader and Leber developed a new chiliastic doctrine by adopting Jewish messianic calculations—to which they had access indirectly via the writings of Christian Hebraists. Just as Leber was first confirmed in his imminent expectation of the Last Judgment by his Jewish teachers in Worms, so he and Bader later attempted for their part to interest Jews in their millennial program of change.

Thus in the German-speaking lands, the close cultural and social contacts between Jews and Christians gave their relationship a distinctly messianic aspect. By demonstrating the dialogical relation of Jewish messianism to its Christian environment, the present study elucidates an important field of communication between Jews and Christians of that time. The interweaving of Jewish-Christian messianism in the zone of German language and culture in the sixteenth century is equal parts conflict, rejection, and cultural transfer. While it is true that, here too, the majority determined the discourse more strongly than did the minority, nevertheless the influence of Judaism on Christian apocalypticism is not to be underestimated. The processes described in the present study certainly impeded, on the one hand, the free expression of Jewish messianic longing; and yet, on the other hand, they also fostered the flowering of apocalyptic expectation on both sides.

This literary and practical interaction in messianic matters reflects the cultural entanglement of Jewish and Christian society. The mechanisms of reception, the reciprocal transfer of messianic ideas and its limits—all contributed in significant ways to the social formation of both groups, to the shaping of their theological and cultural concepts, and to the determination of their options for political action. The case of Bader attained empire-wide notoriety not least of all because of the Christian identification of subversive Jewish messianic hope allegedly lurking behind the Anabaptists' activities. The doctrine of Cellarius and Capito ultimately even entered the central confession of belief of the Lutheran Church, since this new chapter in the Jewish-Christian discourse on the advance of the Red Jews made necessary a definitive rejection of the unorthodox doctrine of the restitution of Israel.

Ultimately, the investigation of messianism opens new perspectives on significant moments in German-Jewish history during the century of the Reformation. Here one ought to mention the anti-Jewish campaign of the convert Johannes Pfefferkorn, the political context of Antonius Margaritha's influential text *Der ganz jüdisch glaub*, and the background of Josel of Rosheim's activities in the year 1530. Framing all three cases is the Jewish-Christian debate about the Messiah, which till now has not been sufficiently taken into account. Pfefferkorn, who himself had converted to Christianity along with his family, out of disappointment at the failed repentance called for by Lemlein, placed his own experiences at the service of an aggressive mission to the Jews. While the popularity of Margaritha's pamphlet profited by the Bader affair, which appeared to prove the allegations of a Jewish-Turkish conspiracy, the revelations of this same court case were what motivated Josel of Rosheim to compose the letter of justification he then conveyed to the emperor and his brother, Ferdinand, in Innsbruck, defending the Jews against the accusation of being disloyal subjects of the Habsburgs.

In the seventeenth and eighteenth centuries, Jews and Christians observed each other's apocalyptic thinking and messianic activity with continued interest. Mechanisms of interaction and confrontation—similar to the ones so decisively in play in the interlacing history of Judaism and Christianity in the Ashkenazic world of the sixteenth century—appear to have remained to some degree effective throughout the early modern period. Indeed, the long lists of false messiahs, deceitful prophets, and failed messianic movements were compiled with greater frequency in the seventeenth century, and the ethnographic literature on the practices of contemporary Jews reached its zenith in the first half of the eighteenth century. A large role in this discourse was now played by the disappointed expectations surrounding Shabtai Zvi and the year 1666, the next high point in parallel apocalyptic hopes. After the failure of the Sabbatian movement, a number of Jews began to reexamine the Jewish doctrine of the Messiah in light of Christian doctrine and arrived finally at the same explanation of events given in Christian polemics.[9] From this perspective the Jewish messianic movement could lend renewed strength to Christian apocalyptic expectation by being read as a prequel to the Christian version of the end.[10]

Although the genre of ethnography retained its tendentious character and its basic purpose of denigrating Judaism, the representations gradually lost their anti-Jewish bias in the post-Reformation period. This was a reflection of changed political and religious views during a time when the effort to transform society had less impact on the treatment of Jews than in the early Reformation period.[11] With the turn of the seventeenth century, the escalating conflict between the various Christian confessions pushed its way increasingly into the foreground, and in this internal struggle Judaism no longer played the role it had played during the century of the Reformation—or, at most, only as a negative example. Thus, the Hebraist Johannes Buxtorf, in his *Synagoga Ivdaica* (Jewish Synagogue, Basel, 1603), the first ethnography written by a born Christian, accused the Jews, as his predecessors had, of blasphemy; in contrast to Margaritha, however, he no longer saw in the Jews and their religion any social or political threat and refrained from any fundamental questioning of their right to exist. This is in line with the tendency among many Protestant princes in the seventeenth century to at least tolerate the Jews. Buxtorf's criticism was above all theological. His ethnography was intended to serve the purposes of missionary work among the Jews and to aid in the censorship of their books; for both, a detailed familiarity with Judaism was necessary.[12]

Compared to the beginning of the early modern period, Christian responses to Jewish messianism in the seventeenth century and later were determined to a much greater degree by the missionary impulse. The mission in the first generations of the Reformation enjoyed, despite Luther's initial hopes, more symbolic value than high practical priority; the seventeenth century, by contrast, saw an increase in serious efforts to convert the Jews.[13] While the Lutheran orthodoxy tended to distance itself from the question of the millennial conversion of the Jews, and in certain quarters even called it into question, the advent of Pietism brought a decisive turn. For Pietists, the expected conversion of the Jews at the end of time was a hard and fast fact; under their influence, this element of the apocalyptic scenario finally became a theological commonplace in Protestantism. Thus the fomenting zenith of the Pietist mission among the Jews falls in the early eighteenth centuries.[14] The new emphases in Christian eschatology, as well as the shifts in Christian perceptions of Jews and Judaism briefly sketched here, also had an effect on the relation to Jewish messianism.[15] The Pietist approach to convince the Jews that their Messiah had already come profoundly changed the common language that enabled Jews and Christians to communicate in. In the eighteenth century, the Reformation-era dispute about the end of days would become an amicable exchange of like-minded people who saw piety as the road to redemption.[16]

EXCURSUS IN NUMISMATICS

The medal in question . . . was intended to commemorate the predictions
of Asher Lemlein respecting the arrival of the Messiah in the year 1503.
— Louis Loewe, *Memoir on the Lemlein Medal*, 1856/57

In search of unknown or misunderstood sources on Asher Lemlein, one finds in the third volume (published in 1859) of Isaak Markus Jost's *Geschichte des Judenthums und seiner Secten* (History of Judaism and Its Sects) an unexpected reference that ultimately points not to Lemlein but to a nineteenth-century scholarly debate. In a note on the "history of Lämlein," Jost reports on a bit of numismatic insight that was at the time quite fresh: in June 1857 the Orientalist Louis Loewe had reevaluated a medal with Hebraic inscription and found a connection to the messianic episode associated with Lemlein. As Jost notes, however, he finds this interpretation risky, since the medal "could scarcely originate with the Lemlein incident." But Loewe's suggestion might still hold true, Jost admits, under certain presuppositions. The object itself was particularly interesting to Jost, since in his view it appeared to represent the handiwork of a Christian.[1] The mysterious medal, which had been discovered in 1656 during excavations in Lyon at the foot of the Fourvière hill (hence its name: "the Fourvière medal"), had piqued the curiosity and imagination of scholars in various disciplines long before Loewe and Jost, and in the mid-nineteenth century it was at the center of a lively scholarly debate that involved some of the most important representatives of Judaic studies at the time—among them, Leopold Zunz and Abraham Geiger.[2]

The cast bronze medal, which is now preserved in the National Library of France, is unusual for its size alone, measuring eighteen centimeters in diameter. Moreover, it is exceptionally thick and weighs more than two kilograms, including a sturdy eyelet, added after the initial casting, so that it can be hung on a cord or chain.[3] The face of the medal (fig. 13) shows the portrait of a young man in high relief. This idealized image, in the antique *laureatus* style with laurel wreath, is pictured in right-facing profile. Around the edge of the medal is an inscription in Hebrew consisting of several lines: "בגזרת נוהג ית׳ מרצון נצחי בחק כל משפט העדר הצורה ראיתי אורך לזמן ישיגהו הקץ ואתבונן בהשגחת אלי רומי השאיר רשומם ואעלוז פדותך אוחיל יוי שדי רב וסלח. ו"י ג"ח ו"ע ע"י." The text (up to the abbreviation) can be translated as follows:

> Because of the decision by the controller of worlds, praised be he, according to his eternal will, through [his] law[4]—the form is missing from all justice—I have seen the length of time. It will reach the end. I shall glimpse the providence of my God, my highest; he has left the trace of it. And I shall be joyful. I hope for your salvation, almighty God, great and merciful.

Appearing from the mouth of the man is the sequence of letters, "מ"י ב"ת א ש"ע ת"ל ח"ו." On either side of the head is a perpendicular line of text: "ב"ן ימ"ן" and "ב"ב כר"ש" respectively.[5] Beneath the portrait stands the Latin inscription "[H]VMILITAS" (humility). The Greek sequence beneath this, "ΤΆωύροςις," exhibits orthographic problems that won't be examined here, but it is to be assumed that what is meant is the equivalent of the Latin concept: ταπείνωσις (*tapeinosis*). The center of the reverse side of the medal (fig. 14) is unworked. On a smooth, raised edge appears a short inscription in Latin: "Post tenebra[s] spero lucem felicitatis iudex dies ultimus" (After the darkness I hope for light. The last day is the judge of

Figure 13. "Lemlein Medal," Italy, n.d., obverse. (BnF, Paris, Série iconographique, Très Grands Modules, no. 5085)

Figure 14. "Lemlein Medal," Italy, n.d., reverse. (BnF, Paris, Série iconographique, Très Grands Modules, no. 5085)

happiness). The year D III M follows. The unusual form of dating, by which the thousand is named last, was certainly not chosen by accident. The naming of D in the first position, closing as it does directly on "dies ultimus" while being spatially set somewhat apart from III M, seems intended to express the idea that the number of the year simultaneously stands for the last day referred to in the Latin inscription.

The first to describe the medal was the Jesuit father Claude Ménestrier forty years after its discovery. Ménestrier believed he recognized in the portrait the facial features of Louis the Pious, and he connected the medal with the Jews in Lyon, where it had been discovered.[6] Ménestrier's interpretation remained essentially uncontested for nearly 150 years.[7] Although the *London Magazine* published a drawing of the medal along with a request for scholarly clarification in 1772,[8] the call appears to have gone unanswered. Only in 1836 did Gerson Lévy raise the reasonable objection that no medals with the likeness of a French king are known to have been made before the time of Charles VII. Therefore, the picture could hardly portray Louis the Pious, and the medal itself could by no means date back to the ninth century.[9]

Leopold Zunz eventually came closer to solving the riddle. In 1840, the famous Berlin scholar intervened in the discussion with an important discovery, one that enabled him to place the medal in fifteenth-century Italy. Zunz pointed out that what Ménestrier had misunderstood as abbreviations of the name of God, that is, the double points above the first letter of each word of the inscription, in fact indicate an acrostic: "Benjamin, son of the most honored master, the sage R. Elijah Beer, the physician. May he live many good years" (בנימן בן כבוד מעלת הרב החכם רבי אליהו באר הרופא יחיה שנים רבות וטובות).[10] Zunz identifies Elijah Beer as one of the most famous Jewish physicians of the Renaissance, namely Elijah b. Shabtai Beer, or Elia Fonte di Sabato da Fermo as he was called in Italian, who lived in Rome in the first half of the fifteenth century. (Accordingly, the medal has since been known as the Beer Medal.[11]) Zunz recognizes quite correctly that the awkwardly rendered, apparently confusing, and partly incomprehensible inscription does not accord well with the skillfully cast portrait, and as explanation he brings messianic hope into the game of interpretation: Benjamin, the son of the physician, had calculated the date of redemption, according to Zunz, "and carved his words announcing Israel's victory into a memorial of Roman greatness," which stood for the enemy power of Edom and which the Messiah would overthrow.[12] Seventeen years later, in 1857, at the annual meeting of the Royal Numismatic Society in London, Louis Loewe gave a lecture with the programmatic title "The Lemlein Medal." Loewe was likewise convinced that the inscription gives expression to the hope for an imminent advent of the Messiah. In this sense he was able to decode the abbreviation at the end of the main inscription, which Zunz had left unidentified. In fact "ו״י ג״ח ו ע״ע י״י" is an acronym from Job 19:25: "But I know that my Vindicator lives; in the end He will testify on earth."[13]

To begin with, Loewe poses two questions that ineluctably arise concerning the medal. In the first four words of the Latin inscription on the rear face, Eljakim Carmoly had already correctly recognized the Vulgate translation of the second half verse of Job 17:12: "Noctem verterunt in diem et rursum, post tenebras spero lucem" (They have turned night into day, and after darkness I hope for light again).[14] Loewe rightly asks why a Jewish author would have preferred Jerome's Latin version to the original Hebrew or, at the very least, to a literal translation into Latin, especially since such linguistic facility would have been the rule for the Jewish upper class in Italy during the Renaissance.[15] And why exactly did he date the expected advent of the Messiah according to a calendar that refers to the birth of the Christian savior (D III M read as MDIII)?[16] Loewe finds the answer in the large number of Christians he assumes to be among Asher Lemlein's followers:[17] the reverse side of the medal was presumably intended for them, to propagate Lemlein's prediction of the advent of the messianic age in 1503. In fact, according to Loewe, the inscription contains a reference to Lemlein's name: He reads "אלי רומי" as an abbreviation of "אשר לעמלין יהודי רומי," Asher Lemlein, a Roman Jew, that is, one who lives in a part of the former *Imperium Romanum*.[18] The likeness of the Roman *laureatus* serves in Loewe's imaginative theory as a diversionary tactic intended to keep Lemlein's secret plans hidden from the authorities. Thus, too, the unusual form of the date is explained, as well as the naming of Beer and son, in reality fictional code names that would have been understood only by the initiates.[19]

Loewe's theory is rather too fantastical to be convincing. Jost's summary is thus a synthesis of Loewe and Zunz: the text of the inscription originates with Benjamin Beer but attained a new relevance with Lemlein's prophecy of the imminent redemption. A Christian artisan had ultimately stumbled on these words and, by adding the Latin inscription and the likeness, had created a rather remarkable collector's item, "which through its strangeness might tempt many a lover."[20] Nevertheless, a connection to Asher Lemlein is hardly made more likely with this suggestion, for neither did the year 1503 play a role, according to present scholarship, in Lemlein's message, nor had he appeared by 1497, as Jost alternatively dates the medal.[21]

Abraham Geiger repudiated Loewe's reading immediately and in the strongest terms and rejected the whole idea of a messianic interpretation of the medal. After his own examination of the object, he was "pleased finally to have arrived at the end of this long snarl of illiterate and nonsensical translations and childish, bastardized views."[22] He presented a completely new interpretation: Elijah Beer consecrated the medal as a memorial to the early death of his son Benjamin in the year 1503. The likeness, according to Geiger, portrays the young Benjamin with a laurel wreath as victor at the end of life's journey, while the inscription lent expression to his trust in the immortality of the soul.[23] In Geiger's well-intended interpretation, belief in individual salvation in eternity is reflected also in the inscription on the reverse side, "which is represented pictorially in the rays of light breaking forth from the darkness of the grave."[24] Several years later Geiger added to his interpretation "a new fact confirming the current findings and a small correction of the same."[25] Since Benjamin had already followed in his father's medical footsteps by the middle of the fifteenth century, he must have reached an advanced age by 1503, so advanced in fact that the elder Beer could hardly still have been numbered among the living.[26] Thus Benjamin had had his own likeness immortalized on the medal.[27] "Admittedly, it has now forfeited its historical relation and significance," Geiger concludes. "No general messianic expectation, no belief in a Lemlein proclaiming the Messiah to come after him. . . . Yet the riddles that [the medal] seemed to contain have been solved. . . . And what thick darkness has surrounded it these hundred and fifty years!"[28] Jost had something to say about this, having apparently grown rather fond of the medal. He objected, as Zunz had before him, that the medal "is worth no especial notice" to Geiger.[29] This was incomprehensible for Jost, since "through the Geigerian view, which despite all remarks against details may still have its correctness, the coin must rather gain than forfeit its worth, and instill yet more interest in the lover." Although Jost thought "the Geigerian conjecture has, we readily admit it, rather more likelihood" than the theories of either Zunz and Loewe,[30] nevertheless he demanded further reliable evidence of its correctness. "Till then we stand in the area of mere suppositions."[31] For Jost, despite all attempts at interpretation and despite his own inclination to throw his weight onto Geiger's side, the medal ultimately remained "still mysterious."[32]

In the same issue of the *Zeitschrift der Deutschen Morgenländischen Gesellschaft* (Journal of the German Oriental Society), in which Geiger and Jost discussed the medal in 1858/59, the editorial board printed a supplement by Raphael Kirchheim to explain the medal. Kirchheim credits the chief rabbi Cahan of Marseille, who had decoded the last uncertain abbreviation. In "מ״י ב״ע ת״ת ש״ע ת״ל ח״ו," he had discovered the initial letters of a further passage from the Book of Job: "O that you would hide me in Sheol, conceal me until your anger passes, set me a fixed time to attend to me" (Job 14:13). Otherwise, writes Kirchheim, "literature on the so-called Lemlein-Medal" has been enriched to the tune of a brochure, while "our understanding of the same has come not one step further." Cahan's conclusion, that is, that the medal is in fact a petition by the prisoner Jean-Lois de Couches (בנימין בן כוש) in medal form, ranks honorably, in Kirchheim's opinion, among the previous interpretations in terms of creative fantasy.[33]

With this, the German Oriental Society considered "the file relating to this overall rather insignificant object to be, for our journal, closed."[34] And, in fact, the heated discussion of the medal came essentially to an end. At the beginning of the twentieth century there followed a number of solitary and little-noticed attempts at new interpretation. The supposedly obscure and darkly represented head on the reverse of the medal, from which rays of light emanate, was sometimes interpreted as a symbol for Judaism and its past, present, and future,[35] sometimes as the portrait of a ruler—in which, after Louis the Pious, now also Augustus,[36] Vespasian,[37] and Emperor Maximilian[38] were recognized. The more recent literature has, in essence, taken one of the two positions that had crystallized in the middle of the nineteenth century: on one side, the universal-messianic interpretation of Zunz and Loewe and, on the other, the individual-eschatological interpretation of Geiger. Thus, Daniel Friedenberg situates the medal in the context of messianic expectations at the beginning of the sixteenth century and even stops short of excluding the possibility of a connection to Lemlein in the sense proposed by Loewe.[39] By contrast, Samuel Kottek, who, in the 1980s, was the last scholar to dedicate a brief study to the medal, denies it any messianic connotation and treads again the well-trodden path laid out by Geiger.[40] Along the way, Kottek cleans up a few of the problems with Geiger's theory. Since it would be a considerable stretch to see in the head immortalized in bronze the likeness of an aged man,[41] the portrait can by no means be related directly to Benjamin. Furthermore, Kottek refers the eulogy "may he live many good years" again to the father Elijah as the one who commissioned the medal after the death of his son.

Thus we reach the end of a long line of interpretations of the Fourvière, Beer, or Lemlein Medal, none of which has been able to convince completely. Apart from the explanations that dispense with any basis whatsoever, the fully unmessianic variations by Geiger and Kottek are especially problematic. Although it is possible in principle to read the inscription and the quotations from Job in the sense of belief in the immortality of the soul and in just recompense after death, fundamental objections remain against the summary attribution of the medal to the Beer family, as has been assumed continuously since Zunz.

First of all, the dating on the reverse side speaks against it. The Roman numerals D III M can only be read as either 1503 (500 + 3 + 1000) or 1497 (500 + 1000 − 3). It is extremely doubtful that the elder Beer was still alive at that time or that he could have commissioned a medal for his son, since Elijah was serving as a private doctor to the pope nearly a hundred years earlier, as well as treating Henry IV in England in 1410. If, on the other hand, as Geiger suspected, it was indeed Benjamin himself who had the medal fabricated around 1500, then one would expect the name of the deceased father to be followed by a formula consecrating him to pious memory. Since nothing like this is found in the inscription, however, Elijah must still have been living at the time of the text's composition. In all likelihood, he died shortly after 1460.[42] It would appear, then, that the text that later became the inscription on the medal was itself composed decades earlier.

In point of fact, the text that contains Benjamin's name seems not to have been originally intended as the inscription for a medal at all. Alone the length of the text supports this. The text is indeed so long that even on the rather large surface of the medal it only has room by being arranged in a spiral. This sort of lettering is unusual for a medal; as a rule, the inscriptions are pithy, so that they comprise at most a circle around the disk's rim. In the rare cases of a longer inscription, the text is generally arranged upright in block form and is more frequently placed on the reverse side.[43] Moreover, Jost characterized the linguistic style of the medal as "the most abominable eccentricity"[44] and attributed the "forced, obscure expression" to the artifice, as Zunz explained, of the acrostic form.[45] The text is by no means the work of a gifted writer. One would expect better from the son of a cultured house, who was himself a trained physician. Moreover, the execution of the Hebrew inscription bespeaks no especial artistic talent.[46]

The Hebrew letters were obviously not formed by a practiced hand. Their appearance is noticeably awkward: On the one hand, the form of a given letter differs from instance to instance, while, on the other, different letters that resemble each other orthographically are here hardly distinguishable in their appearance. Not only does the inscription exhibit little in the way of artistry, but the entire composition of the medal is clumsy at best. Neither is the portrait centered, nor was the space necessary for the Hebrew inscription correctly estimated during fabrication of the casting mold. Both of the last two letters of the main inscription are so compressed above the portrait's head as to be hardly legible, while on the right-hand side a large area remains unused. Moreover, several abbreviation points are missing, the middle of the reverse side is left unworked, and the eyelet is remarkably crude in its workmanship.

The only element of the medal that possesses any artistic value is the portrait itself. The question again arises that Zunz had posed before, namely, how this fits with the amateurish remainder. He came to the conclusion that the picture and the text have nothing to do with each other—an assessment that Kottek shares. According to Kottek's thesis, the medal is based upon the casting of an older portrait medal characteristic of the artistry of the Renaissance around 1470.[47] And, in fact, around the portrait itself a concentric circle can be drawn, approximately twelve centimeters in diameter, which would have corresponded to the size of the original model cast. The medalist thus appears first to have copied the front face of another artist's cast and then, with the help of this copy, to have produced a new cast with an enlarged face and the addition of the inscription in the triad of the classical languages, typical of pseudo-antique medals of the Renaissance. The result was the singular object we see. This explains as well the medal's unusual size and thickness.

If one compares the medal with the works of master artisans in the field, such as the Venetian medalist Giovanni Boldu (whose creations impress as much for their overall effect as for the delicacy of their inscriptions in Latin, Greek, and Hebrew), then it becomes obvious that we are dealing here with no artist of Boldu's caliber.[48] But for a medal intended as honorary object or given in commission by a member of the famous and revered Beer family—cultured, wealthy, and without doubt interested in a representation appropriate to their status—one would expect that a less amateurish medalist could certainly have been found.[49]

What remains after all is thus collective redemption and apocalyptic hope, as Zunz first suspected was at the heart of the medal. To be sure, the longing cast here in bronze is apparently a Christian parody (perhaps by a convert from Judaism?). Around the turn of the sixteenth century, a time during which Jewish and Christian end-time expectations were equally widespread, the medal aimed a polemical message at Jews by turning their messianic hope literally on its head. At first glance, namely at the front face, the medal appears to be genuinely Jewish—in particular, because of the use of Hebrew. Only when the observer turns the medal over do the use of the Vulgate translation of the only complete Bible quotation (i.e., not only abbreviated using initial letters) and the anno Domini date reveal the presumed Christian provenance.[50] By announcing the expected date of redemption according to the Christian calendar, the inscription places it explicitly in the era of a messianic kingdom that has already taken place and thus mocks as hopelessly belated the Jewish expectation of another Messiah. At the same time, one can point to a missionary subtext: there is hope for redemption even for the Jews groping in messianic darkness. If yet again a longed-for year of redemption, in this case either 1503 or 1497, has passed without bringing with it the Messiah, then this might still enlighten them as to their error. They might yet recognize the Christian truth, convert to Christianity, and thereby bring the Jewish history of suffering to a happy ending: "After the darkness I hope for light. The judge of happiness is the last day."

Further evidence for a missionary purpose is the prominence of the Book of Job, represented on the medal by three quotations. Job 19:25, in particular, has a central significance in Christian theology, since the enigmatic verse is typically interpreted with reference to the Christian understanding of redemption through the resurrection of the crucified Jesus: with his death, Jesus has paid for the sins of mankind and secured eternal life for the faithful. This reading is enforced by the programmatic translation of the Vulgate, which Luther and many others followed. The second half verse, departing markedly from the Hebrew original, appends to the Christian soteriology the doctrine of the resurrection of the dead at the end of time: "But I know that my redeemer lives, *and he shall awaken me hereafter out of the earth*."[51] Correspondingly, in the other two quoted passages, which deal with the otherwise uncharacteristic optimism of the biblical hero, the theme is the belief in the messianic resurrection of the dead to new life.[52] The Christological interpretation of Job 19:25 was taken up in the Lutheran Formula of Concord, in catechisms, and in chants and remained uncontested in both the Protestant and the Catholic Church into the seventeenth century.[53] By contrast, the same verse appears with a strongly anti-Christian connotation in Jewish polemics of the Middle Ages, which proceed from the assumption that the Christian redeemer is dead, unlike the Jewish Messiah, who will yet arrive, be it in the distant future.[54] Appropriate to this finding is the unusual orthography of the Greek word on the front face of the medal, which presumably does not exist at all in this form. ΤΑωύροςις functions as an eye-catcher for readers who know Greek. At the very least, the combination of alpha and omega would have been familiar in the Christian context and may well have suggested, with reference to the Apocalypse of John, the imminent return of Jesus: "I am Alpha and Omega, the beginning and the end, the first and the last."[55]

The origin of the medal in a Christian milieu is finally supported by the historical development of the art of medal casting during the early modern period. While Jewish medals in the strict sense, that is, medals fabricated for Jews by Jewish artisans or commissioned by Jewish patrons, first appeared in the 1550s in Italy,[56] Christian medals had by that time already enjoyed a hundred-year history there. In other European lands, including France, the Netherlands, and Germany, Christians were casting and striking medals around the turn of the sixteenth century.[57]

One question above all remains open: Why did the creator of the medal choose such an unusual object to express his message? Did he intend to fulfill literally the wish of Job, who wanted to know that his words were written down for prosperity? "O that my words were written down; would they were inscribed in a record, incised on a rock forever with iron stylus and lead!" (Job 19:23–24). Doubtless—given the eyelet affixed to it—the medal was intended to be hung up and displayed. But where was its place? Was it perhaps a sort of home amulet, protecting the residents from calamity and evil spirits through its messianic blessing?[58] And is the medal's message put in the mouth of a *laureatus*, more or less in the form of a speech bubble, possibly because such an image symbolizes the king Messiah?[59]

Despite all investigations and hypotheses, the medal remains a riddle even today. Clearly, however, it bears neither the name "Beer Medal" nor the name "Lemlein Medal" with any justification. Although a connection to Asher Lemlein cannot be proved, the medal appears nevertheless to have originated in the context of apocalyptic expectation around the year 1500—as a Christian parody of Jewish messianic hope, combined with a final attempt at converting that people led so far astray in the question of the Messiah: the Jews.

ABBREVIATIONS

BnF Bibliothèque nationale de France (National Library of France)

BSB Bayerische Staatsbibliothek (Bavarian State Library)

GJ II *Germania Judaica*. Edited by Zvi Avneri. Vol. 2: *Von 1238 bis zur Mitte des 14. Jahrhunderts*. Tübingen: Mohr Siebeck, 1968.

GJ III *Germania Judaica*. Edited by Arye Maimon, Mordechai Breuer, and Yacov Guggenheim. Vol. 3: *1350–1519*. Tübingen: Mohr Siebeck, 1987–95.

HAB Herzog August Bibliothek (Herzog August Library)

IMHM Institute for Microfilmed Hebrew Manuscripts

JTS Jewish Theological Seminary of America

MN Moses Maimonides, *Moreh nevukhim*

MT Moses Maimonides, *Mishneh torah*

MTA Magyar tudományos akadémia (Hungarian Academy of Sciences)

NLI National Library of Israel

PL *Patrologia Latina*. Edited by Jacques-Paul Migne. Paris: Garnier, 1841–55.

RSL Russian State Library

WA Weimarer Ausgabe (Weimar Edition of Luther's works)

NOTES

INTRODUCTION

1 Essential for the topic of Jewish-Christian apocalypticism is McGinn, Collins, and Stein, *Encyclopedia of Apocalypticism*, vol. 1. On Christian chiliasm in the sixteenth century, see the overview in Bauckham, *Chiliasmus*. On Jewish messianism in the same period, see Aescoly, *Messianic Movements*, chap. 6; Lenowitz, *Jewish Messiahs*, chaps. 5–6; Silver, *Messianic Speculation*, chap. 6.

2 In the interest of clarity, the anachronistic term "Germany" will be used as a synonym for the geographical area in which German language and culture were dominant. During the period in question, this area coincided roughly with the Holy Roman Empire.

3 On Luther's interpretation of the Antichrist, see Leppin, *Antichrist und Jüngster Tag*, 214–20; on his apocalyptic expectations, see Hofmann, *Luther*. Moeller, "Frühzeit der Reformation," places Luther's position within the context of the eschatological orientation of early Reformation preaching in general. On the apocalyptic influence of Lutheranism, see Barnes, *Prophecy and Gnosis*; Leppin, *Antichrist und Jüngster Tag*; Roettig, *Reformation als Apokalypse*; Kaufmann, *Ende der Reformation*.

4 For an introduction, see Lerner, "Millennialism." See also Wilken, "Restoration of Israel."

5 Klaassen, *Living at the End*; List, *Chiliastische Utopie*; Patschovsky, "Chiliasmus." See also Williams, *Radical Reformation*.

6 On the origin and development of Jewish messianic ideas, see Charlesworth, *Messiah*; Neusner, Green, and Frerichs, *Judaisms*; Oegema, *Der Gesalbte*. See also the classic studies by Klausner, *Messianic Idea*; Mowinckel, *He That Cometh*; and Zobel, *Gottes Gesalbter*.

7 Chap. 2 offers an extensive examination of the messianic excitement associated with Lemlein. On Re'uveni and Molkho, see chaps. 3.2, 3.5.

8 Since Bloch, *Thomas Münzer*, and Cohn, *Pursuit of the Millennium*, both of which appeared in the late 1950s, research has flourished around the topic of the millenarianism of the radical Reformation. Little attention, by contrast, has been given to

Jewish messianism in Germany during the same period, with the notable exceptions of Elisheva Carlebach (see below) and Zimmer, "Collaboration." On the messianism of R. Judah Löw b. Bezalel of Prague, see also Gross, *Messianisme juif*; Gross, *Netzah Yisrael*; Schatz Uffenheimer, "Maharal's Doctrine"; Sherwin, *Mystical Theology*, esp. 142–60. The numerous investigations of the Sabbatian movement of the seventeenth century cover the German-speaking lands as well, albeit to a lesser extent; e.g., the standard work by Scholem, *Sabbatai Sevi*, 546–91. See also Carlebach, *Divided Souls*, 76–85. The Emden-Eibeschütz Controversy has also been comparatively well researched, most recently by Hayoun, "Emdens Autobiographie"; Oron, "Gehalei Esh."

9 On the question of Jewish messianic hope in the emancipation debate, see Roemer, "Colliding Visions," esp. 272–77.

10 Graetz, *Geschichte der Juden*, 205.

11 On the Sephardim as cultural model in nineteenth-century German-Jewish thinking, see Schorsch, "Sephardi Supremacy," and Marcus, "Sephardi Mystique."

12 Cf. Jost, *Geschichte des Judenthums*, 3:214, 217.

13 Ibid., 3:215. Cf. Graetz, *Geschichte der Juden*, 205.

14 Thus Neubauer, "Where Are the Ten Tribes?," 408; Aescoly, *David Reubeni*; Aescoly, *Story*, 195–220.

15 Cf., e.g., Scholem, *Jewish Mysticism*, chaps. 7–8; Schatz Uffenheimer, "Outline"; Elior, "Messianic Expectation"; Baer, "Messianic Movement"; Dinur, *Israel and the Diaspora*; Ben-Sasson, "Exile and Redemption"; Ben-Sasson, "Generation"; Tishby, "Messianism." A partial translation of Tishby's article into English is included in Saperstein, *Essential Papers*, 259–86; I am referencing this edition unless otherwise noted. See also Aescoly, *Messianic Movements*, 253–302, esp. 260–62.

16 Cohen, "Messianic Postures," 206, 219. This influential study, now a classic, has appeared in print four times to date: twice in 1967, in 1991, and in 1992.

17 Cohen, "Messianic Postures," 222–25.

18 Introduction to Saperstein, *Essential Papers*, 20. Cf. Sharot, *Messianism, Mysticism and Magic*, chap. 5, esp. 71, 75.

19 Eidelberg, "Permutations," 25. Eidelberg claims that among the Ashkenazic Jews in Germany even the Sabbatian movement was little more than a fleeting episode; ibid., 33. Others proceed likewise from the messianic passivity of the Ashkenazic Jews, e.g., Schäfer, "Idea of Piety," 15–17; Cohen, *Under Crescent and Cross*, 175, 188; Necker, "Brennende Landschaft," 50, 61–63; Detmers, *Reformation und Judentum*, 82.

20 Cohen, "Messianic Postures," 203, 221.

21 For a comparison of the Sephardic "proselytizing redemption" with the Ashkenazic "vengeful redemption," see Yuval, *Two Nations*, 93–115. On the latter, see in detail in chap. 1. Both events (conversion and retribution), however, belong to the traditional apocalypticism that is represented—albeit with different emphases—in the eschatological ideology of the two cultural communities. See Grossman, "Redemption by Conversion."

22 Yuval, *Two Nations*, 288.

23 Carlebach, *Between History and Hope*. See also Carlebach, "Sabbatian Posture," 9–20. On the academic controversy between Cohen and Carlebach, see Berger, "Sephardic and Ashkenazic Messianism."

24 Carlebach, "Sabbatian Posture," 18–20. Scholem has previously pointed to a self-censorship out of concern over the negative Christian perception in the context of the Sabbatian movement; Scholem, *Sabbatai Sevi*, 5, esp. 763–65n205. Cohen, "Messianic Postures," 209, on the contrary sees his typology confirmed in the indirect tradition of messianic calculations in Ashkenaz.

25 Cf. Cohen, "Messianic Postures," 229n11. Nevertheless, Cohen included Sephardic messianic movements in his observations, although the transmission of the source materials is, according to his own criteria, just as dubious.

26 Ruderman, "Hope against Hope." The beginnings of a comparative approach appear in Scholem, *Sabbatai Sevi*, 93–102, and Yerushalmi, *From Spanish Court to Italian Ghetto*, chap. 7, esp. 306–13.

27 Idel, *Messianic Mystics*, chap. 4, esp. 141, 152–54n77. See also Idel, "Introduction," 16–28; Idel, "Particularism," 335–37; Idel, "Religion, Thought and Attitudes."

28 The comparative and connected approach has been put forward by Roni Weinstein in treating Lurianic Kabbalah and its alleged messianism in the context of Catholic reform; Weinstein, *Kabbalah and Jewish Modernity*, 142–65.

29 See, e.g., the contributions in Goldish and Popkin, *Jewish Messianism*, and Elior, *Sabbatian Movement*.

30 Dan, "Ha-sifrut ha-apokaliptit," 18–25, in contrast, compares Jewish and Christian apocalypticism during the Reformation from a purely phenomenological point of view.

31 See, e.g., Goldish, *Sabbatean Prophets*; Idel, *Messianic Mystics*, esp. 142–44; Idel, "Attitude to Christianity"; Popkin, "End of the Career"; Popkin, "Christian Interest"; Popkin, "Jewish-Christian Relations"; Popkin, "Unused Sources"; Ruderman, "Hope against Hope"; Schubert, *Täufertum und Kabbalah*; van der Wall, "Petrus Serrarius"; van der Wall, "Precursor of Christ." Cf. also Sharot, "Jewish Millennial-Messianic Movements," 71–73.

32 E.g., the readmittance of Jews to England in the seventeenth century possessed messianic significance for both Jews and Christians; Katz, *Philosemitism*; Popkin, "Jewish Messianism"; Fisch, "Messianic Politics."

33 The turning point and, ultimately, the renunciation of the traditional notion of Jewish isolation, passivity, and victimization were marked in the mid-1990s by the work of Israel Yuval and of Ivan Marcus; Yuval, *Two Nations*; Marcus, *Rituals of Childhood*. A discussion of this trend in research is offered by Rosman, *Jewish History*; Berger, "Generation of Scholarship"; and, newly, Perry and Voß, "Approaching Shared Heroes." For an initial overview of research on early modern Germany cf. also Diemling, "Jewish-Christian Relations."

34 Among more recent studies on cultural entanglement in the Middle Ages and the early modern times are Baumgarten, *Mothers and Children*; Carlebach, *Palaces of Time*; Idelson-Shein, *Difference of a Different Kind*; Kaplan and Teter, "Out of the

(Historiographic) Ghetto"; Perry, *Tradition and Transformation*; Shyovitz, *Remembrance of His Wonders*.

35 The concept of *histoire croisée* was developed by Bénédicte Zimmermann and Michael Werner; Werner and Zimmermann, "Beyond Comparison"; Werner and Zimmermann, "Vergleich, Transfer, Verflechtung." Recent studies in Jewish history strike out in a similar direction, e.g., Schäfer, *Mirror of His Beauty*, 229–35; Myers, *Resisting History*, 163–70; esp. Perry, "Imaginary War."

36 Carlebach, "Sabbatian Posture," 2–4, 9.

37 Cf. Idel's suggestion of a division between East and West, in which Italy would receive special significance; Idel, *Messianic Mystics*, 20–22, 380n8. See also Yerushalmi, "Messianic Impulses," 468; Roth, *History*, 179; Shulvass, *Rome*, 41–67.

38 The model of "connected histories" through migration and print, among others, was recently applied to early modern Jewish cultures by David Ruderman; Ruderman, *Early Modern Jewry*.

39 Cf. Gow, *Red Jews*, esp. 288–90.

40 Recent studies have posited that Protestant theologians commonly assigned apocalyptic thought a greater importance than did their Catholic colleagues. It should be noted, however, that Catholic apocalypticism has till now received comparatively little scholarly attention. Cf. Smolinsky, *Deutungen der Zeit*; Pohlig, "Konfessionskulturelle Deutungsmuster"; Kaufmann, "Jubeljahr 1600"; Holzem, "Zeitenwende."

CHAPTER I

1 On this polemic in Antiquity and the Middle Ages, see the overview by Williams, *Adversus Judaeos*; Schreckenberg, *Adversus-Judaeos-Texte*.

2 See Carlebach, "Messianische Haltung," 246–50. See also Carlebach, *Divided Souls*, chap. 4; Carlebach, "Last Deception." On anti-Jewish texts in German from the fourteenth century, see Niesner, *Wer mit juden well disputieren*.

3 On the Red Jews, see chap. 3.1.

4 Mangelsdorf, *Der gläserne Schatz*. See also, e.g., the frequently republished picture book *Der Antichrist* (first appearing in Strasbourg in 1480), in which the Jews are the first to pay homage to the Antichrist; Boveland, Burger, and Steffen, *Antichrist*, vol. 1, chap. 5.2.

5 Gow, "Gefolge des Antichristen," 107. See also Weber, *Antichristfenster*, 85–88.

6 Gow, *Jewish Antichrist*, 278–82. On anti-Judaism in the drama of the late Middle Ages, see Wenzel, *Do worden die Juden alle geschant*; Bartoldus, "We dennen menschen." On the role of Jews in the Antichrist dramas in particular, see Aichele, *Antichristdrama*, 140–48. Aichele observes that the anti-Jewish tendency in German plays sharpened significantly toward the end of the fifteenth century; Aichele, *Antichristdrama*, 147.

7 Cf. Wenzel, "Representation of Jews," 395.

8 Ibid., 399–400.

9 See the overview of the beginnings of printing in Müller, "Formen literarischer Kommunikation." See also Hirsch, *Printing*; Febvre and Martin, *Coming of the Book*. On the medium of the German-language pamphlet, see Köhler, *Massenmedium*, and esp.

Cole, "Reformation Pamphlet." See further Ozment, "Pamphlet Literature." Edwards, *Printing*, investigates the way the printed materials and pamphlets in particular turned the Reformation into a mass movement.

10 On visual propaganda in the spread of the Reformation, see Scribner, *Simple Folk*. In a society in which only a fraction of the populace was able to read, written material was also disseminated orally; Ozment, "Pamphlet Literature," 89–90. On the reading culture of the common man, see also Chartier, "Reading Matter."

11 Cf., e.g., the anti-Judaism of fifteenth-century German theologians, which largely eschewed any concern with the actual Jewish other for a preoccupation with routine biblical exegesis; Ocker, "German Theologians."

12 On this genre, see esp. Deutsch, *Judaism in Christian Eyes*; Deutsch, "Polemical Ethnographies"; Deutsch, "View of the Jewish Religion"; Deutsch, "Von der Iuden Ceremonien"; Diemling, "Christliche Ethnographien"; Diemling, "Anthonius Margaritha."

13 On Pfefferkorn, see Kirn, *Bild vom Juden*, chap. 4.1–2; on his writings, see also Martin, *Johannes Pfefferkorn*. On Victor von Carben, see Diemling, "Christliche Ethnographien."

14 "Ir schalckhait sag ich vnnd wil mich des nit schamenn die lang zeit verborgen gewest ist als ich thün bedeütenn das wil ich yetz offenbarn allen Cristen leüten dann ich bin mit yren hebraischen schrifften wol verwart, und dem verkerten geschleht die warhait nit gespart."

15 On Margaritha's work, see Diemling, "Christliche Ethnographien"; Diemling, "Anthonius Margaritha"; Burnett, "Distorted Mirrors," esp. 277–80; Walton, "Anthonius Margaritha"; Walton, *Anthonius Margaritha and the Jewish Faith*. Since the seventeenth century, Christian Hebraists have written corresponding studies, beginning with Johannes Buxtorf. On Buxtorf's work, see Burnett, *Christian Hebraism*, chap. 3; Burnett, "Distorted Mirrors," esp. 280–84.

16 Deutsch, "Von der Iuden Ceremonien," 346–47; Deutsch, *Judaism in Christian Eyes*, 323–24.

17 In general, the information provided by converts is reliable and finds confirmation in the Hebrew source materials of the time. See, e.g., Carlebach, *Anti-Christian Element*, 15, 17; Deutsch, "Von der Iuden Ceremonien," 339; Diemling, "Anthonius Margaritha," 327.

18 On the Jews' loss of their status as the chosen people of God and their replacement by the church, see Hruby, *Juden und Judentum*, 33–54; Simon, *Verus Israel*. As early as 1339, the Dominican Alfonso de Buenhombre (Alfonsus Bonhominis) makes use of the argument of dispersal in his edition of the *Epistula ad R. Isaak de adventu Messiae* (also known as *Epistola Samuelis Maroccani*), which is attributed to the eleventh-century convert Samuel of Fez; PL 149:333–68. This popular epistle, whose historical authenticity is contested, was translated into numerous European languages. Printed versions in German appeared among other places in Augsburg, Colmar, and Zwickau in 1524. On this text, see Kaufmann, "Flugschriftenpublizistik," 432–42, 459–61.

19 Carlebach, *Divided Souls*, 73–82. As early as ca. 1280, in his *Pugio fidei*, Raymond Martini attacked the Jews for their belief in false Messiahs.

20 "Weil sie den rechten vnd wahren Messiam nicht wollen erkenn noch annemen/ verhengt der gerecht Gott vber sie/ daß sie vilmals von denselbs auffgeworffnen falschen Messien vnnd Verführern schändtlich betrogen/ vnd vmb Leib vnd Leben ellendiglich gebracht werden"; Scherer, *Postill*, 61.

21 "Wen jhr mehr für einen Messiam wolltet annemen . . . wol dem/ der von ander leut schande witzig wirdt"; Weidner, *Sermon*, fol. 18v–19r (my pagination). A transcription of this sermon in Hebrew letters can be found in a manuscript collection from the seventeenth century; Bodleian Library, Oxford, MS Mich. 121 (= IMHM, F 19963), fol. 276r–324r, here fol. 287r–v. On the expression "grow clever" (witzig werden) see Grimm, *Dictionary*, 30:894. On Weidner, see Diamant, *Paulus Weidner*.

22 Soldan, *Entdeckunge*. Cf., e.g., Müller, *Greuel der falschen Messien/ wie auch/ Schatz= Kammer des Wahren Messiae Jesu Christi. das ist: Eine ziemliche Lista der Jenigen falschen Messien, [. . .]/ dadurch bewiesen und dargethan wird/ daß Jesus Chrjstus der Rechte Messjas und Erlöser [. . .] sey. Denen Jüden zur Erkäntnis und Reue/ allen rechtschaffenen Christen aber zum Trost ans Licht gegeben.* On the science of lists as a polemical tool, see Wasserstrom, *Between Muslim and Jew*, 98–99; on the list as a literary genre, see Smith, *Imagining Religion*, 36–53.

23 In 1562, Weidner makes reference to a Hebrew epistle that presumably describes seven false Messiahs "at length" (nach der leng) and that was exhibited in one of his Latin works; Weidner, *Sermon*, fol. 19r (my pagination). He mentions the number 7 in ibid., fol. 18v. Unfortunately, I was unable to discover this list; in any event, it is not to be found in his *Loca praecipva Fidei Christianae.* In 1608, Costerus quotes Weidner in his own list, *Historie*, 90–91. For this last reference, I wish to thank Yaacov Deutsch.

24 Carlebach, *Divided Souls*, 76–87. See also Roemer, "Colliding Visions," 268–69, with many additional sources. Numerous studies deal with the Christian perception of Shabtai Zvi, as early as Aescoly, "Newsletter"; Scholem, *Sabbatai Sevi*, 354–71. More recent studies include, e.g., Åkerman, "Queen Christina"; Swiderska, "Polish Pamphlets"; van Wijk, "Rise and Fall." Christian reaction in the German-speaking lands is documented by a comprehensive collection in the Zurich Central Library; see Popkin, "Christian Interest," 93.

25 "Mancherley münd= und schrifftliche Zeitungen . . . / welche aber nach und nach für gantz falsch/ erdichtet und erlogen befunden/ und unsere darob in allzugrosser Leichtgläubigkeit geschöpffte Freude verlohren/ ja in eine allgemeine Verspottunge verwandelt worden"; Bon, *Wolgemeintes Sendschreiben*, 3. Cf. Scholem, *Sabbatai Sevi*, 469–70.

26 Gerson, *Jüden Thalmud*, 399. On Gerson's life and work, see Hüttenmeister, "Jüdische Familie." Gerson serves as source for, e.g., Bischoff, *Gründlicher Bericht*, passim; Soldan, *Entdeckunge*, 579; Buchenroeder, *Messias Juden-Post*, passim; von Lent, *Schediasma*, passim. On Lemlein, see chap. 2; on Re'uveni, see chaps. 3.2, 3.5.

27 On Gans and his work, see Breuer, "Modernism and Traditionalism"; Breuer, introduction to the edition of Gans, *Zemah David*; Neher, *Jewish Thought*. On ibn Yaḥya, see David, "Gedalia Ibn Yahya"; David, *Historiographical Work*; David, "Gedalya ibn Yahya's Shalshelet Hakabbalah."

28 On the Bar Kokhba revolt against the Romans, see Schäfer, *Bar Kokhba Aufstand*; Schäfer, *Bar Kokhba War Reconsidered*; Yadin, *Bar-Kokhba*. Considered in particular as a messianic revolt, see Aescoly, *Messianic Movements*, chap. 2; Lenowitz, *Jewish Messiahs*, 25–29. On Mordechai of Eisenstadt, see Scholem, "Prakim apokaliptiyim."

29 Von Lent's list in turn serves as a basis for Eisenmenger, *Entdecktes Judenthum*, 2:647–66; Müller, *Greuel der falschen Messien*; Schudt, *Jüdische Merckwürdigkeiten*, pt. 2, bk. 6, chap. 27. On Eisenmenger's writings, see Rohrbacher, "Gründlicher und Wahrhaffter Bericht."

30 "Dieses neue Messias=Juden=Geschrey sey den Jüden schädlich/ doch etlichen am Ende nützlich. . . . welches dann auch wir Christen von Hertzen gern den Jüden wüntschen und gönnen"; Buchenroeder, *Messias Juden-Post*, fol. 24r.

31 See Carlebach, *Divided Souls*, 68, 82–85.

32 Rom. 11:25–26. On the different positions of the church fathers on this question, see Hruby, *Juden und Judentum*, 55–65.

33 For a thorough analysis of the association of the Antichrist with Jews, see Gow, "Jewish Antichrist." A cogent overview is to be found in Trachtenberg, *The Devil and the Jews*, 32–43. In the copious literature on the Antichrist, the standard introduction remains Bousset, *Antichrist*. On the origins of the Antichrist tradition, see also Jenks, *Origins*. For an overview of the later development, see Rauh, *Bild des Antichrist*; McGinn, *Antichrist*.

34 Carlebach, "Endtime," 333–35. On the general increase of anti-Judaism in fifteenth-century folklore, see Rubin, *Gentile Tales*; Ocker, "Contempt," 133–39; Bell, *Sacred Communities*, 99–113.

35 See Carlebach, "Endtime," 336–40, and Wenzel, "Representation of Jews," 414–15.

36 Frankl, *Jude*, 66.

37 Bebel, *Facetien*, bk. 2, no. 46.

38 Folz, *Reimpaarsprüche*, no. 9a, 9b. See Wenzel, "Judenproblematik," 86–87. On Folz's anti-Jewish polemic, see also Schiel, "Antijudaismus in Fastnachtspielen."

39 The repellent association of Jews with excrement, which marked the Jews as a "filthy" people, was a special topos of popular fecal humor; see Wenzel, "Representation of Jews," 415–16. Further examples are to be found in Zöller, "Judenfeindschaft," 356–57. On the stereotype of the unclean Jew, see Detmers, *Reformation und Judentum*, 54–55. See also the controversial book by Dundes, *Life Is Like a Chicken Coop Ladder*, in which the author posits an "anal fixation" in German culture as such.

40 The motif of the Jewish Messiah's impure conception was widespread in the sixteenth century. Pfefferkorn's *Wie die blinden Juden yr Ostern halten*, fol. 8v–9r, connects the stereotype of Jewish sexual deviancy with Jewish messianic hope, asserting that at the beginning of Passover, the Jews "cavort the same night immodestly, as each hopes to beget the Messiah himself" (tryben die selben nacht grosse vnkeusch dan eyn yder hofft Messias sol von ym gebarn werden).

41 Emmerson, *Antichrist*, 81–82. One variation on the theme involves an incestuous union, e.g., between father and daughter. In other versions, the devil himself is the biological father of the Antichrist. On the different variations, see Aichele,

Antichristdrama, 113–14. The motif of the Messiah as bastard, conceived in an adulterous act, is also found in *Toldot Yeshu* (The Life of Jesus), a Jewish parody of the Jesus story, widespread in the Middle Ages and the early modern period, that evinces many similarities to the Antichrist vita. On *Toldot Yeshu*, see the standard work by Krauss, *Leben Jesu*, and recently, the collected volume by Schäfer, Meerson, and Deutsch, *Toledot Yeshu.*

42 Caesarius of Heisterbach, *Dialogus miraculorum*, vol. 1.2, chap. 24. German translation of the same, *Von Geheimnissen*, chap. 2, no. 12. In the sixteenth century, the story appeared in the version by Rasch, *Ein hübsch Liedt*, multiple times as a single print (1530, ca. 1552, 1555). Rasch, we might mention, expected the birth of the Antichrist in 1588; see Leppin, *Antichrist und Jüngster Tag*. Schudt's *Jüdische Merckwürdigkeiten*, pt. 1, bk. 5, chap. 11, 411–17, adduces numerous versions from the seventeenth and eighteenth centuries.

43 Kirchhof, *Wendunmuth*, vol. 1.2, no. 50.

44 Folz, *Reimpaarsprüche*, no. 12. See also Schöner, *Judenbilder*, 178–81; Wenzel, "Judenproblematik," 79–80.

45 See Carlebach, "Endtime," 337.

46 "Weicht auß, tret umbe und ruckt von stat! / Ir habt lang genug innen gehabt / Gewalt, herschaft und regiment, / Das nu alles wurd sein end"; von Keller, *Fastnachtspiele*, 1:171.

47 "Das ist schlecht davon der sin, das ich ein ent der Cristen bin"; ibid., 1:173.

48 Ibid., 1:179–80. Cf. Gengenbach, *Nollhart*, 78–81; Pfefferkorn, *Iuden peicht*, fol. 3v–4r.

49 "Er solle uns Heiden durch jren Messia alle tod schlahen und vertilgen, damit sie aller Welt Land, güter und Herrschafft kriegten. . . . Wündschen uns, das Schwert und Kriege, angst und alles unglück uber uns verfluchten Gojim kome"; Luther, *Von den Juden und ihren Lügen*; WA 53:417–552, here 519–20. Cf. Eidelberg, "Passage."

50 "Sie hassen die Cristen vill mer dan andre völcker wie wol sie sich fruntlich gegen vns Cristen erzaigen so ist es doch nit aus hertzen Ursach. . . . das wir cristen an Jesum cristum gelauben vnd den halten für den waren messiam/ das ist größlich/ wider sy"; Pfefferkorn, *Juden veindt*, fol. 2v–3r (my pagination).

51 "Die Juden haben damahls zur Zeit Trajani . . . viel 1000. vom Volck ermordet/ dero Fleisch gefressen/ ihre Häute getragen/ und mit ihren noch blutenden Därmen sich umgürtet"; Schudt, *Jüdische Merckwürdigkeiten*, pt. 2, bk. 6, chap. 17, 298. On Schudt, see Deutsch, "Johann Jacob Schudt"; and the collected papers in Cluse and Voß, *Frankfurt's "Jewish Notabilia."*

52 Berger, *Jewish-Christian Debate*, no. 242. On the Ashkenazic concept of vengeful redemption, see Yuval, *Two Nations*, 93–109.

53 On the equation of Esau/Edom with Rome, see Cohen, *Esau as Symbol*. See also Yuval, *Two Nations*, 10–20; Stemberger, "Beurteilung Roms"; Hadas-Lebel, "Jacob et Esau"; Zeitlin, "Origin."

54 The doctrine of the four kingdoms is traced back to Daniel's visions of the statue (Dan. 2:31–45) and the four beasts (Dan. 7:1–27). See Flusser, "Four Empires."

On the prevalent Jewish-Christian interpretation of the last world empire as a reference to the *Imperium Romanum*, see Adamek, *Endreich*; Swain, "Four Monarchies"; Zeeden, "Daniel." On the historical periodization of the four world empires in sixteenth-century Hebrew historiography, see Degani, "Structure."

55 "Alle der juden hoffnunge vnd betten ist dahin gerichtt/ das der Christen Scepter hinweck genommen/ vnd zu nichten werden sol"; Margaritha, *Gantz Jüdisch glaub*, fol. 27r (my pagination). On the doctrine of the transfer of rule, see Thomas, "Translatio imperii."

56 Abravanel, *Perush*, on Zech. 2:4. On the identification of the four blacksmiths with the four messianic figures in rabbinical literature, see the concordance in Strack and Billerbeck, *Kommentar*, 4:464–65. Specifically on the figure of the first Messiah, who was to fall in the war before the coming of the second, true Messiah ben David, see Berger, "Typological Themes," 143–48; Fishbane, "Midrash and Messianism."

57 Schudt, *Jüdische Merckwürdigkeiten*, pt. 1, bk. 5, chap. 11, 411. Schudt attributes the story of the birth of the Messiah, which in some versions (e.g., that of Caesarius of Heisterbach) takes place in Worms, to this Jewish hope. See also Abravanel, *Yeshu'ot meshiho*, 55, "that the King Messiah will be born in the Christian lands that favor the religion of Rome in the West." The corresponding quote in the Talmud is bSan 98a. On Jewish messianic hopes linked with Worms, see Voß, "Rom am Rhein."

58 "Wie Haman/ ist zerbrochen, und uff geriben worden, also muse auch das Römisch/ Reich uhr plötzlich zertreten werden, zu grund und boden gehen"; Worms City Archives, Abt. 1 B, no. 2021/21, fol. 1r–2v, here fol. 2r (Letter of the Craft Guilds to the Elector of Pfalz [transcript], Worms, April 1615). In some communities, the custom of smashing a plate during an engagement ceremony was likewise associated with the hope "das ir Gott die Christen also sol zerschmettern und gantz zu nicht machen" (that their God shall thus smash the Christians and utterly destroy them); Staffelsteiner, *Etliche Artickel*, fol. A2v. See, by contrast, the traditional explanation as to the origin of this custom in Regensburg: shards bring good luck, because loud noises drive off evil spirits; Margaritha, *Gantz Jüdisch glaub*, fol. H2r. On this custom, see Sperber, *Minhagei Yisra'el*, 6:58–61. Thanks go to Ursula Reuter and Yaacov Deutsch for this reference.

59 "Rach vber die gantz gemain der cristlichen kirchen vnd in sunderhait das das Römisch reich verwust zerbrochen vnd verstört wird"; Pfefferkorn, *Juden veindt*, fol. 2r (my pagination). On *Birkat ha-minim* as anti-Christian curse, cf. Yuval, *Two Nations*, 115–19. For further rituals of cursing in the weekly and festival liturgies, see Yuval, *Two Nations*, chap. 3.3–4.

60 On the textual development of *Birkat ha-minim* and on the question of its intended object at various stages of development, see Schäfer, "Synode von Jabne."

61 "Bald deine prächtige Macht . . . zu schauen, dass die Greuel von der Erde schwinden"; Haim b. Bezalel, *Iggeret ha-tiyyul*, pt. 3, s.v. "barukh." The explication involves a pun on the Hebrew word *amen*: "ואין לנו לענות רק אמן ולהאמין בכל זאת אמונת אומן שנזכה במהרה לראות בתפארת עוזך ומלכות שמים להעביר גילולים מן הארץ." The quoted apocalyptic passage is taken from the introduction to the second part of

the *Alenu* prayer, which concludes every Jewish service. On *Alenu le-shabbeah* (Our Duty to Praise) as anti-Christian polemic, see Yuval, *Two Nations*, esp. 193–202; Wieder, "Gematria"; Elbaum, "Textual Emendations"; Ta-Shma, "Alenu le-shabeah."

62 Margaritha, *Gantz Jüdisch glaub*, fol. 14v (my pagination).

63 Ps. 79:6.

64 Yuval, *Two Nations*, 123–30. Cf. Gutmann, "Messiah at the Seder"; Gutmann, "Wenn das Reich Gottes kommt"; Rosenthal, *"David Redivivus,"* 36. See also Yuval, *Two Nations*, 100–101, on the custom of spilling wine on the floor for each of the ten plagues that God visited upon the Egyptians; on the burning of leavened bread as symbolic destruction of Edom, see Yuval, *Two Nations*, chap. 5.2.

65 Kitzingen, *Hag ha-pessah*, fol. 15v (quoted in Tamar, "Calculations," 932), with a quotation from Eccles. 9:8. Kitzingen refers here to bShab 153a.

66 A parallel is to be found in Acts 6:9–11, where messianic retribution is likewise associated with a white garment, which God gives the martyrs to wear until Judgment Day. See Yuval, *Two Nations*, 95–96. Ibid., 135–59, Yuval shows how the blood of the martyrs of the Rhineland Crusades pogroms of 1096, as evidence of Christian guilt, began to function as a means of calling forth the Messiah to exact revenge. See below, p. 111.

67 Although Elijah is traditionally the harbinger of salvation, here he functions as a second Messiah, taking on the role of judge on Judgment Day (expressed explicitly in Pfefferkorn, *In Lob und eer*, fol. 15v) which typically is reserved for Messiah ben David. The latter functions here, in turn, as the first Messiah, while the figure of Messiah ben Joseph is missing entirely; ibid., fol. 14r. Pfefferkorn deduces this unusual image from Mal. 3:23. In the apocrypha and rabbinical literature, this verse on the eschatological return of the prophet is usually referred to Elijah's preparatory (intra-Jewish) function in the restitution of Israel; see Klausner, *Messianic Idea*, 451–55; Mowinckel, *He That Cometh*, 278, 299; Moore, *Judaism*, 2:358–59. By contrast, see Tanhuma mishpatim 18 (106b), where this verse is connected with the punishment of the kings of the nations by Elijah on the Day of the Lord. Furthermore, a special function is afforded to the prophet with respect to the resurrection of the dead; Klausner, *Messianic Idea*, 456.

68 "Auch habt yr das auß erwelte volck gottes die Juden schwerlich gequellet vnd gepeynigt. vnd dartzu so seit yr nit mit weissen claydern beclaydet"; Pfefferkorn, *In Lob und eer*, fol. 15v–16r (my pagination).

69 Gutmann, "Messiah at the Seder," 35–36; Gutmann, "Wenn das Reich Gottes kommt," 24.

70 Margaritha, *Kurtzer Bericht*, fol. 2v. Victor von Carben makes obvious allusion to this legend in his *Hier inne wirt gelesen*, 21–22 (my pagination). A pictorial translation of the legend can be found in, e.g., the *Washington Haggadah*; see Yuval, *Two Nations*, 125. On Moses as prototype of the Messiah, see Berger, "Typological Themes," 42–43; Teeple, *Eschatological Prophet*.

71 Historical Museum, Frankfurt am Main, C 10154. This etching is a mirror-image replica on a single leaf.

72 On the motif of the *Judensau*, which was especially widespread in Germany, see Shachar, *Judensau*; Fabre-Vassas, *Singular Beast*. On the *Judensau* as satirical portrayal of the messianic donkey, see Yuval, *Two Nations*, 127–28.

73 On the ritual murder case in Trent, see Treue, *Trienter Judenprozess*; Hsia, *Trent 1475*.

74 This also applies even if one sees end-time expectations not merely as the expression of social discontent and the movements arising from it not merely as an instance of class struggle by the wretched masses. This, in an nutshell, is the basis for Cohn's investigation in *Pursuit of the Millennium*. Rather, we must speak here more generally of a connection between religious motivation and political-social action; van Dülmen, *Reformation als Revolution*, 8.

75 Most recently, Wunderli, *Peasant Fires*.

76 Bloch, *Thomas Münzer*. See esp. Elliger, *Thomas Müntzer*; Schwarz, *Apokalyptische Theologie*; Seebaß, *Reich Gottes*; Goertz, "Thomas Müntzer."

77 Klötzer, *Täuferherrschaft*; van Dülmen, *Täuferreich*; Cohn, *Pursuit of the Millennium*, chap. 12.

78 "Das jnen got wölt sendenn Messiam welcher soll mit grosser macht vnd gewalt kommen/ eyn vberwinder der Cristenheyt"; Pfefferkorn, *Handt Spiegel*, fol. 4r (my pagination).

79 Of general relevance here: Chazan, *Daggers of Faith*; Chazan, *Medieval Stereotypes*; Cohen, *Friars*; Cohen, *Living Letters*; Dahan, *Intellectuels chrétiens*. See also Lasker, "Jewish-Christian Polemics."

80 Diemling, "Anthonius Margaritha," 327. See also, e.g., the intention expressed in Pfefferkorn, *Juden veindt*, fol. 9v (my pagination). Friedrich, *Abwehr und Bekehrung*, 46n146, correctly characterizes the ethnographies as "Warnschriften," works that warned about the dangers that Jews and Judaism represented.

81 Kaufmann, "Luther and the Jews," 92–96; Diemling, "Anthonius Margaritha," 328–29; Osten-Sacken, *Martin Luther und die Juden*.

82 On the disputation, see most recently Carlebach, *Divided Souls*, 50–51. See also Diemling, "Anthonius Margaritha," 328–31; Stern, *Josel von Rosheim*, 99–101. See below, pp. 137–39, on the political background.

83 See also Carlebach, "Sabbatian Posture," 21–22.

84 See Gow, "Jewish Antichrist," 280. On the social context of the Nuremberg plays prior to the expulsion of the Jews, see also Habel, "Prototyp und Variation"; Ragotzky, "Fastnacht und Endzeit"; Schiel, *Antijudaismus in Fastnachtspielen*, 164. On the expulsion of the Nuremberg Jews, see Toch, "Umb gemeyns nutz"; Wenninger, *Man bedarf keiner Juden mehr*, 135–54.

85 "Damit sie an der Christen blut jr mütlin heimlich kületen"; WA 53:520. Yuval, *Two Nations*, 161–89, suggests with good reason that the impression made by the concept of salvation by retribution on the Christian environment played a role in the origins of the accusation of ritual murder in the twelfth century.

86 Gow, *Red Jews*, 225–27.

87 "Unterstanden sich dieselben mit Gift auszureuten, stahlen unser Sakrament des Leibes und Blutes Christi, warfen es in die Backöfen, schmiedeten es auf

den Ambossen und trieben viel anderes Gespött damit"; Aventinus, *Baierische Chronik*, 175.

88 On this topic, see Yuval, *Two Nations*, chap. 6. See also Burnett and Gautier Dalché, *Attitudes towards the Mongols*. On the Frankfurt events of 1241, known as the "first Jews battle" (erste Judenschlacht), and its eschatological background, see, most recently, Schnur, "Weltuntergang."

89 Cf. Carlebach, "Endtime," 335.

90 *Von Michel Juden tode*; printed in Aufgebauer, *Michel von Derenburg*, 394–99. On Michel von Derenburg, see ibid., esp. 390–91.

91 Ibid., 395.

92 Ibid., 397.

93 "Ich lasse mir sagen, Es solle ein Reicher Jüde itzt auff dem Lande reiten mit zwelff Pferden (der will ein Kochab werden) und wuchert Fürsten, Herrn, Land und Leute aus, das grosse Herrn scheel dazu sehen"; Luther, *Von den Juden und ihren Lügen*, in WA 53:524. Cf. Aufgebauer, *Michel von Derenburg*, 388.

94 "Darumb haben die verarmeten fürsten dissen reichen Juden/ für jhren patron vnd nothülffer gehalten vnd höher geacht/ weder vnsern Herrn Christum"; Aufgebauer, *Michel von Derenburg*, 395.

95 In a similar way, the financier Isaac of Norwich was caricatured in England. A drawing on the list of debts by the royal exchequer from 1233 portrays Isaac with three faces and a crown on his head, in my view an allusion to the false Trinity of the Antichrist. Beneath the omnipotent Isaac, the scene shows his agent Moses Mokke and another Jew who holds a scale in his hand, the instrument of the money lender. Both are surrounded by demons, one of whom appears to blow a shofar. A reproduction can be found in Lipman, *Jews of Medieval Norwich*, fig. 10; Roth, *Portraits*, fig. 5. Cf. also the north German reformer Urbanus Rhegius, who polemicized against the opulence in which the Jews lived. According to him, they had risen to great esteem as advisers to the princes, had built magnificent synagogues, and had summoned rabbis from foreign lands, such that they believed they lived in messianic times and possessed even the impudence to proselytize among the Christians; Rhegius, *Gründtlick Bewiss*, fol. 3v (my pagination). On the reformer and his attitude toward the Jews, see Hendrix, *Toleration*.

96 "Des Römischen Widderchrists reübischen vnd blutdürstigen hauffen"; "vnsers herrn Christi feinde/ vnd der Juden freunde . . . Judisten/ papisten . . . vnd falsche christen"; Aufgebauer, *Michel von Derenburg*, 395–96.

97 "Frumme ehrliche leüte"; ibid., 395.

98 "Die Christen müsten jhrer gnaden leben/ . . . pfey dich schelm Christe/ du hast verloren wir haben gewonnen/ deine Goim sind zu schanden worden"; ibid., 396–97.

99 Ibid., 398.

100 See, e.g., bSan 97b; bKet 110a. Also Schäfer, "Die messianischen Hoffnungen," 225, 228, 230, 234.

101 Such considerations were familiar to Jewish community leaders in the Islamic world as well. See, e.g., Moses Maimonides in his *Epistle to Yemen* (1172), where he advises

the Yemeni communities to distance themselves from a messianic pretender who had appeared in the country at that time, suggesting they hide him away for a certain period and spread meanwhile the rumor of his insanity. As a consequence, the non-Jews would not take him seriously, and the Jewish community would thereby avoid being harmed by the affair. If, on the contrary, the non-Jews were to learn of the presumptuous claims of the man, the Jews would "incur their wrath"; Maimonides, *Epistle to Yemen*, xviii. By way of warning, Maimonides adverts to the rage of the Muslims in other cases of messianic movements under Islamic rule. The reprisals he describes, however, in contrast to those carried out under Christian rule, turned out to be rather mild; ibid., xix–xx.

102 Scholem, *Sabbatai Sevi*, 497–99, 508, 509–11. On the rabbinical persecution of the Sabbatians in the eighteenth century, see Carlebach, *Pursuit of Heresy*.

103 See Scholem, *Sabbatai Sevi*, 763n205.

104 Carlebach, "Sabbatian Posture," 25–29; Carlebach, "Messianische Haltung," 238–40. Cf. Yuval, *Two Nations*, 275. Berger, "Typological Themes," 162n82, also proposes the thesis that the Jews living in Christian lands, where the claims of a false Messiah were constantly being rejected, were possibly less prepared to lend credence to a messianic pretender.

105 Scholem, *Sabbatai Sevi*, 584.

106 Carlebach, "Messianische Haltung," 239.

107 Yuval, *Two Nations*, 275–76. On the messianic motivation of the so-called immigration of the three hundred rabbis, see ibid., 270–71, with further references.

108 Judah he-Ḥasid, *Buch der Frommen*, no. 212. Cf. Yuval, *Two Nations*, 276–77; Carlebach, "Sabbatian Posture," 21; Necker, "Brennende Landschaft," 50–51.

109 "Do not proclaim it to all the world"; Judah he-Ḥasid, *Buch der Frommen*, no. 212. See Dan, *Esoteric Theology*, 241–45. It is certainly no accident that the editor of the printed anthology of Yiddish narratives, *Mayse bukh* (Basel, 1602), which contains a hagiographic cycle about Judah he-Ḥasid and his father, Samuel, omitted the story of their failed attempts shortly before death to reveal the end after all. The story appears in the handwritten precursors to the first Basel edition; NLI, Jerusalem, Ms. Heb. 8° 5245 (= IMHM, F 52209), and BSB, Munich, Cod. hebr. 495 (= IMHM, B 63). I wish to thank Lucia Raspe for bringing this to my attention. A Hebrew version of the legend is reprinted in Dan, *Ḥasidut Ashkenaz*, 2:208. On the *Mayse bukh*, see Meitlis, *Ma'assebuch*; see, more recently, the introduction to the French translation by Starck, *Beau livre d'histoires*. On the Jerusalem and Munich manuscripts, see Zfatman, "Mayse-Bukh"; Timm, "Frühgeschichte."

110 Adler, *Jewish Travellers*, 68–69. In the earlier Warsaw manuscript, the censored passage can still be found; David, *Sivuv*, 257. Cf. David, *Sivuv*, 240–43; Kuyt, "Die Welt aus sefardischer und ashkenazischer Sicht," 225–26.

111 See Dan, "Problem of Martyrdom."

112 On Jewish self-censorship of anti-Christian passages, see in general Popper, *Censorship*, s.v. "self-censorship"; Benayahu, *Copyright*, 81, 195. See also Raz-Krakotzkin, *Censor*, on the formation of the modern Jewish canon through the combination of

internal and external censorship. Specifically on the (self-)censorship during the printing of Hebrew books in Germany in the sixteenth century, see Burnett, "German Jewish Printing," 518, 526–27; Burnett, "Regulation"; Künast, "Hebräisch-jüdischer Buchdruck," 286, 289.

113 Similarly, the story of the Messiah of vengeance, who stands menacingly before the gates of the imperial administrative seat, comes to us not through the literature of Ashkenazic Jews, but through Schudt, a Christian, and Abravanel, a Sephardic Jew. See above, pp. 28–29.

114 Edited by David, "Tales," no. 6. In fact, the plague persecutions overtook the Jewish community in Worms as well; see Reuter, "Warmaisa," 670.

115 Pfefferkorn, *In lob und eer*, fol. 10v–11r (my pagination).

116 Ibid.

117 On such processions in the Middle Ages and early modern period, see Raspe, "Sacred Space." See also Horowitz, "Speaking to the Dead."

118 On the desecration of the cemetery, see Friedrichs, "Anti-Jewish Politics," 135.

119 Carlebach, "Messianische Haltung," 241–46.

120 Sambari, *Divrei Yosef*, 293–302. See the source texts in Aescoly, *Messianic Movements*, 424–26, 430. On Joseph ha-Kohen and his work, see David, "Iggrono." His two prominent historical works have now been put out by Robert Bonfil in new critical edition in four volumes; ha-Kohen, *Chronicle*; ha-Kohen, *Vale of Tears*. Below, however, I am referencing two older editions, since Bonfil's set came out after completion of this book manuscript.

121 Fraenkel-Goldschmidt, *Historical Writings*, no. 17 (if not otherwise noted, I refer to the English edition rather than the Hebrew).

122 Gans, *Zemah David*, 138–39.

123 In his agitation against Shabtai Zvi and the prophet Nathan of Gaza, Jacob Sasportas refers to events such as the failed repentance movement of Lemlein: "and the catastrophe that will result from it is enormous—apostasy and the endangerment of the souls of the People of Israel! Even if the majority holds fast to their belief, individuals have sinned against it, as you can see from episodes such as those documented in *Shalshelet ha-kabbalah* of ibn Yaḥya"; Sasportas, *Ẓiẓat novel Ẓvi*, 46–47; cf. 116. On Sasportas's fight against Sabbatianism, see Dweck, *Dissident Rabbi*; Moyal, *Sasportas*. On the motif of conversion linked to the Lemlein episode, see below, chap. 2.

CHAPTER 2

1 As early as the middle of the sixteenth century, Mordechai Dato recognized the interreligious meaning of the turn of the century in 1500; Jacobson, *Along the Paths*, 187. In general on the patterns of fear and expectation at a century's end, see Schwartz, *Zeitenwende*. See also the contributions in Jakubowski-Tiessen, *Jahrhundertwenden*.

2 On the apocalyptic undertones of the peasant rebellions, see Cohn, *Pursuit of the Millennium*, chap. 11.

3 On messianism among the conversos, see Lenowitz, *Jewish Messiahs*, 98–99; Baer, *Messianic Movement*, 71–77; Beinart, "Converso Community"; Beinart, *Chapters*, 2:543–88; Carrete Parrondo, "Idealismo y realidad"; Carrete Parrondo, "Judeoconversos"; Levine Melammed, *Heretics*, chap. 3. See, more broadly, Goldish, "Patterns."

4 On Christian responses to the expansion of the Ottoman Empire, see Kaufmann's definitive *Türckenbüchlein*. See also Göllner, *Turcica*; Höfert, *Den Feind beschreiben*; Schwoebel, *Shadow of the Crescent*. For an overview of the Ottoman wars in Europe, see Matschke, *Das Kreuz und der Halbmond*.

5 Ez. 38–39, Apoc. 20. On various Christian interpretations, see Kaufmann, *Türckenbüchlein*, chap. 7. Pohlig, "Konfessionskulturelle Deutungsmuster," esp. 88–291, analyzes for the first time specific attitudes toward the Turkish threat among different Christian confessions. See also Miyamoto, "Influence of Medieval Prophecies"; Lellouch and Yerasimos, *Traditions apocalyptiques*.

6 The Dominican Peter Schwarz, for example, avers that "etlich lügenhaftige jüden haben yen vorgesagt, das nach dem als Constantinopolis ist den cristen abgewunnenn so solt der Meschiah kummen Vnd das bestercket ir hofnung vnd meynen das Wenn der Türck zuerstört das römisch reich als sie denn hofnen das es yn eyner kürcz geschee" (many deceitful Jews have prophesied, that after Constantinople was wrested from the Christians, the Messiah should come and that strengthens their hope and belief that the Turk will destroy the Holy Roman Empire and that this will happen soon); Schwarz, *Stella Meshi'aḥ*, fol. 82r. Cf. Baer, "Messianic Movement," 61–62; Robinson, "Kabbalist and Messianic Visionary," 88, with additional sources given in n. 6. See also Silver, *Messianic Speculation*, 112–13; Yerushalmi, "Messianic Impulses."

7 See Ruderman, "Hope against Hope," 303.

8 Kurze, *Johannes Lichtenberger*.

9 With this, Dato explains why so many—himself included—preferred to use Abravanel's calculation; quoted in Jacobson, *Along the Paths*, 186n170. The frequently asserted dependence of Asher Lemlein on Abravanel (and in general on the Spanish Expulsion especially in earlier research) has not, however, been proven. Thus, e.g., Aescoly, *Messianic Movements*, 271; Tishby, *Messianism*, 276; Silver, *Messianic Speculation*, 143. Idel alludes to the discrepancy in the source findings in "Introduction," 23; Idel, *Messianic Mystics*, 140–41; Idel, "Particularism," 336–37. See also Lawee, "Messianism of Isaac Abarbanel," 4, according to which the importance of Abravanel for the messianic movements of the sixteenth and seventeenth centuries is, in fact, significantly less than heretofore assumed. On Abravanel's messianism, see Netanyahu, *Don Isaac Abravanel*, 195–257; Silver, *Messianic Speculation*, 116–30.

10 "זמן קץ הגאולה בא לזרע אברהם/ זמרו לי"י חסדיו"; RSL, Moskau, Ms. Günzburg 722 (= IMHM, F 47566), fol. 7v. See Song of Sol. 2:11, Joel 2:10 and 4:15. The surviving copy of the poem was presumably inscribed not long after the origin of the text by Meshullam b. Moses Jacob Cusi (the colophon on fol. 132r names March 31, 1501). The scribe was likely a grandson of the man of the same name who

founded a Hebrew press in 1475 in Piove di Sacco near Padua; see Turniansky and Timm, *Yiddish in Italia*, 93–95, no. 46.

11 "משיח הולך ובא בשנת נזר"ו עלינו יציץ"; RSL, Moskau, Ms. Günzburg 722 (= IMHM, F 47566), fol. 7v, my emphasis. Cf. Ps. 132:18.

12 The lines of each respective stanza begin and end on the same letters. The text is written in two columns, such that the terminal letters of one stanza serve simultaneously as the beginning of the stanza opposite. The acrostic reads: זה האלפים מאיר עם יוחנן טוב הוא משיח הולך ובא. At the edge of the page, the Gematria is explained, i.e., the principle of hermeneutic interpretation based upon the numerical value of the letters: ה' אלפים are 5000, זה מאיר and עם יוחנן טוב הוא both have the value of 263, producing a sum of 5263, which in turn corresponds to the Christian year 1502/3: then, as the last part of the acrostic prophesies, the Messiah will come.

13 "Der Krebs wirdt ettlich bald abschutten/ Die lang zeit habent sanfft geritten/ Vil vnstet wesen wirt er machen/ Groß vngesell in kryegs sachen." Brant, *Von den Wunderlichen zamefugung*. On the astrological interpretation of planetary conjunctions and comets in the sixteenth century, see Brosseder, *Im Bann der Sterne*; Zambelli, *Astrologi hallucinati*. See also Schechner, *Comets*; Thomas, *Decline of Magic*, chaps. 10–12.

14 "Der wirdt ein Lerer vnd ein Merer/ Vil übels/ vnd ein welt verkerer/ Vnd doch in frummen schein sich zaygen/ Byß er sein falscheyt recht thüt aygen." Brant, *Von den Wunderlichen zamefugung*. Cf. Kurze, *Johannes Lichtenberger*, 26.

15 Virdung, *Pracitca*, fol. 1v. Unlike Brant, who calculates the date of the conjunction written on the back of the crab in his illustration for June 1504, Virdung and others correctly point to October 1503. In June 1504, contrary to the broadside, Mars was not located near the other two planets.

16 Related by Dato, quoted in Tishby, *Messianism* (Hebr.), 73n226. On Bonet de Lattes, see Goldschmidt, "Bonetto Latis." Another Jewish astrologer in Italy, Yohanan b. Isaac Alemanno, interpreted the unusual conjunction of heavenly bodies similarly as an announcement of the arrival of the herald of the Messiah, making use word for word of a corresponding prediction by a Christian; Beit-Arié and Idel, "Treatise," 182. See also Idel, "Johanan Alemanno."

17 The study by Goldish, *Sabbatean Prophets*, esp. chaps. 1–2, sheds light on the significance of prophecy for early modern messianism.

18 Weinstein, *Savonarola*. In general, see Niccoli, *Prophecy and People*; Reeves, *Prophetic Rome*; esp. Niccoli, "Prophetic Culture." For a representative example of Jewish perceptions of Christian prophets, see Ruderman, "Giovanni Mercurio da Correggio."

19 Quoted in Tishby, *Messianism* (Hebr.), 73n226.

20 In an anonymous Hebrew chronicle from early seventeenth-century Prague, it is one of the few events that do not have to do exclusively with the Jews in Bohemia; David, *Chronicle*, 24, no. 11. Hebrew edition under the same title. I refer to the English edition throughout.

21 Sambari, *Divrei Yosef,* 266.

22 "An. 1500. quidam Iudaeus nomine Lemlen imposuit Iudaeis quibusdam (credo in Germania) se esse verum Christum, quem expectabant." Génebrard, *Chronographia,* to 1500.

23 On Lemlein's messianic activity, see Aescoly, *Messianic Movements,* 271–72, 329–34; Lenowitz, *Jewish Messiahs,* 99–100; Silver, *Messianic Speculation,* 143–45. The most recent contribution on Lemlein is Benmelech, *Shlomo Molkho,* 58–69. Campanini, "Neglected Source," draws attention for the first time to a highly interesting source that sheds light on important aspects of Lemlein's activity. Lemlein's own writings are preserved in a manuscript collection; MTA, Budapest, Ms. Kaufmann A 179 (= IMHM, F 4513), partly edited by Kupfer, "Visions."

24 Cf. Lemlein's own testimony: "Now I am already old and gray and have taken leave of my youth"; Kupfer, "Visions," 422.

25 See Lohrmann, Wadl, and Wenninger, "Überblick"; Ioly Zorattini, "Insediamenti ebraici"; Frejdenberg, "Jews in Slovenian Lands." A good overview of Jewish history in the region is to be found in the essay collection edited by Todeschini, *Mondo ebraico,* and esp. Toaff, "Migrazioni." For further references, see the geographically arranged bibliography by Todeschini, *Mondo ebraico,* 585–96.

26 Roth, *History,* 124. In early 1500, a letter reached Lemlein here; see Kupfer, "Visions," 407. See also Giustiniani, *Precatio* (quoted in Campanini, "Neglected Source," 101), who claims that Lemlein was active near Iustinopolis, today's Koper (Ital. Capodistria). Istrien as Lemlein's area of activity is also asserted by ibn Yaḥya, *Shalshelet ha-kabbalah,* 103; ha-Kohen, *Divrei ha-yamim,* pt. 1, fol. 40r; ha-Kohen, *'Emeq ha-Bakhah,* 67; Sambari, *Divrei Yosef,* 266. "Austria" (אוסטריאה) in later sources is a reading error (correctly: איסטריאה), e.g., in Gerson, *Jüden Thalmud,* 403; ha-Kohen, *Ma'aseh Tuviyah,* fol. 18r; JTS, New York, Ms. 2482 (= IMHM, F 28735), fol. 176r (Joseph of Damascus, *To'ei ru'aḥ*).

27 See, on the one hand, the correspondence between Lemlein and Moses Ḥefeẓ (Gentili) from Fano in the spring and early summer of 1500; Kupfer, "Visions," esp. 408, 419–20. See, on the other hand, the honorary title given to Lemlein by Joseph ibn Shraga, although he sharply criticizes Lemlein's answers to Ḥefeẓ; reprinted in part in Marx, "Asher Laemmlein," 137. On ibn Shraga's writings, see Idel, "Encounters," esp. 214–15. On Lemlein as mystic, see initial observations in Idel, *Messianic Mystics,* 140–42.

28 RSL, Moskau, Ms. Günzburg 652 (= IMHM, F 44117), fol. 211r. This version differs considerably from the *editio princeps,* Venice 1587, where the quoted passage is omitted. For a description of the manuscript, see David, "Historiographical Work," 103–4.

29 Quoted in Kupfer, "Visions," 390n20.

30 Cf. also the superscript of a copy of ibn Shraga's attack on Lemlein; Bodleian Library, Oxford, MS Opp. Add. Qu. 40 (= IMHM, F 17404), fol. 129v.

31 See Giustiniani, *Precatio* (quoted in Campanini, "Neglected Source," 102). The Jewish year 5260 (1499/1500) is given by ibn Yaḥya, *Shalshelet ha-kabbalah,* 103; Gans, *Zemah David,* 137; Kitzingen, *Ḥag ha-pessaḥ,* fol. 27v (quoted in Tamar, "Asher

Lemlein," 400); Isaac, *De Astrologia*, fol. 37v (Hebr.), 38r (Lat., my pagination); von Lent, *Schediasma*, 54.

32 Giustiniani, *Precatio* (quoted in Campanini, "Neglected Source," 102). Two of Lemlein's visions from a later time have been preserved; see below. On the visionary Kabbalah of the sixteenth century, see Elior, "Messianic Expectations." Idel situates Lemlein in the line of Abraham Abulafia's ecstatic messianism, whose primary activity was personal ecstasy as prophetic experience; Idel, *Messianic Mystics*, esp. 140–42. On Abulafia's messianism, see Idel, *Messianic Mystics*, chap. 2. On Idel's theoretic systematization of kabbalistic messianism, see his "Redemptive Activities."

33 Gans, *Zemah David*, 137. On Lemlein's magic use of holy names, see his responsum on the manufacture of amulets (1509); MTA, Budapest, Ms. Kaufmann A 179 (= IMHM, F 4513), 133–36. In another responsum, he considers also the various kinds of parchment and describes their use for Torah scrolls, tefillin, and mezuzot (1505); MTA, Budapest, Ms. Kaufmann A 179 (= IMHM, F 4513), 130–33. See Idel, "Neoplatonic Interpretations," 194, on Lemlein's familiarity with non-Jewish writings about sorcery. Cf. the central importance of miracles as evidence for recognizing a true prophet in MT, bk. 1, *Hilkhot yessodei ha-torah*, chap. 7.7.

34 Ha-Kohen, *Divrei ha-yamim*, pt. 1, fol. 40r; ha-Kohen, *'Emeq ha-Bakhah*, 67: "The prophet was distraught, the inspired man driven mad" (Hosea 9:7). Similarly in Giustiniani, *Precatio* (quoted in Campanini, "Neglected Source," 101): "Malus demon huic sue extasi se immisceret."

35 "With his little wisdom and the deeds that he accomplished, and also with the help of his disciples, he lead the whole region astray with the advent of the redeemer"; quoted in Loewinger, "Recherches," 35. On Farissol's dismissive stance toward messianic speculation in general, cf. Ruderman, *World of a Renaissance Jew*, 137–39.

36 Giustiniani, *Precatio* (quoted in Campanini, "Neglected Source," 102). Cf. ibn Yahya, *Shalshelet ha-kabbalah*, 103.

37 Ha-Kohen, *Divrei ha-yamim*, pt. 1, fol. 40r; ha-Kohen, *'Emeq ha-Bakhah*, 67–68, with quote from Isa. 11:12.

38 Farrissol, quoted in Loewinger, "Recherches," 35. In David, *Chronicle*, 5, no. 11, it reads "all communities of Israel." Likewise, Gans, *Zemah David*, 137; Schudt, *Jüdische Merckwürdigkeiten*, pt. 2, bk. 6, chap. 27, *57 (new pagination starting from chap. 25). Idel's claim that the messianic uproar left the Sephardim in Italy largely unmoved (*Messianic Mystics*, 141) is not supported by the available sources, since none differentiate between the reactions of Ashkenazim and Sephardim. Others deduce this view likewise only from secondary sources. E.g., Kupfer, "Visions," 395, refers to Lemlein's later anti-Sephardic stance, and Jost, *Geschichte des Judenthums*, 3:215, proceeds in a way similar to Idel from the premise of the Ashkenazic character of messianism. On this point, cf. my introduction.

39 Pfefferkorn, *Speculum*, fol. 6r (my pagination).

40 Ibn Yahya, *Shalshelet ha-kabbalah*, 103.

41 Kitzingen, *Hag ha-pessah*, fol. 27v (quoted in Tamar, "Asher Lemlein," 400). Tuvia ha-Kohen of Metz, who had lived in Cracow and Frankfurt an der Oder, likewise

adds to his source ibn Yahya that many communities in the "land of Ashkenaz" hearkened to Lemlein's voice; ha-Kohen, *Ma'aseh Tuviyah*, fol. 18r. On Tuvia ha-Kohen's life and work, see Ruderman, *Jewish Thought*, 229–55.

42 Génebrard, *Chronographia*, to 1500. In the framework of a portrayal of the Sabbatian movement, *Sippur halomot kez ha-pela'ot*, which originated in the last decades of the eighteenth century, Lemlein's activity ultimately appeared as merely a matter of the "German territories in the land of the west"; according to a later edition, *Me'ora'ot Zvi*, 72.

43 Pfefferkorn, *Speculum*, fol. 5v (my pagination). Margaritha similarly builds upon the reader's personal memory, when, in his commentary on Isa. 53 in the context of the sinfulness of the Jews, he alludes to the well-known episode: "So seyt es mir ye grosse narren das jr euch so lanng plagen vnd peynigen last vnnd das jr euch nicht ain mal zum guetten wendet/ Jr habt ye feylich ethwan versuecht das jr begert habt frumb zusein vnnd widerumb zu Gott kheren/ Als nemblich da der lemblin den Moschiach verkhündiget vnnd anzaygete/ theten jr gar vill vnd grosse theschupho"; Margaritha, *Erklerung*, fol. 74v–75r.

44 "Die gewart haben auff das xv. hunderst iair, in wilchem gewiß der messias komen solt"; Pfefferkorn, *Juden Spiegel*. Unless otherwise noted, I quote from the second expanded edition of the German original, Cologne, 1508, edited in the appendix to Kirn, *Bild vom Juden*, 205–30, here 211.

45 "Dan yderman werde in der zeyt so vill mit ime selbst zu thun haben. Das man keyn achtung vff sy haben soll"; Victor von Carben, *Hier inne wirt gelesen*, 94 (my pagination). Similarly, Maimonides on the advent of the Messiah: "the mere report of his advent will strike terror into the hearts of all the kings of the earth, and their kingdoms will fall, neither will they be able to war or revolt against him. They will neither defame nor calumniate him, for the miracles he will perform will frighten them into complete silence"; Maimonides, *Epistle to Yemen*, xvii.

46 Gans, *Zemah David*, 137.

47 Ibid. Likewise Kitzingen, *Hag ha-pessah*, fol. 27v (quoted in Tamar, "Asher Lemlein," 400).

48 "Vill kryg aufrure vnd ander widderwartickeyt entsteen wirt"; "mert sich noch der unfridt von tag zu tage"; Victor von Carben, *Hier inne wirt gelesen*, 95–97 (my pagination). Michael Buchenroeder also knew that, through rumors about the true advent of the Messiah, simple-minded Christians could come to doubt about the truthful savior Jesus Christ ("einfaltige Christen im Zweifel von dem rechten waaren/ und einigen Messia Jesu Christo"); Buchenroeder, *Messias Juden-Post*, fol. 3r. Thus, he conceived his treatise on Shabtai Zvi and Nathan of Gaza as "Gründliche Widerlegung des heutigen Gedichts von den neuerstandenen Messia der Juden/ . . . Denen Christen allerseits/ und ins gemein zu Staerckung ihres Glaubens" (Thorough refutation of the present fantasy of the newly appearing Messiah of the Jews. . . . For all Christians and in general for the strengthening of their faith); Buchenroeder, *Messias Juden-Post*, title page. Buchenroeder even refers to a supposed example of Christians turning into Jews ("Exempel daß Christen zu Jüden worden") in Gerson, *Jüden Thalmud*, bk. 1, chap. 33.

49 Giustiniani, *Precatio* (quoted in Campanini, "Neglected Source," 102). On Giustiniani, see, e.g., Secret, "Dominicains," esp. 321–24; Salone, "Agostino Giustiniani." On Ceresara, see Comboni, "Paride Ceresara."

50 *Me'ora'ot Ẓvi*, 72. This probably also lies behind Lemlein's designation as "the Messiah of Padua" in Dato's *Migdal David*; quoted in Tishby, *Messianism* (Hebr.), 73n226.

51 The key passages that are sometimes cited in the critical literature as evidence of Lemlein's messianic claim are far from unambiguous. When Lemlein is heard to say that the Messiah has already come (Loewinger, "Recherches," 35), he is arguing, in my view, in accordance with the conception that the Messiah will be the reincarnation of the soul of Adam. Lemlein reads ADaM as an acrostic for Adam, David, Messiah and concludes from this that the soul of the first human being, which first put on the form of the biblical King David, will finally pass into the Messiah, assuming that Israel's sins no longer hinder it. Thus, in Lemlein's first response to Ḥefeẓ; Kupfer, "Visions," 410, 413. This reasoning was first formulated by Moses de Leon; Scholem, "Gilgul," 211. See also the interpretations in *Me'ora'ot Ẓvi*, 72.

52 "Sollte eyn fewrene sewl mit eynen finsteren wolcke alle iuden vmbgeben, glicher weyse, wie by pharaonis tzyten geschehen was, vnd sy also weder gen Hierusalem foren, doselbst dan der tempel weder vff gebawtn vnd opferhand/ gegeben werden solt"; Pfefferkorn, *Juden Spiegel*; reprinted in Kirn, *Bild vom Juden*, 218–19. Cf. Exod. 13:21. On messianic penance, cf. also bSan 97b and 98a. Precisely these passages are quoted in Fagius, *Liber fidei*, 99–100, § 77 (Hebr.), 108, § 78 (Lat.), in connection with the Lemlein movement.

53 Kupfer, "Visions," 416–17, with quote from bBer 18b.

54 MTA, Budapest, Ms. Kaufmann A 179 (= IMHM, F 4513), 164–67. The belief that there are righteous individuals who achieve eternal life appears already in the late thirteenth century in Azriel of Gerona; see Scholem, "Kabbalat R. Ya'akov," 237–39n8. In addition to the righteous and the sinners, Lemlein also recognizes a third group, the pious (also the "simple righteous"); Kupfer, "Visions," 415. Although these have a place in the garden of Eden at death, they have not achieved eternal life. They, too, will be resurrected in the end-times in order to perfect their souls; MTA, Budapest, Ms. Kaufmann A 179 (= IMHM, F 4513), 167. On the gradation of the two types of the righteous, cf. Tishby, *Wisdom of the Zohar*, 2:655–67, 686–88.

55 "וזה היה כמה פעמים שעשו תשובה גדולה בכל לבבם ובכל נפשם ובכל מאודם לגלות לֹהם הקץ"; Fagius, *Liber fidei*, 98, § 75 (Hebr.), 106, § 76 (Lat.). The Hebraist Paulus Fagius published the Hebrew text together with his Latin translation in 1542 in Isny under the title *Liber fidei*. Thus far there has been no satisfactory investigation of the work; the important pioneering study remains Steinschneider, "Livre de la foi." See also Friedman, *Most Ancient Testimony*, 245–50, and more recently Burnett, "Dialogue of the Deaf," 172–74. Because of a remark that appears to refer to the activity of David Re'uveni (see chap. 3.2), I would date the work between 1523/24 and 1529, since it served Sebastian Münster as source for his *Vikku'aḥ*. As *terminus post quem*, 1502 has been accepted till now; see Prijs, *Handschriften*, 56–57. On Fagius and his printing press, see Raubenheimer, *Paul Fagius*; Habermann, "Press of Paul Fagius."

56 "בשביל ביאת המשיח כמעט שנה תמימה נער וזקן טף ונשים אשר לא נעשה מעולם
    חשובה כזו שעשו בימים ההם"; Fagius, *Liber fidei*, 99, § 76 (Hebr.), 106, § 77 (Lat.).

57 Ibn Yaḥya, *Shalshelet ha-kabbalah*, 103. כלו after the *editio princeps*, fol. 45r, corrected
    to פלי. Ibn Yaḥya's dating of 5260 refers to the prophetic appearance of Lemlein,
    not to the year of penance, which can be positively dated at 1501/2 from other sources;
    all the above-cited report of the eyewitness Pfefferkorn, *Juden Spiegel* (reprinted in
    Kirn, *Bild vom Juden*, 218). This finds confirmation in von Lent, *Schediasma*, 56; Faris-
    sol, *Magen Avraham* (reprinted in Loewinger, "Recherches," 35); Fagius, *Liber fidei*,
    99, § 76 (Hebr.), 107, § 77 (Lat.); David, *Chronicle*, 5, no. 11. Joseph ha-Kohen's
    dating also points toward 1502; ha-Kohen, *Divrei ha-yamim*, pt. 1, fol. 40r; ha-Kohen,
    'Emeq ha-Bakhah, 67 (incorrectly given in the commentary as 1503).

58 Giustiniani, *Precatio* (quoted in Campanini, "Neglected Source," 101).

59 Cf. the date of a responsum that Lemlein sent from Safed via Jerusalem to one Samuel
    Kohen Ẓedek in Salonika: "נכתב לפרשת והיה הו"א ותמורתו יהיה קדש. ר"ל תיבת
    הו"א, ותמורתו בא"ת ב"ש יעלה צפת, יהיה קדש לביאת הגואל במהרה ר"ל כי במדינת
    צפת בגליל העליון כתבתי זאת"; MTA, Budapest, Ms. Kaufmann A 179 (= IMHM, F
    4513), 136. By contrast, a fictitious place of mystical reality is suspected here by Kup-
    fer, "Visions," 392. See also Idel, *Messianic Mystics*, 141. In 1505 Lemlein maintained a
    correspondence with one Jacob Ashkenazi in Egypt; MTA, Budapest, Ms. Kaufmann
    A 179 (= IMHM, F 4513), 130–33. The last page of an incunable of the Hebrew Bible
    from the Soncino Press (Brescia, 1494) contains the following handwritten note:
    "On July 23, 1504 the pious and righteous R. Lemlein died in blessed remembrance
    and was buried on the same day in Padua" (י"ב אב רס"ד נפטר החסיד והצדיק הר
    לעמליין ז"ל ונקבר באותו יום בפדואה); Biblioteca Palatina, Parma, De Rossi 293, fol.
    583v. But here we are not dealing with testimony about the prophet Asher Lemlein,
    as Perani, *Ebrei a Castel Goffredo*, 150–51, suspects. The information arising from
    Giustiniani's more nearly contemporary description, which appears to be quite well
    informed about Lemlein's activities and coincides not only with external sources but
    also with Lemlein's own manuscripts, makes such an interpretation untenable. By
    contrast, Ibn Yaḥya, *Shalshelet ha-kabbalah*, 103, the only source who otherwise (and
    relatively late) writes of Lemlein's death shortly after 1502, is not reliable on this
    point; see below.

60 Reprinted in Kupfer, "Visions," 397–402.

61 Ibid., 398–99; cf. also 402. The identification of prayer with the *Shekhinah* (the pres-
    ence of God), which is personified in the visionary form of a woman, first appears in
    the second half of the twelfth century in the mystical tradition of *Ḥasidei Ashkenaz*;
    Necker, "Brennende Landschaft," 60. See also Dan, *Esoteric Theology*, 123–28.

62 Kupfer, "Visions," 398.

63 Ibid., 399. For examples of the corrupted passages in the prayer book, see ibid.,
    399–402.

64 Ibid., 398, 402.

65 Ibid., 399, 401.

66 Ibid., 402.

67 Cf. Necker, "Brennende Landschaft," 58–59, with additional references. See also Dan, *Esoteric Theology*, 16–17.

68 MTA, Budapest, Ms. Kaufmann A 179 (= IMHM, F 4513), 136–49. The close of the text (147–49) is reprinted in Kupfer, "Visions," 405–7.

69 Kupfer, "Visions," 405. On the origin, meaning, numerical value, and written form of the individual letters, see MTA, Budapest, Ms. Kaufmann A 179 (= IMHM, F 4513), 141–47. Thus, Lemlein derides the Sephardim for writing the letter *gimel* in a way that looks almost like a *nun*; MTA, Budapest, Ms. Kaufmann A 179 (= IMHM, F 4513), 141.

70 MT, bk. 2, *Hilkhot tefillah ve-birkat kohanim*, chap. 8.12. Maimonides speaks explicitly only of the distinction between *alef* and *ayin*, and he is referring to the Talmudic discussion concerning the question of who should be allowed to be called to read from the Torah, whereby the phonetic equation of *heh* and *ḥet* is also considered a disqualification; see bMeg 24b and yBer 2.4.

71 Kupfer, "Visions," 405–7.

72 Ibid., 406.

73 Ibid.

74 Ibid.

75 See Bonfil, *Rabbis*, 291–92.

76 On this point, see Ben-Sasson, "Exile and Redemption," 220. Abravanel complains, e.g., of the ignorance of the Hebrew language among Ashkenazim, who in his view expressed themselves unclearly and incomprehensibly. See also Zimmels, *Ashkenazim and Sephardim*.

77 The other vision that testifies to Lemlein's later activities polemicizes with a similar severity against the study of the Halachah; Kupfer, "Visions," 402–5. According to Bonfil, *Rabbis*, 266, 284, even the most enthusiastic kabbalists did not typically agitate with such vehemence for the preference of mysticism over traditional Talmudic erudition.

78 Aemilius, *Widerlegung*, fol. 14v. By questioning the use of repentance in general, Aemilius also discredits the conceptions associated with the ten annual days of repentance.

79 See ha-Kohen, *'Emeq ha-Bakhah*, 68; ibn Yaḥya, *Shalshelet ha-kabbalah*, 103; Sambari, *Divrei Yosef*, 267.

80 "All ihr Gut armen Leuten gegeben"; Weidner, *Sermon*, fol. 18v (my pagination).

81 "Wol widerumb reich vnd zu großen Herrn machen würde"; ibid. Although in the conversion sermon that he delivered in 1561 in Prague, Weidner does not mention Lemlein by name, the emphasis on prayer, fasting, and charity makes clear that the messianic call of Lemlein is intended. Weidner certainly would have known of Lemlein firsthand, since he was born in 1525 in Udine in Friuli Venezia Giulia, as the memory of the failed prophet would have been still fresh in this region quite close to the area of Lemlein's main activity. See also Gans, *Zemah David*, 137; von Lent, *Schediasma*, 56.

82 On the disciplines of repentance among Ḥasidei Ashkenaz, see Marcus, *Piety and Society*, 39. Concerning their influence on penitential practices during the early modern

period in Germany and Poland, see Elbaum, *Repentance*. A tabulation of penitential punishments for specific sins is to be found in Juda he-Ḥasid, *Buch der Frommen*, esp. pt. 17–26, 37–43, 52–53, 72–74.

83 Aemilius, *Widerlegung*, fol. 14v; ha-Kohen, *'Emeq ha-Bakhah*, 68. Cf. chap. 1, pp. 30–31.

84 See Loewinger, "Recherches," 35.

85 Ha-Kohen, *'Emeq ha-Bakhah*, 68. See also Kitzingen, *Ḥag ha-pessaḥ*, fol. 27v (quoted in Tamar, "Asher Lemlein," 400).

86 Aemilius, *Widerlegung*, fol. 14v. Similarly, Schudt, *Jüdische Merckwürdigkeiten*, pt. 1, bk. 6, chap. 27, *57 (new pagination with chap. 25), writes that "the Jews almost throughout the world declared in 1502 a three-day fast" (die Juden fast durch die gantze Welt an. 1502. eine allgemeine dreytägige Fasten anstellten). Sambari, *Divrei Yosef*, 267, speaks of both fasting in general (צומות) and of fasting periods of several days (הפסקות). On the concept of *hafsakah* (pause, interruption), see Tishby, *Paths of Faith and Heresy*, 30–42. See also ibn Yaḥya, *Shalshelet ha-kabbalah*, 103; Dato, *Migdal David* (quoted in Tishby, *Messianism* [Hebr.], 73n226).

87 In his letter to Samuel Kohen Ẓedek, Lemlein himself later regretted that his activity had truly been no blessing for him, but rather a curse, since he was accused of being a charlatan: "והבאתי עלי כ״מ קללה ולא ברכה. . . . יאמרו עליו החזון אשר הוא חוזה לימים רבים ולעתים רחוקים הוא נבא. ומי יכחישנו. כי כך דרכי המשקרים שהם תולים עדותם בדרך רחוקה או באורך הזמנים"; MTA, Budapest, Ms. Kaufmann A 179 (= IMHM, F 4513), 132.

88 The long-disregarded text is preserved in a collection of manuscripts written circa 1501/3 in Portogruaro in eastern Venetia; Biblioteca de San Lorenzo, El Escorial, G-III-11 (= IMHM, F 8837). On fol. 128r–129v (incorrect pagination, actually 138r–139v) we find only the first half, while a complete copy in another hand is inserted on fol. 131r–134v (actually 141r–144v). I use the latter version here, fol. 131r (actually 141r), with the quote from Ezek. 1:4. Lemlein is not mentioned by name in the manuscript but described metaphorically as "lamb without blemish" (שה תמים); ibid., 131v (actually 141v). See Exod. 12:5. The manuscript was recently also evaluated by Benmelech, *Shlomo Molkho*, 63–64.

89 Biblioteca de San Lorenzo, El Escorial, G-III-11 (= IMHM, F 8837), fol. 132r–v (actually 142r–v), with quote from Dan. 11:14. See Giustiniani, *Precatio* (quoted in Campanini, "Neglected Source," 101).

90 Biblioteca de San Lorenzo, El Escorial, G-III-11 (= IMHM, F 8837), fol. 132r–v (actually 142r–v). Whether Lemlein, in fact, never explicitly presented himself as a prophet cannot be determined, since no self-declaration on this question has been preserved; all sources attest only to the perceptions of others. Only Sambari, *Divrei Yosef*, 266, claims to quote Lemlein's own words: "he said, that the Lord had sent him as leader to his people Israel." In fact, Sambari merely puts the judgment of Lemlein's followers that is quoted in Yosef ha-Kohen in Lemlein's own mouth; cf. above, p. 53.

91 "לצוות על דבר או להזהר ממנו"; Biblioteca de San Lorenzo, El Escorial, G-III-11 (= IMHM, F 8837), fol. 131v (actually 141v).

92 "לכו והלחמו מלחמה פלו' בשם פל'"; ibid.

93 "קנאה תחרות התנשאות ומחלוק' אונאות רכילו' הוצאת שם רע מסירות ג"ע טרפות";
ibid.

94 "They wield the sharpness of their tongue like sword and lance to mar what is sacred,
so that they can say of a lamb without blemish, 'it is an offensive thing, it will not be
acceptable' (קשת לשונם ידרוכו עם חרב וחנית להטיל מום בקדושי' למען יאמ' על
(שה תמים פגול הוא לא ירצה)"; ibid., fol. 131v–132r (actually 141v–142r), with quote
from Lev. 19:7.

95 Biblioteca de San Lorenzo, El Escorial, G-III-11 (= IMHM, F 8837), fol. 132v
(actually 142v).

96 "השקר הנגלה אין הסבה בו כי אם אהבת הרשות תחרות ונצוח"; ibid., fol. 131v (actually 141v). See ibid., fol. 132v (actually 142v): "For firstly he indicates that he allegedly boasted of prophecy. But that is the invented lie upon which his entire argument
is based" (כי ראשונה ירמוז כאלו התפאר בנבוא'. והוא הכזב המכוזב אשר עליו בנה)
(מאמריו כלם).

97 "כמעט נגד רצון הראשים. אבל השומעם לדברי השלם הזה ומאמריו לבד"; ibid., fol.
132v (actually 142v).

98 Sambari, *Divrei Yosef*, 266–67.

99 On the sensitivity among rabbis in matters of honor and regard as well as for the preservation of rabbinical tradition and of traditional scholarship in the persecution of the
Sabbatians in the eighteenth century, cf. the study by Carlebach, *Pursuit of Heresy*. See
also Goldish, *Sabbatean Prophets*, 144–49.

100 "ובסור הצורך אל השופט יפחת כבודו ומעלתו אצל ההמון"; Biblioteca de San
Lorenzo, El Escorial, G-III-11 (= IMHM, F 8837), fol. 132r (actually 142r).

101 All three causes that, according to Alexander of Aphrodisias, divide human beings
from the truth apply to Lemlein's critics: "First is ambition and self-righteousness,
which prevent the human being from recognizing the truth, the way something is.
The second is the subtlety in itself of the thing to be recognized, its depths and the difficulty of comprehending it. But the third is the incomprehension of the one wishing
thus to recognize, and the insufficiency of his mental powers to recognize something,
the recognition of which is thus impossible for him" (אחת מהם אהבת הרשות והנצוח
המונעי' האדם מהשגת האמת כפי מה שהוא והשני[ת] דקות העניין המושג בעצמו ועומק
(וקשה השגתו. והשלשי[ת] סכלות המשיג וקוצר יד שכלו מהשיג מה שאי אפשר השגתו);
ibid., fol. 131r (actually 141r). Joseph refers to MN, bk. 1, chap. 31. Joseph's argumentation on the second cause is found in Biblioteca de San Lorenzo, El Escorial,
G-III-11 (= IMHM, F 8837), fol. 132v–133v (actually 142v–143v). On the nature of
prophecy, cf. MN, bk. 2, chaps. 32–48, here chaps. 36–38. On Maimonides's understanding of prophecy, see Reines, *Maimonides*. On the third cause, Joseph adverts to
several examples of the incomprehension of his adversary; Biblioteca de San Lorenzo,
El Escorial, G-III-11 (= IMHM, F 8837), fol. 133v–134r (actually 143v–144r). Cf.
MN, bk. 2, chaps. 43–44, 46–47. Joseph intentionally alters the text of Maimonides
from אפשר (possible) to אי אפשר (impossible) to emphasize the mental limitation
of his adversary. This reading does not correspond to the original Arabic text, nor is it
to be found among the known variations of Samuel ibn Tibbon's Hebrew translation;

cf. Even-Shemuel, *Moreh nevukhim*, 1:133 (list of variations at the back of the volume). I wish to thank Bernard Septimus for this information.

102 Joseph nevertheless implies Lemlein's prophetic qualification whenever he refers to his master's perfection: "his piety, his abstinence and humility as well as the depth of his knowledge of hidden things" (חסידותו פרישותו וענוותנותו ועומק השגתו) בידיעת הנעלמות); Biblioteca de San Lorenzo, El Escorial, G-III-11 (= IMHM, F 8837), fol. 132r (actually 142r). According to Maimonides, intellectual and moral perfection are fundamental prerequisites for the prophet's calling. See MN, bk. 2, chaps. 32, 36; and MT, bk. 1, *Hilkhot yessodei ha-torah*, chap. 7.1.

103 Pfefferkorn, *Juden Spiegel*; reprinted in Kirn, *Bild vom Juden*, 219. This motif in not uncommon in the apocalyptic context; see, e.g., Scholem, *Sabbatai Sevi*, 266–67. Possibly Lemlein meant also the structural collapse of the houses of God as a consequence of their abandonment when the Christians recognize the true Messiah and turn away from Jesus. Cf. the same formulation Pfefferkorn uses in a different context: "Weyter werden sie [die Christen] saghen. wyr wellen mit euch geen vnnd vns auch eweren Messias vnterwurffyg machen. vnd man wyrt dan nit mer myt den glocken laeuten. noch meß halten nach Christlicher gewonhait vnd ordenung. Auch sollen alßdann alle kyrchen nyder vallen" (Furthermore, they [the Christians] will say, we wish to go with you and do obeisance to your Messiah, and then the bells will no longer be rung and mass no longer be held according to Christian habit and ordinance. And thereupon all churches will fall to the ground); Pfefferkorn, *In Lob und eer*, fol. 14r (my pagination).

104 See chap. 1.

105 "אפילו אות אחת או רמיזה אחת וכ"ש ממשות"; Fagius, *Liber fidei*, 99, § 76 (Hebr.), 107, § 77 (Lat.).

106 Ibid., 98, § 75 (Hebr.), 106, § 76 (Lat.). To support his argument, the author points to the dissent among the rabbis in bSan 97b–98a, as to whether the advent of the Messiah depended upon the righteousness of the people; Fagius, *Liber fidei*, 99–100, § 77 (Hebr.), 107–8, § 78 (Lat.).

107 Ibid., 99, § 76 (Hebr.), 107, § 77 (Lat.). Münster makes multiple use of the polemical potential of this text; Münster, *Vikku'ah*, 12 (my pagination); Münster, *Messias Christianorvm et Iudaeorum*, fol. 18v–20r (Hebr., my pagination), 43–46 (Lat.); Münster, *Hebraica Biblia*, 3. He takes on the sharpest tone in the missionary treatise that precedes his Hebrew translation of the Gospel of Matthew; Münster, *Evangelium Secundum*, 26–27. On the life of Münster, see Burmeister, *Sebastian Münster*. On his work, see Burnett, "Dialogue of the Deaf"; Friedman, *Most Ancient Testimony*, 221–34.

108 Gerson, *Jüden Thalmud*, 403–4; Scherer, *Postill*, 62; Buchenroeder, *Messias Juden-Post*, fol. 6v; von Lent, *Schediasma*, 54–56; Eisenmenger, *Entdecktes Judenthum*, 2:666, 671; Müller, *Greuel der falschen Messien*, 16. Presumably also in Weidner's unidentified list; cf. above, 201n23. The reference to Christiani, *De Messia*, who names Lemlein alongside other false Messiahs, I owe to Yaacov Deutsch. Schudt, *Jüdische Merckwürdigkeiten*, pt. 2, bk. 6, chap. 27, *57–58 (new pagination from chap. 25), even finds in Lemlein's name a synonym for a certain churlish ne'er-do-well, *Lümmel* ("Lemmel")

in German. Cf. Grimm, *Wörterbuch*, 12:742, 1290. Significantly, by contrast, many of the lists fail to mention David Re'uveni and Solomon Molkho, as in Buchenroeder, *Messias Juden-Post*; Schudt, *Jüdische Merckwürdigkeiten*.

109 Soldan, *Entdeckunge*, 579. See ShemR 25.12 (47b). The figure of speech is explained by a complementary close in music, whereby the melody falls from the sixth pitch level (designated *la* in the solmization scheme) to the third (*mi*), producing a mournful mood; see Grimm, *Wörterbuch*, 12:83.

110 Ibn Yaḥya, *Shalshelet ha-kabbalah*, 103.

111 Aescoly, *Messianic Movements*, 271, 331, and Necker, "Brennende Landschaft," 56, both consider the information as a fictitious addition. By contrast, see Carlebach, *Divided Souls*, 74; Lenowitz, *Jewish Messiahs*, 99.

112 This paragraph is based on an unpublished seminar paper by Lucia Raspe, which the author has generously made available to me; Raspe, "Schalschelet ha-Kabbalah," esp. 22–23.

113 Ibn Yaḥya, *Shalshelet ha-kabbalah*, 262. Here, ibn Yaḥya leans on Usque, *Consolation*, 188; ibn Verga, *Schevet Jehuda*, chap. 6.

114 Usque, *Consolation*, 170–71.

115 Ibn Yaḥya, *Shalshelet ha-kabbalah*, 261.

116 Ibid., 260. There are, in fact, examples of conversions; in certain communities such as Trier and Regensburg, they are considerable in number. Jewish and Christian sources are unanimous, however, in attesting that the number of martyrs significantly exceeded the number of converts. See Toch, *Juden im mittelalterlichen Reich*, 56; Cohen, *Sanctifying the Name of God*, 4–5 et passim; Chazan, *European Jewry*, 99–136; Chazan, *In the Year 1096*, chap. 4; Haverkamp, *Hebräische Berichte*, 9–24. The Hebrew chronicles of the Crusades are edited and translated in Haverkamp, *Hebräische Berichte*.

117 Ibn Yaḥya, *Shalshelet ha-kabbalah*, 100–109, here 102.

118 Ibid.

119 Ibid., 102–3; see 109 on the burning of Solomon Molkho at the stake.

120 Ibid., 102.

121 Ibid., 103.

122 Only a few abbreviated messianic calculations are given there, e.g., from Molkho, without, however, naming their negative consequences. Any reference to Lemlein is also missing; RSL, Moskau, Ms. Günzburg 652 (= IMHM, F 44117), fol. 78r–79v.

123 Ibid., fol. 211r.

124 Thus Kitzingen, *Ḥag ha-pessaḥ*, fol. 27v (quoted in Tamar, "Asher Lemlein," 400); Sasportas, *Ẓiẓat novel Ẓvi*, 46–47; ha-Kohen, *Ma'aseh Tuviyah*, fol. 18r–v; *Me'ora'ot Ẓvi*, 72; JTS, New York, Ms. 2482 (= IMHM, F 28735), fol. 176r (Joseph of Damaskus, *To'ei ru'aḥ*); Sambari, *Divrei Yosef*, 267.

125 See chap. 1. Added to this was certainly also the generally very negative attitude toward conversion in Ashkenaz during the Middle Ages; on this point, see Carlebach, *Divided Souls*, chap. 1.

126 Gerson, *Jüden Thalmud*, 404; Buchenroeder, *Messias Juden-Post*, fol. 6v, 24v; von Lent, *Schediasma*, 55–56; Müller, *Greuel der falschen Messien*, 16.

127 Aemilius, *Widerlegung*, fol. 14v–15r.

128 Pfefferkorn, *Juden Spiegel*; reprinted in Kirn, *Bild vom Juden*, 230. This interpretation is also found in Carlebach, *Divided Souls*, 74, and Campanini, "Neglected Source," 95. The remark by Jost, *Geschichte des Judenthums*, 3:215n2, i.e., that the failed repentance led many communities in the Crimea to convert to Islam, is based on a misunderstanding. Jost bases his remark on ibn Yaḥya's report on Muslims in "Tauros" (in Jost: *Tauris*, the historical name of the Crimean Peninsula), who closed their shops on the Sabbath. Ibn Yaḥya dates the episode in 1500 and yet does not mention Lemlein in this context. No less speculative is the assertion by Graetz that the conversions of three other Jews from Germany and Italy, whom he names, also took place as a result of the Lemlein movement; Graetz, *Geschichte der Juden*, 69n2.

129 "Da aber das Jar umbher kommen ist . . . ists gleich geweßt darnach als dauor"; Aemilius, *Widerlegung*, fol. 14v.

130 "Hartte schwere penitencie des gleichen ir nit gelebet noch auch gelesen habt. Ach wie iemerliche wir betrogen sein!"; Pfefferkorn, *Juden Spiegel*, Nuremberg 1507, fol. 10r. Significantly, in the Low German and Latin editions (both Cologne, 1507), which were directed at a Christian readership, Pfefferkorn uses the personal pronoun in the second-person plural: e.g., in the second Low German edition (Cologne, 1508), "Ach, wie iemerlich wurdt *yr* betrogen!" Reprinted in Kirn, *Bild vom Juden*, 219 (my emphasis).

131 See Pfefferkorn, *Juden Spiegel*; reprinted in Kirn, *Bild vom Juden*, 227; Pfefferkorn, *In Lob und eer*, fol. 20v–21r (my pagination).

132 Pfefferkorn, *In Lob und eer*, fol. 3v–4r (my pagination).

133 In 1513, Pfefferkorn received an appointment as hospital administrator in Cologne, which he apparently held until his death (after 1521); Kirn, *Bild vom Juden*, 10.

134 It is true, of course, that in the tradition of Christian *adversus-judaeos* literature the Jews appear, above all, as a fictive readership, whereas the texts were, in fact, directed at Christians in order to confirm their beliefs about the negative mirror image of the Jews. See Frey, "Juden Spiegel"; Martin, *Johannes Pfefferkorn*, 47, 50, 62, 73–74, 81. Nevertheless, Pfefferkorn's texts are marked by his missionary experiences and therefore offer insights into his activity. On Pfefferkorn's writings during these years, see Martin, *Johannes Pfefferkorn*, chap. 2.

135 "Myn hertzallerliebsten bruder! . . . vberdenckt, das yr betrogen syt, wo blybt ewr messias?!" Pfefferkorn, *Juden Spiegel*; reprinted in Kirn, *Bild vom Juden*, 218.

136 Ibid., 219. In his second publication, *Iuden peicht* (The Jews' Confession), which seems by no means accidentally concerned with Jewish penance, Pfefferkorn attempts to discredit the usefulness of repentance itself for the Jews; cf. Aemilius above, 226n78.

137 Pfefferkorn, *Juden veindt*, fol. 10r (my pagination). On forbidding usury, see ibid., chap. 2. Already in *Juden Spiegel* Pfefferkorn appeals to the authorities to expel the Jews; reprinted in Kirn, *Bild vom Juden*, 222. The fundamental ambivalence between proselytizing among the Jews and anti-Judaism is something Pfefferkorn shares with the Christianity of his time; Oberman, *Wurzeln des Antisemitismus*, 43.

138 Pfefferkorn, *Juden Spiegel*; reprinted in Kirn, *Bild vom Juden*, 224–25.

139 See Carlebach, *Divided Souls*, 48, 178, on this practice.

140 At the same time, Maximilian obtained the opinions of experts. In his testimony, the humanist Johannes Reuchlin objected fundamentally to Pfefferkorn's intention and caused thereby dispute that increased in vehemence over the years and finally culminated in the *Epistolae Obscurorum Virorum* (Letters of Obscure Men). On the argument between the two parties, which was conducted with polemical writings and counter-writings, see Bartoldus, "Humanismus und Talmudstreit"; Rummel, *Case*; Martin, *Johannes Pfefferkorn*, chaps. 3–4.

141 See Carlebach, *Divided Souls*, 48–50. Adding to Pfefferkorn's aggression were certainly also the self-hatred of the convert and the contemporary mistrust of newcomers to Christianity, which often prompted the denunciation of one's former faith as proof of one's sincerity. See Frey, "Juden Spiegel," 178–80.

142 "Vngezweiyfelt nach solcher handlung wurden sy ain andernn sin vnnd gemüt an sich nemen. vnnd also bekant werden zuverlassenn yr falschheit vnnd nachuolgen der warhidt vnnsers glaubens"; Pfefferkorn, *Juden veindt*, fol. 10r (my pagination).

143 "Auch andern frunden durch seyn tzuraytzung den Judischen yrthumb verlassen vnd den Cristen gelawben an sich genommen"; Pfefferkorn, *In Lob und eer*, fol. 3v (my pagination).

144 Loewinger, "Recherches," 35, with quotation from Eccles. 1:14.

145 Ibn Yaḥya, *Shalshelet ha-kabbalah*, 103.

146 "Es ist unser grossen sunden schult"; Victor von Carben, *Hier inne wirt gelesen*, 94 (my pagination). Cf. also the sociological field study on the reaction patterns of religious groups to the failure of apocalyptic expectation; Festinger, Riecken, and Schachter, *When Prophecy Fails*. One possible reaction is the persistence in believing in prophecies after their obvious failure or even an intensified sense of mission; Festinger, Riecken, and Schachter, *When Prophecy Fails*, esp. 1–33, 230–37.

147 Gans, *Zemah David*, 137. On Eliezer Treves, see Brüll, "Geschlecht der Treves," 105–6; Horovitz, *Frankfurter Rabbinen*, 22–24. In accordance with this, Mordechai Dato writes retrospectively in Italy, "My heart tells me that it was not this matter alone," i.e., a failed attempt to bring about the end. For him the events had a deeper meaning in the cosmic perspective: they were part of the redemption process, which occurs in sixty-year cycles; Dato, *Migdal David* (quoted in Tishby, *Messianism* [Hebr.], 73n226). Cf. Jacobson, *Along the Paths*, 168–69n172.

148 This conjecture has frequently been expressed; Tishby, *Messianism*, 280n25; Roth, *History*, 191; Roth, *Venice*, 74. Idel, *Messianic Mystics*, 134, 142, 151, connects Lemlein with the later activity of the kabbalist Abraham ha-Levi in Jerusalem and Solomon Molkho. See, recently, Benmelech, *Shlomo Molkho*, 164–70, on Lemlein's influence on Molkho.

149 See Zimmer, "Collaboration," 74, according to which the family came to Germany from Italy no later than the beginning of the sixteenth century.

150 Monday and Thursday are the traditional days of fasting in Judaism; Elbogen, *Jewish Liturgy*, 68–69.

151 This prayer and penance movement was presumably inspired by Abraham ha-Levi, in whose apocalyptic thinking prayer and repentance played a prominent role. He

introduced special prayers and night vigils to ease the birth pangs of the Messiah, whom he expected in either 1530 or 1531; Robinson, "Messianic Prayer Vigils," 39–40. By contrast, Graetz, *Geschichte der Juden*, 512n5; Klausner, "Movement"; and Zimmer, "Collaboration," 82–83, erroneously connect the awakening portrayed by Treves with the appearance of Molkho. But the "holy writings" in question are presumably letters, not manuscripts of Molkho; see Brüll, "Geschlecht der Treves," 105.

152 "שנת רצ"א בא אלי מכתב מבני יקירי הר"ר אליעזר טריוש יצ"ו אשר העתיק כתבי" קדש הובאו מקא"פו לק' 'בודקו ומשם 'קרקוב אשר בני הנ"ל דר שם ע"ד הגאולה כי התחילה וכבר החילו בני ברית עם קדש ירושלים עד שלוניקי תקנו תעניות ותשובה בה"ב בכל שבוע וסדרו בכל קהל וקהל לפחות עדה מנין אחת להתפלל גם הנשים ישפכו לבם בצום וז"ל ובמזמור ה' אל באפך תוכיחני הש"צ יכוין לשם היוצא ממנו "והאריך מאד בסדר התשובה אין עת להאריך עב"ל; Treves, *Dikduk tefillah*, fol. 78r. On this work, see Zimmer, "Collaboration," 75–76. On Naphtali Hirtz Treves, see Zimmer, "Collaboration," 74–79, 84–86; Horovitz, *Frankfurter Rabbinen*, 28–30, 32, 35, 271–72, 278. On the *taḥanun*, the last part of the morning prayer, see Elbogen, *Jewish Liturgy*, 66–72.

153 This anonymous portrayal is edited by [Kracauer], *Jüdischer Bericht*, 427. The quoted passage is missing from Kracauer's translation of the Hebrew text. Over the course of the next two years, as Schweinfurt was besieged multiple times, the Jews in Frankfurt likewise set days of fasting on every Monday and Thursday and spoke the selihot and *taḥanunim*. On the siege of the two cities, see Kracauer, *Geschichte der Juden*, 1:302–8.

154 Wetzlar, *Libes Briv*, 64–65 (Yid.); 111–13 (Engl.). On Wetzlar and his Yiddish social critique, *Libes briv* (Love Letter), see Faierstein, "Liebes Brief"; Rohrbacher, "Isaak Wetzlar in Celle"; most recently, Voß, "Love Your Fellow as Yourself." A new critical edition with a historical introduction and commentary is Aptroot and Voß, *Libes briv*.

155 See Berliner, *Einheitsgesang*, 14–16; Elbogen, *Jewish Liturgy*, 72; Davidson, *Thesaurus*, 3:485, no. 1676.

156 Wetzlar, *Libes Briv*, 65 (Yid.); 113 (Engl.).

157 Ibid., 69 (Yid.); 117 (Engl.).

158 Feidel (Feiel, Feit) zum Esel is documented as having been in Frankfurt from 1550 to 1560. It is presumed that he died in 1561, the year in which there is first mention of his widow. In 1554, he appears as a rabbi, when he is accused by Israel zum Engel of having cast a spell on him; Institut für Stadtgeschichte, Frankfurt am Main, Rechneiamt, Bücher 398, Diurnalia 1550–1555, 1554, fol. 31v–32r and an inserted page (separate page numbering according to year); Andernacht, *Regesten*, no. 944. I wish to thank Wolfgang Treue for the identification of the name.

159 [Kracauer], *Jüdischer Bericht*, 427. From this source we know that Mannes died sometime between 1552 and 1554. It is possible that the man in question here is Gershom b. Jacob Israel, called Mannes Bek, who is listed among the appointed rabbis and heads of the rabbinical court of the Worms community. I wish to thank Ursula Reuter for this reference. The list can be found in the Worms *Memorbuch*, reprinted in Berliner, *Hazkarat neshamot*, 5. On the question of the identification of this person,

see also the introduction by Peles in Kirchheim, *Customs*, 29n5, who dates, without evidence, the period of Mannes's appointment to 1512–36. In 1512, Mannes is named as an assessor in the rabbinical court; GJ III.2, 1680, no. 9. The so-called R. Mannes Mahl, a feast that was held in Worms on the second to last evening before a wedding and that involved the relatives of the bridal couple and prominent members of the community, may have been named for this same Mannes; Yuspa Shammes, *Minhagbuch*, no. 229. On the siege of Worms, see Boos, *Geschichte der rheinischen Städtekultur*, 4:309–17.

160   Elbogen, *Jewish Liturgy*, 70; Davidson, *Thesaurus*, 1:35, no. 708.

161   Exod. 15:1–18 (given in the source as פרק השירה). See Elbogen, *Jewish Liturgy*, s.v. "Song of the Sea." Drawing children into this ritual reflects a literal enactment of Ps. 8:3: "From the mouth of infants and sucklings You have founded strength on account of Your foes, to put an end to enemy and avenger." I wish to thank Elisabeth Hollender for bringing this to my attention. There are other examples of the special role of children in Jewish ritual. On their function on Simchat Torah, where the children as a group are called up to the Torah and blessed, see Yaari, *Simḥat torah*, 160–65; on the ceremony of the Hollekreisch, in which a baby is given a non-Jewish name, see, e.g., Baumgarten, *Mothers and Children*, 93–99.

162   See chap. 3.4.

163   [Kracauer], *Jüdischer Bericht*, 427.

164   Aescoly, *Messianic Movements*, 340–42, 365–67.

165   See below, p. 90.

166   On his relationship with Molkho, see Aescoly, *Story*, 167 (Hebr. numbering).

167   See ibid., 53–59, 90–99 (Hebr. numbering). A collection of the letters is to be found in Aescoly, *Messianic Movements*, 338–40, 362–67. On their connection to Re'uveni, see chap. 3.2.

168   "בזאת ג״ב נעשה שנת ר״ס מיהודי אחד ששמו לימלן: ואולי בעת אחר א״י״ה אתן לאורה" "כל אותו המעשה עם ענין ר' דוד שביומי גם משום פלאותיו נשרף"; Isaac, *De Astrologia*, fol. 37v–38v (Hebr.); 38r (Lat., my pagination). The marginalia refers to Maimonides's report on a Jew in Yemen, who in the twelfth century had announced the imminent advent of the Messiah (cf. Maimonides, *Epistle to Yemen*, xiv–xviii). Clearly, Isaac never followed through on his announcement, however: at the end of the seventeenth century, Johann von Lent lamented that such a work "is not yet to be seen either in print or in manuscript" (quam videre sive editam, sive nondum impressam, hactenus non licuit); von Lent, *Schediasma*, 56. On Isaac, see Carlebach, *Divided Souls*, esp. 60–61; Fraenkel-Goldschmidt, "Periphery," 627–35.

CHAPTER 3

1   See Talkenberger, *Sintflut*, 235–39. Drummers and pipers played an important role in the peasants' struggle against the authorities; Wohlfeil, "Bauernkrieg," 57.

2   The Hebrew text is reprinted in Roth, "Abraham Zacut," 447–48, here 448; later in part in Aescoly, *Messianic Movements*, 334–35. The planetary conjunction of 1524 was

the subject of more than a hundred publications, many of which gave it an apocalyptic interpretation; Smoller, "Apocalyptic Calculators."

3 *Gesprech*; reprinted in Clemen, *Flugschriften*, 1:387–422. On the dating at January or February, see Clemen, *Flugschriften*, 1:376–77. On this pamphlet, see also Kaufmann, "Flugschriftenpublizistik," 448–55.

4 "Vnnßer Messiah werd kommen dann es bedeut etwas der Rumor vnter euch"; Clemen, *Flugschriften*, 1:397–98.

5 "Ya die letzt zukunfft vnßers Christi hoffen wir do mit er richten wirt die welt/ vnd den hymelischen ewigen tempel beschlissen"; ibid.

6 See, e.g., Aescoly, *Messianic Movements*, 433.

7 Ben-Sasson, "Reformation," 257–70, 313–15. On Jewish reactions to the Reformation, see also Ben-Sasson, "Disputation," 385–89; Schreiner, "Jüdische Reaktionen"; Cohen, "Martin Luther"; David, "Lutheran Reformation"; Bodian, "Reformation."

8 The Jewish interlocutor in Güttel, *Strafen und Plagen*, confirms that he himself and other Jews had, in fact, read Luther's text; preserved in the microfilm collection of Köhler, *Flugschriften*, no. 1990, fol. 20r (my pagination).

9 "Sie haben mit den Juden gehandelt, als weren es hunde und nicht menschen, haben nichts mehr kund thun denn sie schelten und yhr gutt nehmen"; reprinted in WA 11:314–36, here 315. On Luther's much-debated stance toward the Jews and Judaism, see, most recently, Kaufmann, *Luther's Jews*; Kaufmann, *Luthers "Judenschriften"*; Kaufmann, "Luther and the Jews." Further important studies include Bienart, *Luther und die Juden*; Kremers, *Die Juden und Martin Luther*; Lewin, *Luthers Stellung zu den Juden*; Maurer, "Zeit der Reformation."

10 "Blut freund, vettern und bruder unsers hern . . . Will man yhn helffen, so muss man nicht des Babsts, sonder Christlicher liebe gesetz an yhn uben und sie freuntlich annehmen"; WA 11:315, 336.

11 "Sy trösten sich yetz zumal gar vast/ das sy etlich Christen ain zeyther etwas freundtlich gegen ynen erzeiget/ vnd mer gemainschafft mitt yhnen/ auch das sie yetz an etlichen orten offentlich handlen/ vnnd wandlen dürffen/ da sy vorzeytten gar nicht hin gedurfft haben/ vnd dergleychen geschickt ynen yetzung vil guthait/ die ynen vorzeytten seltzam gwesen wer/ darauß volgt aber/ das sy nur destermer Cristum vnd alle die jm anhangen verfluchen vnd verachten"; Margaritha, *Gantz Jüdisch glaub*, fol. 97r; cf. fol. 61v (my pagination). Such a reception of the Reformation possibly even led to messianically motivated Jewish proselytizing work among Christians; see Kaufmann, "Theologische Bewertung," 201–2; Detmers, *Reformation und Judentum*, 81–82. In any case, as Luther reports in *Wider die Sabbather*, numerous Judaizing Christians in Moravia had had themselves circumcised in 1532, after having been seduced by Jews into the belief that the Messiah had in truth not yet come; reprinted in WA 50:312–37, here 312. See, by contrast, Brecht, *Martin Luther*, 332–35.

12 See Ben-Sasson, "Reformation," 285–93, 315; Ben-Sasson, "Disputation," 385–87; David, "Lutheran Reformation," 126–30. Beyond Luther's immediate area of activity, however, a positive evaluation of the Reformation was retained; see Ben-Sasson, "Reformation," 258–60, 273–85; David, "Lutheran Reformation," 130–39.

13 Van Dülmen, *Reformation als Revolution*. On Müntzer in particular and the Münster Rebellion, see the references chap. 1, nn76–77.

14 On Hut, see the significant study by Seebaß, *Müntzers Erbe*.

15 Clasen, *Anabaptism*, 157–60.

16 On Hoffmann, see Deppermann, *Melchior Hoffmann*.

17 The most important study on Re'uveni and Molkho remains the annotated source collection by Aescoly, *Story*; based upon this, Aescoly, *Messianic Movements*, 273–301, 357–436. See also the introduction to Sestieri, *David Reubeni*. An overview is given in Eliav-Feldon, "Invented Identities," 209–18; Lenowitz, *Jewish Messiahs*, 103–23; Silver, *Messianic Speculation*, 145–50. See also chaps. 3.1 and 3.5.

18 "Klaine Hebreische vnd teutsche büchlin"; Margaritha, *Gantz Jüdisch glaub*, fol. 98r (my pagination).

19 For a summary of the legend of the Ten Tribes with comprehensive references to source materials and other scholarship, see Ben-Amos and Noy, *Folktales*, 450–72. The most recent study on the Lost Tribes is by Ben-Dor Benite, *Ten Lost Tribes*. On the historical fate of the northern tribes, see Barmash, "History and Memory."

20 Yuval, *Two Nations*, 35. Cf. above, p. 28.

21 Dan, *Hebrew Story*, 54–55. The two most important classic studies and textual editions on Eldad ha-Dani are Epstein, "Eldad ha-Dani," and Müller, "Recensionen." See, more recently, Perry, *Eldad's Travels*; Morag, "Linguistic Examination"; Loewenthal, *Eldad il Danita*. English translations of Eldad's travel report can be found in Adler, *Jewish Travellers*, 4–21.

22 "Kommen auß dem Landt hinterm Fluß Sambation . . . mit dem Stamm Ephraim/ Manasse/ Benjamin vnd einem Theil der Kinder Gad . . . / sich zu Feld begeben/ den König zu Edom/ den Gog vnd Magog angreiffen/ das ist/ das Römische Reich/ den Keyser vnd Türcken/ tilgen vnd verwüsten"; Fabronius, *Bekehrung der Jüden*, 47–48.

23 See Kaufmann, "Rumour," 503; Perry, "Imaginary War," 21.

24 "Die Roten iuden weren langst komen vnd hetten vns erlost"; Victor von Carben, *Hier inne wirt gelesen*, 36 (my pagination). Cf. Margaritha, *Gantz Jüdisch glaub*, fol. 98r (my pagination). On the Jewish hopes that in the thirteenth century were connected with the onslaught of the Mongols, who were believed to be the Ten Tribes, see Yuval, "Messianic Expectations"; Yuval, *Two Nations*, 284–88; Menache, "Tartars." In addition, see also Breslau, "Juden und Mongolen."

25 "Die selben iuden sint die Roten iuden vnd starcken. Welcher so vyl mer dan aller Cristen in der gantzer cristenheyt synt als vyl ytzo Ewr cristen mer dan vnser sint als ir dan wol mercken mugt. . . . Dar by ist wol zu mercken wie groß der menig der x. geslecht seyn muß . . . die vnß noch wol konnen helffen. Vnd vns vß vnser gefengknis erledigen werden"; Victor von Carben, *Hier inne wirt gelesen*, 35 (my pagination). The idea that the Ten Tribes would take revenge on Christians for the Jewish blood that had been spilled existed also outside the German-speaking areas; see Perry, "Imaginary War," 21–22.

26 On the Christian version of the Red Jews, see Gow, *Red Jews*. On late medieval Christian cognizance of the Jewish concept regarding the apocalyptic function of the Ten Tribes, see Perry, "Imaginary War," 20.

27 This equation spread in the West via the extremely influential Latin translation of
Pseudo-Methodius (ca. 700); Gow, *Red Jews*, 25; Anderson, *Alexander's Gate*, 49–50.
The standard edition remains Sackur, *Sibyllinische Texte*, 59–96, here 72–75. See,
more recently, the comprehensively introduced and annotated edition by Aerts and
Kortekaas, *Pseudo-Methodius*; English translation by Garstad, *Apocalypse of Pseudo-
Methodius*. On the textual transmission, see in detail Anderson, *Alexander's Gate*,
chap. 2. See also Cary, *Medieval Alexander*; Ross, *Alexander Historiatus*. An English
translation of the Alexander story comes from Stoneman, *Alexander Romance*.

28 Victor von Carben, *De vita et moribus Judaeorum*, fol. 78r (BnF, A–2963 [5]); quoted
according to Margolin, "Bibliothèque de Postel," 128.

29 "Das nimptt mich aber groß wunder/ warumb man dise zehen geschlecht die rotten
Juden haist"; Margaritha, *Gantz Jüdisch glaub*, fol. 98r (my pagination); first instanti-
ated in Victor von Carben, *Hier inne wirt gelesen*, 36 (my pagination). Gow, in contrast,
reads the use of the term in these convert writings as a mere reception of the Christian
expression; Gow, *Red Jews*, 136. For the Middle Ages and the early modern period, he
erroneously restricts the notion of the Red Jews to the Christian world and sees the
Jewish usage beginning only in the eighteenth century; Gow, *Red Jews*, 139, 186–87.
I discuss the emergence of the Red Jews in Old Yiddish in detail in Voß, "Entangled
Stories."

30 A connection was already suspected by Zfatman, "Iggrot," 249n35. Note that in Old
Yiddish the moniker "Ten Tribes" also continued to occur; see, e.g., the Yiddish translation of Eldad ha-Dani, first Constantinople 1668; Yidls, *Gliles erets Yisroel*.

31 See Raspe, "Vom Rhein nach Galiläa," 438. On Ashkenazic piyyut commentary, see
Hollender, *Piyyut Commentary*. On the link with the piyyut, see also below.

32 The manuscript, which originated in Italy, is reprinted in Yassif, "Early Versions,"
here 218.

33 Cf. Zfatman, *Yiddish Narrative Prose*, 30n9. The printing is mentioned in the book
lists of the Jews of Mantua, which was compiled by the ecclesiastical censor in 1595;
see Romer-Segal, "Yiddish Literature," 783, 788n25; Baruchson, *Books and Readers*,
156. On these lists, see also Simonsohn, "Books and Libraries."

34 Cf. Zfatman, *Marriage*, 24n27. The type of hagiographic legend in which the narrative
of the Red Jews here appears typically involves a three-step process of transmission:
oral material is first written down in the context of religious liturgy, before later being
detached from this context and transmitted independently. See Raspe, *Jüdische Hagiographie*, 192–96.

35 "Terra russorum iudeorum inclusorum inter montes caspios"; Biblioteca Apostolica
Vaticana, Cod. Pal. lat. 1362 b. On the Jewish tribes in cartography, see Gow, "Gog
and Magog."

36 In the time of the Mongolian onslaught in Europe, Meshullam de Piera of Spain composed a poem, "On the Rumors of Our Enclosed Brothers" (הגנוזים); Shirmann,
Ha-shirah ha-ivrit, 317–18, n. 350, here 317; Epstein, "Messianic Movement," 218. A
letter in the Cairo Genizah (likely from Sicily in the early fifteenth century) expresses
a similar hope for rescue by "the enclosed ones" (הגנוזים); Mann, *Texts and Studies*,

1:34–44, here 43; reprinted in Aescoly, *Messianic Movements*, 308–11. On the contested dating of the text, see especially Aescoly, *Messianic Movements*, 264 (with note by Idel, 266–67n30); Aescoly, "Sicily." See, recently, Zeldes, "Magical Event"; Yuval, *Two Nations*, 286–87. On the expression "enclosed Jews," see also Farissol, quoted in Neher, *Jewish Thought*, 132.

37 In later versions of *Sefer Yosippon*, which contains *Ma'aseh Alexandros*, the Ten Tribes found their way into the narrative of Alexander's journey into the Land of Darkness, known in these texts as the "Mountains of Darkness"; see the Mantua edition of 1480. This change is likely influenced by rabbinical pronouncements concerning Alexander, in which he is associated with the Mountains of Darkness, as, e.g., BerR 33.1 (ed. Theodor and Albeck, 301); Nikolsky, "Rechabites," 38. Already BamR 16.25 (71b) locates the Ten Tribes beyond the Mountains of Darkness. For the early modern period, see Zfatman, "Iggrot," 236; Victor von Carben, *Hier inne wirt gelesen*, 36 (my pagination); Gerson, *Jüden Thalmud*, 390, 404. *Ma'aseh Alexandros* is edited in Flusser, *Yossifon*, 1:461–91. On this text, see Flusser, *Ma'aseh Alexandros*. On the Hebrew tradition regarding Alexander, see also van Bekkum, "Medieval Hebrew Versions."

38 "Berg Caspij verschlossen gog magog"; "das rot mer da die rotten iuden in"; Rüst, *Mappa mundi*.

39 Yidls, *Gliles erets Yisroel*, 85.

40 "Die rotten Juden stellen am freytag vil söck mitt pfeffer an das port dises wassers/ so komen dann die Haiden an den Sabbath vnd pringen alls vil korn an die stat"; Margaritha, *Gantz Jüdisch glaub*, fol. 98r–v (my pagination). The same in Gerson, *Jüden Thalmud*, 390. Accordingly, Abraham Farissol reports that the Jewish tribes by whom David Re'uveni had been sent lived by the spice trade; Aescoly, *Story*, 152–55. The motif of trade is already present in the Eldad ha-Dani tradition; see Bin Gorion, *Born Judas*, 5:32–35.

41 "Am Sabbath/ sey er gantz stille/ da führen die benachbarte Christen vnd Heyden den verschlossenen Juden/ wie sie genent werden/ Speise zu/ jhnen die zu verkeuffen/ dieweil aber die Juden auff den Sabbath nicht reisen dürffen"; Fabronius, *Bekehrung der Jüden*, 48.

42 Yidls, *Gliles erets Yisroel*, 87.

43 Ibid., 84. Eldad ha-Dani had already reported on the affluence of the Lost Tribes, claiming his tribe lived "where there is gold" (Gen. 2:11); Epstein, "Eldad ha-Dani," 38.

44 "וגם אנכי הכותב שמואל זנוויל ראה ראיתי בעיר לינץ ... אויז שרייאר שהיה על חנתו צנצנת שהיה בו חול ואבני' קטנים מנהר סמבטיון והיה החול והאבני' מגלגלי' ומרקדין וביום השבת היה שובת ונח"; Bodleian Library, Oxford, MS Mich. 121 (= IMHM, F 19963), fol. 249r, in the marginalia. See also Carlebach, "Endtime," 331.

45 See Augusti, *Geheimnisse*, 15–18.

46 See, e.g., Abraham Yagel in *Be'er Sheva*, quoted in Neubauer, "Where Are the Ten Tribes?," 411; Menasseh ben Israel, *Hope of Israel*, 136–37. Schudt, *Jüdische Merckwürdigkeiten*, pt. 2, bk. 6, chap. 34, 262, transmits a parallel Christian legend regarding a mill whose wheel stands still on Sundays and cannot be moved even with force.

47 Yidls, *Gliles erets Yisroel*, 85.

48 Benjamin's report is edited in Adler, *Itinerary*; that of Petahya in Grünhut, *Rundreise*. English translations in Adler, *Jewish Travellers*. On Eldad, see 236n21. Steinschneider, *Jüdisch-deutsche Literatur*, no. 154, names a German edition of Benjamin of Tudela, Amsterdam, 1691 (reprint Frankfurt, 1711).

49 The Latin and German versions are edited in Zarncke, *Priester Johannes*; Wagner, *Epistola presbiteri Johannis*; the Hebrew versions in Ullendorf and Beckingham, *Hebrew Letters*. Deserving special mention among the extensive literature on Prester John are Bejczy, *Lettre du Prêtre Jean*; Beckingham and Hamilton, *Prester John*; Knefelkamp, *Priesterkönig Johannes*; Ramos, *Essays in Christian Mythology*. On the textual relation between the traditions of Eldad and Prester John, see Perry, "Imaginary War." By contrast, see Wasserstein, "Eldad ha-Dani."

50 Aescoly, *Messianic Movements*, 336–50; Gross, "Expulsion"; Gross, "Rumors and Investigations." On the location of the Ten Tribes in various parts of the world, see Ruderman, *World of a Renaissance Jew*, chap. 11; Neher, *Jewish Thought*, 119–48; Greenberg, "American Indians"; Katz, *Philosemitism*, chap. 4; Pollak, "Revelation." For Christians, see also Rogers, *Quest for Eastern Christians*, 185–93.

51 David, *Chronicle*, 27, no. 19.

52 *Von ainer grosse meng vnnd gewalt der Juden die lange zeyt mit vnwonhafftigen Wüsten beschlossen vnd verborgen gewesen/ Yetzunder auß gebrochen vnd an tag kommen seyn*; Köhler, *Flugschriften*, no. 2636. Different versions are reprinted in the appendix to Gow, *Red Jews*, 266–69 (English translation, 269–72); Clemen, *Flugschriften*, 1:342–44 (erroneous pagination; actually 442–44); Scheiber and Tardy, "Echo," 599–601. On the different printings, see Gow, *Red Jews*, 148n58; 266n56; Kaufmann, "Flugschriftenpublizistik," 442n81.

53 "Ettliche Christen wissen auch viel von roten Jüden/ welche sie doch nicht gesehen haben/ zu reden/ daher dann der falscher wahn geschöpffet wird/ es könne der Messias noch wol aus dem Stamm Juda/ von den roten Juden gebohren werden"; Gerson, *Jüden Thalmud*, 391.

54 Gow, *Red Jews*, 269–70.

55 Kaufmann, "Flugschriftenpublizistik," 445, reads "Trient" and identifies the person named as Bernhard of Cles, bishop of Trent and chancellor of the Archduke Ferdinand.

56 Sanuto, *Diarii*, 35:105–6.

57 Kramer, *Vnderredung*; reprinted in Köhler, *Flugschriften*, no. 1988. A further edition from Halle an der Saale is reprinted with a short commentary in Clemen, *Flugschriften*, 1:323–40 (erroneous pagination; actually 423–40); in part, with an English translation, in the appendix to Gow, *Red Jews*, 255–58. In radically curtailed form also in the second edition of Victor von Carben's ethnography bearing the title *Juden Büchlein* (1550); reprinted and translated in Gow, *Red Jews*, 259–60. By contrast, the date given in Clemen, *Flugschriften*, 1:425n1 (December 2, 1523), does not, in my view, refer to the date of publication but rather to the date of the original conversation. Several things suggest an actual event behind the text: the precise enumeration

of the date, time, place, participants, and speech characteristics as well as, perhaps most importantly, the fact that the episode does not end with the Jew's conversion; see Kaufmann, "Flugschriftenpublizistik," 448n105. See also Kramer's preface, in which he claims he has "diesen Dyalogum nach geschryebett/ in weyße wie ergangen" (inscribed this dialogue the way it happened); Kramer, *Vnderredung*, fol. 1r.

58 "Von der landt art . . . auß dem alten testament"; Kramer, *Vnderredung*, fol. 1v–2r.

59 Ibid., fol. 5v. On the Jewish-Christian debate surrounding the interpretation of these verses, see Posnanski, *Schiloh*. See also Cohen, *Living Letters*, 30–35.

60 Kramer, *Vnderredung*, fol. 5v; translation according to Gow, *Red Jews*, 257.

61 Wagner, *Epistola presbiteri Johannis*, 361n41. The counter-historical construction was first recognized by Epstein, "Eldad ha-Dani," 15. Similarly, Perry, "Imaginary War," esp. 13–15. The convert Margaritha denies any historical truth whatsoever to the existence of a Jewish community beyond the Sambatyon: "I have questioned many well-traveled merchants and others, who know not at all how it should be possible that in twenty-two hundred years not a thing is known about such a great people and miraculous river" (Ich hab vil erfarne kauffleut vnd andere geforschet/ wissenn aber gar nicht daruon/ wie möcht es müglich sein/ das man in zwayvndzwaintzig hundert jaren nit etwas von solchem grossem volck vnd wunderbarlichen bach erfaren hett). The hope for the red redeemers is, he argues, a self-deception, since the Ten Tribes as a group had long ago ceased to exist. Partly they had assimilated themselves among the nations after having been led into exile by the Assyrians (for which reason they were likely to be found among the early Christians), and partly they had been absorbed into the southern kingdom of Judah; Margaritha, *Gantz Jüdisch glaub*, fol. 98v (my pagination).

62 "Daher desselbigen Lands Jüden genennt werden/ die Roten Jüden"; Joseph, *Gründlicher beweiß*, fol. 21v (my pagination).

63 "Durch die rothen Jüden verstehen sie sicherlich die Einwohner jenseits des Flusses Sambathjon, welchen sie diesen unter ihnen so hoch geachteten und prächtigen Namen beylegen, sowol wegen der rothen lebhaften Farbe ihres Angesichts, als der köstlichen Purpur-Kleidung, womit sie als ein freyes Volck herum giengen, um sie von allen andern in elende lebenden zu unterscheiden. [Anmerkung:] Die Europäischen, und Asiatischen Jüden dürffen keine rothe Kleider tragen, weil sie noch in trauer stehen, wegen des Tempels und der Stadt Jerusalem, die rothe Farbe ist bey denen Jüden ein Zeichen der Freyheit, wie auch der grösten Freudigkeit. Die Königlichen Kinder haben dieses zum voraus gehabt, daß man sie an dieser Farbe von andern hat pflegen zu unterscheiden. Die rothen Jüden hingegen sagen sie, haben kein Galuth, kein Chorban ausgestanden, d.i. keine Gefangenschaft, keine Verwüstung; diese Jüden kleiden sich in den schönsten Purpur, ihnen darf es niemand wehren"; Augusti, *Geheimnisse*, 27–29.

64 See, e.g., the standard dictionaries for modern Yiddish; Weinreich, *Dictionary*; Niborski and Vaisbrot, *Dictionnaire*. Even Simon Lazar, in his book promising to solve the riddle of the Ten Tribes (1908), restricts the expression erroneously to the Polish Jews; Lazar, *Ḥidot*, 79. See on the term "Red Jews" in Old Yiddish for the first time, Voß, "Entangled Stories."

65 Mendele, *Masoes Binjomin*; English translation by Frieden and Miron, *Tales of Mendele the Book Peddler*.

66 Funkenstein, "Counterhistory," 69. Funkenstein deploys the concept "counterhistory" for the first time in "Anti-Jewish Propaganda."

67 These older theories are cross-referenced in Lazar, *Ḥidot*, 79–80.

68 Brook, *Jews of Khazaria*.

69 Biale, "Counter-History."

70 Thus, Gow, *Red Jews*, 66–69, explains the name of the Red Jews. Of particular importance on the topic of color theory and symbolism, with further references to comprehensive scholarship, are two articles by Gage, "Colour in History" and "Color in Western Art."

71 Mellinkoff, *Outcasts*, vol. 1, chap. 2.

72 Mellinkoff, "Judas's Red Hair"; Mellinkoff, *Outcasts*, vol. 1, chap. 7.1. See also Pfeifer, *Etymologisches Wörterbuch*, 3:1442, s.v. "rot"; Grimm, *Wörterbuch*, 8:1296.

73 See Mellinkoff, "Judas's Red Hair," 32; people with red hair are seen as dangerous and warlike.

74 In the colored version of the procession of the Messiah as well (fig. 2), the Jews riding on the back of the messianic donkey are red-haired, a stark contrast to the blond heads of the Christians who ride on the tail.

75 The legend of the Sons of Moses is no invention of Eldad's but rather seems to have been common currency in his time among Jews in Islamic countries. The first textual evidence is, however, of Islamic origin; e.g., the Sons of Moses are mentioned in the Qur'an; Ben-Amos and Noy, *Folktales*, 455–56. On the tradition of *Bnei Moshe*, see also Ginzberg, *Legends*, 4:316–18; Lazar, "Aseret ha-shevatim"; Lazar, *Ḥidot*, 13–16, 74–77; Rubin, *Between Bible and Qur'an*, 26–30, 46–48, 50–52.

76 Weber, "Antichristfenster," 87.

77 See above.

78 So, too, the implicitly counter-historical definition in Yuval, *Two Nations*, 275.

79 Gen. 25:23.

80 On the early typology, see Yuval, *Two Nations*, chap. 1.2. On the later equation of Edom with Rome, see above, p. 28.

81 Rom. 9:6–13. For a comprehensive treatment of the Christian exegesis, see Simon, *Verus Israel*.

82 "And Esau said to Jacob, 'Give me some of that red stuff to gulp down, for I am famished'—which is why he was named Edom." Gen. 25:30.

83 "The first one emerged red, like an hairy mantle all over; so they named him Esau." Gen. 25:25.

84 See Schorsch, "Maoz Zur," 462.

85 MHG Ber 25.25 (ed. Margulies, 439). The discussion in *Sefer nizzaḥon (yashan)*, which arose at approximately the same time as the Christian representation of the Red Jews in Germany, identifies the Christians with red as the color of menstruation, hence of impurity; Berger, *Jewish-Christian Debate*, no. 238. I wish to thank Yaacov Deutsch for this reference.

86   See Cohen, "Esau as Symbol," 264n43.

87   "Doch bedünkt mich/ das durch dis wort/ Rote Juden/ sey angezeigt/ das sie Edom seien/ denn Edom heist rot"; Jonas, *Siebend Capitel Danielis*, fol. 15r. On the life and work of Jonas, see Delius, *Lehre und Leben.*

88   Similarly in Brenz, *Türcken Büchlein*, fol. 10r: "rotte Jüden/ das ist blut hunde vnd mörder" (Red Jews, i.e., blood hounds and murderers).

89   "Vielleicht von Edom/ odder jhrem Blutdorst. Darumb sind die Jüden in Europa jn heimlich günstig/ vnd hoffen/ sie wöllen durch sie frey werden/ vnd wider in jhr Land komen. Sie frewen sich auch wenn der Türcke auff ist/ wider die Christenheit/ vnnd hoffen/ denn sol der Christen Scepter hinweg genomen werden. Denn all jr Scribenten sagen/ dieweil die Edomitter das Scepter haben/ können sie nicht wider zu jhrem Reich kommen/ Also nennen sie aber vns Christen"; Nigrinus, *Jüden Feind*, 88–89.

90   Furthermore, the equation of the Ten Tribes with the impure peoples of the Alexander myth negates the Jewish representation of their life in paradisical holiness. On this point, see Yaniv, "Ha-ḥevrah ha-utopit," 281–82.

91   1 Sam. 16:12.

92   1 Sam. 17:42.

93   First in Rivkind, "Megillat"; taken up in Dan, "Hebrew Source"; Dan, "Hebrew Aqdamoth Story."

94   Elbogen, *Jewish Liturgy*, 257–58; Davidson, *Thesaurus*, 1:332, no. 7314. The text with English translation in Salamon, *Akdamus Millin*, 257–58. On Meir Shatz, see also Zunz, *Literaturgeschichte*, 145–52; Grossman, *Early Sages*, 292–96. On Meir Shatz as the hero of hagiographic tradition, see Raspe, "Vom Rhein nach Galiläa."

95   Raspe, *Jüdische Hagiographie*, 192, 195, argues that the attachment to a piyyut not only lent the narrative legitimacy but also ensured its regular recitation. Cf. Raspe, "Vom Rhein nach Galiläa," 437–38.

96   Baruchson, *Books and Readers*, 156. On the transmission of the text, see above, p. 84.

97   Bodleian Library, Oxford, MS Opp. 714 (= IMHM, F 20496); see Zfatman, *Yiddish Narrative Prose*, 19, no. 2ה. *Ma'aseh Akdamut* is edited synoptically with a later printing of 1694 Fürth in Rivkind, "Historical Allegory." For the Fürth edition, see Zfatman, *Yiddish Narrative Prose*, 66–67, no. 48. The date is incorrect in Zinberg, *Jewish Literature*, 177n16.

98   *Ayn sheyn vunderlikh mayse*, Fürth, 1694; *Mayse dos da heyst Megiles Rebe Meyer*, Amsterdam, 1660 (obviously a reprinting of the first edition from Cremona, also lost; see Zfatman, *Yiddish Narrative Prose*, 44–45, no. 23; Rivkind, *Megillat*, 508); *Ayn sheyn mayse dos iz die geshikhtnis fun Rebe Meyer. Un fun den rotn yudlayn. Un fun den shvarzn minkh*, Amsterdam, 1704; *Die geshikhtnis fun Rebe Meyer Shats un fun den rotn yudlayn un fun den shvartsn minkh*, [Amsterdam, 1805]; see Zfatman, *Yiddish Narrative Prose*, under *Megiles Reb Meyer.*

99   Synoptically edited with Bodleian Library, Oxford, MS Opp. 714 (= IMHM, F 20496) in Zfatman, "Iggrot," 228–47.

100 A detailed paraphrase is offered in Zinberg, *Jewish Literature*, 178–80. Beside *Akdamut*, another liturgical piece, *Shir ha-yiḥud li-vnei Moshe*, came to Europe,

according to legend, from the land beyond the Sambatyon; reprinted in Habermann, *Shirei ha-yihud*, 131–50. The authorship is attributed to the Sons of Moses themselves, who live beyond the Sabbath River: "היחודים שתקנום בני משה מעבר לנהר הובאו ומשם וסמבטיון"; Bodleian Library, MS Opp. 649 (= IMHM, F 17708 G), fol. 102r. Habermann (131–32) suggests a Sephardic origin of the song of unity and dates it in the seventeenth century. In fact, however, we are likely dealing here with an early Ashkenazic composition, since the first evidence is a later insertion between Yom Kippur and Sukkot in a Siddur manuscript of the western Ashkenazic rite from the early fourteenth century in Frankfurt am Main; Bodleian Library, MS Opp. 649 (= IMHM, F 17708 G), fol. 100v–102v. See Ta-Shma, "Machsor Vitri," 85, who, however, is not aware that the text in question is a later addition. The earliest manuscripts and printings of *Shir ha-yihud li-vnei Moshe* come entirely from Germany or northern Italy; Bodleian Library, Oxford, MS Opp. 712 (= IMHM, F 20523), fol. 243v–246r (without ending), as well as printed in Venice in 1600 and Hanau in 1620. Apparently, an earlier printing has been lost; see the final page of the 1600 edition from Venice. Steinschneider, *Catalogus*, nos. 2821 and 3319, mentions further Venetian printings from the seventeenth century. For later printings, see Davidson, *Thesaurus*, 2:74, no. 1658.

101 If not otherwise noted, I quote according to the printing Fürth 1694; Rivkind, "Historical Allegory," 20, 22, 24. See Jer. 31:8, which explicitly includes, among the remnant of Israel that will be gathered from the coasts of the earth, "the blind and the lame."

102 Zfatman, "Iggrot," 240.

103 1 Sam. 17:42. See 1 Sam. 16:12: "He was ruddy-faced, bright-eyed, and handsome."

104 David Kimhi on 1 Sam. 17:42. In the nineteenth century, Meir Löw (Malbim) interpreted David's redness explicitly as "not warlike"; *Mikra'ot gedolot*.

105 Rashi on Song of Sol. 5:10 and Lam. 4:7–8. For this reference, I thank Bernard Septimus.

106 The motif of a sorcery contest between a Jew hater and a Jew, whose victory rescues his people from a deadly menace, is widespread in Hebrew literature and has been documented in numerous variations. As Joseph Dan has shown, it appeared for the first time in Judah he-Ḥasid; Dan, "Sippurim demonologiyim," 288–89n29. Grözinger, "Jüdische Wundermänner," 202–3, counts sixteen versions over a time span of six hundred years. See also Dan, "Hebrew Source"; Dan, "Hebrew Aqdamoth Story."

107 1 Sam. 17:8–9.

108 Rivkind, "Historical Allegory," 16.

109 Ginzberg, "Haggadot ketu'ot," 44.

110 Rivkind, "Historical Allegory," 22, 24.

111 1 Sam. 17:44, in Yassif, "Early Versions," 223.

112 Yassif, "Early Versions," 223. Cf. 1 Sam. 17:46.

113 Rivkind, "Historical Allegory," 32. Cf. 1 Sam. 17:50. The contest of sorcery is described in detail in Rivkind, "Historical Allegory," 23–32. On the motif of the supernatural powers of the rescuers beyond the Sambatyon, see Yaniv, "Moshi'a,"

128. Already in the salvation story of the Exodus from Egypt, the enemy is harmed through the holy names: According to ShemR 1:29 (7b) Moses kills an Egyptian with the help of the name of God.

114 1 Sam. 17:25.

115 The structure of motifs from the story of David and Goliath appears also to have influenced the dream in *Ma'aseh Akdamut* through which a scholar in Worms, in his effort to find a suitable contender for the duel, first hits upon the idea of the Red Jews. In his metaphorical dream, a deep darkness brings misery and suffering over the world. One day, however, a bright star penetrates the darkness. A great bear appears, symbolizing the black magician, along with a little goat, symbolizing the little Red Jew. The two animals fight and the bear is killed (Rivkind, "Historical Allegory," 15–18). The selection of these two animals in particular to face off in the vicarious battle also appears to be grounded in the biblical story, in which David reassures Saul that, just as he has protected his master's flock by killing a lion and a bear, so too will he slay Goliath (1 Sam. 17:34–36).

116 See Ginzberg, *Legends*, 6:247n13.

117 2 Sam. 8:14.

118 Rivkind, "Historical Allegory," 20, with Obad. 1:21. On this designation of the Red Jews, cf. David, *Chronicle*, 27, no. 19.

119 On the Song of the Sea, see above, p. 73.

120 BerR 75.4 (ed. Theodor and Albeck, 882). Lazar, *Ḥidot*, 80, also adverts to the Midrash as the source for the Yiddish expression "Red Jews," albeit without being aware of the Christian counterpart. Lazar identifies the red avengers with the Ten Tribes and their equation with fire by virtue of an intratextual interpretation in bBB 123b: here it is written "that the descendants of Esau will only fall into the hand of the descendants of Joseph, since it is said, 'the House of Jacob shall be fire, and the House of Joseph flame, and the House of Esau shall be straw.'" See BerR 73.7 (ed. Theodor and Albeck, 851), with quote from Obad. 1:18.

121 LeqT 36.21–22 (ed. Buber, 185) with quote from 1 Sam. 16:12.

122 See Ginzberg, *Legends*, 6:247n13.

123 1 Sam. 16:12.

124 Rivkind, "Historical Allegory," 32. In the Midrash and esp. in liturgical poetry in Ashkenaz, God's garment is likewise red, namely, with the blood of those whom he destroys; see Yuval, *Two Nations*, 33, 97–98.

125 Rivkind, "Historical Allegory," 22.

126 BerR 97 (*shitah ḥadashah*) (ed. Theodor and Albeck, 1218).

127 See Dan, *Hebrew Story*, 55–57. See also Bin Gorion, *Born Judas*, 5:29–31.

128 Hill, "Antichrist." See also Bousset, *Antichrist*, 108–15; Emmerson, *Antichrist*, 79–80; Jenks, *Origins*, 77–79, 83–86, 183–84.

129 See Bousset, *Antichrist*, 115.

130 I quote from the English translation of an Ashkenazic version of *Toldot Yeshu* in Meerson and Schäfer, *Toledot Yeshu*, 1:170–74. A Hebrew edition is found in ibid., vol. 2. In both narratives one even finds the motif of a millstone, which both Yeshu and the

black magician employ for their tricks; ibid., and Rivkind, "Historical Allegory," 26. On the reception of *Toldot Yeshu* in Ashkenaz, see Carlebach, *Anti-Christian Element*, 13; as example of a classic counter-history, see Biale, "Counter-History."

131 Voluminous anti-Christian material is documented in Yiddish culture for the early modern period; see Carlebach, *Anti-Christian Element*. On further inversion narratives, see also Stow, "Medieval Jews on Christianity." Of interest in general on the concealed testimonies of oppressed groups, reflecting a quite different assessment of the situation than their official stance and thus offering a form of resistance, see Scott, *Domination*.

132 See Gow, *Red Jews*, 69–70.

133 Yassif, "Early Versions." *Ma'aseh Akdamut* was later translated multiple times into Hebrew; e.g. *Sefer ma'aseh gvurat ha-shem*, Lviv, 1916; redacted in *Sefer Akdamut*, Warsaw, 1902, 41–42. See Rivkind, "Megillat," 508. The title of the edition from Lviv, [1839], *Mayse gvures hashem* (see Rivkind, "Historical Allegory," 10, no. 5), suggests that it, too, was based on a lost Hebrew edition. In Hasidic circles, *Ma'aseh Akdamut* continues to be reprinted today in both Hebrew and Yiddish.

134 E.g., an exempla collection written in a Spanish hand from the seventeenth century, included in Gaster, *Exempla*, no. 369; an oriental manuscript collection from the eighteenth century, ibid., no. 445; a further manuscript collection from Italy in 1785, printed in Ginzberg, "Haggadot ketu'ot," 43–45, no. 4 (Hebr. numbering). For the reference to Gaster, I wish to thank Elisheva Schönfeld.

135 Menasseh ben Israel, *Hope of Israel*.

136 See Carlebach, *Anti-Christian Element*, 18.

137 Schwarz, *Stella Meshi'aḥ*, fol. 48v. On Schwarz, see Ocker, "German Theologians," 46–59; Walde, *Christliche Hebraisten*, chap. 4.

138 See Yagel's work *Be'er sheva*, preserved in manuscript; quoted in Neubauer, "Collections," 39. On Yagel's biography, see Ruderman, *Kabbalah, Magic, and Science*. Ruderman, *Kabbalah, Magic, and Science*, 13, dates the contact with the Gerson family at ca. 1576. Compare with the megillah, "welche man in Deutschland am Pfingsten recitire" (which one recites in Germany on Pentecost), already in Steinschneider, *Geschichtsliteratur*, 80, no. 91a.

139 The censor's lists note several copies in the possession of the Port (Katz) family; Romer-Segal, "Yiddish Literature," 788, no. 25.

140 Yerushalmi, *Zakhor*, 46–48.

141 Turniansky, "Megillas Vints," 126. The text is edited in Ulmer, *Turmoil, Trauma and Triumph*. On the place of Yiddish in the domestic liturgy, see Baumgarten, *Introduction*, chap. 9. Weinreich, "Internal Bilingualism," examines the failed attempt to introduce Yiddish liturgy in synagogue. See also Fishman, "On Prayer in Yiddish."

142 Contrary to the assumption of Rivkind, "Historical Allegory."

143 Raspe, "Vom Rhein nach Galiläa," 440–41; Raspe, *Jüdische Hagiographie*, 196n226. On the fasting days, see Zimmer, "Persecutions of 1096." Hoffman, "Akdamut," 171–73, has recently also placed the history of this piyyut in the context of the crusade persecutions. For Hoffman, the commemoration of 1096 explains the longevity of the piyyut in Ashkenazic liturgy, since this catastrophe actualized and thus

strengthened the comforting power of poetry for future generations, especially in light of its originary legend.

144 Yuval, *Two Nations*, 135–59. On this messianic-activist function of commemoration, cf. above, 214n66.

145 See above, p. 72.

146 Raspe, "Vom Rhein nach Galiläa," 447. Cf. Zunz, *Ritus*, 69; Fleischer, "Prayer and Piyyut," 75; Fraenkel, *Maḥzor shavu'ot*, 28 (Hebr. numbering), n. 167. On the Worms Mahzor, see Beit-Arié, "Worms Mahzor" (1985); Beit-Arié, "Worms Mahzor" (1993); Kogman-Appel, *Mahzor from Worms*. Facsimile edition *Worms Mahzor*.

147 Yuspa Shammes, *Minhagbuch*, 1:112; Kirchheim, *Customs*, 258.

148 Yuspa Shammes, *Minhagbuch*, 2:174.

149 Kirchheim, *Customs*, 258n8. Yuspa Shammes by contrast without mentioning reasons; see Epstein, "Wormser Minhagbücher," 289n6; Eidelberg, *Juspa*, 25–26.

150 Yuspa Shammes, *Mayse nissim*, Amsterdam 1696, fol. 31r: "עז איז איין מעשה גדרוקט זאגט אם שבועות דש מן אקדמות פון." The occasion of the reference is the motif of a wheel of fortune that appears both in Yuspa's narrative no. 22 and in *Ma'aseh Akdamut*; see the Hebrew translation by Eidelberg, *Juspa*, 86 (Hebr. numbering), missing in the English part.

151 Accordingly, in the manuscript of Yagel's *Be'er sheva*, the part in which the *Ma'aseh Akdamut* is retold is rendered largely incomprehensible by censorship; cf. Neubauer, "Where Are the Ten Tribes?," 411. By contrast, Raspe, "Vom Rhein nach Galiläa," 448, explains the absence of *Akdamut* in Worms liturgy by noting the general discontinuation of Aramaic piyyutim. The loss of the liturgical pegs also explains the absence, according to Raspe, of a Worms version of *Ma'aseh Akdamut* in the early modern period. Cf. Fleischer, "Prayer and Piyyut," 75.

152 In 1748, the convert Augusti of Thuringia published a collection of letters, under the title *Geheimnisse der Jüden von dem Wunder-Fluß Sambathjon, wie auch von denen rothen Juden* (Secrets of the Jews from the Miraculous Sambatyon River as Well as of the Red Jews), in which he claimed to have exchanged with his former fellow believers on the topic of the Red Jews; Augusti, *Geheimnisse*.

153 Zfatman, *Yiddish Narrative Prose*, 166, nos. 173, 174.

154 Friden and Miron, *Tales of Mendele the Book Peddler*, 333.

155 The fascinating role of the Red Jews and their vicissitudes in Jewish culture has thus far gone entirely unexplored. My monograph on the motif of the Red Jews in Jewish culture from the Middle Ages to today is forthcoming.

156 The Hildesheim chronicle of the cleric Johann Oldecop confirms the advance of the Red Jews in the summer of 1561; Euling, *Chronik*, 490: news from Constantinople reached Venice that the Red Jews, whom Alexander had enclosed in the mountains, had broken out, conquered Babylonia, and were now advancing toward the Holy Land, to all of which the Jew Lefman could supposedly testify. For this reference, I wish to thank Wolfgang Treue.

157 On the news of the conquests of the Ten Tribes in the Muslim East at the time of Shabtai Zvi, cf. Scholem, *Sabbatai Sevi*, 327–54.

158 Cf. Gow, *Red Jews*, chap. 6.5. Concurrently, Gow adverts to the biblical criticism of the reformers, which gradually led to the diminished credibility of the myth of the Red Jews. For another example of the revaluation of a millennial people's eschatological role, in this case the Mongols, see Schmieder, "Mongols."

159 "Es seint xij. geschlecht genßerhalb des meerß gewest in Egipten/ vnd nicht mehr dan eylffthalb geschlecht seint erüber komen im außgange"; Kramer, *Vnderredung*, fol. 5v, translation according to Gow, *Red Jews*, 257.

160 "Diesen vergangnen Sommer hatt Gott sie mit gnaden heym gesucht/ dan das wasser . . . diesen Sommer auff ein zeyt hatß angefangen auff den Saboth/ vnd acht tage in rugen gestanden/ So habenn die Propheten zum volcke gerufenn/ das sie sollen ansehen/ das sie Gott erlößen wollte/ drumb sollen sie außgehenn in das gelobtthe landt/ das yhn Gott versprochen hatte"; Kramer, *Vnderredung*, fol. 5v–6r, translation according to Gow, *Red Jews*, 257–58.

161 Re'uveni's travel report is edited in Aescoly, *Story*, 7–32. A sharply abbreviated English translation is accessible in Adler, *Jewish Travellers*, 251–328. The riddle of Re'uveni's true identity cannot be solved. On the basis of (in every case) very weak evidence, it is supposed that he came from the Arabian Peninsula, from the Land of Israel, from Yemen, from Ethiopia, from India, or, finally, from Europe. Shohat, "Notes," 70n1, summarizes these different points of view. See also Eliav-Feldon, "Invented Identities," 213, and, more recently, on Re'uveni's native language, Díaz Esteban, "Problemas."

162 Gow, *Red Jews*, 150, 152–53, points out that this representation might also have been influenced by the efforts of Charles V to form an anti-Turkish alliance with the Persian Shah, as well as by the rebellion of Mameluckes of Egypt against the Ottoman rulers.

163 On the two pamphlets (Kramer, *Vnderredung*, and *Von ainer grosse Meng*), see above, pp. 89–94. Rohrbacher and Schmidt, *Judenbilder*, 190, have previously suggested a historical source; later, Kaufmann, "Flugschriftenpublizistik," 444. Similarly, Scheiber and Tardy, "Echo," 595. By contrast, Gow, *Red Jews*, 142, 150, maintains that the pamphlets merely reproduce common images of the Red Jews. On the letters as a source for Re'uveni's activities, see also Cassuto, "David Reubeni."

164 Aescoly, *Story*, 19.

165 Ibid., 22–27.

166 Ibid., 26. Schubert, "Jenseits von Edom," draws attention for the first time to Re'uveni's alleged signs and wonders.

167 Cassuto, "David Reubeni," 353. On Abraham Raphael b. Azriel Trabot, see Frumkin, *Toldot*, 1:85.

168 The letter, which is preserved in a manuscript by the copyist of messianic texts, Judah de Blanis, has already been mentioned in connection with Lemlein's later writings (see above, p. 74). The text is reprinted in Neubauer, "Collections," 35–37; English translation in Lenowitz, *Jewish Messiahs*, 111–12. See relevant material in Cassuto, "David Reubeni"; Aescoly, "David Reubeni," 19–20; Aescoly, *Story*, 54–59, 93–100 (Hebr. numbering). Vogelstein and Rieger, *Geschichte*, 1:42, and Scheiber and Tardy, "Echo," 596–97, generally connect letters from Damascus to Jews in Hungary with

the appearance of Re'uveni. These letters, which were known to Sanuto (see above, p. 90), also report of the advance of the Ten Tribes.

169 Neubauer, "Collections," 36.

170 Ibid.

171 "Das er jn jr alt vnnd Vätterlich erblandt das ist terrapromissionis widerumb zuaygne wa aber nit/ Wöllenn sy das selb mit gewalt vnnd streyt selbst eynnemen"; *Von ainer grosse meng*, fol. 2r; English translation according to Gow, *Red Jews*, 270.

172 Cf. *Von ainer grosse meng*, fol. 3v.

173 "Ain grosse menge vnd macht der Juden Nemlich biß in die fünff oder sechß mal hundert Tausent inn das Egypten landt ankommen vnnd sich dafür Jherusalem xxx tag rayß weyt gelegert oder nydergeschlagen"; ibid., fol. 2r; translation according to Gow, *Red Jews*, 270.

174 Neubauer, "Collections," 36. The choice of Mount Hor is not accidental; this was a station on the Israelites' journey during the Exodus, just before they reached the Land of Canaan; Num. 33:37.

175 "Die weylls yrer vatter ist gewest vnnd von Gott yhn gegebenn, er wollte es yn verkauffen. darauf die Juden widder geantwort: Gott hett es yn gegeben, darumb wollten sie es nicht kauffen, sunder mit dem schwerdt gewyn"; Kramer, *Vnderredung*, fol. 6r; translation according to Gow, *Red Jews*, 258.

176 Aescoly, *Story*, 33–35. Beginning in the late Middle Ages, false diplomats from exotic lands had been appearing in Europe to offer Christian authorities aid against the Ottomans; see Schmieder, *Europa und die Fremden*, 73–180.

177 This assertion is found in the famous disputation with the convert Pablo Christiani in Barcelona; Eisenstein, *Ozar*, 88. Prior to Re'uveni, Abraham Abulafia had sought out the pope in messianic matters; see Idel, *Messianic Mystics*, 61–62. On the theme in rabbinical literature of the Messiah in Rome, see Berger, "Captive at the Gate of Rome."

178 Exod. 7:26.

179 Aescoly, *Story*, 33. On this point, see Schubert, "Jenseits von Edom."

180 Cf. Cohen, "Esau as Symbol," 245.

181 Thus, for the first time, Yerushalmi, "Messianic Impulses," 485–86n29. As Benmelech, *Shlomo Molkho*, chap. 2, has recently and convincingly demonstrated, Re'uveni did indeed seek to bring about the fall of Christendom in this way, leaning heavily thereby on the apocalyptic scenario laid out by the famous Abraham ha-Levi, who at that time was living in the Land of Israel. On the general influence of ha-Levi's prophesies on Re'uveni's messianic plan, see already Cassuto, "David Reubeni," 351–53.

182 "Der Keyser der Turcken/ vnd die rothen Juden yetzundt mit dem schwerdt vmb das gelobthe land fechten"; Kramer, *Vnderredung*, fol. 6r; translation according to Gow, *Red Jews*, 258. In the original German edition of this book, I quoted also another pamphlet with similar content, which I erroneously dated to 1524; cf. also Voß, "Jüdische Irrlehre," 10. Tardy and Scheiber, "Echo," 597, cite its correct year, 1574. This pamphlet, therefore, is not relevant to the present discussion.

183 The millenarians of the ancient church (esp. Irenaeus, Tertullian, Victorinus, and Lactantius) expected the literal fulfillment of Old Testament prophecy concerning

Israel in a kingdom of God on earth, at the center of which a new temple would stand in a new Jerusalem. They referred such utterances unambiguously to the millennial kingdom of Christ and by no means expected the return of the Jews to the Holy Land, much less the founding of a new Jewish kingdom. A single alleged exception in Heid, *Chiliasmus*, 55.

184 "Ja yr ist zu sechßmal hundermall tausent/ das byn ich gewyß"; Kramer, *Vnderredung*, fol. 5v–6r; translation according to Gow, *Red Jews*, 258.

185 "Jacob ich laße zu das yr Jherusalem widder vberkommet/ Aber ich laße nicht zu das yr das königkliche Cepter widder erlanget/ sunder die öberkeyt/ denn Turcken oder Christen bleyben wirdt. Dann die Heyden haben nyhe keinen Judischenn könig wollt habenn noch leyden/ sunder alwegen sich mit gewallt widder sie gesatzt. Allein von diesem Schylo/ oder Messias stehet geschrieben/ das yn die Völker vnd Heyden werden zufallenn"; Kramer, *Vnderredung*, fol. 6r; translation according to Gow, *Red Jews*, 258.

186 "Welcher könig ist auff erdenn ye so gewaldig/ vnd so angenem gewest/ an den die Heyden so hefttigklich geglaubtt hettenn/ alls ann den Judischenn könig Christum/ vmb welchs willen viel tausent Heydenn seindt gemartert"; Kramer, *Vnderredung*, fol. 6r.

187 "Jacobs knecht stehet auff satteln vnnd Jacob nymbt seynn abscheydt vom Pfarherr/ vnnd reytht"; ibid., fol. 6v.

188 "אם על ידי התשובה יהיה קבוץ גליותכם לעולם לא תגאלו מאחר אתם תמיד הייתם עם הערף הקשה ומורד"; Münster, *Vikku'aḥ*, 21 (my pagination). See Fagius, *Liber fidei*, 99, § 76 (Hebr.), 107, § 77 (Lat.). In my view, Münster, *Vikku'aḥ*, 16, even makes implicit reference to Re'uveni's audience with the pope in February 1524 by having the Jewish disputant claim that the redemption is imminent on the basis of the Messiah's approach to the pope.

189 A summary of the work's contents can be found in Williams, "Martin Cellarius," 479–86. On the doctrine of restitution, see Seifert, "Reformation und Chiliasmus," and, more recently, Schubert, *Täufertum und Kabbalah*, appendix 2. A biography of Cellarius is a desideratum. A brief overview can be found in Seifert, "Reformation und Chiliasmus," 478–79, and in Friesen, "Martin Cellarius." See also the bibliography in Backus, "Martin Borrhaus."

190 "... quae Israeli post Apostolos per Romanus in umbra contigerunt, Israeli secundum promissionem, in ueritate acciderunt." Cellarius, *De operibus Dei*, fol. 75v.

191 See ibid., fol. 83r: "Ita nunc restituendus, & ab aereo suo caelo & terra ferrea liberandus, eiusdem post tantam indignationem liberationem, successura benedictione maledictioni, gratia irae ignominia gloriae (sic!) praefigurabit, ut res semel respondeat, hoc est, simul de toto Israele ac semine Abraham secundum carnem dici possit, id quod de domo Iacob, quae uere domus Iacob est, dicitur, quod cum umbra non pugnat, nihil enim uetat esse secundum carnem & promissionem de semine Abraham. . . ." Ibid., fol. 86v: "Ut Israel, qui iam profugus & toto orbe dispersus . . . captiuitate Zion redempta, iuxta ceteros, in terram suam reducatur, ut hoc modo electorum resurrectionem, & a quattuor orbis angulis eorundem in regnum gloriae congregationem, quae in aduentu maiestatis futura est, praefiguret."

192 Cellarius was not the first to hypothesize on a consistent typological basis the restitution of a Jewish kingdom of Israel as precondition for Christian redemption. In the
fourteenth century, the Franciscan Jean de Roquetaillade espoused similar views; see
Lerner, "Millennialism," 353. On parallels in the late medieval period, see also Voß,
"Jüdische Irrlehre."

193 Reprinted in Krebs and Rott, Quellen, 118–21. Capito makes no explicit mention,
however, of Cellarius's doctrine of restitution. On the relation between Cellarius and
Capito, see Baum, Capito und Bucer, 280–82, 406–12.

194 On the origins of the manuscript, see Baum, Capito und Bucer, 406–12. Seifert, "Reformation und Chiliasmus," 239–41, offers a succinct summary. Unfortunately, an
investigation of Capito's Israel doctrine in its entirety does not at present exist; in lieu,
see Detmers, Reformation und Judentum, 269–72.

195 To sidestep the contradiction between the rejection of the external Israel and the
fulfillment of its prophecies, Capito assumes that the latter will only hold for those
Jews who are numbered among the elect ("Israel according to the inner covenant"):
"Caeterum Israel, id est, decem tribus, temetsi de semine Abrae, iuxta tamen exter-
nam faciem abdicatur, quod adimantur eis temporalia toties ex foedere promissa.
Vers 9. Et rursus in abscondito, per gratiam, constantißime assumitur, iuxta 10. uer-
sum, hoc est, qui electi sunt, et sine Deo egerunt in mundo, hactenus ad sensum
interni foedere pertinget. Ne quis putet internum foedus rescissum, quod in sempi-
ternum durabit, electio enim Dei immutabilis est." Capito, Commentarius, fol. 27v.

196 "Iam quia cum Israele, in figura omnia contigerunt, & contigent imposterum omnia
quae revera cum pijs & acta sunt & agentur, sequitur promißiones magnificas ei genti
factas, implendas esse, quo verae figurae ueritati certißimae, ut hactenus, quae tamen
hactenus impletae non sunt. Nam in illo populo peculiari, figura, ut dixi praefertur,
tanquam umbra ueritati. Augebitur igitir Israel post hanc diuturnam captivitatem et
figuralis ille populus, una cum gentibus, sed postquam plenitudo gentium intraverit,
ad regnum Christi concedet, numero maximo, sicut est harena maris innumerabilis."
Ibid., fol. 28r. Cf. Schubert, Täufertum und Kabbalah, 329.

197 Capito, Commentarius, fol. 79v: "Neque Israel secundum carnem qui est figura ex toto
salvus est, ut Israel verus secundum spiritum, qui in omnes gentes patet totus servari
Christoque annumerari posset, salvabitur autem externus Israel, ut figura veritati
praeluceat, et ut indicetur Israel in abscondito ex toto adimplendum Christo."

198 ". . . ad terram magno numero regressuri sint." Ibid., fol. 30v; cf. ibid., fol. 74r: "Hic
uides coniuncto Daniele esse tempus, quando Messiah regnet, & Iudaeus tamen car-
nalis, talem neque quaerat, neque agnoscat. Quod pariter documento est, regnum
Christi de hoc saeculo non esse. Tametsi Iudaei tempore Christi in terram quoque
Chananeam cum summa tranquillitate occupabunt, idque od (sic!) figuram ut alias
accuratius enarrabimus, pro modo fidei, & gloriae Dei, duce spiritu, & antea Martinus
Cellarius felicisissime expediuit."

199 ". . . terram suam libere possidebit, cum magno splendore." Ibid., fol. 269v.

200 ". . . in terram quoque Chananeam cum summa tranquillitate occupabunt." Ibid.,
fol. 74r.

201 The issue here was less the doctrine of restitution itself than the doctrine of the sacra-
ments, above all relating to the understanding of baptism. See Schubert, *Täufertum
und Kabbala*, 337–39; Williams, "Martin Cellarius," 491–97, 487–88. On the conflict,
see also Hobbs, "Monitio Amica." On Martin Bucer's hermeneutic criticism of Capito's "Jewish" understanding of the role of the Jews and of the Holy Land in Christian
eschatology, see Hobbs, "Bucer," 157–60.

202 "Vor der Auferstehung der Toten eitel Heilige, Fromme ein weltlich Reich haben";
Bekenntnisschriften, 72. That the article was not directed against the Augsburg Anabaptist Augustin Bader, as had been believed since Bossert, "Augustin Bader" (10),
341, but rather against Cellarius and Capito, was shown by Seifert, "Reformation
und Chiliasmus," 230–32. List, *Chiliastische Utopie*, 178n23, had already suspected
this, but without pursuing it further. By contrast, the not especially convincing thesis that the Lutheran confession of faith was directed against Jewish messianism,
and thus was a reaction to the activities of Re'uveni and Molkho; first in Kolde, *Älteste
Redaktion*, 55; subsequently *Bekenntnisschriften*, 72n3; Scholem, *Sabbatai Sevi*, 100;
Ruderman, "Hope against Hope," 308.

203 See Capito, *A nostre allie*. The treatise "An unsere Verbündeten und Bundesgenos-
sen, das Volk des Sinai-Bundes" is preserved only in a later French translation
appended to the Olivetan Bible; a facsimile reprint is found in Droz, *Chemins de
l'hérésie*, between 110 and 111. The text was for a long time mistakenly attributed
to John Calvin, until Detmers, *Reformation und Judentum*, 268–76, demonstrated
Capito's authorship beyond a doubt. Schubert, *Täufertum und Kabbalah*, 339n48,
correctly remarks, however, that Detmers overlooks the specificity of the restitution
theory, namely, that Capito by no means assumed a millennial conversion of the
elected Jews.

204 "Die Verheißung von Eroberung des gelobten Lands müssen leiblich verstanden war-
den"; *Bekenntnisschriften*, 72. On the different versions of the text, see Wenz, *Bekenntnisschriften*, 576–78.

205 "Die Pentecostes . . . Fertur multa milia Judaeorum ex Egipto & perside convenisse,
pro recup[e]ratione suae terrae olim promissae." Weiss, *Diarium*, 2:686.

206 "Man schreibt von Ferrar, daß die Rothen Juden auskommen seyn, Gog und Magog
und zögen mit großer Menge dem heiligen Land zu"; Bretschneider and Bindseil,
Philippi Melanthonis opera, 10:130, no. 7112. Melanchthon likely learned this from
Georg Burkhardt Spalatin, who was also present in the city for the imperial diet; see
Kolde, *Älteste Redaktion*, 55.

207 ". . . quandam fabulae simillimiam, sed certam et veram historiam de Judeis, qui infi-
nitum exercitum contraxerunt ad invadendam Palaestinam." Bretschneider and Bindseil, *Philippi Melanthonis opera*, 2:119, no. 732. Bietenhard, *Das tausendjährige Reich*,
92, misses the historical context.

208 See Schubert, *Täufertum und Kabbalah*, 342. Kolde, *Älteste Redaktion*, 55, already
suspected that the absence of the passage regarding a Jewish return to the Land of
Israel is explained by the rumors of the Red Jews.

209 See Wengert, "Melanchthon and the Jews," 127–30.

210 The first comprehensive treatment of the life and activity of Augustin Bader is Schubert, *Täufertum und Kabbalah*. His study fills in important lacuna in the research on Anabaptism. Moreover, Schubert contextualizes Bader's biography within both south German Anabaptism and Jewish messianic tradition. Packull, *Mysticism*, 130–38, offers a brief overview of Bader's activity.

211 On this point, see Schraepler, *Behandlung der Täufer*.

212 The court records are edited in Bossert, "Augustin Bader." Likewise reprinted in Bossert, *Quellen*, 921–88; a partial reprinting of the court confessions is found in Laube, *Flugschriften*, 2:984–96.

213 On the imperial political dimension of the Bader case, see Schubert, *Täufertum und Kabbala*, 171–81.

214 On these efforts, see Press, "Württembergische Restitution"; Press, "Epochenjahr."

215 Schubert, *Täufertum und Kabbalah*, 171–81.

216 "Davon sie vil hilf und vertrostung gehabt haben"; Steglich, *Bundestage*, 792.

217 On Leber, see Schubert, *Täufertum und Kabbalah*, chap. 2.3. Stern, *Josel von Rosheim*, 81–82, suggests erroneously that Bader, too, learned Hebrew in Worms.

218 On Christian Hebraism in general, see Burnett, *Christian Hebraism*; Coudert and Shoulson, *Hebraica Veritas*; Friedman, *Most Ancient Testimony*; Rummel, "Humanists, Jews, and Judaism." On sixteenth-century Germany, see Geiger, *Studium der Hebräischen Sprache*. On the pre-Reformation period, see Kluge, "Hebräische Sprachwissenschaft"; Walde, *Christliche Hebraisten*. On the Christian fascination with Jewish teachings, particularly in the 1520s, see Detmers, *Reformation und Judentum*, 64–76. On Christian Kabbalah, see Secret, *Kabbalistes chrétiens*; Secret, *Zohar*.

219 In general, see Burnett, "Jüdische Vermittler." On the well-known philologist and poet Elijah Levita, who counted among others Egidio da Viterbo, the cardinal of Rome, as his student, see, e.g., Weil, *Elie Levita*.

220 Rohrbacher, "Medinat Schwaben," 96.

221 See a letter from Isaac to Amman; BSB, Munich, Cod. hebr. 426 (= IMHM, F 1653), fol. 206v (reprinted in Zimmer, "Collaboration," 88, no. 5). A transcription of the beginning of the letter is also preserved in BSB, Munich, Cod. hebr. 827 (= IMHM, F 38866), fol. 47r.

222 See a letter from Bacharach to Amman that addresses religious questions; BSB, Munich, Cod. hebr. 426 (= IMHM, F 1653), fol. 204v–205r; preserved in a further transcription in BSB, Munich, Cod. hebr. 827 (= IMHM, F 38866), fol. 46v–47r.

223 Letter from Treves to Amman; BSB, Munich, Cod. hebr. 426 (= IMHM, F 1653), fol. 196v, 197r (Lat.); reprinted in Zimmer, "Collaboration," 85–86, no. 2. A partial transcription is also preserved in BSB, Munich, Cod. hebr. 827 (= IMHM, F 38866), fol. 48r. The contact was obviously brought about through R. Raphael Wolf, a former student of Treves who at this time was rabbi in Hagenau in Alsace and brother of the rabbi in Worms, Samuel b. Eliezer Mize'a; BSB, Munich, Cod. hebr. 426 (= IMHM, F 1653), fol. 190v; reprinted in Zimmer, "Collaboration," 84–85, no. 1; see also 77–79. On the physician in Günzburg, who had contacts to the

highest Christian circles, among others the royal court in Innsbruck and the bishop of Augsburg, see Rohrbacher, "Medinat Schwaben," 85–86.

224 BSB, Munich, Cod. hebr. 426 (= IMHM, F 1653), fol. 191v, 192v; reprinted in Zimmer, "Collaboration," 87–88, no. 3 and 4. The beginning of the second letter is also preserved in a transcription in BSB, Munich, Cod. hebr. 827 (= IMHM, F 38866), fol. 49r. On these letters, see Zimmer, "Collaboration," 79. Schubert, *Täufertum und Kabbalah*, 79n274, corrects Zimmer's dating of the letters at 1520. Cf. Geiger, *Studium der hebräischen Sprache*, 75n2, who likewise dates the correspondence evidently at the beginning of the 1520s.

225 Cf. Zimmer, "Collaboration," 76.

226 Schubert, *Täufertum und Kabbalah*, 78–80. James Beck examines another example of Jewish-Anabaptist cooperation in Worms: the case of Hans Denck and Ludwig Hätzer, who in 1527 completed their famous translation of the so-called *Prophets of Worms*; Beck, "Anabaptists." Since this translation of the biblical prophets hews very close to the Hebrew original and often abstains from Christological interpretations, Beck assumes that the authors leaned heavily on Jewish exegetical traditions to which they would have been exposed in direct interaction with Jewish scholars in Worms. Driedger, "Intensification," 282, objects that Beck bases his argument above all on internal textual criticism. In fact, Denck and Hätzer refer to Jewish sources in several brief explanatory passages; see Goeters, *Ludwig Hätzer*, 99–100.

227 Scholem, "Prakim mi-toldot sifrut ha-kabbalah," 445.

228 The relevant passage from the letter is quoted in David, "Jerusalemite Epistle," 59. On Abraham ha-Levi's refusal, see also Idel, *Messianic Mystics*, 134; Robinson, *Kabbalist and Messianic Visionary*, 135. On the treatise in question, see Robinson, "Two Letters," 403–22; Scholem, "Introduction," 36–37. Similarly, the Sabbatian Ber Perlhefter also declined to explicate certain messianic Midrashim to the Christian Hebraist Johann Christoph Wagenseil; Carlebach, *Divided Souls*, 80. In general on this reluctance, see Idel, "Particularism," 327–31.

229 On this form of active messianism, see, in particular, Zimmer, "Collaboration," esp. 81; thereafter, Rohrbacher, "Medinat Schwaben," 97. Numerous references have been made to a corresponding justification for revealing mystical secrets to non-Jews; Stow, *Catholic Thought*, 251; Ruderman, "Hope against Hope," 305, 309–10. In addition, one must consider the humanistic ideal of the universal scholar (*ḥakham kolel*), who was also educated in Hebrew literature, as a further motivation for cooperation with Christians; see, e.g., Bonfil, *Epoca del Rinascimento*, 149–51.

230 Cf. Zika, *Reuchlin*, 129.

231 Messianic significance was attributed to this year by, e.g., Abraham ha-Levi (Silver, *Messianic Speculation*, 131; Idel, "Introduction," 25; Tishby, *Messianism* [Hebr.], 133–34), Joseph ibn Shraga (Tishby, *Messianism* [Hebr.], 90–91), and Solomon Molkho (Idel, *Messianic Mystics*, 149). Isaac Abravanel had calculated 1530/31 as a possible date for the advent of the Messiah; Netanyahu, *Don Isaac Abravanel*, 225–26.

232 "Der hab Oßwalten die verenderung allen nach der leng angezaigt vnd hab der Jud gesagt, das solchen verenderung vf das jar [1530] gescheen sol"; Bader's testimony, in Bossert, "Augustin Bader" (11), 46.

233 "Hab man zu Wormbs lang nit erlauben wollen, bis er solichs mit recht erhalten"; ibid.

234 "Vnd im anzaigt, in welchem hauß vnd in welcher gassen er in alda findt"; ibid. See also Bader's statement in ibid., 128: "Es sy ouch sunst ein Jud von Worms vß gen Jherusalem gezogen, der lang vor dem, ehe Oßwalt zu im Augustin komen, anzaigt, wan vf das dryssigst jar kein verenderung kom, so soll der tufel mer vf eine warten."

235 See above, p. 71.

236 Schubert, *Täufertum und Kabbalah*, 91–100. On the Anabaptist community of Strasbourg, see Deppermann, *Melchior Hoffmann*, 139–94, 236–71; Deppermann, "Täufergruppen"; Müsing, "Anabaptist Movement"; Derksen, *From Radicals to Reformers*.

237 See Schubert, *Täufertum und Kabbalah*, 101–2n381.

238 "Fröwet euch von gantzem hertzen, und von ganzen krefften, und danckend und lobend Gott, wann der herr hat uns brüdern eröffnet, in was zeyt er die straffen wöll, die euch verfolgt und zerströwet haben." Thus in an epistle to the brothers in Augsburg, reprinted in Laube, *Flugschriften*, 1:838.

239 Seebaß, *Müntzers Erbe*, 350–52. On the Anabaptist community in Augsburg, see Deppermann, "Täufergruppen"; Guderian, *Täufer in Augsburg*; Uhland, *Täufertum und Obrigkeit*.

240 Schubert, *Täufertum und Kabbalah*, 104–8.

241 "Der Oßwald der pfaff hab in vil vnderricht vnd gesterckt in der verenderung"; Bossert, "Augustin Bader" (11), 46.

242 For a thorough examination of Bader's views and teachings, see Schubert, *Täufertum und Kabbalah*, chap. 3. On the reception of Jewish theologumena, see ibid., esp. chaps. 3.4 and 5. Laube, *Flugschriften*, 2:994n19, and List, *Chiliastische Utopie*, 174–78, already point out a Jewish influence on Bader's teachings. Seifert, "Reformation und Chiliasmus," handles this question in depth but inadvertently gives the impression that Bader's ideas had no Jewish background at all.

243 "Welt nyemand, weder Juden, heiden, Turcken in der verenderung ußgeschlossen haben, dann er wißte nit, wen gott zu solchem berieft, dann Paulus hab geschriben: hat er des edlen zwygs nit verschont und abgeschnitten, noch vil weniger wird er deß willden verschonen." Bossert, "Augustin Bader" (11), 132. Cf. the olive tree metaphor in Rom. 11:21.

244 4 Ezra 13:25–52. An English edition is Charlesworth, *Old Testament Pseudepigrapha*, 1:517–60.

245 Schubert, *Täufertum und Kabbalah*, 149, 234.

246 See Bossert, "Augustin Bader" (10), 45, 132, and Schubert, *Täufertum und Kabbalah*, 142–53.

247 See Rohrbacher, "Medinat Schwaben"; Rohrbacher, "Ungleiche Partnerschaft." On the structural transformation of Jewish life and settlement in the transition from the

late Middle Ages to the early modern period, see Rohrbacher, "Landgemeinden"; Rohrbacher, "Stadt und Land"; Rohrbacher, "Medinot Aschkenas."

248   Cf. above, p. 131.

249   Bossert, "Augustin Bader" (11), 45–46 (Bader's testimony), 59 (Gall Vischer's testimony). Süßlin was born in Günzburg; after 1504, he received permission from the city council of Ulm to settle in nearby Leipheim, from which the Jews had been expelled in 1503; see GJ III.1, 480, 482n35; Bossert, "Augustin Bader" (10), 213. In addition to Süßlin's family, there was only one other Jewish family in Leipheim at that time. I wish to thank Stefan Rohrbacher for this information.

250   "Deß namb im unwissend"; Bossert, "Augustin Bader" (11), 131.

251   "Wie ire altar vnd opfer nichts wern, ouch der wucher kein nutz, vnd es wurd ein verenderung komen, die wer ouch schon vorhanden. Daruf der Jud geantwurt, er welts gern wissen vnd by im syn"; ibid.

252   "Het gern gewißt, wa er vnd seine gsellen sich enthalten, so welt er zu in ziechen, er habs inen aber dazumal nit anzaigen wellen"; ibid., 45, 59.

253   See the testimony of the miller of Westerstetten, in whose mill the group lived temporarily; ibid., 42. "Würzburg" is presumably to be amended here as "Günzburg."

254   "Zu hand weren sie nachgeloffen vnd grosse ere empotten vnd gestrichen, er were der reht vnd sollte mer mit im reden"; ibid., 42.

255   Thus the suspicion by Stern, Josel von Rosheim, 82. Ibid., 81, however requires emendation from "Leipzig" to "Leipheim." See also Bossert, "Augustin Bader" (10), 213–14.

256   Cf. above, e.g., on the year 1523. See also Ruderman, "Hope against Hope."

257   "Weder vom alten glauben, dem widertauf, von der Luterschen noch newen ler nichzit gehalten"; Bossert, "Augustin Bader" (11), 41 (testimony of the miller of Westerstetten and his wife).

258   "Mer vf der Juden dan vf unsern glauben"; ibid., 43. The couple hung their testimony above all on the fact that Bader, in accordance with the suspension of baptism announced by Hut in the millennial time of suffering, had not had his newborn child baptized and that he had been of an anti-Trinitarian mind.

259   4 Ezra 11:34–46.

260   Schubert, Täufertum und Kabbalah, 148.

261   Ibid., 231.

262   Jews were welcome in the Ottoman Empire, because they brought with them important expertise for economic development and were widely regarded as being a neutral minority that did not stand under suspicion of sympathizing with the European powers; on this point, see Epstein, Ottoman Jewish Communities. Nevertheless, Ottoman politics were by no means fundamentally friendly to Jews, even though the romanticizing view of a Muslim-Jewish symbiosis found for a long time widespread acceptance among scholars. Thus, e.g., Shaw, Jews of the Ottoman Empire, 29–30. This cliché was critiqued fairly early, however, by Joseph Hacker; Hacker, "Ottoman Policies."

263   See, e.g., Rohrbacher and Schmidt, Judenbilder, 242; Fraenkel-Goldschmidt, Historical Writings, 172–73. On the contemporary myth of close Jewish-Turkish relationships and of Jewish influence in Muslim countries, see, in general, Braude, "Myths,"

18–22. See also Braude, "Contes persans," esp. 1133–37. On the dangers that Jews and Muslims supposedly posed to Christians, see Lewis, *Cultures in Conflict*, chap. 2.

264 See Carlebach, "Endtime," 338, on a motif in Folz.

265 While Luther, WA 30.2:224, considered the Turks to be the descendants of the Red Jews, for Jonas the term is merely a metaphorical designation for the Turks. In reality, according to him, the Turks are no born Jews at all; only their customs resemble those of the Jews; Jonas, *Siebend Capitel Danielis*, fol. 15r. Similarly, Brenz, *Türcken Büchlein*, fol. 9v. See also Gow, *Red Jews* 157–58; Köhler, *Melanchthon*, 67–68.

266 "Der Oßwald hab zum Juden von Gintzburg gesagt, der Durch sy jer vetter vnd von jerem geschlecht"; Bossert, "Augustin Bader" (11), 46.

267 "Dan er hab zu Kronweissenburg die Juden erwurckt, vnd wa er solches nit thon, hetten sie in fur dien gehapt vnd angenommen, der die verenderung vfrichten vnd die Christenhait abthon vnd zerstairn soll"; ibid.

268 "Allem anseen nach die gröst prakticken dieser erschrockenlichen handlungen von den Juden ausgeen vnd angericht sein möchten"; ibid., 52.

269 See Fraenkel-Goldschmidt, *Historical Writings*, 102–3n120.

270 Thus, e.g., Rhegius, *De Restitutione Regni Israelitici*; reprinted in Stupperich, *Schriften*, 137–57, here 153, no. 83. See Bossert, "Augustin Bader" (11), 52.

271 "Wie sy dann yetz in des Türcken kryeg ayn vberflüssige freüd gehabt vnd verhofft/ das scepter der Christen solt hingenommen worden sein"; Margaritha, *Gantz Jüdisch glaub*, fol. 27r (my pagination). On the rumors and the information politics of the regional government in Stuttgart during the court proceedings, see Schubert, *Täufertum und Kabbalah*, 185–86.

272 Carlebach, *Divided Souls*, 180.

273 Fraenkel-Goldschmidt, *Historical Writings*, 178–79. See also above, p. 35.

274 Bossert, "Augustin Bader" (11), 52.

275 "Damit die selbige Juden zu gefengnus pracht vnd die warhait irs furnemens aigentlichen erlernet werden mug"; "damit dan solh pose handlung andern zu ainem exempel ernstlich gestraft vnd darin nyemands verschont werde"; ibid., 104.

276 Quoted in Müller, "Aus fünf Jahrhunderten," 82–83.

277 Ibid., 83.

278 The contents are cross-referenced in ibid., 83–85.

279 David, *Chronicle*, 37, no. 34. The dating of the events at 1529 in this chronicle is based on the fact that the Bader proceedings, as Peutinger confirms, were seen to have proved the accusations that had been made in that year.

280 Fraenkel-Goldschmidt, *Historical Writings*, 321, no. 14. For the original Hebrew text of Josel's chronicle, see Fraenkel-Goldschmidt, *Historical Writings* (Hebr.), 293.

281 Fraenkel-Goldschmidt, *Historical Writings*, 321, no. 14.

282 Ibid., 174–75; Feilchenfeld, *Josel von Rosheim*, 116; Stern, *Josel von Rosheim*, 82. On the connection with Bader, see Stern, *Josel von Rosheim*, 80–81; Schubert, *Täufertum und Kabbalah*, 192–93.

283 On Ferdinand's treatment of the Jews, see Fraenkel-Goldschmidt, *Historical Writings*, 174–75.

284 On Bader's execution, see Schubert, *Täufertum und Kabbalah*, 197–202.

285 On Josel's activity, see Stern, *Josel von Rosheim*; Feilchenfeld, *Josel von Rosheim*; as well as the edition of his chronicle, introduced and annotated by Fraenkel-Goldschmidt, *Historical Writings*. Avraham Siluk investigates Josel's work in the broader context of Jewish politics in sixteenth-century Germany; Siluk, *Die Juden im politischen System des Alten Reichs*.

286 On the phenomenon of the "royal alliance" that guaranteed stability in Jewish political history, see Yerushalmi, *Diener von Königen*; Yerushalmi, "Servants of Kings." His theory is evaluated by Dubin, "Royal Alliance."

287 The literature on the Last Emperor prophecy and related themes is vast. The fundamentals of the field were established by Kampers, *Kaiseridee*; Sackur, *Sibyllinische Texte*. For a more recent treatment, see Möhring, *Weltkaiser*. See also Alexander, "Medieval Legend."

288 The origin of the prophecy lies in the so-called Constantine Vaticinium, a prophecy about Constantine the Great, which is transmitted at the end of a Latin version of the Tiburtine Sibyl; Alexander, "Medieval Legend," 17–53.

289 Sackur, *Sibyllinische Texte*, 39–41. The Syrian Apocalypse of Pseudo-Methodius soon spread in translation into Byzantium and Europe, and along with the biblical Book of Daniel and the Apocalypse of John was one of the most influential apocalyptic texts in the Middle Ages. On its interpretation, see Reinink, *Concept of History*; Alexander, *Byzantine Apocalyptic Tradition*, 13–38.

290 Möhring, *Weltkaiser*, 217–309; Reeves, *Influence of Prophecy*, 304–92. On the characterization of the third state of humanity, see Reeves, *Influence of Prophecy*, 135–44; Töpfer, *Reich des Friedens*, 52–80.

291 In a Yiddish glossary to the Bible, dated paleographically to around 1410, the mysterious king in Prov. 30:31 is called a "kunek von Rom" (king of Rome) and his name, Alkum, is a sequence of initials of the kings Otto, Louis, Conrad, Frederick, and Messiah. The historical monarchs referred to are a ruler from the Ottonian dynasty, Louis the VII of France or Lothar of Sachsen-Supplinburg (altered to Louis by a copyist's error), Conrad III, and Frederick Barbarossa. The prophecy must therefore stem from the twelfth century, since Barbarossa died in 1190. See Timm, *Jiddische Semantik*, 42.

292 On these texts, see Reeves, *Trajectories in Near Eastern Apocalyptic*, 106–10. I have dealt with the Jewish Last Emperor prophecy in greater detail in an expanded version of this chapter; Voß, "Charles V as Last World Emperor."

293 Hebrew editions in Jellinek, *Bet ha-Midrasch*, 2:58–63; Even-Shemuel, *Midreshei ge'ullah*, 318–23. English translation in Reeves, *Trajectories in Near Eastern Apocalyptic*, 124.

294 *Otot R. Shimon b. Yoḥai*, Hebrew edition in Marmorstein, "Signes," 181–86. English translation in Reeves, *Trajectories in Near Eastern Apocalyptic*, 113.

295 According to the version in Even-Shemuel, *Midreshei ge'ullah*, 320, Armilus is described as the one "whom the non-Jews call Antichrist." By itself, however, this does not constitute evidence of Christian influence. On the Jewish anti-Messiah, see Dan, "Armilus"; Berger, "Typological Themes," 155–62.

296 Alexander, *Byzantine Apocalyptic Tradition*, 151–84, presumes a Jewish source for the idea of the Last Emperor. See also Alexander, "Medieval Legend." Already in the Syriac *Apocalypse of Baruch*, which originated (likely from a Hebrew original) in the second century in Palestine, the last Roman emperor is led in bondage to Mount Zion, where he is slain by the Messiah. The Jewish idea that Rome's power will end with the return of the crown to God is traceable in the third century. See Möhring, *Weltkaiser*, 50, 369. Moreover, it is prophesied that Messiah ben Joseph will lay down his wreath upon *even ha-shtiyyah* (the foundation stone), the Jewish counterpart to the Christian Golgatha; Even-Shemuel, *Midreshei ge'ullah*, 312.

297 See Möhring, *Weltkaiser*, 291–310; Reeves, *Influence of Prophecy*, 359–74. In particular on the expectation of a second Charlemagne, see Reeves, *Influence of Prophecy*, 320–31. On Charlemagne as Last Emperor, see Möhring, "Karl der Große." Charles V presented himself—just as did his adversary Suleiman—as the last world ruler; Finlay, "Prophecy and Politics"; Subrahmanyam, "Du Tage au Gange," 58–60; Parker, "Messianic Visions," 5–6.

298 I use the version reprinted in Aescoly, *Messianic Movements*, 390, and Aescoly, *Story*, 156. On the transmission history, see Sambari, *Divrei Yosef*, 38. Several versions attribute the vision to Sherira Gaon or his son Hai Gaon, respectively. The dating is deduced from the mention of Charles's coronation by the pope in 1530. Aescoly, *Messianic Movements*, 390, by contrast dates it in the 1520s.

299 The prophecy comes down to us through Abraham ha-Levi, reprinted in Scholem, "Prakim mi-toldot sifrut ha-kabbalah," 442–48; later in Aescoly, *Messianic Movements*, 354.

300 On the expectations regarding Frederick, which depending on one's standpoint identified the ruler either with the Last Emperor or with the Antichrist, see Möhring, *Weltkaiser*, 217–68; Reeves, *Influence of Prophecy*, 306–19, 332–46. On Frederick II in particular, see also Wies, *Friedrich II*; Cohn, *Pursuit of the Millennium*, chap. 5. In general on the expectation of a vanished or deceased ruler's return, see Bercé, *Roi caché*. Bercé, *Roi caché*, 346, draws attention to an interesting analogy to the continuing secret existence and reemergence of the Ten Tribes.

301 On this episode, see Rohrbacher, *Juden in Neuss*, 21–22; Struve, "Die falschen Friedriche," 323–24. See also Wisplinghoff, *Neuss*, 75–76; GJ II.2, 581.

302 Also quoted by Abraham ha-Levi; Aescoly, *Messianic Movements*, 354–55.

303 Cf. Möhring, *Weltkaiser*, 244; Reeves, *Influence of Prophecy*, 360–61.

304 Aescoly, *Messianic Movements*, 390; Aescoly, *Story*, 156. Because Mic. 2:12 lies at the basis of the text in the form of an acrostic, the year is given in abbreviated form; צ is therefore more sensibly expanded to ר״ץ, thus [5]290, or 1530 according to the Christian calendar: "כתר קארולוש במלחמו[ת] צריו אנשא קיסר בתוך [ר]צ׳ שנה׳ אשמיד רומי תורקאי." Shtober in Sambari, *Divrei Yosef*, 144n11, expands the year in the version transmitted by Sambari in the same way. Nevertheless, he draws no connection to the coronation.

305 The imperial coronation also served Joseph of Orly as an indication of the coming beginning of messianic time. Since the ceremony took place at Charles's behest

and against the pope's, it appeared to signal the demise of the papacy; see Graetz, *Geschichte der Juden*, 527–28n5.

306 On the alliance with the sultan, see Hochedlinger, "Französisch-osmanische Freundschaft." See also Vaughan, *Europe and the Turk*, 104–34; Inalcik, *Ottoman Empire*, 35–37.

307 On the Francophobic tendency in German expectations regarding the Last Emperor, see Möhring, *Weltkaiser*, 306; Kampers, *Kaiseridee*, 53–59. Francophilic prophecies of the Last Emperor were often directed in contrast against the Holy Roman Empire; see, e.g., Möhring, *Weltkaiser*, 277, 283–84, 296.

308 The outcome of the Battle of Pavia was largely perceived as confirmation of Charles as Last Emperor; see Möhring, *Weltkaiser*, 306; Reeves, *Influence of Prophecy*, 364.

309 The greatest significance was attributed to this outcome. Chastel, *Sack of Rome*, 82, counts for the decade between 1520 and 1530 a total of 133 pamphlets by fifty-six authors concerned with the destruction of Rome and the papacy in an eschatological context. Depending upon one's perspective, Charles could, of course, also appear as the Antichrist or his harbinger; see Reeves, "Note on Prophecy"; Niccoli, *Prophecy and People*, 175–77. Jews likewise saw a messianic significance in the *Sacco di Roma*; see, e.g., Beit-Arié, "Letter," 372–74.

310 Möhring, *Weltkaiser*, 307. See also Duchhardt, "Tunisunternehmen."

311 See Reeves, *Trajectories in Near Eastern Apocalyptic*, 113.

312 Aescoly, *Messianic Movements*, 390; Aescoly, *Story*, 156.

313 The text has been placed in connection with the activity of Re'uveni and Molkho. See Aescoly, *Messianic Movements*, 390; Aescoly, *Story*, 227–30 (Hebr. numbering), who speculates that the prophecy dates back to Molkho himself. A connection cannot be ruled out, since their plan involved the defeat of the Turks as well as the annihilation of Rome, and they purposely worked toward an alliance with Charles V. In my view, however, the significance of the text lies less in this discussion than in its place in the contemporary tradition of the Last Emperor.

314 Fraenkel-Goldschmidt, *Sefer Hammiknah*, 73. Fraenkel-Goldschmidt has pointed out that this is the only place in Josel's writings where he gives expression to a messianic expectation; Fraenkel-Goldschmidt, *Sefer Hammiknah*, 67 (Hebr. numbering).

315 Josel adopts the Catholic standpoint; see ibid., 68 (Hebr. numbering) and 74n56. Ben-Sasson, "Reformation," 291, by contrast, suggests that behind Josel's critique lie generally fundamentalist motives.

316 A common wordplay upon Luther's name: לוטר—לא טהור.

317 Fraenkel-Goldschmidt, *Sefer Hammiknah*, 73–74. On Josel's loyalist stance on the Schmalkaldic War, see also Fraenkel-Goldschmidt, *Historical Writings*, 294, 298. On Frankfurt in the Schmalkaldic War, see Kracauer, *Geschichte der Juden*, 1:299–300.

318 Deut. 30:3.

319 Fraenkel-Goldschmidt, *Sefer Hammiknah*, 75.

320 See ibid., 37 (Hebr. numbering). On Josel's dependence upon Bibago, see ibid., 34–35 (Hebr. numbering). On the contents in general, see ibid., 13–39 (Hebr. numbering); Feilchenfeld, *Josel von Rosheim*, 139–42.

321 Fraenkel-Goldschmidt, *Sefer Hammiknah*, 75.

322 Evidence for this is the materiality of the book. The page in question is double-sided, and the writing is more compressed, involving smaller letters than the other pages; see ibid., 12 (Hebr. numbering). The difference from Josel's description of the same events in his chronicle is indicative. Whereas in *Sefer ha-miknah* he speaks of a miracle, of divine guidance and mercy, in the chronicle he describes the siege in the context of the Schmalkaldic War in terms that are prosaic and sober; Fraenkel-Goldschmidt, *Historical Writings*, 339, no. 29.

323 Edited in Fraenkel-Goldschmidt, *Historical Writings* (Hebr.), 393–94; in the English edition, 418–23.

324 Thus runs the assessment in ibid., 418.

325 Ibid., 420; in the Hebrew, 393.

326 Ibid., 393 (Hebr.); 421 (Engl.). Josel holds up two instances as exemplary. For one, he names the release of Jewish prisoners during the wars of the imperial troops in the Mediterranean in the 1530s. See also the chronicle entry for 1532–35; ibid., 325–26, no. 19, with commentary; 213–19. For another, Josel reminds his readers of the protection of the community in Hagenau in Alsace, when in May 1552 a French army stormed the city; ibid., 423.

327 Ibid., 421 (Engl.), 393 (Hebr.). Fraenkel-Goldschmidt notes that after the phrase "to this day," Josel left himself plenty of space, in which he possibly wished to enter a date—perhaps the date of salvation?

328 Ibid., 421 (Engl.), 393–94 (Hebr).

329 Ibid., 421 (Engl.), 394 (Hebr.).

330 Ibid., 421–22 (Engl.), 394 (Hebr.).

331 Ibid., 421 (Engl.), 394 (Hebr.).

332 On this text, see Reeves, *Influence of Prophecy*, 369–72. On Lazius himself and his historiographical work, see Schmidt, "Lazius."

333 See Reeves, *Influence of Prophecy*, 369–70. Although Lazius identifies the arch-heretic and false pope with Luther, he interprets one of the Pseudo-Methodius prophecies explicitly with reference to the Schmalkaldic League; ibid., 370n2. Lazius devotes another work exclusively to the history of the Schmalkaldic War; see Schmidt, "Lazius"; on the date of compilation, whether 1550 or 1551, see ibid., 128.

334 See Reeves, *Influence of Prophecy*, 372.

335 Dan. 11. Contrary to Fraenkel-Goldschmidt, *Historical Writings*, 422n22, which refers here to Judg. 9:23 and Ezek. 1:4, although they fit less will with the overall impression of the text.

336 Fraenkel-Goldschmidt, *Historical Writings*, 422 (Engl.), 394 (Hebr.). See above, p. 71, for further evidence of the messianic significance of the siege of Frankfurt by the margrave's army.

337 Fraenkel-Goldschmidt, *Historical Writings*, 422–23 (Engl.), 394–96 (Hebr.).

338 See ibid., 392–94.

339 Dan. 11:45.

340 See Dan. 11:2–4.

341 See Ben-Sasson, "Reformation," 257–70, esp. 314–15, on Luther as savior. See also above, pp. 77–78.

342 Bonfil, "Ebrei d'Italia e la Riforma," examines another case in which the anti-Protestant stance is directly fed by Catholic sources. He points out an analogous influence in Joseph ha-Kohen's *Emek ha-bakhah.*

343 It is possible that the Jewish perception of the French king Charles VIII in messianic contexts is also an echo of Christian Last Emperor prophecy; this would have to be investigated as a separate case. An apocalyptic interpretation of his invasion of Italy, by Joseph Shealtiel b. Moses ha-Kohen of Rome, survives in a brief commentary on the kabbalistic work *Sefer ha-pli'ah* (Book of the Miraculous). The majority of the text, which is found as a later insert in Biblioteca Apostolica Vaticana, Ebr. 187 (= IMHM, F 245), is reprinted in appendix 2 of Krauss, "Charles VIII," 95–96. The name of the author is gleaned from the acrostic in the introductory poem (fol. 77v), which is missing, however, in Krauss. See the suggestion of Christian influence already in Ruderman, "Hope against Hope," 305. Similarly, Yerushalmi, "Messianic Impulses," 469n34, on Joseph ha-Kohen's interpretation in his history of the kings of France and the Ottoman Empire. On the Christian image of Charles VIII, see Möhring, *Weltkaiser,* 299–302; Reeves, *Influence of Prophecy,* 354, 358, 430–35; Weinstein, *Savonarola,* 62–63, 112–15, 166. Additional Jewish interpretations are found in Linder, "Expédition italienne."

344 Reeves, *Influence of Prophecy,* 361–67. See also Reeves, "Egidio of Viterbo." On the person of Egidio, see Campanini, "Cabbalisti cristiani," 149–65; on his eschatology, see Idel, "Egidio da Viterbo."

345 The Christian proponents for the renewal of the crusades advocated for this in similar terms. Since the Turkish conquest of Constantinople, however, they found themselves in the minority; Helmrath, "Pius II."

346 Aescoly, *Story,* 48.

347 Ibid., 66, 69, 94.

348 Ibid., 90.

349 Lenowitz, *Jewish Messiahs,* 104; Nahon, "Judaïsme"; Nahon, "From Algarve to Rivtigo." Chetrit, "Secret," 243, represents the view that Re'uveni's entire intention actually had as its goal the liberation of the conversos.

350 Aescoly, *Story,* 126–35.

351 See Simonsohn, "Second Mission." Cf. also Kaufmann, "Azriel b. Solomon Dayiena."

352 The approximate date emerges from a report by the special papal emissary to Germany, Girolamo Aleander; Müller, *Nuntiaturberichte,* 444. An English translation of the document is found in Fraenkel-Goldschmidt, *Historical Writings,* 195.

353 On Molkho, see Benmelech, *Shlomo Molkho.* See also Aescoly, *Story,* passim; Bernstein, "Schlomo Molcho"; Idel, "Unknown Sermon"; Idel, *Messianic Mystics,* 144–52; Idel, "Molkho as Magician"; Lenowitz, *Jewish Messiahs,* 104–7, 115–20; Sadek, "Molcho and His Teachings."

354 See Lenowitz, *Jewish Messiahs,* 107; Shohat, "Notes," 116.

355 Thus the papal emissary Aleander describes Molkho as the "chief"; Müller, *Nuntiaturberichte,* 444; Fraenkel-Goldschmidt, *Historical Writings,* 195. Other sources likewise

cast Molkho in the leading role in Regensburg or speak even exclusively of him, which leads Eidelberg, *David Reubeni*, to the false assumption that Molkho traveled alone to Regensburg.

356 On the other hand, Simonsohn, "Second Mission," 203, believes that Re'uveni's unmasking was the reason for his later arrest in Regensburg.

357 On this fascinating phenomenon, see Eliav-Feldon, "Invented Identities," which treats the Re'uveni episode among others, and Eliav-Feldon, "Prince or Pauper?"; Bercé, *Roi caché*; Groebner, *Who Are You?*, 214–15; Olsen, *Calabrian Charlatan*.

358 From Sanuto, *Diarii*, 54:145–48, here 148; also reprinted in Aescoly, *Story*, 183–89, here 189.

359 Aescoly, *Story*, 151–52, here 152.

360 Farissol, *Iggeret*; reprinted in Aescoly, *Story*, 154.

361 Aescoly, *Story*, 172, 176.

362 Ibid., 174.

363 Müller, *Nuntiaturberichte*, 426; Fraenkel-Goldschmidt, *Historical Writings*, 194. Accordingly, in Aleander's report to the pope himself, from September 1, 1532; Müller, *Nuntiaturberichte*, 443; Fraenkel-Goldschmidt, *Historical Writings*, 195. On Molkho's attempt to see the pope in 1529, cf. Idel, *Messianic Mystics*, 146–49; Sestieri, "Un Papa in crisi."

364 Fraenkel-Goldschmidt, *Historical Writings*, 195; Müller, *Nuntiaturberichte*, 443.

365 Müller, *Nuntiaturberichte*, 443.

366 Fraenkel-Goldschmidt, *Historical Writings*, 195; Müller *Nuntiaturberichte*, 443–44. Cf. the report to Sanga, in which Molkho is referred to as "head of the army"; Fraenkel-Goldschmidt, *Historical Writings*, 194; Müller *Nuntiaturberichte*, 426.

367 Fraenkel-Goldschmidt, *Historical Writings*, 323, no. 17. There is no reason to assume that Molkho did not have the Jews in the empire in view. Against this, Eidelberg, *David Reubeni*, 149, and Graetz, *Geschichte der Juden*, 527, refer to the conversos in Spain and Portugal.

368 Fraenkel-Goldschmidt, *Historical Writings*, 194; Müller, *Nuntiaturberichte*, 426.

369 See Teply, *Türkische Sagen*, 45; Kurze, *Johannes Lichtenberger*, 61; von Liliencron, *Volkslieder*, 3:359, no. 348; Peuckert, *Große Wende*, 161.

370 Even though the conflict between Christianity and Islam was hardly free of messianic undertones, it was primarily considerations of realpolitik that, for many other European rulers as well, stood in the foreground of the question of whether to accept Re'uveni; see Eliav-Feldon, "Invented Identities," 218, 222; Jacobs, "Zionistisches Experiment."

371 See Möhring, *Weltkaiser*, 202–3, 308. See also Neck, "Diplomatische Beziehungen"; von Palombini, *Bündniswerben*, 63–84, 118–19. The pamphlet discussed above, *Von ainer grosse meng*, fol. 3r–v, refers to Charles's efforts in this regard. By contrast, Kaufmann, "Flugschriftenpublizistik," 446n100, erroneously identifies the "Sophoy" mentioned there not as the Persian monarch but rather, in accordance with a common usage of the time, as the Duke of Savoy.

372 Aulinger, *Reichstag*, 167–75.

373 See Müller, *Nuntiaturberichte*, 425.

374 Ibid.

375 Fraenkel-Goldschmidt, *Historical Writings*, 197.

376 Ibid., 195; Müller, *Nuntiaturberichte*, 444.

377 Fraenkel-Goldschmidt, *Historical Writings*, 192–97. More recently, Lenowitz, *Jewish Messiahs*, 107. See also Aescoly, *Story*, 172–83 (Hebr. numbering).

378 Fraenkel-Goldschmidt, *Historical Writings*, 196.

379 Ibid., 194; Müller, *Nuntiaturberichte*, 426.

380 Clement rescued his protégé from being burned at the stake by having another executed in his place; Lenowitz, *Jewish Messiahs*, 107.

381 Fraenkel-Goldschmidt, *Historical Writings*, 194; Müller, *Nuntiaturberichte*, 426.

382 Fraenkel-Goldschmidt, *Historical Writings*, 195; Müller, *Nuntiaturberichte*, 444.

383 Leone Leoni, *Hebrew Portuguese Nations*, chap. 5.

384 Fraenkel-Goldschmidt, *Historical Writings*, 192.

385 Ibid., 194; Müller, *Nuntiaturberichte*, 426.

386 See Goldish, "Patterns."

387 Fraenkel-Goldschmidt, *Historical Writings* (Hebr.), 324, no. 17. I agree here with Carlebach, *Between History and Hope*, 26n50. The suspicion of a messianic movement in the empire appears also in Rohrbacher, "Medinat Schwaben," 97; Stern, *Josel von Rosheim*, 112. As for its expansion into the central and eastern European areas, this is suggested by the mention of Re'uveni and Molkho in an anonymous list of Jewish trials and tribulations in the empire, in Italy, Bohemia and Moravia, Poland, and Belarus; State and University Library, Hamburg, Cod. hebr. 237 (= IMHM, F 1042), fol. 48r–49v, here fol. 48r. The text, which cannot have been composed before 1653, survives only as a fragment (the beginning and end are missing); the remainder begins partway into the relevant entry, no. 43. By contrast, Fraenkel-Goldschmidt, *Historical Writings*, 198 and 324n259, refers Josel's observation to the conversos without, however, offering sufficient reason.

388 Cf. also Idel, *Messianic Mystics*, 152; Lenowitz, *Jewish Messiahs*, 108.

389 Gans, *Zemah David*, 138–39.

390 Ibid., 138.

391 Carlebach, "Messianische Haltung," 245, points out this connection.

392 Idel, *Messianic Mystics*, 152. Naphtali Hirtz Treves and his son Joseph were also familiar with them; cf. Treves, *Dikduk tefillah*, fol. 71v, as well as Joseph's glosses on the novellas of his father on Baḥya b. Asher's commentary on the Pentateuch, *Naftule elohim*; Treves, *Simanim*, commentary on *Naso* and *Shoftim*. A modern edition appears under the title *Sefer Naftali*.

393 "Dedi te in lucem gentium ut sis salus mea usque ad extrema terrae. Quare iterum vos obsecro, ut scribatis ad me ex Synagoga vestra consilio Rabinorum, quis sit ille unctus, quem vos adhuc expectatis, quandoquidem verus ille Messias Domini ante tot secula venit & implevit prophetias, Obsecro autem ut scribatis clara, solida, & vera. Nam figmenta vestri Nizahon ipse jam pridem legi, quae nihil aliud sunt quam indoctae & impiae fabulae, Stultus enim ille author & historiarum & scripturarum ex

aequo fuit ignarus & vos simplices magis decepit quam Rabbi Schlomoh, quamvis ille vos egregiè seducat, Sicut nos seduxit Papa Romanus." Rhegius, *Epistola*, fol. 4v–5r. Interesting in terms of confessional discourse is the remark that Molkho had seduced not only the Jews but also the head of the church.

394 Isaac, *De Astrologia*, fol. 37v–38v (Hebr.); 38r (Lat., my pagination).

395 More obvious still is this lack of awareness in Müller, *Greuel der falschen Messien*, 16. Müller erroneously assumes that, in 1534, his forty-sixth false Messiah, David Re'uveni, was in Rome and Portugal, while his forty-seventh, Solomon Molkho, was visiting the emperor.

396 Fraenkel-Goldschmidt, *Historical Writings*, 198–99, has rightly shown that the reason for Josel's positive epitaph on Molkho lies in the fact of the latter's martyrdom. She suspects that behind this lay Josel's need to justify himself to posterity for not having been able to rescue Molkho but instead, out of concern for the well-being of the Jewish community, having been forced to turn away from him. On the religious ideal of martyrdom in the period of the Reformation, see Carlebach, "Jewish Responses," 477–80.

397 Jews were not generally excluded from the right to bear arms, and there are examples of Jews both possessing and using weapons in the Middle Ages and the early modern times. Although the Landfrieden of Mainz in 1103 conditionally removed the Jews, as a people in need of imperial protection, from the class of people allowed to carry weapons, the law involved no direct weapons ban. On this controversial theme, see Magin, "Waffenrecht"; Wenninger, "Von jüdischen Rittern"; Litt, "Juden und Waffen."

398 "Propter seditionis Hebraicae." Thus, Widmanstetter in a brief description of one of Molkho's writings, reprinted in a bibliography from 1784; quoted in Fraenkel-Goldschmidt, *Historical Writings*, 191; Aescoly, *Story*, 191.

399 Aleander attests that Molkho and Re'uveni were accompanied by others and that all of them were eventually arrested in Regensburg; Fraenkel-Goldschmidt, *Historical Writings*, 195; Müller, *Nuntiaturberichte*, 443–44. Cf. also on Re'uveni's audience in the Vatican, Lenowitz, *Jewish Messiahs*, 113.

400 Fraenkel-Goldschmidt, *Historical Writings*, 195; Müller, *Nuntiaturberichte*, 443. Cf. also Müller, *Nuntiaturberichte*, 426; Fraenkel-Goldschmidt, *Historical Writings*, 194.

401 Sambari, *Divrei Yosef*, 294; reprinted in Aescoly, *Story*, 165.

402 Fraenkel-Goldschmidt, *Historical Writings*, 194–95; Müller, *Nuntiaturberichte*, 426, 443.

403 See, e.g., Aescoly, *Story*, 101–2, 108, 118.

404 This was the information Re'uveni gave the Portuguese king as to the purpose of the flags; ibid., 100. Cf. also ibid., 128. Incidentally, later pamphlets on the advance of the Red Jews also mention their flags; see, e.g., Scheiber and Tardy, "Echo," 597.

405 Aescoly, *Story*, 57, 128, 146. Cf. also Aescoly, *Messianic Movements*, 410. The description of the banners is found in Aescoly, *Story*, 104–5, 128–29.

406 Some were no longer in his possession by then, as the Baron of Clermont had taken five of them during Re'uveni's second arrest in southern France; Aescoly, *Story*, 146.

407 The flag has often been described and admired; see Foges, *Alterthümer*, 105; Grotte, "Reliquien"; Mayer, "Messianisches Programm"; Sadek, "Etendard."

408 Ps. 79:6, Lam. 3:66, Ps. 94:1 and 47:4 (on the front of the flag). On *Shefokh*, see above, pp. 30–31.

409 Ps. 9:21 and 90:15 (on the back of the flag).

410 With Ps. 47:7–8 (on the back of the flag).

411 2 Sam. 22:35 and 38. Cf. a poem by Molkho that also takes as its theme the destruction of Edom; reprinted in Hebrew in, e.g., Kaufmann, "Poème messianique"; corrected in Idel, "Introduction," xxvii–xxx; English translation in Idel, *Messianic Mystics*, 147; Lenowitz, *Jewish Messiahs*, 119–20.

412 "Hujus vexillus vidi Ratisbonae anno 1541 cum literis מכב׳"; quoted in Aescoly, *Story*, 191; Fraenkel-Goldschmidt, *Historical Writings*, 191.

413 Graetz, *Salomon Molcho*, 245. On the magical significance of the names, see also Idel, "Molkho as Magician," 211–13.

414 That the Jewish-Turkish fraternization was, in fact, the reason for the arrest is assumed already by Feilchenfeld, *Josel von Rosheim*, 52, 116, and Stern, *Josel von Rosheim*, 111, with reference to 1530. They are followed in this by Fraenkel-Goldschmidt, *Sefer Hammiknah*, 67 (Hebr. numbering).

415 See Fraenkel-Goldschmidt, *Historical Writings*, 173.

416 See above, pp. 114–27.

417 See also a source from 1595, which connects the Red Jews not only with the Turks but also with the Tartars; Gow, *Red Jews*, 164.

418 "Sie sind vnd bleiben Christi Feind/ Wie meint jrs vns geneiget seind? // Wenn sie gewalt hetten der Welt/ Wies an sich bringen vnser Gelt. // Vnnd hettens Volck vnnd Heeres macht/ Wie sie begeren Tag vnd Nacht. // Sie würgten vns alle wie tolle hund/ Kein Christen liedens eine stund. // Ein solchen Messiam begert/ Der Jüdisch Hauff auff diser Erdt. // Der vns all morde vnd erstech/ Das jhm kein Mensch nicht widersprech. // Wenn ein Türck kem vom Jüden Stam/ Nemen sien an für Messiam. // Doch sind sie heimlich jhre Freund." Nigrinus, *Jüden Feind*, 19–20.

419 "Die verwandtschafft/ weil sie Gebrüder vnd Geuettern sind. Denn man nennet die Türcken die rotten Jüden/.... Darumb sind die Jüden in Europa jn heimlich günstig/ vnd hoffen/ sie wöllen durch sie frey werden/ vnd wider in jhr Land komen. Sie frewen sich auch wenn der Türcke auff ist/ wider die Christenheit." Ibid., 88. Lombardus, *Gründtlicher Bericht*, fol. 20v–21r, adopts both the poem and the second quoted passage from Nigrinus, albeit without explicit mention of the Red Jews. Lombardus connects the accusation with the (at that time current) fifth Venetian War against the Turks, during which, in 1570, the Turks conquered Cyprus, allegedly with the help of Jewish espionage; Lombardus, *Gründtlicher Bericht*, fol. 9r. Such activities on the part of the Jews were, for Lombardus, already responsible for the Turkish conquest of much of Hungary (1541) and their successes in Transylvania in the 1560s.

420 Stern, *Josel von Rosheim*, 111, has already suggested generally that the accusation of Jewish-Turkish fraternization lies behind Josel's point of view.

421 Fraenkel-Goldschmidt, *Historical Writings*, 323, no. 17.

422 Ibid., 324.

423 See chap. 3.3.

424 See chap. 3.4.

425 See, e.g., Franck, *Chronica*, fol. 291r: "Anno M.D.xxxiii. hat sich ein schedliche sect der Widertäuffer zu Münster inn der hauptstat Westphalen gemehrt/ welche *auff Jüdische munier* die res-titucion Israelis/ hie auff erden verhofften/ und sich ja für die hielten/ die den erdboden von dem gotlosen wesen raumen/ und das reich Israelis das new reich Hierusalem auffrichten sollten mitt dem schwert/ und alleyn im landt sicher wonen." (In the year 1533 a pernicious sect of Anabaptists at Münster has grown in the capital of Westphalia which hope in *the Jewish manner* for the restitution of Israel on earth and which consider themselves the ones who will rid the earth of the godless and establish the kingdom of Israel, the new kingdom of Jerusalem, with the sword, and safely inhabit the land alone). My emphasis. The destructive dangers of Jewish messianism were ever and again being put to use as admonition against millennial tendencies; see Popkin, "Christian Interest," 96–101; Heyd, "Jewish Quaker."

426 Stern, *Josel von Rosheim*, 115.

427 On the court proceeding, see ibid., 115–17; Feilchenfeld, *Josel von Rosheim*, 12–15; most recently, Kaplan, "Negotiating Boundaries." In general on the title, office, and function of the Jewish shtadlan in the early modern period, with special consideration of Josel, see Voß, "Habe die Mission treu erfüllt."

428 "So sollest du doch des unaengesehen, sonderlich jetzund in diesen schweren, schwinden leufen (darin sich ainer schlechter geburt und handwerks königl. Titels angemast) dich ... für einen regierer gemeiner judischait im reich ungeburlicher weis ... angeben, unser Mt. als einigen, rechten regierer gemelter judischait nit zu geringem verkleinern, spot und hohn, auch ander bosen zu ufrurischen exempel und beispil." Reprinted in the appendix to Feilchenfeld, *Josel von Rosheim*, 167–68, no. X, here 167.

429 "Aller christen verderpnuns, abgang und genzlich vertielgung gewislich vil lieber dan itzund das widerspiel vor Augen sehen wollte und begert; auch wo inen forcht der peen und gewalt der oberkeit nit abschreckte, on allen zweifel mit andern juden iren nutz und unser aller verderben zu schaffen gern understen und vornemen wurde"; ibid., 173–75, no. XIII, here 174–75.

430 Fraenkel-Goldschmidt, *Historical Writings*, 195; Müller, *Nuntiaturberichte*, 444.

431 Ha-Kohen, *Divrei ha-yamim*, pt. 2, fol. 23r.

432 Lenowitz, *Jewish Messiahs*, 107. On Re'uveni's end, see Lipiner, "Inyanim." See also the partially contradictory older literature; Kayserling, *Geschichte*, 225–27; Rodriguez-Monino, "Judaisants"; Roth, "Martyre"; Révah, "David Reubeni."

433 See Sambari, *Divrei Yosef*, 294. Shtober in Sambari, *Divrei Yosef*, and Graetz, *Salomon Molcho*, 214n7, read עיר פולוניא as Bologna.

434 The time frame for the removal of the relics is determined on the basis of a letter dated 1666, which speaks of "nearly 122 years"; reprinted in Scholem, "Sabbatian Gleanings," 144. A partial translation is found in Scholem, *Sabbatai Sevi*, 563. This fits with Widmanstetter's claim to have seen one of the two flags still in Regensburg in 1541; see above.

435 Neher, *Jewish Thought*, 146. Heřman, "Prague Jewish Community," 32, sees behind this a dig at Josel of Rosheim, the decided adversary of Molkho, who since 1534

had often been called upon as negotiator of the Prague community in conflicts with the Horowitz family. On this affair, see Fraenkel-Goldschmidt, *Historical Writings*, 219–30. On the political and cultural significance of Molkho's relics, see, most recently, Goldish, "Jews and Habsburgs."

436 Thus in his commentary on the well-known halachic work *Piskei ha-Rosh* in the context of the minhag of the color of the fringes: "ומ"מ פה ק"ק פראג בבה"כ דפנחס שהייתי רגיל בה קודם שנתמניתי לאב"ד יש ארבע כנפות ממשי בצבע ירוק כחלמון ביצה וכן הציציות שבו ג"כ ממשי ירוק כחלמון ביצה, והובא לכאן מרעגנשבורק, והוא של הקדוש שלמה מלכו הי"ד. עוד שני דגלים שלו וגם סרגינוס שקורין קיטל"; Lipmann Heller, *Ma'adannei Yom Tov, Hilkhot ẕiẕit*, no. 25 (reprinted in Romm's traditional Vilna edition of the Talmud, fol. 126r). Perhaps the second flag, which no longer survives, was the one bearing the inscription "Maccabi." On Lipmann Heller, see Davis, *Yom-Tov Lipmann Heller*.

437 Molkho's aristocratic and sumptuous clothing in the style of non-Jews was criticized by Jewish contemporaries in Venice; see a letter by Azriel Diena, who defends Molkho against such criticism. The Hebrew letter is reprinted with a partial translation into German in Sonne, "Neue Dokumente," 128 (Germ.), 132 (Hebr.).

438 Inventory no. 32.754. Like the flag, it is part of the permanent exhibit in the Maisel Synagogue. The coat, which Lipmann Heller fails to mention, is named in the 1666 letter; Scholem, "Sabbatian Gleanings," 144.

439 Possibly they survived until as late as the Holocaust. Voos, *David Reubeni*, 63, writes in 1933 that Molkho's possessions remain "to the present day" in Prague. Because of his dependence on Heller—Voos likewise fails to mention Molkho's coat—he may have merely presumed the continued existence of the items since the seventeenth century, sight unseen.

440 Scholem, "Sabbatian Gleanings," 144.

441 See Brod, *Rëubëni*, 524. The photograph is reprinted in Grotte, "Reliquien," 169. The *kitl* and the coat have often been confused. Foges, *Alterthümer*, 105, believes he is describing the former, when, in fact, what he appears to have seen is the coat "of white linen." Although Grotte, "Reliquien," 169, recognizes that Foges's description disagrees with his own, he fails to realize that this discrepancy points to the existence of another article of clothing altogether. Fraenkel-Goldschmidt, *Historical Writings*, 191n392, correctly pointed out that the image of the garment reprinted in Grotte is not identical with the coat preserved in the Prague museum.

442 "על דבר הדגל הנמצא בבה"כ פנחס בין שאר בגדי קדש אשר רבים אומרים משבחים ומפארים שהוא הדגל של הקדוש ר' שלמה מלכו הי"ד" (On the matter of the flag housed in the Pinkas Synagogue among other holy garments, many say in praise and admiration that it is the flag of the holy R. Solomon Molkho, the Lord will avenge his blood). *Pinkas min yarẕeiten be-veit ha-knesset Pinḥas*; Jewish Museum, Prague, ms. 445.

443 The reverence of Molkho as martyr was not restricted to communities in the empire. His execution also made a deep impression on, e.g., Joseph Karo, author of the *Shulḥan arukh*; he dreamed that God gave him the honor of following in Molkho's

footsteps and being burned at the stake to the glory of God's Name; Werblowsky, *Joseph Karo*, 97–100.

444 All quotes below according to the edition of the text in Scholem, "Sabbatian Gleanings," 144–45. As early as 1714 the Christian theologian Hermann von der Hardt had published a Latin version of the letter; von der Hardt, *De usu et abusu*. The enduring influence of Molkho's messianic message is attested also by Jacob Kitzingen. He concludes his tally of messianic calculations with the remark that all those named had erred, with the one exception of Molkho, who had placed the end in the year 1600; Kitzingen, *Ḥag ha-pessaḥ*, fol. 28r (quoted in Tamar, "Calculations," 934). The year 1600 had not yet come and gone at the time Kitzingen wrote. Kitzingen bases his work on ibn Yaḥya, *Shalshelet ha-kabbalah*, 107.

445 לקרות corrected to לקרוא.

446 Cf. Grotte, "Reliquien," 168.

EPILOGUE

1 Cf. Barnai, "Social Aspects," 82–83. See also his important monograph, *Sabbatianism*.

2 See chap. 1.

3 See Yuval's discussion in particular of the events of the year 1240; above, p. 36.

4 Bodleian Library, Oxford, MS Opp. 712 (= IMHM, F 20523), fol. 160r–161v. On fol. 243v–246r is also found a partial copy of *Shir ha-yiḥud li-vnei Moshe* (see 243n100), which is possibly also to be read in a messianic context. A description of the manuscript is offered by Fraenkel-Goldschmidt, *Sefer Hammiknah*, 11–13 (Hebr. numbering).

5 See above, 216–17n101.

6 Yuval, *Moses redivivus*.

7 Hofmann, *Luther*, 633–35; Cohn, *Pursuit of the Millennium*, 260–62; van Dülmen, *Reformation als Revolution*, 32–39.

8 Although examples can be found of the rejection of an active messianism among social elites, it does not follow vice versa that messianic movements arose only among the common people. Scholem, in particular, espouses the view of a contrast between messianic movements and the rabbinical elite; cf. Scholem, "Crisis of Tradition"; Scholem, *Messianic Idea*. An extreme use of the messianism-versus-rabbinism construct is found in Kochan, *Jews, Idols and Messiahs*. Kochan postulates a fundamental tension between Jewish communities guided by the Halachah and those informed by the messianic idea. For a more nuanced picture of the rabbinical establishment, see Carlebach, *Pursuit of Heresy*; Carlebach, "Rabbinic Circles."

9 Numerous examples in Carlebach, *Divided Souls*, 82–85; Carlebach, "Sabbatianism." Especially instructive are the successes of Esdras Edzard in Hamburg and Johann Heinrich Callenberg in Halle, both of whom leaned explicitly on disappointed Sabbatian hopes. See below, 269n14.

10 This is how Edzard, e.g., interpreted the Sabbatian movement; see Carlebach, *Divided Souls*, 81. This ought not to obscure the fact, however, that in the sixteenth century as well the millennial expectations of both Catholics and Protestants were nearly always

closely connected with the theme of the imminent conversion of the Jews; cf. Ruderman, "Hope against Hope," 306–7, with additional references.

11 Friedman, *Most Ancient Testimony*, 195–209. While the ethnographic texts composed right at the beginning of the seventeenth century were indeed guided by an anti-Jewish tendency, this impetus became more marginalized as the century proceeded; Deutsch, "Von der Iuden Ceremonien," 353. See also Deutsch and Diemling, "Christliche Ethnographien." On the difference between sixteenth- and seventeenth-century ethnographies, see also Burnett, "Distorted Mirrors," esp. 283–87. Naturally, the fact that beginning in the seventeenth century Christian Hebraists also wrote ethnographies played a significance role here: the sharp polemic due to personal disagreement of a convert with his former fellow believers generally fell away.

12 Cf. Friedrich, *Abwehr und Bekehrung*, 19–25. Nevertheless, the blasphemy of the Jews remained a decisive factor in the Protestant discussion of tolerance well into the eighteenth century; Arnoldi, *Pro Iudaeis*, 26–27.

13 On the Protestant mission in the seventeenth and eighteenth centuries, see Friedrich, *Abwehr und Bekehrung*; Clark, *Politics of Conversion*.

14 Jung, *Württembergische Kirche*, 101–2. One should mention, in particular, Callenberg's Institutum Judaicum in Halle. On this, see Rymatzki, *Hallischer Pietismus*. The project of Edzard, pastor at the Lutheran St. Michael's Church in Hamburg, should also be emphasized here; over the course of thirty-five years, Edzard baptized nearly 150 Jews; Carlebach, *Divided Souls*, 81.

15 For this later period, there is significant work of a comparative nature. See, among others, Carlebach, "Sabbatianism"; Goldish, *Sabbatean Prophets*; Heyd, "Jewish Quaker"; Kaplan, "Coenen in Smyrna"; Marriott, *Transnational Networks*; Popkin, "Jewish-Christian Relations."

16 For the encounter between Jews and Pietist missionaries, see Voß, "Jewish-Pietist Network."

EXCURSUS IN NUMISMATICS

1 "Schwerlich von dem Lämlein-Erreignis herrühren dürfte"; Jost, *Geschichte des Judenthums*, 215–16n2.

2 Moritz Steinschneider traces the debate in *Hebräische Bibliographie* 1 (1858), 60, 123; 2 (1859), 53. The medal has frequently been pictured and described also outside the quoted specialist literature. It receives as much attention in European numismatics and Jewish art history as in overviews of Jewish history and in studies of the history of medicine; e.g., Armand, *Médailleurs italiens*, 2:142n16; Hill, *Corpus*, n. 878; Künzl, "Jüdische Kunst," 86–88; Shulvass, *Jews*, 236n3; Roth, *Renaissance*, between 148 and 149; Holzmair, *Katalog*, 72–73; Waddington, "Graven Images." Friedenwald, *Jews and Medicine*, 2:566–67, 570, even reproduces an image of the medal on the title page of the first volume.

3 Cabinet des Médailles, BnF, Paris, Série iconographique, Très Grands Modules, no. 5085. In the early twentieth century, a dealer in Paris is supposed to have possessed

a second example of the medal, but this cannot be verified; Charvet, *Médailles*, 309. Aftercasts are found in various museums, libraries, and private collections in Europe, the United States, and Israel, e.g., in the British Museum, London; the Jewish Museum, New York; and the Friedenwald Collection in the National Library of Israel in Jerusalem. Among the writings of the seventeenth-century Christian kabbalist Christian Knorr von Rosenroth a drawing of the medal is found; HAB, Wolfenbüttel, Cod. Guelf. 30.4 Extrav., fol. 4r. I thank Yossi Chajes for this reference.

4 In general, "בתם" is read. A comparison of letters shows, however, that we are more likely dealing here with *ḥet* and a somewhat compressed *kuf*. Both Derenbourg, "Médaille" and Férarès, "Médaille," 205, read it this way.

5 *Resh* is uncertain here. Since both letters in the inscription are very similar, it could also be a *dalet*.

6 Ménestrier, *Histoire civile*, 219–23.

7 Adopted by Boissi, *Dissertations*, 68–74; Carmoly, *Mémoire*; Loewisohn, *Vorlesungen*, 31–32.

8 Explanation of the Annexed Plate.

9 Lévy, "Mémoire."

10 Zunz, "Medaille" (17), 149.

11 On Elia di Sabato, see Castaldini, *Mondi paralleli*, 120–22.

12 Zunz, "Medaille" (18), 156–57. Zunz finds the messianic date in the word הקץ (the end), whose numerical value produces the year 1430. The origin of the medal in fifteenth-century Italy is supported by the choice of abbreviations; ibid. (17), 149.

13 Loewe, "Lemlein Medal," 258. Loewe's further decoding of the inscription rests however on a mistaken reading and is thus invalid; cf. Cahen, *Nouvelle explication*; Carmoly, *Mémoire*, VI; Zunz, "Medaille," 157. Loewe erroneously reads *kaf* instead of *bet* and *heh* instead of *tav*, thus "מ'י כ'ת ה ע'," which he deciphers as "מעשה ידי כתיבת הענו" (the work of my hands, the script of Anav). Here Loewe connects the letters that are placed at the side of the portrait's head. He solves "ב'ן ימ'ן ב'ן כר'ש" as "בנימין בן כבוד רבי שבתי" (Benjamin, son of the honored R. Shabtai). This (fictive) Benjamin b. Shabtai Anav (Ital. Delli Mansi), who has nevertheless persisted in the scholarship ever since, is according to Loewe's interpretation the supposed artificer of the medal; Loewe, "Lemlein Medal," 260–62.

14 Cf. Loewe, "Lemlein Medal," 263. I have unfortunately been unable to determine which work by Carmoly is being referred to here; in any event, it is not his *Mémoire*.

15 Loewe, "Lemlein Medal," 263. Literally, "the light is near—in face of darkness."

16 Ibid., 264–65; cf. also 267–68.

17 Ibid., 266–67.

18 Ibid., 268–69.

19 Ibid., 268. Worms, "Date certaine," likewise interprets the medal in a messianic context connected with Lemlein and the year 1503.

20 Jost, "Neues," 123–24.

21 Ibid.

22 Geiger, "Aus einem Briefe," 490.

23 Ibid., 490–91.

24 Geiger, "Medaille," 693.

25 Geiger, "Abhandlungen," 173.

26 In 1447/48 Benjamin is referred to as a doctor in Hebrew translations of Averroes's commentaries on Aristotle that had been copied out for him. The manuscripts are housed in BnF, ms. heb. 933 (= IMHM, F 30917), and ms. heb. 1147 (= IMHM, F 31367). Benjamin's exact date of birth (May 21, 1428) is mentioned in a medical miscellany by Bernhard of Gordon, which was in his father's possession; BnF, ms. heb. 1185. For this reference I wish to thank Moti Benmelech.

27 Geiger, "Abhandlungen," 173–74.

28 Geiger, "Medaille," 693.

29 Jost, "Zu dem Aufsatze," 272.

30 Ibid., 274.

31 Ibid., 275.

32 Jost, Geschichte des Judenthums, 3:216n2.

33 Kirchheim, "Nachtrag." Cf. Cahen, Nouvelle explication.

34 Kirchheim, "Nachtrag."

35 Gottheil and Broydé, "Beer," 632.

36 Férarès, "Médaille," 218–19.

37 Explanation of the Annexed Plate.

38 Steyert, Histoire de Lyon, 666–67.

39 Friedenberg, Jewish Medals, 76. For Friedenberg, the purpose and statement of the image as well as the identities of the persons in question remain to be clarified. The temporal gap between the well-known physician Elijah Beer and the "Benjamin" of the medal is in his view too great for it be about Beer's own son; ibid., 74–75.

40 Kottek, "Humilitas," 46. See also Kottek, "Ha-rofeh ha-Anav."

41 Cf. Férarès, "Médaille," 216.

42 Castaldini, Mondi paralleli, 120–21.

43 See, e.g., the reproductions in Steguweit, Europäische Medaillenkunst, no. 20, 125; Friedenberg, Jewish Medals, 63, 90–91.

44 Jost, "Zu dem Aufsatze," 274.

45 Zunz, "Medaille," 149.

46 Kottek, "Humilitas," 44.

47 Ibid., 45.

48 Cf., e.g., the reproductions in Friedländer, Die italienischen Schaumünzen, table XV, no. 1; Steguweit, Europäische Medaillenkunst, 79, fig. 105; Friedenberg, Jewish Medals, 89–90.

49 See, by contrast, the perfection of the famous portrait medal of Doña Gracia Nasi (1558); Friedenberg, Jewish Medals, 45.

50 See ibid., 77–78, 92–93, on other cases in which Christians produced medals then given out as the work of Jews.

51 Following Luther, Heilige Schrifft: "Aber ich weis das mein Erlöser lebet vnd er wird mich hernach aus der Erden auffwecken." My emphasis. The JPS Hebrew-English Tanakh in contrast translates the second part: "In the end He will testify on earth."

52 On the doctrine of the resurrection and its biblical basis in Christianity and in Judaism, see Madigan and Levenson, *Resurrection*. See also Levenson, *Resurrection*.

53 Weiser, *Hiob*, 153.

54 Cf., e.g., at the end of Abraham ibn Ezra's piyyut *Nishmat kol ḥai*, which is part of the morning worship service on the Sabbath and on holidays; Elbogen, *Jewish Liturgy*, 96; Davidson, *Thesaurus*, 3:231–32n769. For this reference I would like to thank Yacov Guggenheim.

55 Apoc. 22:13; cf. 1:8. I am indebted to Anselm Schubert for this observation.

56 Friedenberg, *Jewish Medals*, 42–46.

57 Cf. the influential overview by Scher, *Currency of Fame*, 13–28.

58 Cf. Jost, "Neues," 123, on the use of relevant texts to strengthen the belief in redemption as a talisman. Cf. also Zunz, "Medaille," 157.

59 The explanation that the portrait stands as symbolic epitome of pride and arrogance, in contrast to the humility that is actually appropriate for mankind, does little to convince. Thus, e.g., Kottek, "Humilitas," 44–45.

BIBLIOGRAPHY

MANUSCRIPTS

Biblioteca Apostolica Vaticana
Cod. Pal. lat. 1362 b
Ebr. 187

Biblioteca de San Lorenzo, El Escorial
G-III-11

Biblioteca Palatina, Parma
De Rossi 293

BnF, Paris
A-2963 (5)
Ms. heb. 933
Ms. heb. 1147
Ms. heb. 1185

Bodleian Library, Oxford
MS Mich. 121
MS Opp. 649
MS Opp. 712
MS Opp. 714
MS Opp. Add. Qu. 40

BSB, Munich
Cod. hebr. 426
Cod. hebr. 495
Cod. hebr. 827

HAB, Wolfenbüttel
Cod. Guelf. 30.4 Extrav.

IMHM, Jerusalem
B 63 (= BSB, Cod. hebr. 495)
F 245 (= Biblioteca Apostolica Vaticana,
    Ebr. 187)
F 1042 (= State and University Library,
    Hamburg, Cod. hebr. 237)
F 1653 (= BSB, Cod. hebr. 426)
F 4513 (= MTA, Ms. Kaufmann A 179)
F 8837 (= Biblioteca de San Lorenzo,
    G-III-11)
F 17404 (= Bodleian Library, MS Opp. Add.
    Qu. 40)
F 17708 G (= Bodleian Library, MS Opp.
    649)
F 19963 (= Bodleian Library, MS Mich. 121)
F 20496 (= Bodleian Library, MS Opp. 714)
F 20523 (= Bodleian Library, MS Opp. 712)
F 28735 (= JTS, Ms. 2482)
F 30917 (= BnF, Ms. heb. 933)
F 31367 (= BnF, Ms. heb. 1147)
F 38866 (= BSB, Cod. hebr. 827)
F 44117 (= RSL, Ms. Günzburg 652)
F 47566 (= RSL, Ms. Günzburg 722)
F 52209 (= NLI, Ms. Heb. 8° 5245)

Institut für Stadtgeschichte, Frankfurt am
   Main
Rechneiamt, Bücher 398, Diurnalia 1550–55

NLI, Jerusalem
Ms. Heb. 8° 5245

JTS, New York
Ms. 2482

Jewish Museum, Prague
Ms. 445

MTA, Budapest
Ms. Kaufmann A 179

RSL, Moskau
Ms. Günzburg 652
Ms. Günzburg 722

State and University Library, Hamburg
Cod. hebr. 237

City Archives, Worms
Abt. 1 B, Nr. 2021/21

PRINTED SOURCES

Abravanel, Isaac. *Perush ha-tanakh*. Vol. 4, *Perush al nevi'im aḥaronim*. Jaffa: Hoẓa'at sefarim torah ve-da'at, 1960.

———. *Sefer yeshu'ot meshiḥo*. Jerusalem: Hoẓa'at sefarim torah ve-da'at, 1999.

Adler, Elkan N. *Jewish Travellers*. London: RoutledgeCurzon, 1930. Reprint, New York: Routledge, 2014.

Adler, Marcus N., ed. *The Itinerary of Benjamin of Tudela: Critical Text, Translation and Commentary*. London: Henry Frowde, 1907. Reprint, New York: P. Feldheim, n.d.

Aemilius, Paulus. *Widerlegung/ vnd ablainung etlicher fürnemster Articul/ vnd vrsachen/ darumb die Juden/ iren und der gantzen welt rechten/ warhaftigen Messiam Jesum Christum nit annemen*. Ingolstadt: Alexander Weißenhorn, 1548.

Aerts, Willem J., and George A. A. Kortekaas, eds. *Die Apokalypse des Pseudo-Methodius: Die ältesten griechischen und lateinischen Übersetzungen*. 2 vols. Corpus Scriptorum Christianorum Orientalium 569/70, Subsidia 97/98. Leuven: Peeters, 1998.

Aescoly, Aaron Z. *Jewish Messianic Movements: Sources and Documents on Messianism in Jewish History from the Bar-Kokhba Revolt until Recent Times in Two Volumes*. Vol. 1, *From the Bar-Kokhba Revolt until the Expulsion of the Jews from Spain*. 2nd ed. Jerusalem: Bialik Institute, 1987. [Hebrew]

———. *The Story of David Hareuveni: Copied from the Oxford Manuscript*. 2nd ed. Jerusalem: Bialik Institute, 1993. [Hebrew]

Andernacht, Dietrich. *Regesten zur Geschichte der Juden in der Reichsstadt Frankfurt am Main von 1520–1616*. Edited by Helga Andernacht. 2 vols. Hannover: Hahn, 2007.

Aptroot, Marion, and Rebekka Voß, eds. *Libes briv (1748/49): Isaak Wetzlars pietistisches Erneuerungsprogramm des Judentums. Textedition, Übersetzung, Kommentar und historische Beiträge*. Hamburg: Buske, 2021.

Augusti, Friedrich Albrecht. *Geheimnisse der Jüden von dem Wunder-Fluß Sambathjon, wie auch von denen rothen Juden, in einem Brief-Wechsel mit denen heutigen Jüden, zur Erläuterung 2 Reg. 17,6 abgehandelt, und dem Druck überlassen*. Erfurt: Verlag der Jungnicolischen Erbin Buchhandlung, 1748.

Aulinger, Rosemarie, ed. *Der Reichstag in Regensburg und die Verhandlungen über einen Fried-stand mit den Protestanten in Schweinfurt und Nürnberg 1532.* Deutsche Reichstagsakten, Jüngere Reihe 10. Göttingen: Vandenhoeck & Ruprecht, 1992.

Aventinus, Johannes. *Baierische Chronik.* Edited by Georg Leidinger. Jena: E. Diederichs, 1926.

Ayn sheyn mayse dos iz die geshikhtnis fun Rebe Meyer. Un fun den rotn yudlayn. Un fun den shvarzn minkh. Amsterdam: Süsskind Alexander b. Kalonymus Weilen, 1704.

Ayn sheyn vunderlikh mayse. Fürth: Zvi Hirsch b. Joseph ha-Levi, 1694.

Baruchson, Shifra. *Books and Readers: The Reading Interests of Italian Jews at the Close of the Renaissance.* Ramat Gan: Bar-Ilan University Press, 1993. [Hebrew]

Bebel, Heinrich. *Facetien: Drei Bücher.* Edited by Gustav Bebermeyer. Leipzig: K. W. Hiersemann, 1931.

Beit-Arié, Malachi. "A Letter Concerning the Ten Tribes by the Kabbalist R. Abraham ben Eliezer ha-Levi from the Year [5]288." *Kobez al Yad* n.s. 6 (1966): 369–78.

Die Bekenntnisschriften der evangelisch-lutherischen Kirche. Edited by Deutscher Evangelischer Kirchenausschuss. 12th ed. Göttingen: Vandenhoeck & Ruprecht, 1998.

Berger, David, ed. *The Jewish-Christian Debate in the High Middle Ages: A Critical Edition of the Nizzahon Vetus.* Philadelphia: Jewish Publication Society of America, 1979.

Berliner, Abraham. "Sefer hazkarat neshamot kehillat Warmaisa." *Kobez al Yad* 3 (1887): 1–62.

Bin Gorion, Micha J. *Der Born Judas: Legenden, Märchen und Erzählungen.* 6 vols. Leipzig: Insel-Verlag, 1919–21.

Bischoff, Melchior. *Gründlicher Bericht Von Christlicher Tauffe Johannis Christiani, eines gebornen Jüden von Franckfurt am Mayn/ vor seiner Widergeburt Elias genant/ geschehen zu Coburg in der Pfarrkirchen/ am Palm Sontage/ den 5. April. Anno 1612 [. . .].* Erfurt: Joachim Mechler, 1614.

Bon, Daniel Jacob. *Wolgemeintes Sendschreiben/ Mein Daniel Jacob Bon/ bekehrten Judens/ Nunmehr unter dem Namen Claus Andreas von Osteroda/ [. . .] abgelassen An meine hertzlich=geehrte Eltern/ nahmentlich Jacob Bon/ und Sarah Wolff/ [. . .] Darin ihnen die Ursach meines Abtrits vom Jüdenthum [. . .] fürgestellet wird.* Nordhausen: August Martin Hynitzsch, 1694.

Bossert, Gustav. "Augustin Bader von Augsburg, der Prophet und König und seine Genossen, nach den Prozeßakten von 1530." *Archiv für Reformationsgeschichte* 10 (1912/13): 117–65, 209–41, 297–349; 11 (1914): 19–64, 103–33, 176–99.

———, ed. *Quellen zur Geschichte der Wiedertäufer.* Vol. 1, *Herzogtum Württemberg.* Quellen und Forschungen zur Reformationsgeschichte 13. Leipzig: M. Heinsius Nachfolger Eger & Sievers, 1930.

Boveland, Karin, Christoph P. Burger, and Ruth Steffen, eds. *Der Antichrist und Die Fünfzehn Zeichen vor dem Jüngsten Gericht: Faksimile der ersten typographischen Ausgabe eines unbekannten Straßburger Druckers, um 1480.* 2 vols. Hamburg: Wittig, 1979.

Brant, Sebastian. *Von den Wunderlichen zamefugung der öbersten Planeten.* [Pforzheim], 1504.

Brenz, Johannes. *Türcken Büchlein: Wie sich Prediger vnd Leien halten sollen/ so der Türck das Deudsche Land vberfallen würde. Christliche vnd nottürfftige vnterrichtung.* Wittenberg: Georg Rhau, 1531.

Bretschneider, Carl G., and Heinrich E. Bindseil, eds. *Philippi Melanthonis opera quae supersunt omnia.* 28 vols. Corpus Reformatorum 1–28. Halle: Schwetschke, 1834–60. Reprint, Nieuwkoop: De Graaf, 1968.

Buber, Salomon, ed. *Lekah tob (Pesikta sutarta): Ein agadischer Commentar zum ersten und zweiten Buch Mosis von R. Tobia ben Elieser.* Vilnius: Wittwe & Gebrüder Romm, 1884. Reprint, Jerusalem: S. Monzon, 1960. [Hebrew]

Buchenroeder, Michael. *Eilende Messias Juden-Post/ Oder Gründliche Widerlegung des heutigen Gedichts von den neuerstandenen Messia der Juden/ und seines Propheten Nathans: Wie auch/ von andern dergleichen sich mehrmahls entbörenden jüdischen Rebellen [. . .].* Nuremberg: Wolf Eberhard Felssecker, 1666.

Buxtorf, Johannes. *Synagoga Ivdaica: Das ist/ Jüden Schul: Darinnen der gantz Jüdische Glaub vnd Glaubensvbung/ mit allen Ceremonien/ Satzungen/ Sitten vnd Gebräuchen/ wie sie bey jhnen offentlich vnd heimlich im Brauche: Auß jhren eigenen Bücheren vnd Schrifften/ so den Christen mehrtheils vnbekandt vnnd verborgen sind/ [. . .] grundlich erkläret: Item Ein Außführlicher Bericht von Jhrem zukünfftigen Messia [. . .].* Basel: Wilhelm Antonius, 1603.

Caesarius of Heisterbach. *Dialogus miraculorum.* Edited by Joseph Stange. Cologne: J. M. Heberle, 1851.

———. *Von Geheimnissen und Wundern.* Edited by Helmut Herles. 2nd ed. Bonn: Bouvier, 1991.

Capito, Wolfgang. *In Hoseam Prophetam V F Capitonis Commentarius/ Ex Quo Peculiaria Pro/phetias, & hactenus fortaßis nusquam/ sic tractata, si uersam pagellam/ & indicem percurris, co/gnoscere potes.* Strasbourg: Johannes Herwagen, 1528.

———. "V[oulphgang] F[abricius] C[apito] a nostre allie et confedere le peuple de l'alliance de Sinai." In *La Bible qui est toute la sainte Escripture. En laquelle sont contenus/ le Vieil Testament & le Nouveau/ translatez en francoys: Le Vieil/ de lebrieu: & le Nouveau/ du grec.* Translated by Pierre Robert Olivétan. Neuchâtel: Pirot Picard, 1535.

Cellarius, Martin. *De operibus Dei.* Strasbourg: Johannes Herwagen, 1527.

Charlesworth, James H., ed. *The Old Testament Pseudepigrapha.* Vol. 1: *Apocalyptic Literature and Testaments.* Peabody, MA: Hendrickson, 1983.

Christiani, David. *De Messia Dispvtationes IV: in qvibus agitur: I. De Messia eiusque adventu in genere. II. De duobus Messiis, quos Judaei praestolantur & comminiscuntur. III. De Pseudo-Messiis variis, quos seculis diversis coeci ac cervicosi Judaei commenti, ac Meßiae exiomate dignati sunt. IV. De miraculis X. Meßiae adventum praecessuris in genere. Accessit sive tractatvs de paradiso, historice, geographice, philologice & theologice delineato.* Gießen: Chemlin, 1657.

Clemen, Otto. *Flugschriften aus den ersten Jahren der Reformation.* 4 vols. Halle: Haupt, 1906–11. Reprint, Nieuwkoop: De Graaf, 1967.

Costerus, Abraham. *Historie der Joden.* Amsterdam: Gerrit Willemsz, 1608.

David, Abraham, ed. *A Hebrew Chronicle from Prague c. 1615.* Jerusalem: Dinur Center, 1984. [Hebrew]

———, ed. *A Hebrew Chronicle from Prague, c. 1615.* Tuscaloosa: University of Alabama Press, 1993.

———. "Sivuv R. Petaḥya mi-Regensburg be-nusaḥ ḥadash." *Kobez al Yad* n.s. 13 (1996): 235–69.

———. "Tales Concerning Persecutions in Medieval Germany." In *Papers on Medieval Hebrew Literature: Presented to A. M. Habermann on the Occasion of His 75th Birthday*, edited by Zvi Malachi, 69–83. Jerusalem: Mass, 1977.

Droz, Eugénie. *Chemins de l'hérésie: Textes et documents*. Vol. 1. Genf: Slatkine, 1970.

Dülmen, Richard van, ed. *Das Täuferreich zu Münster 1534–1535: Berichte und Dokumente*. Munich: Deutscher Taschenbuch Verlag, 1974.

Eisenmenger, Johann Andreas. *Entdecktes Judenthum, oder: Gründlicher und Wahrhaffter Bericht, welchergestalt die verstockten Juden Die Hochheilige Dreyeinigkeit, Gott Vater, Sohn und Heiligen Geist erschrecklicherweise lästern und verunehren*. 2 vols. [Frankfurt am Main]: 1700–42.

Eisenstein, Yehuda D. *Oẓar Vikkuḥim*. New York: Reznick, Menschel, 1928.

Eldad ha-Dani. *Seyfer Eldad ha-Dani*. Constantinople, 1668.

Epstein, Abraham. "Eldad ha-Dani: Seine Berichte über die zehn Stämme und deren Ritus in verschiedenen Versionen nach Handschriften und alten Drucken mit Einleitung und Anmerkungen nebst einem Excurse über die Falascha und deren Gebräuche." In *The Literary Works of Abraham Epstein*, edited by Abraham M. Habermann, 1:1–211, 2nd ed. Jerusalem: Mossad Harav Kook, 1965. [Hebrew]

Epstein, Jacob N. "Regarding the Messianic Movement in Sicily." *Tarbiz* 11 (1940): 218–19. [Hebrew]

Euling, Karl, ed. *Chronik des Johan Oldecop*. Bibliothek des Literarischen Vereins in Stuttgart 190. Tübingen: H. Laupp, 1891.

Even-Shemuel, Yehuda. *Midreshei ge'ullah: Pirkei ha-apokalipsah ha-yehudit mi-ḥatimat ha-talmud ha-Bavli ad reshit ha-elef ha-shishi*. 2nd ed. Jerusalem: Bialik Institute, 1954.

———, ed. *Sefer moreh nevukhim le-rabeinu Moshe b. Maimon*. Translated by Samuel ibn Tibbon. Vol. 1. Tel Aviv: Shvil, 1935.

Fabronius, Hermann. *Bekehrung der Jüden: Vnd Von Mancherley Abergläubischen Ceremonien/ vnnd seltzamen Sitten/ so die zerstreweten Jüden haben: Vnd wie sie in der Christenheit zu dulden seyn [...]*. Erfurt: Fritzsch, 1624.

Fagius, Paulus. *Liber fidei: Preciosvs bonvs et ivcvndvs, qvem aedidit vir qvidam israelites, sapiens & prudens, ante multos annos, ad docendum & comprobandum in eo, argumentis sufficienti-bus & euidentibus, quod fides Christianorum [...] perfecta, recta & indubitata sit, collocata super fundamentum legis, prophetarum & hagiographorum, ideo uocauit nomen eius Sepher Aemana [...]*. Isny, 1542.

Farissol, Abraham b. Mordechai. *Iggeret orḥot olam*. Venice: Di Gara, 1586.

Flusser, David, ed. *Sefer Yossipon*. 2 vols. Jerusalem: Bialik Institute, 1978–80. [Hebrew]

Folz, Hans. *Die Reimpaarsprüche*. Edited by Hanns Fischer. Munich: Beck, 1961.

Fraenkel, Jonah, ed. *Maḥzor shavu'ot le-fi minhagei bnei Ashkenaz le-khol anfeihem*. Jerusalem: Koren, 2000.

Fraenkel-Goldschmidt, Chava, ed. *The Historical Writings of Joseph of Rosheim: Leader of Jewry in Early Modern Germany*. Studies in Jewish History and Culture 12. Leiden: Brill, 2006.

————, ed. *Iosephi de Rosheim: Sefer Hammiknah.* Jerusalem: Mekiṭẓei Nirdanim, 1970. [Hebrew]

————, ed. *Joseph of Rosheim: Historical Writings.* Jerusalem: Magnes Press, 1996. [Hebrew]

Franck, Sebastian. *Chronica zeitbuch unnd Geschichtsbibell von anbegyn bisz in diss gegenwertig M.D.xxxvi. iar verlengt [...].* Ulm: Varrnier, 1536. Reprint, Darmstadt: Wissenschaftliche Buchgesellschaft, 1969.

Friedländer, Julius. *Die italienischen Schaumünzen des fünfzehnten Jahrhunderts 1430–1530: Ein Beitrag zur Kunstgeschichte.* Berlin: Weidmann, 1880. Reprint, Bologna: Forni, 1976.

Gans, David. *Zemah David: A Chronicle of Jewish and World History (Prague, 1592).* Edited by Mordechai Breuer. Jerusalem: Magnes Press, 1983. [Hebrew]

Garstad, Benjamin, ed. *Apocalypse of Pseudo-Methodius: An Alexandrian World Chronicle.* Dumbarton Oaks Medieval Library. Cambridge, MA: Harvard University Press, 2012.

Gaster, Moses. *The Exempla of the Rabbis: Being a Collection of Exempla, Apologues and Tales Culled from Hebrew Manuscripts and Rare Hebrew Books.* London: Asia Publishing House, 1924. Reprint, New York: Ktav, 1968.

Génebrard, Gilbert. *Chronographia in duos libros distincta: Prior est de Rebus veteris Populi: Posterior recentes historias praesertimque: Ecclesiasticas complectitur.* Paris: Iuvenus, 1567.

Gengenbach, Pamphilius. *Der Nollhart.* Edited by Violanta Werren-Uffer. Schweizer Texte 1. Bern: Lang, 1977.

Gerson, Christian. *Der Jüden Thalmud Fürnembster innhalt/ vnd Widerlegung/ In Zwey Bücher verfasset. Im Ersten Wird die gantze Jüdische Religion/ vnd falsche Gottesdienste beschrieben. Im Andern Werden dieselbe/ beydes durch die schrifft des Alten Testaments/ vnd des Thalmuds selbst/ gründlich widerlegt vnd vmbgestossen.* Goslar: Johan Vogt, 1607.

Die geshikhtnis fun Rebe Meyer Shats un fun den rotn yudlayn un fun den shvartsn minkh. [Amsterdam, 1805].

Ein gesprech auff das kurtzt zwuschen eynem Christen vnd Juden/ auch eynem Wyrthe sampt seynem Haußknecht/ den Eckstein Christum betreffendt/ so noch Götlicher schrifft abkkunterfeyt ist/ wie alhie bey gedruckt figur auß weyßet. Erfurt: Michael Buchführer, 1524.

Ginzberg, Louis. "Haggadot ketu'ot." *Me'assef le-ḥokhmat Yisra'el* 9 (1922): 43–45.

————, ed. *The Legends of the Jews.* 6 vols. Philadelphia: Jewish Publication Society of America, 1909–55. Reprint, Hildesheim: Olms, 2000.

Giustiniani, Agostino. *Precatio Pietatis plena ad Deum omnipotentem composita ex duobus et septuaginta nominibus divinis Hebraicis et Latinis una cum interprete commentario.* Venice: Alessandro Paganino, 1513.

Grünhut, Lazar, ed. *Die Rundreise des Rabbi Petachjah aus Regensburg.* Sippurei nos'im ivriyim 1. Frankfurt am Main: Kauffmann, 1904/5. Reprint, Jerusalem, 1967. [Hebrew]

Güttel, Caspar. *Von den Strafen und Plagen/ die etwan Gott uber die Juden/ und auch zeyt/ ytzt aber ynn sonderheit uber uns Christen hat verhangen und ausgehen lassen.* Zwickau: Gabriel Kantz, 1529.

Habermann, Abraham M. *Shirei ha-yiḥud ve-ha-kavod.* Jerusalem: Mossad Harav Kook, 1948.

Haim b. Bezalel. *Sefer iggeret ha-tiyyul ha-shalem.* Jerusalem: Ehrenreich, 1956–57.

Ha-Kohen, Joseph. *Chronicle of French and Ottoman Kings.* 3 vols. Edited by Robert Bonfil. Jerusalem: Magnes Press, 2020. [Hebrew]

———. *Sefer divrei ha-yamim le-malkei ẓarfat u-malkei bet ottoman ha-togar.* Jerusalem: Bialik Institute, 1967.

———. *Sefer 'Emeq ha-Bakhah (The Vale of Tears): With the Chronicle of the Anonymous Corrector.* Edited by Karin Almbladh. Uppsala: Uppsala University Press, 1981.

———. *The Vale of Tears.* Edited by Robert Bonfil. Jerusalem: Magnes Press, 2020. [Hebrew]

Ha-Kohen, Tuvia b. Moses. *Ma'aseh Tuviyah.* Venice: Bragadin, 1708.

Hardt, Hermann von der. *De usu et abusu Psalmi CXIX apud Judaeos: De R. Schlomo Malchu, deque novissimo inter Judaeos anno praesenti MDCCXIV adventus Messiae termino […].* Helmstedt: Hamm, 1714.

Haverkamp, Eva, ed. *Hebräische Berichte über Judenverfolgungen während des Ersten Kreuzzugs.* MGH: Hebräische Texte aus dem mittelalterlichen Deutschland 1. Hannover: Hahn, 2005.

Ibn Verga, Solomon. *Schevet Jehuda: Ein Buch über das Leiden des jüdischen Volkes im Exil.* Translated by Me'ir Wiener, edited by Sina Rauschenbach. Berlin: Parerga, 2006.

Ibn Yaḥya, Gedalya. *Shalshelet ha-kabbalah.* Venice: Di Gara, 1587. Reprint, Jerusalem: Hoẓa'at ha-dorot ha-rishonim ve-korotam, 2000.

Isaac, Johannes. *De Astrologia: Rabbi Mosis Filii Meimon Epistola elegans, & cum Christiana religione congruens, Hebraea, nunc primum edita & latina facta.* Cologne: Soter, 1555.

Jellinek, Adolph, ed. *Bet ha-Midrasch: Sammlung kleiner Midraschim und vermischter Abhandlungen aus der ältern jüdischen Literatur.* Leipzig/Vienna, 1853–77. Reprint, Jerusalem: Bamberger & Wahrmann, 1938. [Hebrew]

Jonas, Justus. *Das siebend Capitel Danielis von des Türcken Gotteslesterung vnd schrecklich morderey.* Wittenberg: Hans Lufft, 1529.

Joseph, Paul. *Gründlicher beweiß/ auß dem alten Testament/ vnd zum theil auß dem Jüdischen Talmud/ Wie daß Christus Jesus der Jungfrau Marie Son/ sey der wahre verheissene Messias vnd Heyland der Welt/ vnd die ander Person inn der heiligen Dreyfaltigkeit […].* Altdorf, 1612.

Judah b. Samuel he-Ḥasid. *Das Buch der Frommen nach der Rezension in Cod. de Rossi No. 1033.* Edited by Jehuda Wistinetzki and Jakob Freimann. Frankfurt am Main: Wahrmann, 1924. Reprint, Jerusalem: Wahrmann, 1969. [Hebrew]

Keller, Adelbert von, ed. *Fastnachtspiele aus dem 15. Jahrhundert.* 4 vols. Bibliothek des Litterarischen Vereins in Stuttgart 28–30, 46. Stuttgart: Litterarischer Verein, 1853–58. Reprint, Darmstadt: Wissenschaftliche Buchgesellschaft, 1965/66.

Kirchheim, Judah Löw. *The Customs of Worms Jewry.* Edited by Israel M. Peles. Jerusalem: Mif'al torat ḥakhmei Ashkenaz, Mekhon Yerushalayim, 1987. [Hebrew]

Kirchhof, Hans W. *Wendunmuth.* Edited by Hermann Oesterley. 5 vols. Tübingen: Laupp, 1869. Reprint, Hildesheim: Olms, 1980.

Kitzingen, Jacob b. Joseph. *Ḥag ha-pessaḥ.* Cracow, 1597.

Köhler, Hans-Joachim, ed. *Flugschriften des frühen 16. Jahrhunderts (1501–1530).* Zug: Inter Documentation, 1978–87.

Kolde, Theodor. *Die älteste Redaktion der Augsburger Konfession mit Melanchthons Einleitung: Zum ersten Mal herausgegeben und geschichtlich gewürdigt.* Gütersloh: Bertelsmann, 1906.

[Kracauer, Isidore]. "Jüdischer Bericht über die Belagerung von 1552: Nach einer Handschrift der Stadtbibliothek zu Amsterdam." In *Frankfurter Chroniken und annalistische*

Aufzeichungen der Reformationszeit nebst einer Darstellung der Frankfurter Belagerung von 1552, edited by Rudolf Jung. Quellen zur Frankfurter Geschichte 2. Frankfurt am Main: Jügel, 1888.

Kramer, Michael. *Eyn vnderredung vom glawben, durch Micheln kromer, Pfarherr zu Cunitz, vnd eynem Judischen Rabien, mit namen Jacob vonn Brucks, geschehenn ynß Richters hauße do selbst zu Cunitz: Mitwoch nach Andree M.D.xxiij.* Erfurt: Mathes Maler, 1523.

Krebs, Manfred, and Hans G. Rott, eds. *Quellen zur Geschichte der Täufer.* Vol. 1, *Elsaß*, pt. 1, *Stadt Straßburg 1522–1532*. Quellen und Forschungen zur Reformationsgeschichte 26. Gütersloh: Bertelsmann, 1959.

Kupfer, Ephraim. "The Visions of R. Asher ben R. Meir Called Lemlein Reutlingen." *Kobez al Yad* n.s. 8 (1975): 385–423.

Laube, Adolf, ed. *Flugschriften vom Bauernkrieg zum Täuferreich (1526–1535).* Vol. 2. Berlin: Akademie-Verlag, 1992.

Lent, Johann von. *Schediasma historico-philologicum de Judaeorum Pseudomessiis.* Herborn: J. H. Andreae, 1683.

Liliencron, Rochus von. *Die historischen Volkslieder der Deutschen vom 13. bis 16. Jahrhundert.* 4 vols. Leipzig: Vogel, 1865–69.

Lipmann Heller, Yom Tov. *Ma'adannei Yom Tov.* Prague, 1628.

Loewinger, Samuel. "Recherches sur l'oeuvre apologétique d'Abraham Farissol." *Revue des Études Juives* 105 (1940): 23–53.

Lombardus, Marcus. *Gründtlicher Bericht Vnd Erklärung von der Juden Handlungen vnnd Ceremonien/ schelten vnd fluchen wider vnseren Herren Jesum Christum vnd seine Kirchen [...].* Basel: Apiarius, 1573.

Luther, Martin. *Die gantze Heilige Schrifft deudsch, Wittenberg 1545: Letzte zu Luthers Lebzeiten erschienene Ausgabe.* Edited by Hans Volz. 3 vols. Munich: Rogner & Bernhard, 1972.

———. *D. Martin Luthers Werke: Kritische Gesamtausgabe (Weimarer Ausgabe).* 65 vols. Weimar: Böhlau, 1883–93.

Maimonides, Moses. *Epistle to Yemen: The Arabic Original and the Three Hebrew Versions.* Edited by Abraham S. Halkin. Translated by Boaz Cohen. New York: American Academy for Jewish Research, 1952.

Mangelsdorf, Frank, ed. *Der gläserne Schatz: Die Bilderbibel der St. Marienkirche in Frankfurt (Oder).* 2nd ed. Berlin: Das Neue Berlin, 2007.

Mann, Jacob. *Texts and Studies in Jewish History and Literature.* 2 vols. 2nd ed. New York: Ktav, 1972.

Margaritha, Antonius. *Erklerung: Wie aus dem heylligen. 53. Capittel/ des fürnemigsten Propheten Esaie gründtlich außgefüert/ probiert/ das der verhaischen Moschiach (wellicher Christus ist) schon khomen/ [...].* Vienna: Singrenium, 1534.

———. *Der gantz Jüdisch glaub mit sampt ainer gründtlichen vnd warhafften anzaygunge/ Aller Satzungen/ Ceremonien/ Gebetten/ Haymliche vnd offentliche Gebreuch/ deren sich dye Juden halten/ durch das gantz Jar/ Mit schönen vnd gegründten Argumenten wyder jren Glauben.* Augsburg: Steyner, 1530.

———. *Ain kurtzer Bericht vnd anzaigung wo die Christlich Ceremonien vom Balmesel in bayden Testamenten gegründt sei: Auch etlich erdichte falsche Comment vnd Fabln So die blinden yetz vermainten halßsterrige Juden von jrem zuekünfftigen erdichten Moschiach/ das ist Christus vnd von sein Esel schreiben vnnd liegen.* Vienna: Singrenium, 1541.

Margulies, Mordecai, ed. *Midrash Haggadol on the Pentateuch.* Vol. 1, *Genesis.* Jerusalem: Mossad Harav Kook, 1947. Reprint, Jerusalem: Mossad Harav Kook, 1967. [Hebrew]

Marmorstein, Arthur. "Les signes du Messie." *Revue des Études Juives* 52 (1906): 176–86.

Martini, Raymond. *Pugio fidei adversus Mauros et Iudaeos.* Edited by Joseph de Voisin. Paris: Henault, 1651.

Marx, Alexander. "Le faux messie Ascher Laemmlein." *Revue des Études Juives* 61 (1911): 135–38.

Mayse dos da heyst Megiles Rebe Meyer. Amsterdam, 1660.

Mayse gvures hashem fon ayn gros nes vos yudn is geshehen vos zey zenen nitsl gevorn fun ayn shlekhtn galekh dorkh R. Meyer vos hot gemakht Akdomes un dorkh ayn rot yudn unter dem Sambatyen. Lviv, [1839].

Megiles Reb Meyer. Cremona, [ca. 1560].

Menasseh ben Israel. *The Hope of Israel: The English Translation by Moses Wall 1652.* Edited by Henry Méchoulan and Gérard Nahon. Oxford: Oxford University Press, 1987.

Mendele Moykher Sforim. *Kitser masoes Binyomin hashlishi.* Amherst, MA: National Yiddish Book Center, 1999.

———. *Tales of Mendele the Book Peddler: Fishke the Lame and Benjamin the Third.* Edited by Ken Frieden and Dan Miron. New York: Schocken, 1996.

Me'ora'ot Ẓvi. Warsaw, 1835.

Migne, Jacques-Paul, ed. *Patrologiae cursus completus: Series Latina.* 217 vols. Paris: Garnier, 1841–55.

Mikra'ot gedolot im perush ha-Malbim. Vol. 2, *Shmu'el: Im perush devar Shmu'el.* Jerusalem, 1980/81.

Müller, Gerhard, ed. *Nuntiaturberichte aus Deutschland nebst ergänzenden Aktenstücken: Erste Abteilung 1533–1559.* 2nd supplementary vol. 153, *Legation Lorenzo Campeggios 1532 und Nuntiatur Girolamo Aleandros 1532.* Tübingen: Niemeyer, 1969.

Müller, Johann Christoph. *Greuel der falschen Messien/ wie auch/ Schatz=Kammer des Wahren Messiae Jesu Christi. das ist: Eine ziemliche Lista der Jenigen falschen Messien, so von Anfang der Welt/ biß auff diese ietzige Zeit haben können in Erfahrung gebracht werden. [. . .], in: Ders., Alte und neue Schwarm=Geister=Bruth/ Quäcker=Greuel/ Das ist Gründliche Vorstellung und Glaubwürdige Erzehlung Von denen Alten Quackern Und Neuen Frey= Geistern/ [. . .].* N.p., 1702.

Münster, Sebastian. *En Tibi Lector Hebraica Biblia latina: Latina Planeque Nova Sebastiani Munsteri translatione, post omneis omnium hactenus ubivis gentium aeditiones evulgata, & quoad fieri potuit, Hebraicae veritati conformata: adiectis insuper e Rabinorum commentariis annotationibus [. . .].* Basel: Isengrin and Petrus, 1534.

———. *Evangelium Secundum Matthaeum in Lingua Hebraica cum versione Latina atque succinctis annotationibus [. . .].* Basel: Petrus, 1537.

———. *Messias Christianorvm et Iudaeorum: Hebraicè & Latinè [. . .].* Basel: Petrus, 1539.

———. *Ha-Vikku'aḥ Christiani Hominis cvm Iudaeo pertinaciter prodigiosis suis opinionibus, & scripturae uiolentis interpretationibus addicto.* Basel: Petrus, 1529.

Nigrinus, Georg. *Jüden Feind: Von den Edlen Früchten der Thalmudischen Jüden/ so jetziger zeit in Teutschelande wonen/ ein ernste/ wol gegründte Schrifft/* [. . .]. [Strasbourg?], 1570.

Pfefferkorn, Johannes. *Handt Spiegel: Johannis Pfefferkorn/ wider und gegen die Jüden/ vnd Judischen Thalmudischen schrifftenn So/ sie vber das Cristenlich Regiment/ singen vnd lesen* [. . .] *Solliche artickel zu widerlegen Dargegen ich antwurdt vnd mit bescheidene reden vffgelöst hab.* Mainz: Schöffer, 1511.

———. *Ich bin ain Buchlinn der Juden veindt ist mein namen: ir schalckhait sag ich vnnd wil mich des nit schamenn die lang zeyt verborgen gewest ist als ich thün bedeütenn das wil ich yetz offenbarn allen Cristen leüten dann ich bin mit yren hebraischen schrifften wol verwart, vnd dem verkerten geschleht die warhait nit gespart.* Augsburg: Oeglin, 1509.

———. *In disem buchlein vindet yr ein entlichen furtrag: wie die blinden Juden yr Ostern halten/ vnnd besonderlich wie das Abentmal gessen wirt/ Verner wurde außgedruckt das die Juden ketzer seyn/ des alten vnd neuwen testaments/ Deßhalb sye schuldig seyn des gerichts nach dem gesetz Moysi.* Augsburg: Oeglin, 1509.

———. *In Lob und eer dem Allerdurchleuchtigsten Großmechtigsten Fursten vnd heren hern Maximilian* [. . .] *Romschen kaysers* [. . .]. Cologne: Nuss, 1509.

———. *Jch heyß ein buchlein der iuden peicht: In allen orten vindt man mich leicht/ Vill newen meren synt mir woll bekant/ Jch will mich preyten in allen landt/ Wer mich lyst dem wunsch ich heyl/ Doch das ich den iuden nit werde zu teyl.* Cologne: Johann Landen, 1508.

———. *Der Joeden spiegel.* Cologne, 1507.

———. *Der Juden Spiegel.* Nuremberg: Huber, 1507.

———. *Der Juden Spiegel.* Cologne, 1508.

———. *Speculum adhortationis iudaice ad Christum.* Cologne: von Werden, 1507.

Rasch, Johann. *Ein hübsch Liedt, Wie zu Plonig ein Christen eines Juden Tochter schwanger macht, vnd sie vermeint, sie hette den Messiam empfangen, von einem Engel.* Nuremberg, 1530.

Rhegius, Urbanus. *De Restitutione Regni Israëlitici, contra omnes omnium seculorum Chiliastas* [. . .] *disputatio.* [Augsburg: Steiner], 1536.

———. *Epistola. D. Vrbani Rhegii ad Totam Judeorum Synagogam Brunsuici habitantem, ex Ebraeo in sermonem latinum conuersa. De vero Messia qvod venerit* [. . .]. Hamburg: Wolff, 1591.

———. *Gründtlick Bewiss uth der Propheten/ vnd Apostel schrifften/ dat Jesus Christus/ de rechte ware Messias sy/ tegen der vörstockeden Jöden/ schendige vnde düuelsche lögen.* Lübeck: Balhorn, 1555.

Rivkind, Isaac. "The Historical Allegory of Rabbi Meir Shatz." *Studies in Philology* 3 (1929): 1–42. [Yiddish]

Rüst, Hans. *Mappa mundi: Das ist die mapa mundi un alle land un kungk reich wie sie ligend in der gantze welt.* [Augsburg, ca. 1480].

Salamon, Avrohom Yaacov, ed. *Akdamus Millin: With a New Translation and Commentary Anthologized from the Traditional Rabbinic Literature.* 2nd ed. Brooklyn: Mesorah Publications, 1993.

Sambari, Yosef b. Yitzhak. *Sefer divrei Yosef: Eleven Hundred Years of Jewish History under Muslim Rule.* Edited by Shimon Shtober. Jerusalem: Ben-Zvi Institute, 1994. [Hebrew]

Sanuto, Marino (the Younger). *Diarii.* Edited by Rinaldo Fulin and others. 59 vols. Venice: Visentini, 1879–1903. Reprint, Bologna: Forni, 1969/70.

Sasportas, Jacob. *Sefer ẓiẓat novel Ẓvi.* Edited by Isaiah Tishby. Jerusalem: Bialik Institute, 1954.

Scherer, Georg. *Postill Oder Auslegung der Sontäglichen Euangelien durch das gantze Jahr.* Munich: Henricus, 1610.

Schudt, Johann Jakob. *Jüdische Merckwürdigkeiten: Vorstellende Was sich Curieuses und denckwürdiges in den neuern Zeiten bey einigen Jahrhunderten mit denen in alle IV. Theile der Welt/ sonderlich durch Teutschland/ zerstreuten Juden zugetragen [. . .].* Frankfurt am Main, 1714–18. Reprint, Berlin: Lamm, 1922.

Schwab, Dietrich. *Detectum velum Mosaicum Judaeorum nostri temporis: Das ist: Jüdischer Deckmantel dess Mosaischen Gesetzes, unter welchem die Juden jetzigen Zeit allerley Bubenstück, Laster, Schand und Finantzerey, & üben und treiben, auffgehoben und entdecket.* Mainz: Schwab, 1619.

Schwarz, Peter. *Stella Meshiʻaḥ.* Esslingen: Fyner, 1477.

Sefer akdamut. Warsaw, 1902.

Sefer ma'aseh gvurat ha-shem. Lviv, 1916.

Sefer Yosippon. Mantua, 1480.

Shir ha-yiḥud li-vnei Moshe. Hanau, 1620.

Shir ha-yiḥud li-vnei Moshe. Venice, 1600.

Shirmann, Yefim [Ḥaim], ed. *Ha-shirah ha-ivrit bi-Sefarad u-ve-Provans.* Vol. 2, *Mi-Yosef Kimḥi ad Sa'adya ibn Danan (1150–1492).* Tel Aviv: Dvir, 1956.

Sippur ḥalomot keẓ ha-pla'ot. Lviv, 1804.

Soldan, Justus. *Entdeckunge vnd fürstellung Der Bundsladen vnd Gnadenstuels deß alten Testaments. Das ist: Gründliche Außführunge vnd Kräfftige Beweißthume in zwantzig zweyen Reden begriffen/ daß Jesus Christus/ der Sohn Gottes vnd die andere Person der hochgelobten Dreyeinigkeit/ der rechte versprochene Messias/ [. . .] An die naher Cassel beschriebene vnd versamlete der Judenschafft/ [. . .].* Kassel: Mencke, 1650.

Sonne, Isaiah. "Neue Dokumente über Salomo Molcho." *Monatsschrift für Geschichte und Wissenschaft des Judentums* n.s. 75.2 (1931): 127–35.

Staffelsteiner, Paul. *Etliche Artickel von den Juden als nemlich deren verheiratungen Hochzeiten Ehelichem leben Absterben Begrebnussen Grabsteinen Bahn Viehschlachtung Wein trincken und dergleichen aus irem Hebreischen Talmut unnd Cabolisten.* Heidelberg: [Kohl, 1562?].

Starck, Astrid, ed. *Un beau livre d'histoires: Eyn shön Mayse bukh, Traduction du Yiddish, introduction et notes.* 2 vols. Basel: Schwabe, 2004.

Steglich, Wolfgang, ed. *Die schwäbischen Bundestage zwischen den Reichstagen zu Speyer 1529 und Augsburg 1530: Die Bereitstellung der Reichshilfe zum Türkenkrieg und zur Rettung Wiens 1529.* Deutsche Reichstagsakten, Jüngere Reihe 8.2. Göttingen: Vandenhoeck & Ruprecht, 1971.

Steguweit, Wolfgang. *Europäische Medaillenkunst von der Renaissance bis zur Gegenwart.* Berlin: Mann, 1995.

Stoneman, Richard, ed. *The Greek Alexander Romance.* New York: Penguin, 1991.

Stupperich, Robert, ed. *Die Schriften der Münsterischen Täufer und ihre Gegner*. Vol. 3, *Die Schriften von evangelischer Seite gegen die Täufer*. Veröffentlichungen der Historischen Kommission Westfalens 32. Münster: Aschendorff, 1983.

Theodor, Juda, and Chanoch Albeck. *Midrash Bereshit Rabba: Critical Edition with Notes and Commentary*. 2nd ed. Jerusalem: Wahrmann, 1965. [Hebrew]

Treves, Naphtali Hirtz. *Sefer dikduk tefillah*. Tiengen, 1560. Reprint, New York, 2003.

———. *Sefer Naftali*. London: Ha-makhrikh, 1959. Reprint, in *Sefer rabeinu Bahya al hatorah*. 4 vols. Bne Brak, 1992.

———. *Simanim al ḥidushei ha-Baḥya ve-aḥar kakh gam bi'urim yafim alav*. Heddernheim, 1546.

Ullendorf, Edward, and Charles F. Beckingham. *The Hebrew Letters of Prester John*. Oxford: Oxford University Press, 1982.

Ulmer, Rivka. *Turmoil, Trauma and Triumph: The Fettmilch Uprising in Frankfurt am Main (1612–1616) according to Megillas Vintz: A Critical Edition of the Yiddish and Hebrew Text Including an English Translation*. Frankfurt am Main: Lang, 2001.

Usque, Samuel. *Consolation for the Tribulations of Israel*. Translated by Martin A. Cohen. Philadelphia: Jewish Publication Society of America, 1977.

Victor von Carben. *De vita et moribus Judaeorum Victoris de Carben, olim Judaei nunc Christi miseratione christiani, libellus*. Paris: [Stephanus?], 1511.

———. *Hier inne wirt gelesen wie Her Victor von Carben. Welicher eyn Rabi der Juden gewest ist zu Cristlichem glawbn komen. Weiter vindet man dar Jn: eyn Costliche disputatz eynes gelerten Cristen. vnd eyns gelerten Juden. dar inne alle Jrthumb der Juden durch yr aygen schrifft aufgelost werden*. [Cologne, 1508?].

———. *Juden Büchlein [. . .]*. N.p., 1550.

Virdung, Johannes. *Practica Teutsch Etliche Jar werende: Aus der grossen coniunction der dreier öbersten Planeten Saturni Jouis vnd Martis gezogen. Von der zukunfft eins newen Propheten, vnd anderer grosser geschicht, die durch genante coniunction bezeichnet werden*. Oppenheim, 1503. Reprint, Strasbourg, 1503.

Von ainer grosse meng vnnd gewalt der Juden die lange zeyt mit vnwonhafftigen Wüsten beschlossen vnd verborgen gewesen/ Yetzunder auß gebrochen vnd an tag kommen seyn/ Dreyssig tag reyß von Jherusalem sich nydergeschlagen/ Was sy fürgenommen haben findt man nachlaut dises Sendbrieffs zum tayl glaubliche Vnderricht. [Augsburg?], 1523.

Von Michel Juden tode: Johannes Liechtenbergers prophecey: Meissen wirt heydentzen/ so wirt die Marck Judentzen/ vnd Golt fur Gott anbeten. [Magdeburg?], 1549.

Wagner, Bettina. *Die "Epistola presbiteri Johannis" lateinisch und deutsch: Überlieferung, Textgeschichte, Rezeption und Übertragungen im Mittelalter, Mit bisher unedierten Texten*. Münchener Texte und Untersuchungen zur deutschen Literatur des Mittelalters 115. Tübingen: Niemeyer, 2000.

Weidner, Paul. *Loca praecipva Fidei Christianae, collecta, & explicata à Paulo Weidnero, Philosophiae ac Medicinae Doctore, ex Iudaismo ad fidem Christi conuerso*. Vienna: Hoffhalter, 1559.

———. *Ein Sermon/ durch Paulum Weidner der Ertzney Doctoren/ vnd in der Hochloeblichen Vniuersitet zu Wien Hebraischer sprachen Professoren: den Juden zu Prag Anno M.D.LXI*.

den 26 Aprilis in jrer Synagoga geprediget: dadurch auch etliche Personen zum Christlichen glauben bekert worden. Vienna: Hoffhalter, 1562.

Weiss, Adam. *Diarium, über das sich bey seyner Anwesenheit Auf dem Reichs-Tag zu Augsburg, Anno 1530, zugetragen.* 3 vols. Uffenheimische Neben-Stunden 7. Schwabach: Enderes, 1743.

Wetzlar, Isaak. *The Libes Briv of Isaac Wetzlar.* Edited and translated by Morris M. Faierstein. Brown Judaic Studies 308. Atlanta, GA: Scholars Press, 1996.

The Worms Mahzor: The Jewish National and University Library, Ms. Heb. 4° 781/1. Facsimile reproduction. Vaduz: Cyelar, 1985.

Yassif, Eli. "Two Early Versions of the Aqdamoth Story." *Criticism and Interpretation* 9/10 (1976): 214–26. [Hebrew]

Yidls, Gerson b. Eliezer ha-Levi. *Gliles erets Yisroel: Im tirgum le-ivrit ba-shem iggeret ha-kodesh.* Edited by Yitzhak ben Zvi. Mekorot erez̧ Yisra'el 5. Jerusalem: Mossad Harav Kook, 1953.

Yuspa Shammes. *Seyfer mayse nissim.* Amsterdam, 1696.

———. *Wormser Minhagbuch.* Edited by Benjamin S. Hamburger and Eric Zimmer. 2 vols. Jerusalem: Mif'al torat ḥakhmei Ashkenaz, Mekhon Yerushalayim, 1988–92. [Hebrew]

Zarncke, Friedrich. *Der Priester Johannes.* 2 vols. Abhandlungen der Philosophisch-Historischen Classe der Königlich Sächsischen Gesellschaft der Wissenschaften 7/8. Leipzig: S. Hirzel, 1876–79. Reprint, Hildesheim: Olms, 1980.

Zfatman, Sara. "Iggrot be-yiddish mi-sof ha-me'ah ha-16 be-inyan aseret ha-shevatim." *Kobez al Yad* n.s. 20 (1982): 217–52.

SECONDARY LITERATURE

Adamek, Josef. *Vom römischen Endreich der mittelalterlichen Bibelerklärung.* Würzburg: Triltsch, 1938.

Aescoly, Aaron Z. "David Reubeni in the Light of History." *Jewish Quarterly Review* 28 (1937): 1–45.

———. "A Flandrian Newsletter Concerning the Sabbatian Movement." In *Sefer Dinaburg: Kovez divrei iyyun u-meḥkar muggash le-Ben-Zion Dinaburg,* edited by Yitzhak Baer, 215–36. Jerusalem: Kiryat Sefer, 1949. [Hebrew]

———. "On the Messianic Movement in Sicily." *Tarbiz* 11 (1940): 207–17. [Hebrew]

Aichele, Klaus. *Das Antichristdrama des Mittelalters, der Reformation und Gegenreformation.* Den Haag: Nijhoff, 1974.

Åkerman, Susanna. "Queen Christina of Sweden and Messianic Thought." In *Sceptics, Millenarians and Jews,* edited by David S. Katz and Jonathan I. Israel, 142–60. Leiden: Brill, 1990.

Alexander, Paul J. *The Byzantine Apocalyptic Tradition.* Berkeley: University of California Press, 1985.

———. "The Medieval Legend of the Last Roman Emperor and Its Messianic Origin." *Journal of the Warburg and Courtauld Institutes* 41 (1978): 1–15.

Anderson, Andrew R. *Alexander's Gate, Gog and Magog and the Inclosed Nations.* Cambridge, MA: Medieval Academy of America, 1932.

Armand, Alfred. *Les médailleurs italiens des quinzième et seizième siècles.* 3 vols. Paris: E. Plon et Cie, 1883. Reprint, Bologna: Forni, 1966.

Arnoldi, Udo. *Pro Iudaeis: Die Gutachten der hallischen Theologen im 18. Jahrhundert zu Fragen der Judentoleranz.* Berlin: Institut Kirche und Judentum, 1993.

Aufgebauer, Peter. "Der Hoffaktor Michel von Derenburg (gest. 1549) und die Polemik gegen ihn." *Blätter für deutsche Landesgeschichte* 120 (1984): 371–99.

Avneri, Zvi, ed. *Germania Judaica.* Vol. 2, *Von 1238 bis zur Mitte des 14. Jahrhunderts.* Tübingen: Mohr Siebeck, 1968.

Backus, Irena. *Martin Borrhaus (Cellarius).* Bibliotheca Dissidentium 2, Bibliotheca bibliographica Aureliana 88. Baden-Baden: Koerner, 1981.

Baer, Yitzhak. "The Messianic Movement in Spain in the Period of the Expulsion." *Me'assef Zion* 5 (1933): 61–78. [Hebrew]

Barmash, Pamela. "At the Nexus of History and Memory: The Ten Lost Tribes." *AJS Review* 29.2 (2005): 207–36.

Barnai, Jacob. *Sabbatianism: Social Perspectives.* Jerusalem: Zalman Shazar Center for Jewish History, 2000. [Hebrew]

———. "Social Aspects of the Polemics Between Sabbatians and Their Opponents." In *Millenarianism and Messianism in Early Modern European Culture.* Vol. 1, *Messianism in the Early Modern World,* edited by Matt D. Goldish and Richard H. Popkin, 77–90. Archives internationales d'histoire des idées 173. Dordrecht: Kluwer, 2001.

Barnes, Robin B. *Prophecy and Gnosis: Apocalypticism in the Wake of the Lutheran Reformation.* Stanford: University of California Press, 1988.

Bartoldus, Thomas. "Humanismus und Talmudstreit: Pfefferkorn, Reuchlin und die 'Dunkelmännerbriefe' (1515/17)." In *Judentum und Antijudaismus in der deutschen Literatur im Mittelalter und an der Wende zur Neuzeit: Ein Studienbuch,* edited by Arne Domrös, Thomas Bartoldus, and Julian Voloj, 179–228. Berlin: Jüdische Verlagsanstalt, 2002.

———. "We dennen menschen die schuldig sind: Zum Antijudaismus im geistlichen Spiel des späten Mittelalters." In *Judentum und Antijudaismus in der deutschen Literatur im Mittelalter und an der Wende zur Neuzeit: Ein Studienbuch,* edited by Arne Domrös, Thomas Bartoldus, and Julian Voloj, 121–46. Berlin: Jüdische Verlagsanstalt, 2002.

Bauckham, Richard. "Chiliasmus IV: Reformation." *Theologische Realenzyklopädie,* 36 vols., edited by Gerhard Müller et al., 7:737–45. Berlin: De Gruyter, 1981.

Baum, Johann W. *Capito und Bucer: Straßburgs Reformatoren: Nach ihrem handschriftlichen Briefschatze und anderen gleichzeitigen Quellen dargestellt.* Elberfeld: Friderichs, 1860.

Baumgarten, Elisheva. *Mothers and Children: Jewish Family Life in Medieval Europe.* Princeton, NJ: Princeton University Press, 2004.

Baumgarten, Jean. *Introduction to Old Yiddish Literature.* Translated by Jerold C. Frakes. Oxford: Oxford University Press, 2005.

Beck, James. "The Anabaptists and the Jews: The Case of Hätzer, Denck and the Worms Prophets." *Mennonite Quarterly Review* 75.4 (2001): 407–27.

Beckingham, Charles F., and Bernard Hamilton, eds. *Prester John, the Mongols and the Ten Lost Tribes.* Aldershot: Variorum, 1996.

Beinart, Haim. *Chapters in Judeo-Spanish History*. 2 vols. Jerusalem: Magnes Press, 1998. [Hebrew]

———. "The Converso Community in Sixteenth- and Seventeenth-Century Spain." In *The Sephardi Heritage*, edited by Richard D. Barnett, 457–78. London: Vallentine Mitchell, 1971.

Beit-Arié, Malachi. "The Worms Mahzor: Its History and Its Palaeographic and Codicological Characteristics." In *The Worms Mahzor: The Jewish National and University Library: Ms. Heb. 4° 781/1*, 13–35. Vaduz: Cyelar, Jewish National and University Library, 1985.

———. "The Worms Mahzor: MS Jerusalem, Jewish National and University Library Heb. 4° 781/1: Würzburg? (Germany), 1272." In *The Makings of the Medieval Hebrew Book: Studies in Palaeography and Codicology*, 152–80. Jerusalem: Magnes Press, 1993.

Beit-Arié, Malachi, and Moshe Idel. "Treatise on Eschatology and Astrology by R. Abraham Zacut (Jewish National and University Library Ms. Heb. 8 3935)." *Kirjat Sefer* 54 (1979): 174–94. [Hebrew]

Bejczy, István. *La lettre du Prêtre Jean: Une utopie médiévale*. Paris: Imago, 2001.

Bekkum, Wout J. van. "Medieval Hebrew Versions of the Alexander Romance." In *Mediaeval Antiquity*, edited by Andries Welkenhuysen, Herman Braet, and Werner Verbeke, 293–302. Leuven: Leuven University Press, 1995.

Bell, Dean P. *Sacred Communities: Jewish and Christian Identities in Fifteenth-Century Germany*. Leiden: Brill, 2001.

Ben-Amos, Dan, and Dov Noy, eds. *Folktales of the Jews*. Vol. 1, *Tales from the Sephardic Dispersion*. Philadelphia: Jewish Publication Society, 2006.

Benayahu, Meir. *Copyright, Authorization and Imprimatour for Hebrew Books Printed in Venice*. Jerusalem: Ben-Zvi Institute, 1971. [Hebrew]

Ben-Dor Benite, Zvi. *The Ten Lost Tribes: A World History*. Oxford: Oxford University Press, 2009.

Benmelech, Moti. *Shlomo Molkho: The Life and Death of Messiah ben Joseph*. Jerusalem: Ben-Zvi Institute, 2017. [Hebrew]

Ben-Sasson, Haim Hillel. "Exile and Redemption through the Eyes of the Spanish Exiles." In *Yitzhak F. Baer Jubilee Volume*, edited by Salo W. Baron et al., 216–27. Jerusalem: Historical Society of Israel, 1961. [Hebrew]

———. "The Generation of the Spanish Exiles Considers Its Fate." In *Binah: Studies in Jewish History*, edited by Joseph Dan, 1:83–98. New York: Praeger, 1989.

———. "Jewish-Christian Disputation in the Setting of Humanism and Reformation in the German Empire." *Harvard Theological Review* 59 (1966): 369–90.

———. "The Reformation in Contemporary Jewish Eyes." *Proceedings of the Israel Academy of Sciences and Humanities* 4.12 (1970): 239–326.

Bercé, Yves-Marie. *Le roi caché: Sauveurs et imposteurs: Mythes politiques populaires dans l'Europe moderne*. Paris: Fayard, 1990.

Berger, Abraham. "Captive at the Gate of Rome: The Story of a Messianic Motif." *Proceedings of the American Academy for Jewish Research* 44 (1977): 1–17.

Berger, David. "A Generation of Scholarship on Jewish-Christian Interaction in the Medieval World." *Tradition* 38.2 (2004): 4–14.

———. "Sephardic and Ashkenazic Messianism in the Middle Ages: An Assessment of the Historiographical Controversy." In *From Sages to Savants: Studies Presented to Avraham Grossman*, edited by Joseph R. Hacker, Yosef Kaplan, and Benjamin Z. Kedar, 11–28. Jerusalem: Zalman Shazar Center for Jewish History, 2010. [Hebrew]

———. "Three Typological Themes in Early Jewish Messianism: Messiah Son of Joseph, Rabbinic Calculations, and the Figure of Armilus." *AJS Review* 10.2 (1985): 141–64.

Berliner, Abraham. *Der Einheitsgesang: Eine literar-historische Studie.* Wissenschaftliche Beilage zum Jahresbericht des Rabbiner-Seminars zu Berlin für 1908/09. Berlin: Itzkowski, 1910.

Bernstein, Simon. "R. Shlomo Molkho ha-kadosh mi-Mantova." In *Shomrei ha-Ḥomot*, edited by Simon Bernstein, 11–62, 173–79. Tel Aviv: Miẓpeh, 1938.

Biale, David. "Counter-History and Jewish Polemics against Christianity: The *Sefer toldot yeshu* and the *Sefer zerubavel*." *Jewish Social Studies* 6.1 (1999): 130–45.

Bienart, Walther. *Martin Luther und die Juden: Ein Quellenbuch mit zeitgenössischen Illustrationen, mit Einführungen und Erläuterungen.* Frankfurt am Main: De Gruyter, 1982.

Bietenhard, Hans. *Das tausendjährige Reich: Eine biblisch-theologische Studie.* Zürich: Zwingli, 1955.

Bloch, Ernst. *Gesamtausgabe.* Vol. 2, *Thomas Münzer als Theologe der Revolution.* 2nd ed. Frankfurt am Main: Suhrkamp, 1959.

Bodian, Miriam. "The Reformation and the Jews." In *Rethinking European Jewish History*, edited by Jeremy Cohen and Moshe Rosman, 112–32. Oxford: Littman Library of Jewish Civilization, 2009.

Boissi, Louis M. de. *Dissertations critiques pour servir d'éclaircissemens à l'histoire des juifs, avant et depuis Jesus-Christ.* Paris: Lagrange, 1785.

Bonfil, Robert. "Gli ebrei d'Italia e la Riforma: Una questione da riconsiderare." In *Cultural Change among the Jews of Early Modern Italy*, 47–60. Variorum Collected Studies Series 945. Farnham: Ashgate, 2010.

———. *Gli ebrei in Italia nell'epoca del Rinascimento.* Florence: Sansoni, 1991.

———. *Rabbis and Jewish Communities in Renaissance Italy.* Oxford: Littman Library of Jewish Civilization, 1990.

Boos, Heinrich. *Geschichte der rheinischen Städtekultur mit besonderer Berücksichtigung der Stadt Worms.* Vol. 4. Berlin: Stargardt, 1901.

Bousset, Wilhelm. *Der Antichrist in der Überlieferung des Judentums, des neuen Testaments und der alten Kirche: Ein Beitrag zur Auslegung der Apokalypse.* Göttingen: Vandenhoeck & Ruprecht, 1895. Reprint, Hildesheim: Olms, 1983.

Braude, Benjamin. "Les contes persans de Menasseh Ben Israël. Polémique, apologétique et dissimulation à Amsterdam au xviie siècle." *Annales: Histoire, Sciences Sociales* 49 (1994): 1107–38.

———. "Myths and Realities of Turkish-Jewish Contacts." In *Turkish-Jewish Encounters: Studies on Turkish-Jewish Relations through the Ages*, edited by Mehmet Tütüncü. Turquoise Studies 5. Haarlem: Research Center for Turkistan and Azerbaijan, 2001.

Brecht, Martin. *Martin Luther.* Vol. 3, *Die Erhaltung der Kirche 1532–1546.* Stuttgart: Calwer, 1987.

Breslau, Harry. "Juden und Mongolen 1241." *Zeitschrift für die Geschichte der Juden in Deutschland* 11 (1887): 99–102.

Breuer, Mordechai. "Modernism and Traditionalism in Sixteenth-Century Jewish Historiography: A Study of David Gans' Tzemah David." In *Jewish Thought in the Sixteenth Century*, edited by Bernard D. Cooperman, 49–87. Harvard Judaica Texts and Studies 2. Cambridge, MA: Harvard University Press, 1983.

Brod, Max. *Rëubēni, Fürst der Juden: Ein Renaissance-Roman.* Munich: Wolff, 1925.

Brook, Kevin A. *The Jews of Khazaria.* Northvale, NJ: Jason Aronson, 1999.

Brosseder, Claudia. *Im Bann der Sterne: Caspar Peucer, Philipp Melanchthon und andere Wittenberger Astrologen.* Berlin: De Gruyter, 2005.

Brüll, Nehemias. "Das Geschlecht der Treves." *Jahrbücher für Jüdische Geschichte und Literatur* 1 (1874): 87–122.

Burmeister, Karl-Heinz. *Sebastian Münster: Versuch eines biographischen Gesamtbildes.* Basel/Stuttgart: Halbig & Lichtenhahn, 1963.

Burnett, Charles, and Patrick Gautier Dalché. "Attitudes towards the Mongols in Medieval Literature: The XXII Kings of Gog and Magog from the Court of Frederick II to John de Mandeville." *Viator: Medieval and Renaissance Studies* 22 (1991): 153–68.

Burnett, Stephen G. "A Dialogue of the Deaf: Hebrew Pedagogy and Anti-Jewish Polemic in Sebastian Münster's 'Messiah of the Christians and the Jews' (1529/39)." *Archiv für Reformationsgeschichte* 91 (2000): 168–90.

———. "Distorted Mirrors: Antonius Margaritha, Johann Buxtorf and Christian Ethnographies of the Jews." *Sixteenth Century Journal* 25.2 (1994): 275–87.

———. *From Christian Hebraism to Jewish Studies: Johannes Buxtorf (1564–1629) and Hebrew Learning in the Seventeenth Century.* Leiden: Brill, 1996.

———. "German Jewish Printing in the Reformation Era (1530–1633)." In *Jews, Judaism, and the Reformation in Sixteenth-Century Germany,* edited by Dean P. Bell and Stephen G. Burnett, 503–27. Studies in Central European Histories 37. Leiden: Brill, 2006.

———. "Jüdische Vermittler des Hebräischen und ihre christlichen Schüler im Spätmittelalter." In *Wechselseitige Wahrnehmung der Religionen im Spätmittelalter und in der Frühen Neuzeit.* Vol. 1, *Bericht über Kolloquien der Kommission zur Erforschung der Kultur des Spätmittelalters 2004 und 2005,* edited by Ludger Grenzmann et al., 173–88. Berlin: De Gruyter, 2009.

———. "The Regulation of Hebrew Printing in Germany, 1555–1630: Confessional Politics and the Limits of Jewish Toleration." In *Infinite Boundaries: Order, Disorder, and Reorder in Early Modern German Culture,* edited by Max Reinhart, 329–48. Sixteenth Century Essays and Studies 40, Early Modern German Studies 1. Kirksville, MO: Sixteenth Century Journal Publishers, 1998.

Cahen, M. D. *Nouvelle explication d'une médaille antique ayant une triple inscription hébraique, latine et grecque.* Metz: J. Mayer, 1858.

Campanini, Saverio. "I cabbalisti cristiani del Rinascimento." In *La cultura ebraica,* edited by Patrizia Reinach Sabbadini, 149–65. Turin: Einaudi, 2000.

———. "A Neglected Source Concerning Asher Lemmlein and Paride da Ceresara: Agostino Giustiniani." *European Journal of Jewish Studies* 2.1 (2008): 89–110.

Carlebach, Elisheva. *The Anti-Christian Element in Early Modern Yiddish Culture*. Braun Lectures in the History of the Jews in Prussia 10. Ramat Gan: Bar-Ilan University Press, 2003.

———. *Between History and Hope: Jewish Messianism between Ashkenaz and Sepharad*. Annual Lecture of the Selmanowitz Chair of Jewish History, May 17, 1998, New York.

———. *Divided Souls: Converts from Judaism in Germany, 1500–1750*. New Haven, CT: Yale University Press, 2001.

———. "Jewish Responses to Christianity in Reformation Germany." In *Jews, Judaism, and the Reformation in Sixteenth-Century Germany*, edited by Dean P. Bell and Stephen G. Burnett, 451–80. Studies in Central European Histories 37. Leiden: Brill, 2006.

———. "Jews, Christians and the Endtime in Early Modern Germany." *Jewish History* 14.3 (2000): 331–44.

———. "The Last Deception: Failed Messiahs and Jewish Conversion in Early Modern German Lands." In *Millenarianism and Messianism in Early Modern European Culture*. Vol. 1, *Jewish Messianism in the Early Modern World*, edited by Matt D. Goldish and Richard H. Popkin, 125–38. Archives internationales d'histoire des idées 173. Dordrecht: Kluwer 2001.

———. "Die messianische Haltung der deutschen Juden im Spiegel von Glikls Zikhroynes." In *Die Hamburger Kauffrau Glikl: Jüdische Existenz in der Frühen Neuzeit*, edited by Monika Richarz, 238–52. Hamburg: Christians, 2001.

———. *Palaces of Time: Jewish Calendar and Culture in Early Modern Europe*. Cambridge, MA: Belknap Press of Harvard University Press, 2011.

———. *The Pursuit of Heresy: Rabbi Moses Hagiz and the Sabbatian Controversies*. New York: Columbia University Press, 1990.

———. "Rabbinic Circles as Messianic Pathways in the Post-Expulsion Era." *Judaism* 41.3 (1992): 208–16.

———. "The Sabbatian Posture of German Jewry." In *The Sabbatian Movement and Its Aftermath: Messianism, Sabbatianism and Frankism*, edited by Rachel Elior, 2:1–30. Jerusalem Studies in Jewish Thought 16/17. Jerusalem: Hebrew University of Jerusalem Press, 2001.

———. "Sabbatianism and the Jewish-Christian Polemic." *Proceedings of the Tenth World Congress for Jewish Studies*, Div. C. Vol. 2, *Jewish Thought and Literature* (1990): 1–7.

Carmoly, Eliacin. *Mémoire sur une médaille en l'honneur de Louis-de-Débonnaire: Présenté a l'Académie Royale des Sciences et Belles-Lettres de Bruxelles, le 6 Décembre 1834*. Brüssel: Balleroy, 1835.

Carrete Parrondo, Carlos. "Idealismo y realidad: Notas sobre la noción de Jerusalem entre los judeoconversos castellanos." *El Olivo* 20 (1996): 7–11.

———. "Judeoconversos andaluces y expectativas mesiánicas" In *Xudeus e Conversos na Historica*, edited by Carlos Barros, 1:325–37. Santiago de Compostela, 1994.

Cary, George. *The Medieval Alexander*. Cambridge: Cambridge University Press, 1956. Reprint, New York: Garland, 1987.

Cassuto, M. D. Umberto. "Who Was David Reubeni?" *Tarbiz* 32.4 (1963): 339–58. [Hebrew]

Castaldini, Alberto. *Mondi paralleli: Ebrei e cristiani nell'Italia padana dal tardo Medioevo all'Età moderna*. Accademia nazionale virgiliana di scienze lettere e arti: Classe di scienze morali 2. Florence: Olschki, 2004.

Charlesworth, James H., ed. *The Messiah: Developments in Earliest Judaism and Christianity: The First Princeton Symposium on Judaism and Christian Origins*. Minneapolis: Fortress Press, 1992.

Chartier, Roger. "Reading Matter and 'Popular' Reading: From the Renaissance to the Seventeenth Century." In *A History of Reading in the West*, edited by Guglielmo Cavallo and Roger Chartier. Translated by Lydia G. Cochrane, 269–83. Amherst: University of Massachusetts Press, 1999.

Charvet, Étienne L. G. *Médailles et jetons de la ville de Lyon*. Chalon-sur-Saône: E. Bertrand, 1907–9.

Chastel, André. *The Sack of Rome, 1527*. Bollingen Series 35.26. Princeton, NJ: Princeton University Press, 1983.

Chazan, Robert. *Daggers of Faith: Thirteenth-Century Christian Missionizing and Jewish Response*. Berkeley: University of California Press, 1989.

———. *European Jewry and the First Crusade*. Berkeley: University of California Press, 1987.

———. *In the Year 1096: The First Crusade and the Jews*. Philadelphia: Jewish Publication Society, 1996.

———. *Medieval Stereotypes and Modern Antisemitism*. Berkeley: University of California Press, 1997.

Chetrit, Joseph. "The Secret of David Hareuveni According to a Hebrew Poem from Morocco." *Tarbiz* 6 (1991): 237–63. [Hebrew]

Clark, Christopher M. *The Politics of Conversion: Missionary Protestantism and the Jews in Prussia, 1728–1941*. Oxford: Clarendon, 1995.

Clasen, Claus-Peter. *Anabaptism: A Social History, 1525–1618, Switzerland, Austria, Moravia, and South and Central Germany*. Ithaca, NY: Cornell University Press, 1972.

Cluse, Christoph and Rebekka Voß, eds. *Frankfurt's "Jewish Notabilia" ('Jüdische Merckwürdigkeiten'): Ethnographic Views of Urban Jewry in Central Europe around 1700*. Special issue of *Frankfurter Judaistische Beiträge* 40 (2015).

Cohen, Carl. "Martin Luther and His Jewish Contemporaries." *Jewish Social Studies* 25 (1963): 195–204.

Cohen, Gerson D. "Esau as Symbol in Early Medieval Thought." In *Studies in the Variety of Rabbinic Cultures*, 243–69. Philadelphia: Jewish Publication Society, 1991.

———. "Messianic Postures of Ashkenazim and Sephardim." In *Essential Papers on Messianic Movements and Personalities in Jewish History*, edited by Marc Saperstein, 202–33. Essential Papers on Jewish Studies 6. New York: New York University Press, 1992.

Cohen, Jeremy. *The Friars and the Jews: The Evolution of Medieval Anti-Judaism*. Ithaca, NY: Cornell University Press, 1982.

———. *Living Letters of the Law: Ideas of the Jew in Medieval Christendom*. Berkeley: University of California Press, 1999.

———. *Sanctifying the Name of God: Jewish Martyrs and Jewish Memories of the First Crusade*. Philadelphia: University of Pennsylvania Press, 2004.

Cohen, Mark R. *Under Crescent and Cross: The Jews in the Middle Ages*. Princeton, NJ: Princeton University Press, 1994.

Cohn, Norman. *The Pursuit of the Millennium: Revolutionary Millenarians and Mystical Anarchists of the Middle Ages*. London: Pimlico, 1993.

Cole, Richard G. "The Reformation Pamphlet and Communication Processes." In *Flugschriften als Massenmedium der Reformationszeit: Beiträge zum Tübinger Symposion 1980*, edited by Hans-Joachim Köhler, 139–61. Spätmittelalter und frühe Neuzeit 13. Stuttgart: Klett-Cotta, 1981.

Comboni, Andrea. "Paride Ceresara, mantovano." In *Veronica Gambara e la poesia del suo tempo nell'Italia settentrionale: Atti del Convegno die Brescia-Correggio (17.–19. Okt. 1985)*, edited by Cesare Bozzetti, Pietro Gibellini, and Ennio Sandal, 263–91. Florence: Olschki, 1989.

Coudert, Allison P., and Jeffrey S. Shoulson, eds. *Hebraica Veritas? Christian Hebraists and the Study of Judaism in Early Modern Europe*. Philadelphia: University of Pennsylvania Press, 2004.

Dahan, Gilbert. *Les intellectuels chrétiens et les juifs au moyen âge*. Paris: Éditions du cerf, 1990.

Dan, Joseph. "Armilus: The Jewish Antichrist and the Origins and Dating of the 'Sefer Zerubbavel.'" In *Toward the Millennium: Messianic Expectations from the Bible to Waco*, edited by Peter Schäfer and Marc Cohen, 73–104. Leiden: Brill, 1998.

———. "An Early Hebrew Source of the Yiddish 'Aqdamoth' Story." *Hebrew University Studies in Literature* 1 (1973): 39–46.

———. *The Esoteric Theology of Ashkenazi Hasidism*. Jerusalem: Bialik Institute, 1968. [Hebrew]

———. *Ḥasidut Ashkenaz be-toldot ha-maḥshavah ha-yehudit*. Tel Aviv: Open University, 1990/91.

———. "Ha-sifrut ha-apokaliptit bein yahadut le-naẓrut." In *Milḥemet gog u-magog: Meshiḥiyut va-apokalipsah ba-yahadut be-avar u-ve-yameinu*, edited by David Ariel-Yoel, 11–31. Tel Aviv: Yedi'ot aḥronot, 2001.

———. *The Hebrew Story in the Middle Ages*. Jerusalem: Keter, 1974. [Hebrew]

———. "The History of the Hebrew Aqdamoth Story." *Criticism and Interpretation* 9/10 (1976): 197–213. [Hebrew]

———. "The Problem of Martyrdom in the Theoretical Doctrine Teaching of Ashkenazic Hasidism." In *Holy War and Martyrology: Lectures Delivered at the Eleventh Convention of the Historical Society of Israel, March 1966*, 121–29. Jerusalem: Historical Society of Israel, 1967. [Hebrew]

———. "Sippurim demonologiyim mi-kitvei R. Yehudah he-Ḥasid." *Tarbiz* 30 (1960/61): 271–89.

David, Abraham. "Gedalia Ibn Yahya: Auteur de Shalshelet Ha-Qabbalah." *Revue des Études Juives* 153.1–2 (1994): 101–32.

———. "The Historiographical Work of Gedalyah ibn Yahya, Author of Shalshelet ha-Kabbalah." PhD diss., Hebrew University of Jerusalem, 1976. [Hebrew]

———. "Iggrono shel Yosef ha-Kohen ba'al Emek ha-bakhah." *Italia: Studi e ricerche sulla cultura e sulla letteratura degli ebrei d'Italia* 5 (1985): 7–105.

———. "A Jerusalemite Epistle from the Beginning of the Ottoman Rule in the Land of Israel." In *Jerusalem in the Early Ottoman Period*, edited by Amnon Cohen, 39–60. Jerusalem: Ben-Zvi Institute, 1979. [Hebrew]

———. "The Lutheran Reformation in Sixteenth-Century Jewish Historiography." *Jewish Studies Quarterly* 10.2 (2003): 124–39.

———. "R. Gedalya ibn Yahya's Shalshelet Hakabbalah 'Chain of Tradition': A Chapter in Medieval Jewish History." *Immanuel: A Semi-Annual Bulletin of Religious Thought and Research in Israel* 12 (1980): 60–76.

Davidson, Israel. *Thesaurus of Mediaeval Hebrew Poetry*. 4 vols. New York: Jewish Theological Seminary of America, 1924–33. Reprint, Piscataway, NJ: Gorgias Press, 2017.

Davis, Joseph M. *Yom-Tov Lipmann Heller: Portrait of a Seventeenth-Century Rabbi*. Oxford: Littman Library of Jewish Civilization, 2004.

Degani, Ben-Zion. "The Structure of World History and the Redemption of Israel in Zemah David." *Zion* 45 (1980): 173–200. [Hebrew]

Delius, Walter. *Lehre und Leben: Justus Jonas 1493–1555*. Gütersloh: Bertelsmann, 1952.

Deppermann, Klaus. *Melchior Hoffmann: Soziale Unruhen und apokalyptische Visionen im Zeitalter der Reformation*. Göttingen: Vandenhoeck & Ruprecht, 1979.

———. "Täufergruppen in Augsburg und Straßburg: Ihre soziale Rekrutierung und Theologie." In *Städtische Randgruppen und Minderheiten*, edited by Bernhard Kirchgässner and Fritz Reuter, 161–82, 231–35. Stadt in der Geschichte 13. Sigmaringen: Thorbecke, 1986.

Derenbourg, Joseph. "La médaille de Fourvière." *Revue israélite* 1 (1870): 4–8.

Derksen, John D. *From Radicals to Reformers: Strasbourg's Religious Nonconformists over Two Generations, 1525–1570*. Bibliotheca humanistica reformatorica 61. Utrecht: Hes & de Graaf, 2002.

Detmers, Achim. *Reformation und Judentum: Israel-Lehren und Einstellungen zum Judentum von Luther bis zum frühen Calvin*. Judentum und Christentum 7. Stuttgart: Kohlhammer, 2001.

Deutsch, Yaacov. "Johann Jacob Schudt: Der erste Ethnograph der jüdischen Gemeinde in Frankfurt am Main." In *Die Frankfurter Judengasse: Jüdisches Leben in der Frühen Neuzeit*, edited by Fritz Backhaus et al., 67–76. Frankfurt am Main: Societäts-Verlag, 2006.

———. *Judaism in Christian Eyes: Ethnographic Descriptions of Jews and Judaism in Early Modern Europe*. Oxford: Oxford University Press, 2012.

———. "Polemical Ethnographies: Descriptions of Yom Kippur in the Writings of Christian Hebraists and Jewish Converts to Christianity in Early Modern Europe." In *Hebraica Veritas? Christian Hebraists and the Study of Judaism in Early Modern Europe*, edited by Allison P. Coudert and Jeffrey S. Shoulson, 202–33. Philadelphia: University of Pennsylvania Press, 2004.

———. "'A View of the Jewish Religion': Conceptions of Jewish Practice and Ritual in Early Modern Europe." *Archiv für Reformationsgeschichte* 3 (2001): 273–95.

———. "Von der Iuden Ceremonien: Representations of Jews in Sixteenth-Century Germany." In *Jews, Judaism, and the Reformation in Sixteenth-Century Germany*, edited by Dean P. Bell and Stephen G. Burnett, 335–56. Studies in Central European Histories 37. Leiden: Brill, 2006.

Deutsch, Yaacov, and Maria Diemling. "'Christliche Ethnographien' von Juden und Judentum: Die Konstruktion des Jüdischen in frühneuzeitlichen Texten." In *Die Konstruktion des Jüdischen in Vergangenheit und Gegenwart*, edited by Michael Konkel, Alexandra Pontzen, and Henning Theissen, 15–27. Paderborn: Schöningh, 2003.

Diamant, Paul J. *Paulus Weidner von Billerburg 1525–1585: Kaiserlicher Leibarzt und Rektor der Wiener Universität*. Vienna, 1933.

Díaz Esteban, Fernando. "Problemas de lenguaje en David Rubeni." In *History and Creativity in the Sephardi and Oriental Jewish Communities*, edited by Tamar Alexander et al., 35–49. Jerusalem: Misgav Yerushalayim, 1994.

Diemling, Maria. "Anthonius Margaritha and His 'Der Gantz Jüdisch Glaub.'" In *Jews, Judaism, and the Reformation in Sixteenth-Century Germany*, edited by Dean P. Bell and Stephen G. Burnett, 303–33. Studies in Central European Histories 37. Leiden: Brill, 2006.

———. "'Christliche Ethnographien' über Juden und Judentum in der Frühen Neuzeit: Die Konvertiten Victor von Carben und Anthonius Margaritha und ihre Darstellung jüdischen Lebens und jüdischer Religion." PhD diss., University of Vienna, 1999.

———. "Jewish-Christian Relations in Early Modern Germany: A Review." *EAJS Newsletter* 16 (2005): 34–47.

Dinur, Ben-Zion. *Israel and the Diaspora*. Philadelphia: Jewish Publication Society of America, 1969.

Driedger, Michael. "The Intensification of Religious Commitment: Jews, Anabaptists, Radical Reform, and Confessionalization." In *Jews, Judaism, and the Reformation in Sixteenth-Century Germany*, edited by Dean P. Bell and Stephen G. Burnett, 209–99. Studies in Central European Histories 37. Leiden: Brill, 2006.

Dubin, Lois C. "Yosef Hayim Yerushalmi, the Royal Alliance, and Jewish Political Theory." *Jewish History* 28.1 (2014): 51–81.

Duchhardt, Heinz. "Das Tunisunternehmen Karl V. 1535." *Mitteilungen des Österreichischen Staatsarchivs* 37 (1984): 35–72.

Dülmen, Richard van. *Reformation als Revolution: Soziale Bewegung und religiöser Radikalismus in der deutschen Reformation*. 2nd ed. Frankfurt am Main: Fischer, 1987.

Dundes, Alan. *Life is Like a Chicken Coop Ladder: A Study of German National Character through Folklore*. Detroit: Wayne State University Press, 1989.

Dweck, Yaacob. *Dissident Rabbi: The Life of Jacob Sasportas*. Princeton, NJ: Princeton University Press, 2019.

Edwards, Mark U., Jr. *Printing, Propaganda, and Martin Luther*. Berkeley: University of California Press, 1994.

Eidelberg, Shlomo. "Did David Reubeni Accompany Solomon Molcho on His Journey to Regensburg?" *Tarbiz* 42 (1973): 148–53. [Hebrew]

———. "A Passage in Martin Luther's Writing Regarding Maimonides' Description of the Messianic Age." In *Medieval Ashkenazic History: Studies on European Jewry*. Vol. 2, *Hebrew Essays*, 98–101. Brooklyn, NY: Sepher Hermon Press, 2000. [Hebrew]

———. "Permutations of the Messianic Idea among the Jews of Germany." In *Between History and Literature: Studies in Honor of Isaac Barzilay*, edited by Stanley Nash, 25–54. Bne Brak: Hakibbutz Hameuchad, 1997. [Hebrew]

———. R. *Juspa, Shammash of Warmaisa: Jewish Life in 17th Century Worms*. Jerusalem: Magnes Press, 1991. [Hebrew]

Elbaum, Jacob. "Concerning Two Textual Emendations in the 'Aleinu Prayer.'" *Tarbiz* 42 (1972/73): 204–8. [Hebrew]

———. *Repentance and Self-Flagellation in the Writings of the Sages of Germany and Poland 1348–1648*. Jerusalem: Magnes Press, 1992. [Hebrew]

Elbogen, Ismar. *Jewish Liturgy: A Comprehensive History*. Translated by Raymond P. Scheindlin. Philadelphia: Jewish Publication Society, 1993.

Eliav-Feldon, Miriam. "Invented Identities: Credulity in the Age of Prophecy and Exploration." *Journal of Early Modern History* 3.3 (1999): 203–32.

———. "Prince or Pauper? Impostors and Dupes in Early Modern Europe." *Semanim* 83 (2003): 47–68. [Hebrew]

Elior, Rachel. "Messianic Expectation and Spiritualization of Religious Life in the 16th Century." In *Essential Papers on Jewish Culture in Renaissance and Baroque Italy*, edited by David B. Ruderman, 283–98. Essential Papers on Jewish Studies 5. New York: New York University Press, 1992.

———, ed. *The Sabbatian Movement and Its Aftermath: Messianism, Sabbatianism and Frankism*. 2 vols. Jerusalem Studies in Jewish Thought 16/17. Jerusalem: Posner & Sons, 2001. [Hebrew]

Elliger, Walter. *Thomas Müntzer: Leben und Werk*. Göttingen: Vandenhoeck & Ruprecht, 1975.

Emmerson, Richard K. *Antichrist in the Middle Ages: A Study of Medieval Apocalypticism, Art and Literature*. Seattle: University of Washington Press, 1981.

Epstein, Abraham. "Die Wormser Minhagbücher: Literarisches und Culturhistorisches aus denselben." In *Gedenkbuch zur Erinnerung an David Kaufmann*, edited by Marcus Brann and Ferdinand Rosenthal, 288–317. Breslau: Schottländer, 1900. Reprint, New York: Arno Press, 1980.

Epstein, Mark A. *The Ottoman Jewish Communities and Their Role in the Fifteenth and Sixteenth Centuries*. Islamkundliche Untersuchungen 56. Freiburg: Klaus Schwarz, 1980.

"Explanation of the Annexed Plate." *London Magazine or Gentleman's Monthly Intelligencer* 16 (1772): 460.

Fabre-Vassas, Claudine. *The Singular Beast: Jews, Christians, and the Pig*. Translated by Carol Volk. European Perspectives: A Series in Social Thought and Cultural Criticism. New York: Columbia University Press, 1999.

Faierstein, Morris M. "The 'Liebes Brief': A Critique of Jewish Society in Germany 1749." *Leo Baeck Institute Yearbook* 27 (1982): 219–42.

Febvre, Lucien, and Henri-Jean Martin. *The Coming of the Book: The Impact of Printing 1450–1800*. Translated by David Gerard. 2nd ed. London: Verso, 1990.

Feilchenfeld, Ludwig. *Rabbi Josel von Rosheim: Ein Beitrag zur Geschichte der Juden in Deutschland im Reformationszeitalter*. Strasbourg: Heitz, 1898.

Férarès, S. "La médaille dite de Fourvière et sa légende hébraique." *Revue Numismatique* n.s. 14 (1910): 196–227.

Festinger, Leon, Henry W. Riecken, and Stanley Schachter, eds. *When Prophecy Fails: A Social and Psychological Study of a Modern Group That Predicted the Destruction of the World*. New York: Harper & Row, 1964.

Finlay, Robert. "Prophecy and Politics in Istanbul: Charles V, Sultan Süleyman, and the Habsburg Embassy of 1533–1534." *Journal of Early Modern History* 2 (1998): 1–31.

Fisch, Harold. "The Messianic Politics of Menasseh ben Israel." In *Menasseh ben Israel and His World*, edited by Yosef Kaplan, Henry Méchoulan, and Richard H. Popkin, 228–39. Leiden: Brill, 1989.

Fishbane, Michael. "Midrash and Messianism: Some Theologies of Suffering and Salvation." In *Toward the Millennium: Messianic Expectations from the Bible to Waco*, translated by Peter Schäfer and Marc Cohen, 57–71. Leiden: Brill, 1998.

Fishman, David E. "On Prayer in Yiddish: New Sources and Perspectives." In *Text and Context: Essays in Modern Jewish History and Historiography in Honor of Ismar Schorsch*, edited by Eli Lederhendler and Jack Wertheimer, 133–56. New York: Jewish Theological Seminary of America, 2005.

Fleischer, Ezra. "Prayer and Piyyut in the Worms Mahzor." In *The Worms Mahzor: The Jewish National and University Library, Ms. Heb. 4° 781/1*, edited by Malachi Beit-Arié, 36–78. Vaduz: Cyelar, 1985.

Flusser, David. "The Four Empires in the Fourth Sibyl and in the Book of Daniel." *Israel Oriental Studies* 2 (1972): 148–75.

———. "Ma'aseh Alexandros According to Ms. Parma." *Tarbiz* 21 (1957): 165–84. [Hebrew]

Foges, Benedikt. *Alterthümer der Prager Josefstadt, israelitischer Friedhof, Alt-Neu-Schule und andere Synagogen […]*. Edited by David J. Podiebrad. Vol. 4. Prague, 1882.

Fraenkel-Goldschmidt, Chava. "On the Periphery of Jewish Society: Jewish Converts to Christianity in the Age of the Reformation." In *Culture and Society in Medieval Jewry: Studies Dedicated to the Memory of Haim Hillel Ben-Sasson*, edited by Menahem Ben-Sasson, Robert Bonfil, and Joseph R. Hacker, 623–54. Jerusalem: Zalman Shazar Center for Jewish History, 1989. [Hebrew]

Frankl, Oskar. *Der Jude in den deutschen Dichtungen des 15., 16. und 17. Jahrhunderts*. Mährisch Ostrau: Papauschek & Hoffmann, 1905.

Frejdenberg, Maren. "Jews in Slovenian Lands (Krain and Styria)." *Jews and Slavs* 3 (1993): 239–52.

Frey, Winfried. "Der 'Juden Spiegel': Johannes Pfefferkorn und die Volksfrömmigkeit." In *Volksreligion im hohen und späten Mittelalter*, edited by Peter Dinzelbacher and Dieter R. Bauer, 177–93. Quellen und Forschungen aus dem Gebiet der Geschichte n.s. 13. Paderborn: Schöningh, 1990.

Friedenberg, Daniel M. *Jewish Medals from the Renaissance to the Fall of Napoleon (1503–1815)*. New York: Clarkson N. Potter, 1970.

Friedenwald, Harry. *Jews and Medicine*. 2 vols. Baltimore, MD: Johns Hopkins University Press, 1944.

Friedman, Jerome. *The Most Ancient Testimony: Sixteenth-Century Christian Hebraica in the Age of Renaissance Nostalgia*. Athens: Ohio University Press, 1983.

Friedrich, Martin. *Zwischen Abwehr und Bekehrung: Die Stellung der deutschen evangelischen Theologie zum Judentum im 17. Jahrhundert.* Beiträge zur historischen Theologie 72. Tübingen: Mohr Siebeck, 1988.

Friedrichs, Christopher R. "Anti-Jewish Politics in Early Modern Germany: The Uprising in Worms 1613–17." *Central European History* 23 (1990): 91–152.

Friesen, Abraham. "Martin Cellarius: In der Grauzone der Ketzerei." In *Radikale Reformatoren: 21 biographische Skizzen von Thomas Müntzer bis Paracelsus,* edited by Hans-Jürgen Goertz, 210–22. Munich: Beck, 1978.

Frumkin, Arye Loeb. *Toldot ḥakhmei Yerushalayim mi-shenat 5250 le-yeẓirah ad 5630 le-yeẓirah.* 4 vols. Jerusalem: Salomon, 1928–30. Reprint, Tel Aviv, 1969.

Funkenstein, Amos. "Anti-Jewish Propaganda: Pagan, Medieval and Modern." *Jerusalem Quarterly* 19 (1981): 56–72.

———. "History, Counterhistory, and Narrative." In *Probing the Limits of Representation: Nazism and the "Final Solution,"* edited by Saul Friedländer, 3rd ed., 66–81. Cambridge, MA: Harvard University Press, 1996.

Gage, John. "Color in Western Art: An Issue?" *Art Bulletin* 72 (1990): 518–41.

———. "Colour in History: Relative and Absolute." *Art History* 1 (1978): 104–30.

Geiger, Abraham. "Abhandlungen." Pt. 3, "Der Arzt Benjamin ben Eliahu Beër." *Jüdische Zeitschrift für Wissenschaft und Leben* 4 (1866): 171–74.

———. "Aus einem Briefe des Rabb. Dr. Geiger." *Zeitschrift der Deutschen Morgenländischen Gesellschaft* 13 (1859): 490–92.

———. "Eine mittelalterliche jüdische Medaille." *Zeitschrift der Deutschen Morgenländischen Gesellschaft* 12 (1858): 680–93.

———. *Das Studium der Hebräischen Sprache in Deutschland vom Ende des XV bis zur Mitte des XVI Jahrhunderts.* Breslau: Schletter, 1870.

Goertz, Hans-Jürgen. *Thomas Müntzer: Mystiker, Apokalyptiker, Revolutionär.* Munich: Beck, 1989.

Goeters, J. F. Gerhard. *Ludwig Hätzer ca. 1500 bis 1529: Spiritualist und Antitrinitarier: Eine Randfigur der frühen Täuferbewegung.* Quellen und Forschungen zur Reformationsgeschichte 25. Gütersloh: Bertelsmann, 1927.

Goldish, Matt D. "Jews and Habsburgs in Prague and Regensburg: On the Political and Cultural Significance of Solomon Molkho's Relics." In *Jewish Culture in Early Modern Europe: Essays in Honor of David B. Ruderman,* edited by Richard I. Cohen et al., 28–38. Pittsburgh, PA, and Cincinnati, OH: University of Pittsburgh Press and Hebrew Union College Press, 2014.

———. "Patterns in Converso Messianism." In *Millenarianism and Messianism in Early Modern European Culture.* Vol. 1, *Jewish Messianism in the Early Modern World,* edited by Matt D. Goldish and Richard H. Popkin, 41–63. Archives internationales d'histoire des idées 173. Dordrecht: Kluwer, 2001.

———. *The Sabbatean Prophets.* Cambridge, MA: Harvard University Press, 2004.

Goldish, Matt D., and Richard H. Popkin, eds. *Millenarianism and Messianism in Early Modern European Culture.* Vol. 1, *Jewish Messianism in the Early Modern World.* Archives internationales d'histoire des idées 173. Dordrecht: Kluwer, 2001.

Goldschmidt, Daniel. "Bonetto Latis e i soui scritti latini e italiani." In *Scritti in memoria di Enzo Sereni: Saggi sull'Ebraismo Romano*, edited by Daniel Carpi, 88–94. Jerusalem: Fondazione Sally Mayer, 1970.

Göllner, Carl. *Turcica*. 3 vols. Bukarest: Editura Academiei Republicii Socialiste Romania, 1961–78.

Gottheil, Richard, and Isaac Broydé. "Beer, Benjamin ben Elijah ha-Rofe." In *The Jewish Encyclopedia: A Descriptive Record of the History, Religion, Literature, and Customs of the Jewish People from the Earliest Time to the Present Day*, 12 vols, edited by Isidore Singer et al., 2:631–33. New York: Funk and Wagnalls, 1901–6. Reprint, New York: Funk and Wagnalls, 1925.

Gow, Andrew C. "Das Gefolge des Antichristen: Zur Legende von den 'roten Juden.'" In *Der Antichrist: Die Glasmalereien in der Marienkirche in Frankfurt (Oder)*, edited by Ulrich Knefelkamp and Frank Martin, 102–12. Leipzig: Edition Leipzig, 2008.

———. "Gog and Magog on 'Mappamundi' and Early Printed World Maps: Orientalizing Ethnography in the Apocalyptic Tradition." *Journal of Early Modern History* 2.1 (1998): 61–88.

———. "The Jewish Antichrist in Medieval and Early Modern Germany." *Medieval Encounters* 2.3 (1996): 249–85.

———. *The Red Jews: Antisemitism in an Apocalyptic Age, 1200–1600*. Leiden: Brill, 1995.

Graetz, Heinrich. *Geschichte der Juden von den ältesten Zeiten bis auf die Gegenwart*. Vol. 9, *Von der Verbannung der Juden aus Spanien und Portugal (1494) bis zur dauernden Ansiedelung der Marranen in Holland (1618)*. Leipzig: Oskar Leiner, 1907. Reprint Darmstadt: Wissenschaftliche Buchgesellschaft, 1998.

———. "Salomon Molcho und David Reubeni." *Monatsschrift für Geschichte und Wissenschaft des Judentums* 5 (1856): 205–15, 241–61.

Greenberg, Gershon. "American Indians, Ten Lost Tribes and Christian Eschatology." In *Religion in the Age of Exploration: The Case of Spain and New Spain*, edited by Bryan F. LeBeau, 127–48. Studies in Jewish Civilization 5. Omaha, NE: Creighton University Press, 1996.

Grimm, Jacob, and Wilhelm Grimm. *Deutsches Wörterbuch*. 33 vols. Leipzig: Hirzel, 1854–1971. Reprint, Gütersloh: Bertelsmann, 1991.

Groebner, Valentin. *Who Are You? Identification, Deception, and Surveillance in Early Modern Europe*. New York: Zone Books, 2007.

Gross, Avraham. "The Expulsion and the Search for the Ten Tribes." *Judaism* 41.2 (1992): 130–47.

———. "The Ten Tribes and the Kingdom of Prester John: Rumors and Investigations before and after the Expulsion from Spain." *Pe'amim* (1991): 5–41. [Hebrew]

Gross, Benjamin. *Le Messianisme juif: L'éternité d'Israel du Maharal de Prague (1512–1609)*. Paris: Klincksieck, 1969.

———. *Netzah Yisrael: The Maharal of Prague's Messianic Conception of Exile and Redemption*. Tel Aviv: Dvir, 1974. [Hebrew]

Grossman, Avraham. *The Early Sages of Ashkenaz*. 2nd ed. Jerusalem: Magnes Press, 1988. [Hebrew]

――――. "'Redemption by Conversion' in the Teaching of Early Ashkenazi Sages." *Zion* 59 (1994): 325–42. [Hebrew]

Grotte, Alfred. "Die 'Reliquien' des Salomo Molcho." *Monatsschrift für Geschichte und Wissenschaft des Judentums* 67.5 (1923): 167–70.

Grözinger, Karl E. "Jüdische Wundermänner in Deutschland." In *Judentum im deutschen Sprachraum*, edited by Karl E. Grözinger, 190–221. Frankfurt am Main: Suhrkamp, 1991.

Guderian, Hans. *Die Täufer in Augsburg: Ihre Geschichte und ihr Erbe: Ein Beitrag zur 2000-Jahr-Feier der Stadt Augsburg*. Pfaffenhofen: Ludwig, 1984.

Gutmann, Joseph. "The Messiah at the Seder: A Fifteenth-Century Motif in Jewish Art." In *Studies in Jewish History: Presented to Professor Raphael Mahler on His Seventy-Fifth Birthday*, edited by Shmuel Yeivin, 29–38. Tel Aviv: Sifri'at Po'alim, 1974.

――――. "Wenn das Reich Gottes kommt: Messianische Themen in der Kunst des Mittelalters." In *Wenn der Messias kommt: Das jüdisch-christliche Verhältnis im Spiegel mittelalterlicher Kunst*, edited by Lieselotte Kötzsche and Peter von der Osten-Sacken, 19–26. Veröffentlichungen aus dem Institut Kirche und Judentum 16. Berlin: Institut Kirche und Judentum, [1994].

Habel, Thomas. "Prototyp und Variation: Aufstieg und Fall des Antichrist in Nürnberger Bildertexten und Fastnachtspielen des 15. Jahrhunderts." In *Der Sturz des Mächtigen*, edited by Theodor Wolpers, 149–201. Göttingen: Vandenhoeck & Ruprecht, 2000.

Habermann, Abraham M. "The Press of Paul Fagius and the Books of His Print Shop." In *Studies in the History of Hebrew Printers and Books*, 149–66. Jerusalem: Mass, 1978. [Hebrew]

Hacker, Joseph R. "Ottoman Policies towards the Jews and Jewish Attitudes towards the Ottomans during the 15th Century." In *Christians and Jews in the Ottoman Empire: The Functioning of a Plural Society*, edited by Benjamin Braude and Bernhard Lewis, 1:117–26. New York: Holmes and Meier, 1982.

Hadas-Lebel, Mireille. "Jacob et Esau ou Israel et Rome dans le Talmud et le Midrash." *Revue de l'histoire des religions* 201 (1984): 369–92.

Hayoun, Maurice R. "Rabbi Ja'akov Emdens Autobiographie oder der Kämpfer wider die sabbatianische Häresie." In *Judentum im deutschen Sprachraum*, edited by Karl E. Grözinger, 222–36. Frankfurt am Main: Suhrkamp, 1991.

Heid, Stefan. *Chiliasmus und Antichrist-Mythos: Eine frühchristliche Kontroverse um das Heilige Land*. Hereditas 6. Bonn: Borengässer, 1993.

Helmrath, Johnnes. "Pius II. und die Türken." In *Europa und die Türken in der Renaissance*, edited by Bodo Guthmüller and Wilhelm Kühlmann, 78–137. Tübingen: Niemeyer, 2000.

Hendrix, Scott H. "Toleration of the Jews in the German Reformation: Urbanus Rhegius and Braunschweig (1535–1540)." *Archiv für Reformationsgeschichte* 81 (1990): 189–215.

Heřman, Jan. "The Prague Jewish Community before the Expulsion of 1541." In *Prague Ghetto in the Renaissance Period*, edited by Otto Muneles, translated by Iva Drápalová, 15–42. Jewish Monuments in Bohemia and Moravia 4. Prague: Orbis, 1965.

Heyd, Michael. "The 'Jewish Quaker': Christian Perceptions of Sabbatai Zevi as an Enthusiast." In *Hebraica Veritas? Christian Hebraists and the Study of Judaism in Early Modern Europe*, edited by Allison P. Coudert and Jeffrey S. Shoulson, 234–65. Philadelphia: University of Pennsylvania Press, 2004.

Hill, Charles E. "Antichrist from the Tribe of Dan." *Journal of Theological Studies* n.s. 46.1 (1995): 99–117.

Hill, George F. *A Corpus of Italian Medals of the Renaissance before Cellini*. 2 vols. London: British Museum, 1930. Reprint, Florence: Studio per Edizioni Scelte, 1984.

Hirsch, Rudolf. *Printing, Selling and Reading, 1450–1550*. 2nd ed. Wiesbaden: Harrassowitz, 1974.

Hobbs, Gerald. "Bucer, the Jews, and Judaism." In *Jews, Judaism, and the Reformation in Sixteenth-Century Germany*, edited by Dean P. Bell and Stephen G. Burnett, 137–69. Studies in Central European Histories 37. Leiden: Brill, 2006.

———. "Monitio Amica: Pellican et Capiton sur le danger des lectures rabbiniques." In *Horizons européens de la Réforme en Alsace: Das Elsass und die Reformation im Europa des XVI. Jahrhunderts: Mélanges offerts à Jean Rott pour son 65. anniversaire*, edited by Marijn de Kroon and Marc Lienhard, 81–93. Société savante d'Alsace et des Régions de l'Est 17. Strasbourg: Librairie Istra, 1980.

Hochedlinger, Michael. "Die französisch-osmanische 'Freundschaft' 1525–1792." *Mitteilungen des Instituts für österreichische Geschichtsforschung* 102 (1994): 108–24.

Höfert, Almut. *Den Feind beschreiben: 'Türkengefahr' und europäisches Wissen über das Osmanische Reich 1450–1600*. Campus Historische Studien 8. Frankfurt am Main: Campus, 2003.

Hoffman, Jeffrey. "Akdamut: History, Folklore, and Meaning." *Jewish Quarterly Review* 99.2 (2009): 161–83.

Hofmann, Hans-Ulrich. *Luther und die Johannes-Apokalypse: Dargestellt im Rahmen der Auslegungsgeschichte des letzten Buches der Bibel und im Zusammenhang der theologischen Entwicklung des Reformators*. Tübingen: Mohr Siebeck, 1982.

Hollender, Elisabeth. *Piyyut Commentary in Medieval Ashkenaz*. Studia Judaica 42. Berlin: De Gruyter, 2008.

Holzem, Andreas. "Zeit—Zeitenwende—Endzeit? Anfangsbeobachtungen zum deutschen katholischen Schrifttum um 1700." In *Jahrhundertwenden*, edited by Manfred Jakubowski-Tiessen et al., 213–32. Veröffentlichungen des Max-Planck-Instituts für Geschichte 155. Göttingen: Vandenhoeck & Ruprecht, 1999.

Holzmair, Eduard. *Katalog der Sammlung Dr. Josef Brettauer: Medicina in Nummis*. Vienna, 1937.

Horovitz, Marcus. *Frankfurter Rabbinen: Ein Beitrag zur Geschichte der israelitischen Gemeinde in Frankfurt a.M.* 2nd ed. Jerusalem: Mossad Harav Kook, 1969.

Horowitz, Elliott. "Speaking to the Dead: Cemetery Prayer in Medieval and Early Modern Jewry." *Journal of Jewish Thought and Philosophy* 8 (1999): 303–17.

Hruby, Kurt. *Juden und Judentum bei den Kirchenvätern*. Schriften zur Judentumskunde 2. Zürich: Theologischer Verlag, 1972.

Hsia, Ronnie Po-chia. *Trent 1475: Stories of a Ritual Murder Trial*. New Haven, CT: Yale University Press, 1992.

Hüttenmeister, Nathanja. "Eine jüdische Familie im Spannungsverhältnis zwischen Judentum und Christentum: Der Konvertit Christian Gerson im Konflikt mit seiner jüdischen Verwandtschaft." *Vestische Zeitschrift: Zeitschrift der Vereine für Orts- und Heimatkunde im Vest Recklinghausen* 99 (2002): 47–59.

Idel, Moshe. "The Attitude to Christianity in the Sefer ha-Meshiv." *Zion* 46 (1981): 77–91. [Hebrew]

———. "Egidio da Viterbo and R. Abraham Abulafia's Writings." *Italia: Studi e ricerche sulla cultura e sulla letteratura degli ebrei d'Italia* 2.1 (1981): 48–50. [Hebrew]

———. "Encounters between Spanish and Italian Kabbalists in the Generation of the Expulsion." In *Crisis and Creativity in the Sephardic World, 1391–1648*, edited by Benjamin R. Gampel, 189–222. New York: Columbia University Press, 1997.

———. "Introduction." In *Jewish Messianic Movements: Sources and Documents on Messianism in Jewish History from the Bar-Kokhba Revolt until Recent Times in Two Volumes.* Vol. 1, *From the Bar-Kokhba Revolt until the Expulsion of the Jews from Spain*, edited by Aaron Z. Aescoly, 9–28. 2nd ed. Jerusalem: Bialik Institute, 1987. [Hebrew]

———. "The Magical and Neoplatonic Interpretations of Kabbalah in the Renaissance." In *Jewish Thought in the Sixteenth Century*, edited by Bernard D. Cooperman, 186–242. Harvard Judaica Texts and Studies 2. Cambridge, MA: Harvard University Press, 1983.

———. *Messianic Mystics.* New Haven, CT: Yale University Press, 1998.

———. "Particularism and Universalism in Kabbalah, 1480–1650." In *Essential Papers on Jewish Culture in Renaissance and Baroque Italy*, edited by David B. Ruderman, 324–44. Essential Papers on Jewish Studies 5. New York: New York University Press, 1992.

———. "R. Johanan Alemanno and the Astrological Treatise 'Ma'amar Hoze': A Supplement to 'Treatise on Eschatology and Astrology.'" *Kirjat Sefer* 54 (1979): 825–26 [Hebrew]

———. "Religion, Thought and Attitudes: The Impact of the Expulsion of the Jews." In *Spain and the Jews: The Sephardi Experience 1492 and After*, edited by Elie Kedourie, 123–39. London: Thames and Hudson, 1992.

———. "Shlomo Molkho as Magician." *Sefunot* 3 (1985): 193–219. [Hebrew]

———. "Types of Redemptive Activities in the Middle Ages." In *Messianism and Eschatology: A Collection of Essays*, edited by Zvi Baras, 253–79. Jerusalem: Zalman Shazar Center for Jewish History, 1983. [Hebrew]

———. "An Unknown Sermon of Shlomo Molkho's." In *Exile and Diaspora: Studies in the History of the Jewish People Presented to Professor Haim Beinart*, edited by Aharon Mirsky, Avraham Grossman, and Yosef Kaplan, 430–36. Jerusalem: Ben-Zvi Institute, 1991. [Hebrew]

Idelson-Shein, Iris. *Difference of a Different Kind: Jewish Constructions of Race during the Long Eighteenth Century.* Philadelphia: University of Pennsylvania Press, 2014.

Inalcik, Halil. *The Ottoman Empire: The Classical Age, 1300–1600.* London: Phoenix, 1973.

Ioly Zorattini, Pier Cesare. "Gli insediamenti ebraici nel Friuli veneto." In *Gli ebrei e Venezia secoli XIV–XVIII: Atti del Convegno internazionale organizzato dall' Istituto di storia della società e dello stato veneziano della Fondazione Giorgio Cini (Venice, 5.–10. Juni 1983)*, edited by Gaetano Cozzi, 261–80. Milan: Edizioni di Comunità, 1987.

Jacobs, Martin. "David ha-Re'uveni: ein 'zionistisches Experiment' im Kontext der europäischen Expansion?" In *An der Schwelle zur Moderne: Juden in der Renaissance*, edited by Giuseppe Veltri and Annette Winkelmann, 191–206. Leiden: Brill, 2003.

Jacobson, Yoram R. *Along the Paths of Exile and Redemption: The Doctrine of Redemption of Mordecai Dato*. Jerusalem: Bialik Institute, 1986. [Hebrew]

Jakubowski-Tiessen, Manfred, et al., eds. *Jahrhundertwenden*. Veröffentlichungen des Max-Planck-Instituts für Geschichte 155. Göttingen: Vandenhoeck & Ruprecht, 1999.

Jenks, Gregory C. *The Origins and Early Development of the Antichrist Myth*. Beihefte zur Zeitschrift für die neutestamentliche Wissenschaft 59. Berlin: De Gruyter, 1991.

Jost, Isaak M. *Geschichte des Judenthums und seiner Secten*. 3 vols. Leipzig: Dörffling & Franke, 1857–59.

———. "Neues über die vielbesprochene in Lyon gefundene Medaille." *Der israelitische Volkslehrer: Ein Organ für Synagoge, Schule, Leben und Wissenschaft des Judenthums* 8.4 (1858): 117–24.

———. "Zu dem Aufsatze des Herrn Dr. Geiger: Eine mittelalterliche jüdische Medaille." *Zeitschrift der Deutschen Morgenländischen Gesellschaft* 13 (1859): 272–75.

Jung, Martin. *Die württembergische Kirche und die Juden in der Zeit des Pietismus (1675–1780)*. Studien zu Kirche und Israel 13. Berlin: Institut Kirche und Judentum, 1992.

Kampers, Franz. *Die deutsche Kaiseridee in Prophetie und Sage*. 2nd ed. Munich: Lüneberg, 1896. Reprint, Aalen: Scientia, 1969.

Kaplan, Debra L. *Beyond Expulsion: Jews, Christians and Reformation Strasbourg*. Stanford, CA: Stanford University Press, 2011.

Kaplan, Debra L., and Magda Teter. "Out of the (Historiographic) Ghetto: European Jews and Reformation Narratives." *Sixteenth Century Journal* 50.2 (2009): 365–94.

Kaplan, Yosef. "Thomas Coenen in Smyrna: Reflections of a Dutch Calvinist on the Sabbatean Awakening of the Levantine Jews." In Thomas Coenen, *Vain Hopes of the Jews as Revealed in the Figure of Sabbetai Zevi*, edited by Yosef Kaplan, 7–22. Jerusalem: Dinur Institute, 1998. [Hebrew]

Katz, David S. *Philosemitism and the Readmission of the Jews to England*. Oxford: Clarendon, 1982.

Kaufmann, David. "Azriel b. Solomon Dayiena et la seconde intervention de David Reubeni en Italie." *Revue des Études Juives* 30 (1895): 304–9.

———. "Un poème messianique de Salomon Molkho." *Revue des Études Juives* 34 (1897): 121–25.

———. "A Rumour about the Ten Tribes in Pope Martin V's Time." *Jewish Quarterly Review* 4 (1892): 503–8.

Kaufmann, Thomas. *Das Ende der Reformation: Magdeburgs "Herrgotts Kanzlei" (1548–1551/52)*. Beiträge zur historischen Theologie 123. Tübingen: Mohr Siebeck, 2003.

———. "Das Judentum in der frühreformatorischen Flugschriftenpublizistik." *Zeitschrift für Theologie und Kirche* 95 (1998): 429–61.

————. "Luther and the Jews." In *Jews, Judaism, and the Reformation in Sixteenth-Century Germany*, edited by Dean P. Bell and Stephen G. Burnett, 69–104. Studies in Central European Histories 37. Leiden: Brill, 2006.

————. *Luther's Jews: A Journey into Anti-Semitism*. Oxford: Oxford University Press, 2017.

————. *Luthers "Judenschriften": Ein Beitrag zu ihrer historischen Kontextualisierung*. 2nd ed. Tübingen: Mohr Siebeck, 2013.

————. "Römisches und evangelisches Jubeljahr 1600: Konfessionskulturelle Deutungsalternativen der Zeit im Jahrhundert der Reformation." In *Millennium: Deutungen zum christlichen Mythos der Jahrtausendwende*, edited by Christoph Bochinger et al., 73–136. Kaiser Taschenbuch 171. Gütersloh: Bertelsmann, 1999.

————. "Die theologische Bewertung des Judentums im Protestantismus des späteren 16. Jahrhunderts (1530–1600)." *Archiv für Reformationsgeschichte* 91 (2000): 191–237.

————. *"Türckenbüchlein": Zur christlichen Wahrnehmung "türkischer Religion" in Spätmittelalter und Reformation*. Forschungen zur Kirchen- und Dogmengeschichte 97. Göttingen: Vandenhoeck & Ruprecht. 2008.

Kayserling, Moses. *Geschichte der Juden in Portugal*. Leipzig: Leiner, 1867.

Kirchheim, [Raphael]. "Nachtrag zur Erklärung der mittelalterlichen jüdischen Medaille." *Zeitschrift der Deutschen Morgenländischen Gesellschaft* 13 (1859): 273.

Kirn, Hans-Martin. *Das Bild vom Juden im Deutschland des frühen 16. Jahrhunderts dargestellt an den Schriften Johannes Pfefferkorns*. Texts and Studies in Medieval and Early Modern Judaism 3. Tübingen: Mohr Siebeck, 1989.

Klaassen, Walter. *Living at the End of the Ages: Apocalyptic Expectation in the Radical Reformation*. Lanham, MD: University Press of America, 1992.

Klausner, Joseph. *The Messianic Idea in Israel from Its Beginning to the Completion of the Mishnah*. New York: Macmillan, 1955.

Klausner, Judah A. "On the Movement of Solomon Molcho." *Kirjat Sefer* 15 (1939): 391–92. [Hebrew]

Klötzer, Ralf. *Die Täuferherrschaft von Münster: Stadtreformation und Welterneuerung*. Reformationsgeschichtliche Studien und Texte 131. Münster: Aschendorff, 1992.

Kluge, Otto. "Die Hebräische Sprachwissenschaft in Deutschland im Zeitalter des Humanismus." *Zeitschrift für die Geschichte der Juden in Deutschland* 3 (1931): 81–97, 180–93; 4 (1932): 100–129.

Knefelkamp, Ulrich. "Der Priesterkönig Johannes und sein Reich: Legende oder Realität." *Journal of Medieval History* 14 (1988): 337–55.

Kochan, Lionel. *Jews, Idols and Messiahs: The Challenge from History*. Oxford: Basil Blackwell, 1990.

Kogman-Appel, Katrin. *A Mahzor from Worms: Art and Religion in a Medieval Jewish Community*. Cambridge, MA: Harvard University Press, 2012.

Köhler, Hans-Joachim, ed. *Flugschriften als Massenmedium der Reformationszeit: Beiträge zum Tübinger Symposion 1980*. Spätmittelalter und frühe Neuzeit 13. Stuttgart: Klett-Cotta, 1981.

Köhler, Manfred. *Melanchthon und der Islam: Ein Beitrag zur Klärung des Verhältnisses zwischen Christentum und Fremdreligionen in der Reformationszeit*. Leipzig: Klotz, 1938.

Kottek, Samuel. "Ha-rofeh ha-Anav: He-erot ve-ḥiddushim al medaliyah mi-tekufat ha-Renesans." *Koroth: A Bulletin Devoted to the History of Medicine and Science* 28.7 (1980): 747–53.

———. "Humilitas: On a Controversial Medal of Benjamin Son of Elijah Beer the Physician (1497?–1503?)." *Journal of Jewish Art* 11 (1985): 41–46.

Kracauer, Isidore. *Geschichte der Juden in Frankfurt a.M. (1150–1824).* 2 vols. Frankfurt am Main: Kauffmann, 1925–27.

Krauss, Samuel. "Le Roi de France Charles VIII et les espérances messianiques." *Revue des Études Juives* 51 (1906): 87–96.

Kremers, Heinz, ed. *Die Juden und Martin Luther—Martin Luther und die Juden: Geschichte, Wirkungsgeschichte, Herausforderung.* Neukirchen-Vluyn: Neukirchener Verlag, 1985.

Künast, Hans-Jörg. "Hebräisch-jüdischer Buchdruck in Schwaben in der ersten Hälfte des 16. Jahrhunderts." In *Landjudentum im deutschen Südwesten während der Frühen Neuzeit,* edited by Rolf Kießling and Sabine Ullmann, 277–303. Colloquia Augustana 10. Berlin: Akademie-Verlag, 1999.

Künzl, Hannelore. "Die Jüdische Kunst zwischen Mittelalter und Moderne: Das 16. bis 18. Jahrhundert." In *Schöpferische Momente des europäischen Judentums in der frühen Neuzeit,* edited by Michael Graetz, 75–96. Heidelberg: Winter, 2000.

Kurze, Dietrich. *Johannes Lichtenberger (gest. 1503): Eine Studie zur Geschichte der Prophetie und Astrologie.* Historische Studien 379. Lübeck: Matthiesen, 1960.

Kuyt, Annelies. "Die Welt aus sefardischer und ashkenazischer Sicht: Die mittelalterlichen hebräischen Reiseberichte des Benjamin von Tudela und des Petachja von Regensburg." In *Erkundung und Beschreibung der Welt: Zur Poetik der Reise- und Länderberichte, Vorträge eines interdisziplinären Symposiums vom 19.–24. Juni 2000 an der Justus-Liebig-Universität Gießen,* edited by Xenja von Ertzdorff-Kupffer and Gerhard Giesemann, 211–31. Chloe 34. Amsterdam: Rodopi, 2003.

Lasker, Daniel J. "Jewish-Christian Polemics at the Turning Point: Jewish Evidence from the Twelfth Century." *Harvard Theological Review* 89 (1996): 161–73.

Lawee, Eric. "The Messianism of Isaac Abarbanel, 'Father of the [Jewish] Messianic Movements of the Sixteenth and Seventeenth Centuries.'" In *Millenarianism and Messianism in Early Modern European Culture.* Vol. 1, *Messianism in the Early Modern World,* edited by Matt D. Goldish and Richard H. Popkin, 1–39. Archives internationales d'histoire des idées 173. Dordrecht: Kluwer, 2001.

Lazar, Simon Menachem. "Aseret ha-shevatim." *Ha-shilo'aḥ* 9 (1902): 46–56, 205–21, 352–63, 431–47, 520–28; 10 (1902): 42–56, 156–64, 226–35.

———. *Ḥidot ha-haggadot ha-nifla'ot al davar aseret ha-shevatim u-pitronan.* Drohobycz, 1908.

Lellouch, Benjamin, and Stéphane Yerasimos. *Les traditions apocalyptiques au tournant de la chute de Constantinople: Actes de la Table Ronde d'Istanbul (13–14 avril 1996).* Varia Turcica 33. Paris: Harmattan, 2000.

Lenowitz, Harris. *The Jewish Messiahs: From the Galilee to Crown Heights.* New York: Oxford University Press, 1998.

Leone Leoni, Aron di. *The Hebrew Portuguese Nations in Antwerp and London at the Time of Charles V and Henry VIII: New Documents and Interpretations.* Jersey City, NJ: Ktav, 2005.

Leppin, Volker. *Antichrist und Jüngster Tag: Das Profil apokalyptischer Flugschriftenpublizistik im deutschen Luthertum 1548–1618.* Quellen und Forschungen zur Reformationsgeschichte 69. Gütersloh: Gütersloher Verlagshaus, 1999.

Lerner, Robert E. "Millennialism." In *Encyclopedia of Apocalypticism,* edited by Bernard McGinn, John J. Collins, and Stephen J. Stein, 2:326–60. 3rd ed. New York: Continuum, 2000. Reprint, New York: Continuum, 2003.

Levenson, Jon D. *Resurrection and the Restoration of Israel: The Ultimate Victory of the God of Life.* New Haven, CT: Yale University Press, 2006.

Levine Melammed, Renée. *Heretics or Daughters of Israel? The Crypto-Jewish Women of Castile.* Oxford: Oxford University Press, 1999.

Lévy, Gerson. "Sur le mémoire anuscri à une médaille en l'honneur de Louis-le-Débonnaire par M. Carmoly, grand-rabbin de Bruxelles." *Mémoires de l'Académie royale de Metz* 18 (1837): 163–74.

Lewin, Reinhold. *Luthers Stellung zu den Juden: Ein Beitrag zur Geschichte der Juden in Deutschland während des Reformationszeitalters.* Berlin: Trowitzsch, 1911. Reprint, Aalen: Scientia, 1973.

Lewis, Bernard. *Cultures in Conflict: Christians, Muslims, and Jews in the Age of Discovery.* 2nd ed. New York: Oxford University Press, 1995.

Linder, Amnon. "L'expédition italienne de Charles VIII et les espérances messianiques des Juifs, Temoignage du manuscript B.N. Lat. 5971A." *Revue des Études Juives* 137 (1978): 179–86.

Lipiner, Elias. "Inyanim be-farashat David ha-Re'uveni u-Shlomo Molkho." In *The Story of David Hareuveni: Copied from the Oxford Manuscript,* edited by Aaron Z. Aescoly, 45–48. 2nd ed. Jerusalem: Bialik Institute, 1993.

Lipman, Vivian D. *The Jews of Medieval Norwich.* London: Jewish Historical Society of England, 1967.

List, Günther. *Chiliastische Utopie und radikale Reformation: Die Erneuerung der Idee vom Tausendjährigen Reich im 16. Jahrhundert.* Munich: Fink, 1973.

Litt, Stefan. "Juden und Waffen im 16. und 17. Jahrhundert: Anmerkungen zu einem Alltagsphänomen." *Aschkenas: Zeitschrift für Geschichte und Kultur der Juden* 13.1 (2003): 83–92.

Loewe, Louis. "Memoir on the Lemlein Medal." *Numismatic Chronicle and Journal of the Numismatic Society* 19 (1856/57): 237–70.

Loewenthal, Elena. *Il libro di Eldad il Danita: Viaggio immaginario di un ebreo del medioevo.* Bologna: Fattoadarte, 1993.

Loewisohn, Salomo. *Vorlesungen über die neuere Geschichte der Juden.* Vienna: Beck, 1820.

Lohrmann, Klaus, Wilhelm Wadl, and Markus J. Wenninger. "Überblick über die jüdischen Siedlungen in Österreich." In *1000 Jahre österreichisches Judentum: Ausstellungskatalog,* edited by Klaus Lohrmann, 69–92. Studia Judaica Austriaca 9. Eisenstadt: Roetzer, 1982.

Madigan, Kevin J., and Jon D. Levenson. *Resurrection: The Power of God for Christians and Jews.* New Haven, CT: Yale University Press, 2008.

Magin, Christine. "'Waffenrecht' und 'Waffenverbot' für Juden im Mittelalter: Zu einem Mythos der Forschungsgeschichte." *Aschkenas: Zeitschrift für Geschichte und Kultur der Juden* 13.1 (2003): 17–33.

Maimon, Arye, Mordechai Breuer, and Yacov Guggenheim, eds. *Germania Judaica*. Vol. 3, *1350–1519*. Tübingen: Mohr Siebeck, 1987–95.

Marcus, Ivan G. "Beyond the Sephardi Mystique." *Orim* 1 (1985): 35–53.

———. *Piety and Society: The Jewish Pietists of Medieval Germany*. Leiden: Brill, 1981.

———. *Rituals of Childhood: Jewish Acculturation in Medieval Europe*. New Haven, CT: Yale University Press, 1996.

Margolin, Jean-Claude. "Sur quelques ouvrages de la bibliothèque de Postel annotés de sa main." In *Guillaume Postel 1581–1981: Actes du Colloque International d'Avranches 5–9 septembre 1981*, 109–30. Paris: Editions de la Maisnie, 1985.

Marriott, Brandon. *Transnational Networks and Cross-Religious Exchange in the Seventeenth-Century Mediterranean and Atlantic Worlds: Sabbatai Sevi and the Lost Tribes of Israel*. London: Routledge, 2016.

Martin, Ellen. *Die deutschen Schriften des Johannes Pfefferkorn: Zum Problem des Judenhasses und der Intoleranz in der Zeit der Vorreformation*. Göppinger Arbeiten zur Germanistik 604. Göppingen: Kümmerle, 1994.

Matschke, Klaus-Peter. *Das Kreuz und der Halbmond: Die Geschichte der Türkenkriege*. Düsseldorf: Artemis & Winkler, 2004.

Maurer, Wilhelm. "Die Zeit der Reformation." In *Kirche und Synagoge: Handbuch zur Geschichte von Christen und Juden, Darstellung mit Quellen*, edited by Karl Heinrich Rengstorf and Siegfried von Kortzfleisch, 1:363–452. Stuttgart: Klett, 1968.

Mayer, Reinhold. "Schlomo Molchos messianisches Programm." *Emuna* 5/6 (1974): 333–41.

McGinn, Bernard. *Antichrist: Two Thousand Years of the Human Fascination with Evil*. 2nd ed. New York: Columbia University Press, 2000.

McGinn, Bernard, John J. Collins, and Stephen J. Stein, eds. *Encyclopedia of Apocalypticism*. 3 vols. 3rd ed. New York: Continuum, 2000. Reprint, New York: Continuum, 2003.

Meerson, Michael, and Peter Schäfer, eds. *Toledot Yeshu: The Life Story of Jesus*. 2 vols. Texts and Studies in Ancient Judaism 159. Tübingen: Mohr Siebeck, 2014.

Meitlis, Jakob. *Das Ma'assebuch, seine Entstehung und Quellengeschichte, zugleich ein Beitrag zur Einführung in die altjiddische Agada*. Berlin: Mass, 1933.

Mellinkoff, Ruth. "Judas's Red Hair and the Jews." *Journal of Jewish Art* 9 (1982): 31–46.

———. *Outcasts: Signs of Otherness in Northern European Art of the Late Middle Ages*. 2 vols. Berkeley: University of California Press, 1993.

Menache, Sophia. "Tartars, Jews, Saracens and the Jewish-Mongol 'Plot' of 1241." *History: The Journal of the Historical Association* 81 (1996): 319–24.

Ménestrier, Claude F. *Histoire civile ou consulaire de la ville de Lyon*. Lyon: Jean-Baptiste et Nicolas de Ville, 1696.

Miyamoto, Yoko. "The Influence of Medieval Prophecies on Views of the Turks: Islam and Apocalypticism in the Sixteenth Century." *Journal of Turkish Studies* 17 (1993): 125–45.

Moeller, Bernd. "Was wurde in der Frühzeit der Reformation in den deutschen Städten gepredigt?" *Archiv für Reformationsgeschichte* 75 (1984): 176–93.

Möhring, Hannes. "Karl der Große und die Endkaiser-Weissagung: Der Sieger über den Islam kommt aus dem Westen." In *Montjoie: Studies in Crusade History in Honour of*

Hans Eberhard Mayer, edited by Benjamin Z. Kedar, Jonathan Riley-Smith, and Rudolf Hiestand, 1–19. Variorum 20. London: Variorum, 1997.

———. *Der Weltkaiser der Endzeit: Entstehung, Wandel und Wirkung einer tausendjährigen Weissagung.* Mittelalter-Forschungen 3. Stuttgart: Thorbecke, 2000.

Moore, George F. *Judaism in the First Centuries of the Christian Era: The Age of the Tannaim.* 3 vols. Cambridge, MA: Harvard University Press, 1927–30.

Morag, Shlomo. "A Linguistic Examination of Eldad the Danite's Origin." *Tarbiz* 66 (1997): 223–46. [Hebrew]

Mowinckel, Sigmund. *He That Cometh: The Messianic Concept in the Old Testament and Later Judaism.* Oxford: Basil Blackwell, 1956. Reprint, Grand Rapids, MI: William B. Eerdmans, 2005.

Moyal, Eli. *Rabbi Yaacov Sasportas.* Jerusalem, 1992. [Hebrew]

Müller, David H. "Die Recensionen und Versionen des Eldad ha-Dani." *Denkschriften der Kaiserlichen Akademie der Wissenschaften: Philosophisch-Historische Klasse* 41 (1892): 1–80.

Müller, Jan-Dirk. "Formen literarischer Kommunikation im Übergang vom Mittelalter zur Neuzeit." In *Die Literatur im Übergang vom Mittelalter zur Neuzeit*, edited by Werner Röcke and Marina Münkler, 21–53. Hansers Sozialgeschichte der deutschen Literatur vom 16. Jahrhundert bis zur Gegenwart 1. Munich: Hanser, 2004.

Müller, Ludwig. "Aus fünf Jahrhunderten: Beiträge zur Geschichte der jüdischen Gemeinden im Ries." *Zeitschrift des historischen Vereins für Schwaben und Neuburg* 25 (1898): 1–124; 26 (1899): 81–182.

Müsing, Hans Werner. "The Anabaptist Movement in Strasbourg from Early 1526 to July 1527." *Mennonite Quarterly Review* 51 (1977): 91–126.

Myers, David N. *Resisting History: Historicism and Its Discontents in German-Jewish Thought.* Princeton, NJ: Princeton University Press, 2003.

Nahon, Gérard. "From Algarve to Rivtigo: New Christians During David ha-Re'uveni's Travels in Portugal." In *International Congress: The Expulsion of the Jews from Spain (1474–1516): Abstracts*, 63–64. Jerusalem, 1992.

———. "Judaïsme médiévale et moderne I: Le judaïsme des Marranes espagnols et portugais, Étude de quelques modèles." *Annuaire École pratique des Hautes Études* 87 (1978/79): 241–47.

Neck, Rudolf. "Diplomatische Beziehungen zum Vorderen Orient unter Karl V." *Mitteilungen des Österreichischen Staatsarchivs* 5 (1952): 63–86.

Necker, Gerold. "'Brennende Landschaft der Erlösung': Jüdische Mystik und Messiashoffnung in Mitteleuropa (1200–1500)." In *Die Wehen des Messias: Zeitenwenden in der jüdischen Geschichte*, edited by Eveline Brugger and Martha Keil, 47–66. Berlin: Philo, 2001.

Neher, André. *Jewish Thought and the Scientific Revolution of the Sixteenth Century: David Gans (1541–1613) and His Times.* Oxford: Oxford University Press, 1986.

Netanyahu, Benzion. *Don Isaac Abravanel: Statesman and Philosopher.* 5th ed. Ithaca, NY: Cornell University Press, 1998.

Neubauer, Adolf. "Collections on Matters Pertaining to the Ten Tribes and the Sons of Moses." *Kobez al Yad* 4 (1888): 9–74. [Hebrew]

————. "Where Are the Ten Tribes?" *Jewish Quarterly Review* 1 (1889): 14–28, 95–114, 185–201, 408–23.

Neusner, Jacob, William S. Green, and Ernest Frerichs, eds. *Judaisms and Their Messiahs at the Turn of the Christian Era.* Cambridge: Cambridge University Press, 1997.

Niborski, Yitskhok, and Bernard Vaisbrot. *Dictionnaire Yiddish-Français.* Paris: Bibliothèque Medem, 2002.

Niccoli, Ottavia. "High and Low Prophetic Culture in Rome at the Beginning of the Sixteenth Century." In *Prophetic Rome in the High Renaissance Period*, edited by Marjorie Reeves, 203–22. Oxford: Clarendon, 1992.

————. *Prophecy and People in Renaissance Italy.* Princeton, NJ: Princeton University Press, 1990.

Niesner, Manuela. *"Wer mit juden well disputiren": Deutschsprachige Adversus Judaeos Literatur des 14. Jahrhunderts.* Münchener Texte und Untersuchungen zur deutschen Literatur des Mittelalters 128. Tübingen: Niemeyer, 2005.

Nikolsky, Ronit. "The Rechabites in Ma'aseh Alexandros and in the Medieval Ben Sira." *Zutot: Perspectives on Jewish Culture* 4 (2004): 35–41.

Oberman, Heiko A. *Wurzeln des Antisemitismus: Christenangst und Judenplage im Zeitalter von Humanismus und Reformation.* Berlin: Severin & Siedler, 1981.

Ocker, Christopher. "Contempt for Friars and Contempt for Jews in Late Medieval Germany." In *Friars and Jews in the Middle Ages and Renaissance*, edited by Stephen J. McMichael and Susan E. Myers, 119–46. Leiden: Brill, 2004.

————. "German Theologians and the Jews in the Fifteenth Century." In *Jews, Judaism, and the Reformation in Sixteenth-Century Germany*, edited by Dean P. Bell and Stephen G. Burnett, 33–65. Studies in Central European Histories 37. Leiden: Brill, 2006.

Oegema, Gerbern S. *Der Gesalbte und sein Volk: Untersuchungen zum Konzeptionalisierungsprozess der messianischen Erwartungen von den Makkabäern bis Bar Koziba.* Schriften des Institutum Judaicum Delitzschianum 2. Göttingen: Vandenhoeck & Ruprecht, 1994.

Olsen, H. Eric R. *The Calabrian Charlatan, 1598–1603: Messianic Nationalism in Early Modern Europe.* Basingstoke: Palgrave Macmillan, 2003.

Oron, Michal. "Sefer Gehalei Esh." In *The Sabbatian Movement and Its Aftermath: Messianism, Sabbatianism and Frankism*, edited by Rachel Elior, 1:73–92. Jerusalem Studies in Jewish Thought 16/17. Jerusalem: Hebrew University of Jerusalem Press, 2001. [Hebrew]

Osten-Sacken, Peter von der. *Martin Luther und die Juden: Neu untersucht anhand von Anton Margarithas "Der gantz Jüdisch glaub" (1530/31).* Stuttgart: Kohlhammer, 2002.

Ozment, Steven. "Pamphlet Literature of the German Reformation." In *Reformation Europe: A Guide to Research*, 85–106. St. Louis, MO: Center for Reformation Research, 1982.

Packull, Werner O. *Mysticism and the Early South German-Austrian Anabaptist Movement, 1525–1531.* Studies in Anabaptist and Mennonite History 19. Scottsdale: Herald Press, 1977.

Palombini, Barbara von. *Bündniswerben abendländischer Mächte um Persien 1453–1600.* Freiburger Islamstudien 1. Wiesbaden: Steiner, 1986.

Parker, Geoffrey. "Messianic Visions in the Spanish Monarchy, 1516–1598." *Calíope* 8.2 (2002): 5–24.

Patschovsky, Alexander. "Chiliasmus und Reformation im ausgehenden Mittelalter." In *Ideologie und Herrschaft im Mittelalter*, edited by Max Kerner, 475–96. Wege der Forschung 530. Darmstadt: Wissenschaftliche Buchgesellschaft, 1982.

Perani, Mauro. *Gli ebrei a Castel Goffredo: Con uno studio sulla Bibbia Soncino di Brescia del 1494*. Florence: La Giuntina, 1998.

Perry, Micha. *Eldad's Travels: A Journey from the Lost Tribes to the Present*. Routledge Focus. London: Routledge, 2019.

———. "The Imaginary War between Prester John and Eldad the Danite and Its Real Implications." *Viator: Medieval and Renaissance Studies* 41.1 (2010): 1–23.

———. *Tradition and Transformation: Knowledge Transmission among European Jews in the Middle Ages*. Tel Aviv: Hakibbutz Hameuchad, 2010. [Hebrew]

Perry, Micha, and Rebekka Voß. "Approaching Shared Heroes: Cultural Transfer and Transnational Jewish History." *Jewish History* 30.1–2 (2016): 1–13.

Peuckert, Will-Erich. *Die große Wende: Das apokalyptische Säculum und Luther*. Hamburg: Claassen & Goverts, 1948.

Pfeifer, Wolfgang, ed. *Etymologisches Wörterbuch des Deutschen*. 3 vols. Berlin: Akademie Verlag, 1989.

Pohlig, Matthias. "Konfessionskulturelle Deutungsmuster internationaler Konflikte um 1600: Kreuzzug, Antichrist, Tausendjähriges Reich." *Archiv für Reformationsgeschichte* 93 (2002): 278–316.

Pollak, Michael. "The Revelation of a Jewish Presence in Seventeenth-Century China: Its Impact on Western Messianic Thought." In *The Jews of China*, edited by Jonathan Goldstein. 2 vols. Armonk, NY: Sharpe, 1999.

Popkin, Richard H. "Christian Interest and Concerns about Sabbatai Zevi." In *Millenarianism and Messianism in Early Modern European Culture*. Vol. 1, *Messianism in the Early Modern World*, edited by Matt D. Goldish und Richard H. Popkin, 91–106. Archives internationales d'histoire des idées 173. Dordrecht: Kluwer, 2001.

———. "The End of the Career of a Great Seventeenth-Century Millenarian: John Dury." *Pietismus und Neuzeit* 14 (1988): 203–20.

———. "Jewish-Christian Relations in the Sixteenth and Seventeenth Centuries: The Conception of the Messiah." In *The Frank Talmage Memorial Volume*. Vol. 2, edited by Barry Walfish, 163–77. Haifa: Haifa University Press, 1992/93.

———. "Jewish Messianism and Christian Millenarianism." In *Culture and Politics from Puritanism to Enlightenment*, edited by Perez Zagorin, 67–90. Berkeley: University of California Press, 1980.

———. "Two Unused Sources about Sabbatai Zevi and His Effect on European Communities." In *Dutch Jewish History*. Vol. 2, *Proceedings of the Fourth-Fifth Symposium on the History of the Jews in the Netherlands, 7–10 December, Tel-Aviv, Jerusalem, 1986*, edited by Jozeph Michman, 67–74. Jerusalem: Institute for Research on Dutch Jewry, 1989.

Popper, William. *The Censorship of Hebrew Books*. New York: Knickerbocker Press, 1899. Reprint, New York: Ktav, 1969.

Posnanski, Adolf. *Schiloh: Ein Beitrag zur Geschichte der Messiaslehre*. Vol. 1, *Die Auslegung von Genesis 49,10 im Altertume bis zu Ende des Mittelalters*. Leipzig: Hinrichs, 1904.

Press, Volker. "Ein Epochenjahr der württembergischen Geschichte: Restitution und Reformation 1534." *Zeitschrift für württembergische Landesgeschichte* 47 (1988): 203–34.

———. "Die württembergische Restitution von 1534: Reichspolitische Voraussetzungen und Konsequenzen." *Blätter für württembergische Kirchengeschichte* 87 (1987): 44–71.

Prijs, Joseph. *Die hebräischen Handschriften*. Edited by Bernhard and David Prijs. Publikationen der Universitätsbibliothek Basel 21. Basel: Universitätsbibliothek, 1994.

Ragotzky, Hedda. "Fastnacht und Endzeit: Zur Funktion der Antichrist-Figur im Nürnberger Fastnachtspiel des 15. Jahrhunderts." *Zeitschrift für deutsche Philologie* 121 (2002): 54–71.

Ramos, Manuel João. *Essays in Christian Mythology: The Metamorphosis of Prester John*. New York: University Press of America, 2006.

Raspe, Lucia. "Gedaliah ibn Yahya's Schalschelet ha-Kabbalah and the Expulsion from Spain." Seminar paper, Hebrew University of Jerusalem, 1993.

———. *Jüdische Hagiographie im mittelalterlichen Aschkenas*. Texts and Studies in Medieval and Early Modern Judaism 19. Tübingen: Mohr Siebeck, 2006.

———. "Sacred Space, Local History, and Diasporic Identity: The Graves of the Righteous in Medieval and Early Modern Ashkenaz." In *Jewish Studies at the Crossroads of Anthropology and History: Authority, Diaspora, Tradition*, edited by Ra'anan Boustan, Oren Kosansky, and Marina Rustow. Philadelphia: University of Pennsylvania Press, 2011.

———. "Vom Rhein nach Galiläa: Rabbi Meir Schatz von Worms als Held hagiographischer Überlieferung." *Aschkenas: Zeitschrift für Geschichte und Kultur der Juden* 17.2 (2007): 431–55.

Raubenheimer, Richard. *Paul Fagius aus Rheinzabern: Sein Leben und Wirken als Reformator und Gelehrter*. Grünstadt: Verlag des Vereins für pfälzische Kirchengeschichte, 1957.

Rauh, Horst-Dieter. *Das Bild des Antichrist im Mittelalter: Von Tyconius zum Deutschen Symbolismus*. Beiträge zur Geschichte der Philosophie und Theologie des Mittelalters n.s. 9. 2nd ed. Münster: Aschendorff, 1979.

Raz-Krakotzkin, Amnon. *The Censor, the Editor, and the Text: The Catholic Church and the Shaping of the Jewish Canon in the Sixteenth Century*. Translated by Jackie Feldman. Philadelphia: University of Pennsylvania Press, 2007.

Reeves, John C., ed. *Trajectories in Near Eastern Apocalyptic: A Postrabbinic Jewish Apocalypse Reader*. Leiden: Brill, 2005.

Reeves, Marjorie. "Cardinal Egidio of Viterbo: A Prophetic Interpretation of History." In *Prophetic Rome in the High Renaissance Period*, 91–109. Oxford: Clarendon, 1992.

———. *The Influence of Prophecy in the Later Middle Ages: A Study in Joachimism*. Oxford: Clarendon, 1969.

———. "A Note on Prophecy and the Sack of Rome (1527)." In *Prophetic Rome in the High Renaissance Period*, 271–78. Oxford: Clarendon, 1992.

———, ed. *Prophetic Rome in the High Renaissance Period*. Oxford: Clarendon, 1992.

Reines, Alvin J. *Maimonides and Abrabanel on Prophecy*. Cincinnati, OH: Hebrew Union College Press, 1970.

Reinink, Gerrit J. "Pseudo-Methodius: A Concept of History in Response to the Rise of Islam." In *The Byzantine and Early Islamic Near East*. Vol. 1, *Problems in the Literary Source Material*, edited by Averil Cameron and Lawrence I. Conrad, 149–87. Studies in Late Antiquity and Early Islam 1. Princeton, NJ: Darwin, 1992.

Reuter, Fritz. "Warmaisa—das jüdische Worms: Von den Anfängen bis zum jüdischen Museum des Isidor Kiefer." In *Geschichte der Stadt Worms*, edited by Gerold Bönnen, 664–90. Stuttgart: Theiss, 2005.

Révah, Israel S. "David Reubeni: Exécuté en Espagne en 1538." *Revue des Études Juives* 117 (1958): 128–35.

Rivkind, Isaac. "Megillat R. Me'ir Shaẓ (He'arot le-Ma'aseh Akdamut)." *Ha-do'ar* 9.30 (1930): 207–9.

Robinson, Ira. "Abraham ben Eliezer ha-Levi: Kabbalist and Messianic Visionary of the Early Sixteenth Century." PhD diss., Harvard University, 1980.

———. "Messianic Prayer Vigils in Jerusalem in the Early Sixteenth Century." *Jewish Quarterly Review* 22 (1981): 32–42.

———. "Two Letters of Abraham ben Eliezer Halevi." In *Studies in Medieval Jewish History and Literature*, edited by Isidore Twersky, 2:403–44. Cambridge, MA: Harvard University Press, 1984.

Rodriguez-Monino, Antonio. "Les Judaisants à Badajoz de 1493 à 1599." *Revue des Études Juives* 115 (1956): 73–86.

Roemer, Nils. "Colliding Visions: Jewish Messianism and German Scholarship in the Eighteenth Century." In *Hebraica Veritas? Christian Hebraists and the Study of Judaism in Early Modern Europe*, edited by Allison P. Coudert and Jeffrey S. Shoulson, 266–85. Philadelphia: University of Pennsylvania Press, 2004.

Roettig, Petra. *Reformation als Apokalypse: Die Holzschnitte von Matthias Gerung im Codex germanicus 6592 der Bayerischen Staatsbibliothek in München*. Bern: Peter Lang, 1990.

Rogers, Francis M. *The Quest for Eastern Christians: Travels and Rumours in the Age of Discovery*. Minneapolis: University of Minnesota Press, 1962.

Rohrbacher, Stefan. "Die Entstehung der jüdischen Landgemeinden in der Frühneuzeit." In *Mappot—gesegnet, der da kommt: Das Band jüdischer Tradition seit der Spätantike, Eine Ausstellung der Hidden Legacy Foundation London und der Prähistorischen Staatssammlung München 16.5.1997–14.9.1997, Ausstellungskatalog*, edited by Annette Weber, Evelyn Friedländer, and Fritz Armbruster, 35–41. Osnabrück: Secolo-Verlag, 1997.

———. "Gründlicher und Wahrhaffter Bericht: Des Orientalisten Johann Andreas Eisenmengers Entdecktes Judenthum (1700) als Klassiker des 'wissenschaftlichen Antisemitismus.'" In *Reuchlin und seine Erben*, edited by Peter Schäfer and Irina Wandrey, 171–88. Pforzheimer Reuchlinschriften 11. Ostfildern: Thorbecke, 2005.

———. "Isaak Wetzlar in Celle: Ein jüdischer Reformer vor der Aufklärung," In *Juden in Celle: Biographische Skizzen aus drei Jahrhunderten*, edited by the City of Celle, 33–66. Celler Beiträge zur Landes- und Kulturgeschichte: Schriftenreihe des Stadtarchivs und des Bomann-Museums 26. Celle: Archiv der Stadt Celle, 1996.

———. *Juden in Neuss*. Neuss: Galerie Küppers, 1986.

————. "Die jüdischen Gemeinden in den Medinot Aschkenas zwischen Spätmittelalter und Dreißigjährigem Krieg." In *Jüdische Gemeinden und ihr christlicher Kontext in kulturräumlich vergleichender Betrachtung, von der Spätantike bis zum 18. Jahrhundert*, edited by Christoph Cluse, Alfred Haverkamp, and Israel J. Yuval, 451–63. Forschungen zur Geschichte der Juden A 13. Hannover: Hahn, 2003.

————. "Medinat Schwaben: Jüdisches Leben in einer süddeutschen Landschaft in der Frühneuzeit." In *Judengemeinden in Schwaben im Kontext des Alten Reiches*, edited by Rolf Kießling, 80–109. Colloquia Augustana 2. Berlin: Akademie Verlag, 1995.

————. "Stadt und Land: Zur 'inneren' Situation der süd- und westdeutschen Juden in der Frühneuzeit." In *Jüdisches Leben auf dem Lande: Studien zur deutsch-jüdischen Geschichte*, edited by Monika Richarz and Reinhard Rürup, 37–58. Schriftenreihe wissenschaftlicher Abhandlungen des Leo Baeck Instituts 56. Tübingen: Mohr Siebeck, 1997.

————. "Ungleiche Partnerschaft: Simon Günzburg und die erste Ansiedlung von Juden vor den Toren Augsburgs in der Frühen Neuzeit." In *Landjudentum im deutschen Südwesten während der Frühen Neuzeit*, edited by Rolf Kießling and Sabine Ullmann, 192–219. Colloquia Augustana 10. Berlin: Akademie Verlag, 1999.

Rohrbacher, Stefan, and Michael Schmidt. *Judenbilder: Kulturgeschichte antijüdischer Mythen und antisemitischer Vorurteile*. Reinbek bei Hamburg: Rowohlt, 1991.

Romer-Segal, Agnes. "Yiddish Literature and Its Readers in the 16th Century: Books in the Censors' Lists, Mantua 1595." *Kirjat Sefer* 53.4 (1978): 779–90. [Hebrew]

Rosenthal, Malka. "David Redivivus: Studien zur jüdischen Erlösungsidee in Sicht und Bild des 13. Jahrhunderts." In *Wenn der Messias kommt: Das jüdisch-christliche Verhältnis im Spiegel mittelalterlicher Kunst*, edited by Lieselotte Kotzsche and Peter von der Osten-Sacken, 27–76. Veröffentlichungen aus dem Institut Kirche und Judentum 16. Berlin: Institut Kirche und Judentum, [1994].

Rosman, Moshe. *How Jewish Is Jewish History?* Oxford: Littman Library of Jewish Civilization, 2007.

Ross, David J. A. *Alexander Historiatus: A Guide to Medieval Illustrated Alexander Literature*. Athenäums Monographien: Altertumswissenschaften 168. 2nd ed. Frankfurt am Main: Athenäum, 1988.

Roth, Cecil. *The History of the Jews of Italy*. Philadelphia: Jewish Publication Society of America, 1946.

————. *The Jews in the Renaissance*. New York: Harper & Row, 1959.

————. "The Last Years of Abraham Zacut." *Sefarad* 9 (1949): 445–54.

————. "Le martyre de David Reubeni." *Revue des Études Juives* 116 (1957): 93–95.

————. "Portraits and Caricatures of Medieval English Jews." In *Essays and Portraits in Anglo-Jewish History*, 22–25. Philadelphia: Jewish Publication Society of America, 1962.

————. *Venice*. Philadelphia: Jewish Publication Society of America, 1930. Reprint, New York: Schocken, 1975.

Rubin, Miri. *Gentile Tales: The Narrative Assault on Late Medieval Jews*. New Haven, CT: Yale University Press, 1999.

Rubin, Uri. *Between Bible and Qur'an: The Children of Israel and Islamic Self-Image*. Studies in Late Antiquity and Early Islam 17. Princeton, NJ: Darwin, 1999.

Ruderman, David B. *Early Modern Jewry: A New Cultural History*. Princeton, NJ: Princeton University Press, 2010.

———. "Giovanni Mercurio da Correggio's Appearance in Italy as Seen Through the Eyes of an Italian Jew." *Renaissance Quarterly* 28 (1975): 309–22.

———. "Hope against Hope: Jewish and Christian Messianic Expectations in the Late Middle Ages." In *Essential Papers on Jewish Culture in Renaissance and Baroque Italy*, 299–323. Essential Papers on Jewish Studies 5. New York: New York University Press, 1992.

———. *Jewish Thought and Scientific Discovery in Early Modern Europe*. 2nd ed. Detroit, MI: Wayne State University Press, 2001.

———. *Kabbalah, Magic, and Science: The Cultural Universe of a Sixteenth-Century Jewish Physician*. Cambridge, MA: Harvard University Press, 1988.

———. *The World of a Renaissance Jew: The Life and Thought of Abraham ben Mordecai Farissol*. Cincinnati, OH: Hebrew Union College Press, 1981. Reprint, Ann Arbor: University of Michigan Press, 1996.

Rummel, Erika. *The Case against Johann Reuchlin: Religious and Social Controversy in Sixteenth-Century Germany*. Toronto: University Press, 2002.

———. "Humanists, Jews, and Judaism." In *Jews, Judaism, and the Reformation in Sixteenth-Century Germany*, edited by Dean P. Bell and Stephen G. Burnett, 3–31. Studies in Central European Histories 37. Leiden: Brill, 2006.

Rymatzki, Christoph. *Hallischer Pietismus und Judenmission: Johann Heinrich Callenbergs Institutum Judaicum und dessen Freundeskreis (1728–1736)*. Hallesche Forschungen 11. Tübingen: Niemeyer, 2004.

Sackur, Ernst. *Sibyllinische Texte und Forschungen: Pseudomethodius, Adso und die tiburtinische Sibylle*. Halle: Niemeyer, 1898. Reprint, Turin: Bottega d'Erasmo, 1976.

Sadek, Vladimir. "Etendard et robe de Salomon Molkho." *Judaica Bohemiae* 16 (1980): 65.

———. "Solomon Molcho (c. 1500–1532) and His Teachings." *Judaica Bohemiae* 20.2 (1984): 84–96.

Salone, Anna M. "La fortuna editoriale di mons: Agostine Giustiniani e della sua opera." In *Agostino Giustiniani annalista genovese e I suoi tempi: Atti del Convegno di studi (Genua 28.–31. Maggio 1982)*, 135–46. Genoa: Compagnia dei librai, 1984.

Saperstein, Marc, ed. *Essential Papers on Messianic Movements and Personalities in Jewish History*. Essential Papers on Jewish Studies 6. New York: New York University Press, 1992.

Schäfer, Peter. *Der Bar Kokhba Aufstand: Studien zum zweiten jüdischen Krieg gegen Rom*. Texte und Studien zum antiken Judentum 1. Tübingen: Mohr Siebeck, 1981.

———, ed. *The Bar Kokhba War Reconsidered: New Perspectives on the Second Revolt against Rome*. Texts and Studies in Ancient Judaism 100. Tübingen: Mohr Siebeck, 2003.

———. "The Idea of Piety of the Ashkenazi Hasidim and Its Roots in Jewish Tradition." *Jewish History* 4.2 (1990): 9–23.

———. "Die messianischen Hoffnungen des rabbinischen Judentums zwischen Naherwartung und religiösem Pragmatismus." In *Studien zur Geschichte und Theologie des rabbinischen Judentums*, 214–43. Arbeiten zur Geschichte des antiken Judentums und des Urchristentums 15. Leiden: Brill, 1978.

———. *Mirror of His Beauty: Feminine Images of God from the Bible to the Early Kabbalah.* Princeton, NJ: Princeton University Press, 2002.

———. "Die sogenannte Synode von Jabne." In *Studien zur Geschichte und Theologie des rabbinischen Judentums,* 45–55. Arbeiten zur Geschichte des antiken Judentums und des Urchristentums 15. Leiden: Brill, 1978.

Schatz Uffenheimer, Rivka. "Maharal's Doctrine: Between Existence and Eschatology." In *Messianism and Eschatology: A Collection of Essays,* edited by Zvi Baras, 301–24. Jerusalem: Zalman Shazar Center for Jewish History, 1983. [Hebrew]

———. "An Outline of the Image of the Political-Messianic Arousal after the Spanish Expulsion." *Da'at* 11 (1983): 53–66. [Hebrew]

Schechner, Sara J. *Comets, Popular Culture, and the Birth of Modern Cosmology.* Princeton, NJ: Princeton University Press, 1998.

Scheiber, Alexander, and Louis Tardy. "L'echo de la premiere manifestation de David Reubeni dans les brochures de colportage allemande de l'epoque." *Revue des Études Juives* 32 (1973): 595–601.

Scher, Stehpen K., ed. *The Currency of Fame: Portrait Medals of the Renaissance.* New York: Abrams, 1994.

Schiel, Regine. "Die giftigen würm das seit ir: Antijudaismus in Fastnachtspielen des Nürnberger Meistersängers Hans Folz (Ende 15. Jahrhundert)." In *Judentum und Antijudaismus in der deutschen Literatur im Mittelalter und an der Wende zur Neuzeit: Ein Studienbuch,* edited by Arne Domrös, Thomas Bartoldus, and Julian Voloj, 147–77. Berlin: Jüdische Verlagsanstalt, 2002.

Schmidt, Otto Eduard. "Wolfgang Lazius, ein Geschichtsschreiber des Schmalkaldischen Krieges." *Neues Archiv für sächsische Geschichte* 24 (1903): 111–33.

Schmieder, Felicitas. "Christians, Jews, Muslims—and Mongols: Fitting a Foreign People into the Western Christian Apocalyptic Scenario." *Medieval Encounters* 12.1 (2006): 274–95.

———. *Europa und die Fremden.* Sigmaringen: Thorbecke, 1994.

Schnur, David. "Weltuntergang an der Wende zum Spätmittelalter? Der Frankfurter Pogrom von 1241 und seine Einbettung in jüdische Endzeiterwartungen." In *Endspiele: Zukunftserwartungen zwischen Weltuntergang und Topia,* edited by Nora Eibisch, Hendrik Klinge, and Mark Wittlinger, 109–43. Kontexte: Neue Beiträge zur historischen und systematischen Theologie. Göttingen: Vandenhoeck & Ruprecht, 2015.

Scholem, Gershom. "The Crisis of Tradition in Jewish Messianism." In *The Messianic Idea in Judaism and Other Essays on Jewish Spirituality,* 49–77. New York: Schocken, 1971.

———. "Gilgul: Seelenwanderung und Sympathie der Seelen." In *Von der mystischen Gestalt der Gottheit,* 193–247. Frankfurt am Main: Suhrkamp, 1977.

———. "Introduction." In *Abraham ben Eliezer Ha-Levi: Ma'amar Meshare Qitrin, Constantinople 1510,* edited by Malachi Beit-Arié and Gershom Scholem, 9–42. Jerusalem: Jewish National & University Library Press, 1977. [Hebrew]

———. "Kabbalat R. Ya'akov ve-R. Yiẓḥak bnei R. Ya'akov ha-Kohen (Mekorot le-toldot ha-kabbalah lifnei hitgalut ha-zohar)." *Mada'ei ha-yahadut* 2 (1927): 163–293.

———. *Major Trends in Jewish Mysticism.* Reprinted from the 3rd revised edition. New York: Schocken, 1995.

————. *The Messianic Idea in Judaism and Other Essays on Jewish Spirituality*. New York: Schocken, 1971.

————. "Prakim apokaliptiyim ve-meshihiyim al R. Mordehai mi-Eisenstadt." In *Sefer Dinaburg: Kovez divrei iyyun u-mehkar muggash le-Ben-Zion Dinaburg*, edited by Yitzhak Baer, 237–62. Jerusalem: Kiryat Sefer, 1949.

————. "Prakim mi-toldot sifrut ha-kabbalah: Hakirot hadashot al R. Abraham b. Eli'ezer ha-Levi." *Kirjat Sefer* 7 (1930/31): 149–65, 440–56.

————. *Sabbatai Sevi: The Mystical Messiah, 1626–1676. With a New Introduction by Yaacob Dweck*. Bollingen Series 93. Princeton, NJ: Princeton University Press, 2016.

————. "Sabbatian Gleanings." *Zion* 10.3–4 (1945): 140–48. [Hebrew]

Schöner, Petra. *Judenbilder im deutschen Einblattdruck der Renaissance: Ein Beitrag zu Imagologie*. Saecula Spiritualia 42. Baden-Baden: Koerner, 2002.

Schorsch, Ismar. "A Meditation on Maoz Zur." *Judaism: A Quarterly Journal of Jewish Life and Thought* 37.4 (1988): 459–64.

————. "The Myth of Sephardi Supremacy." *Leo Baeck Institute Yearbook* 35 (1989): 47–66.

Schraepler, Horst W. *Die rechtliche Behandlung der Täufer in der deutschen Schweiz, Südwestdeutschland und Hessen 1525–1618*. Schriften zur Kirchen- und Rechtsgeschichte 4. Tübingen: Fabian Osiander, 1957.

Schreckenberg, Heinz. *Die christlichen Adversus-Judaeos-Texte und ihr literarisches und historisches Umfeld*. 3 vols. Europäische Hochschulschriften Reihe 23. 4th ed. Frankfurt am Main: Peter Lang, 1994–99.

Schreiner, Stefan. "Jüdische Reaktionen auf die Reformation: Einige Bemerkungen." *Judaica* 39 (1983): 150–65.

Schubert, Anselm. "Jenseits von Edom: Zur Messianität David Reubenis." In *Kriminelle —Freidenker—Alchemisten: Räume des Untergrunds in der Frühen Neuzeit*, edited by Martin Mulsow. Cologne: Böhlau, 2014.

————. *Täufertum und Kabbalah: Augustin Bader und die Grenzen der radikalen Reformation*. Schriften des Vereins für Reformationsgeschichte 82. Gütersloh: Gütersloher Verlagshaus, 2008.

Schwartz, Hillel. *Zeitenwende—Weltenende? Visionen beim Wechsel der Jahrhunderte von 990–1990*. Braunschweig: Westermann, 1992.

Schwarz, Reinhard. *Die apokalyptische Theologie Thomas Müntzers und der Taboriten*. Beiträge zur historischen Theologie 55. Tübingen: Mohr Siebeck, 1977.

Schwoebel, Robert. *The Shadow of the Crescent: The Renaissance Image of the Turk, 1453–1517*. New York: de Graf, 1967.

Scott, James C. *Domination and the Arts of Resistance: Hidden Transcripts*. New Haven, CT: Yale University Press, 1990.

Scribner, Robert W. *For the Sake of Simple Folk: Popular Propaganda for the German Reformation*. Oxford: Clarendon, 1994.

Secret, François. "Les dominicains et la kabbale chrétienne à la Renaissance." *Archivum Fratrum Praedicatorum* 27 (1957): 319–24.

————. *Les Kabbalistes chrétiens de la Renaissance*. Paris: Dunod, 1964. Reprint, Milan: Archè, 1985.

——. *Le Zohar chez les kabbalistes chrétiens de la Renaissance*. Paris: Durlacher, 1958.

Seebaß, Gottfried. *Müntzers Erbe: Werk, Leben und Theologie des Hans Hut 1527*. Gütersloh: Gütersloher Verlagshaus, 2002.

——. "Reich Gottes und Apokalyptik bei Thomas Müntzer." *Lutherjahrbuch* 58 (1991): 75–99.

Seifert, Arno. "Reformation und Chiliasmus: Die Rolle des Martin Cellarius-Borrhaus." *Archiv für Reformationsgeschichte* 77 (1986): 226–64.

Sestieri, Lea. *David Reubeni: Un Ebreo d'Arabia in missione segreta nell'Europa del '500*. Collana di saggistica 54. Genoa: Marietti, 1991.

——. "Un papa in crisi e due visionari ebrei 1525–1532: Clemente VII, David Reubeni e Shlomo Molko." In *Hebraica Miscellanea di studi in onore di Sergio J. Sierra per il suo 75. Compleanno*, edited by Felice Israel, 503–16. Turin: Istituto di studi ebraici—Scuola rabbinica S. H. Margulies-D. Disegni, 1998.

Shachar, Isaiah. *The Judensau: A Medieval Anti-Jewish Motif and Its History*. London: Warburg Institute, 1974.

Sharot, Stephen. "Jewish Millennial-Messianic Movements: A Comparison of Medieval Communities." In *Comparing Jewish Societies*, edited by Todd M. Endelman, 61–87. Comparative Studies in Society and History 6. Ann Arbor: University of Michigan Press, 1997.

——. *Messianism, Mysticism, and Magic: A Sociological Analysis of Jewish Religious Movements*. Chapel Hill: University of North Carolina Press, 1982.

Shaw, Stanford J. *The Jews of the Ottoman Empire and the Turkish Republic*. London: Palgrave Macmillan, 1991.

Sherwin, Byron L. *Mystical Theology and Social Dissent: The Life and Works of Judah Loew of Prague*. Rutherford: Fairleigh Dickinson University Press, 1982.

Shohat, Azriel. "Notes on the David Reubeni Affair." *Zion* 35 (1970): 70–116. [Hebrew]

Shulvass, Moses A. *The Jews in the World of the Renaissance*. Translated by Elvin I. Kose. Leiden: Brill, 1973.

——. *Rome and Jerusalem*. Jerusalem: Mossad Harav Kook, 1944. [Hebrew]

Shyovitz, David I. *A Remembrance of His Wonders: Nature and the Supernatural in Medieval Ashkenaz*. Philadelphia: University of Pennsylvania Press, 2017.

Siluk, Avraham. *Die Juden im politischen System des Alten Reichs: Jüdische Politik und ihre Organisation im Zeitalter der Reformation*. Bibliothek altes Reich 36. Berlin: De Gruyter; Oldenbourg, 2021.

Silver, Abba H. *A History of Messianic Speculation in Israel: From the First through the Seventeenth Centuries*. New York: Macmillan, 1927. Reprint, Whitefish, MT: Kessinger, 2003.

Simon, Marcel. *Verus Israel: A Study of the Relations between Christians and Jews in the Roman Empire, AD 135–425*. Oxford: Littman Library of Jewish Civilization, 1996.

Simonsohn, Shlomo. "Books and Libraries of Mantuan Jews, 1595." *Kirjat Sefer* 37.1 (1961): 103–22. [Hebrew]

——. "David Reubeni's Second Mission in Italy." *Zion* 26 (1961): 198–207. [Hebrew]

Smith, Jonathan Z. *Imagining Religion: From Babylon to Jonestown*. Chicago: University of Chicago Press, 1982.

Smolinsky, Heribert. *Deutungen der Zeit im Streit der Konfessionen: Kontroverstheologie, Apokalyptik und Astrologie im 16. Jahrhundert.* Schriften der philosophisch-historischen Klasse der Heidelberger Akademie der Wissenschaften 20. Heidelberg: Winter, 2000.

Smoller, Laura. "Apocalyptic Calculators of the Later Middle Ages." In *Knowing the Time, Knowing of a Time: Proceedings of the Third Annual Conference of the Center for Millennial Studies (Boston, MA, 6.–8. December 1998).* http://www.mille.org/publications/Confpro98/SMOLLER.PDF. Accessed April 15, 2021.

Sperber, Daniel. *Minhagei Yisra'el.* 6 vols. Jerusalem: Mossad Harav Kook, 1998.

Steinschneider, Moritz, ed. *Catalogus librorum hebraeorum in bibliotheca bodleiana.* Berlin: Friedländer, 1852–60. Reprint, Hildesheim: Olms, 1964.

———. *Die Geschichtsliteratur der Juden in Druckwerken und Handschriften.* Frankfurt am Main: Kauffmann, 1905. Reprint, New York: Arno, 1980.

———. *Hebräische Bibliographie: Blätter für neuere und ältere Literatur des Judenthums.* 2 vols. Berlin: Asher, 1858/59.

———. "Jüdisch-deutsche Literatur: Nach einem handschriftlichen Katalog der Oppenheim'schen Bibliothek in Oxford, mit Zusätzen und Berichtigungen." *Serapeum: Zeitschrift für Bibliothekswissenschaft, Handschriftenkunde und ältere Litteratur* 9 (1848–49). Reprint, Jerusalem: Hebrew University of Jerusalem Press, 1961.

———. "Le Livre de la foi: Paulus Fagius et Sébastian Munster." *Revue des Études Juives* 4 (1882): 78–83; 5 (1882): 57–67.

Stemberger, Günter. "Die Beurteilung Roms in der rabbinischen Literatur." In *Aufstieg und Niedergang der römischen Welt: Geschichte und Kultur Roms im Spiegel der neueren Forschung,* edited by Hildegard Temporini and Wolfgang Haase, 19.2:338–96. Berlin: De Gruyter, 1979.

Stern, Selma. *Josel von Rosheim: Befehlshaber der Judenschaft im Heiligen Römischen Reich Deutscher Nation.* Stuttgart: Deutsche Verlags-Anstalt, 1959.

Steyert, André. *Nouvelle histoire de Lyon et des provinces de Lyonnais, Forez, Beaujolais, Franc-Lyonnais et Dombes.* Vol. 2. Lyon: Bernoux et Cumin, 1897.

Stow, Kenneth. *Catholic Thought and Papal Jewry Policy, 1555–1593.* New York: Jewish Theological Seminary of America, 1977.

———. "Medieval Jews on Christianity." *Rivista di storia del Cristianesimo* 4.1 (2007): 73–100.

Strack, Hermann L., and Paul Billerbeck. *Kommentar zum Neuen Testament aus Talmud und Midrasch.* 6 vols. Munich: Beck, 1922–61.

Struve, Tilman. "Die falschen Friedriche und die Friedenssehnsucht des Volkes im späten Mittelalter." In *Fälschungen im Mittelalter: Internationaler Kongress der Monumenta Germaniae Historica, München, 16.–19. September 1986.* Vol. 1, *Schriften,* 317–37. Monumenta Germaniae Historica 33.1. Hannover: Hahn, 1988.

Subrahmanyam, Sanjay. "Du Tage au Gange au XVIe siècle: Une conjoncture millénariste à l'échelle eurasiatique." *Annales: Histoire, Sciences Sociales* 56.1 (2001): 51–84.

Swain, Joseph W. "The Theory of the Four Monarchies: Opposition History under the Roman Empire." *Classical Philology* 35 (1940): 1–21.

Swiderska, Hanna. "Three Polish Pamphlets on Pseudo-Messiah Sabbetai Sevi." *British Library Journal* 15 (1989): 112–16.

Talkenberger, Heike. *Sintflut: Prophetie und Zeitgeschehen in Texten und Holzschnitten astrologischer Flugschriften 1488–1528.* Studien und Texte zur Sozialgeschichte der Literatur 26. Tübingen: Niemeyer, 1990.

Tamar, David. "Calculations of the End in the Work Hag ha-Pesah." *Sinai: A Journal for Torah and Jewish Studies* 100 (1987): 931–35. [Hebrew]

———. "On R. Asher Lemlein." *Zion* 52.3 (1987): 399–401 [Hebrew]

Ta-Shma, Israel. "Al kama inyanei maḥzor Vitri." *Alei Sefer* 11:81–89.

———. "The Source and Location of the Prayer Alenu le-shabeah in the Siddur: The Ma'amadot and the Question of the End of the Prayer." In *The Frank Talmage Memorial Volume*, edited by Barry Walfish, 1:85–98. Haifa: Haifa University Press, 1992/93.

Teeple, Howard M. *The Mosaic Eschatological Prophet.* Philadelphia: Society of Biblical Literature, 1957.

Teply, Karl. *Türkische Sagen und Legenden um die Kaiserstadt Wien.* Vienna: Böhlau, 1980.

Thomas, Heinz. "Translatio Imperii." In *Lexikon des Mittelalters*, edited by Robert-Henri Bautier and Robert Auty, 8:944–96. Munich: Deutscher Taschenbuch Verlag, 2002.

Thomas, Keith. *Religion and the Decline of Magic: Studies in Popular Beliefs in Sixteenth and Seventeenth Century England.* London: Penguin History, 1991.

Timm, Erika. *Historische jiddische Semantik: Die Bibelübersetzungssprache als Faktor der Auseinanderentwicklung des jiddischen und des deutschen Wortschatzes.* Tübingen: Niemeyer, 2005.

———. "Zur Frühgeschichte der jiddischen Erzählprosa: Eine neuaufgefundene Maiśe-Handschrift." *Beiträge zur Geschichte der deutschen Sprache und Literatur* 117 (1995): 243–80.

Tishby, Isaiah. "Messianism in the Time of the Expulsion from Spain and Portugal." In *Essential Papers on Messianic Movements and Personalities in Jewish History*, edited by Marc Saperstein, 259–86. Essential Papers on Jewish Studies 6. New York: New York University Press, 1992.

———. *Messianism in the Time of the Expulsion from Spain and Portugal.* Jerusalem: Zalman Shazar Center for Jewish History, 1985. [Hebrew]

———. *Paths of Faith and Heresy: Essays in Kabbalistic Literature and Sabbatianism.* Ramat Gan: Massada, 1964. [Hebrew]

———, ed. *The Wisdom of the Zohar: An Anthology of Texts.* 3 vols. Oxford: Littman Library of Jewish Civilization, 1989.

Toaff, Ariel. "Migrazioni di ebrei tedeschi attraverso i territori triestini e friulani fra XIV e XV secolo." In *Il mondo ebraico: Gli ebrei tra Italia nord-orientale e Impero asburgico dal medioevo all'età contemporanea*, edited by Giacomo Todeschini, 3–28. Pordenone: Studio Tesi, 1991.

Toch, Michael. *Die Juden im mittelalterlichen Reich.* Enzyklopädie deutscher Geschichte 44. Munich: Oldenbourg, 1998.

———. "Umb gemeyns nutz und nottdurfft willen: Obrigkeitliches und jurisdiktionelles Denken bei der Austreibung der Nürnberger Juden 1498/99." *Zeitschrift für Historische Forschung* 11 (1984): 1–21.

Todeschini, Giacomo, ed. *Il mondo ebraico: Gli ebrei tra Italia nord-orientale e Impero asburgico dal medioevo all'età contemporanea.* Pordenone: Studio Tesi, 1991.

Töpfer, Bernhard. *Das kommende Reich des Friedens: Zur Entwicklung chiliastischer Zukunfts-hoffnungen im Hochmittelalter.* Forschungen zur mittelalterlichen Geschichte 11. Berlin: Akademie Verlag, 1964.

Trachtenberg, Joshua. *The Devil and the Jews: The Medieval Conception of the Jew and Its Relation to Modern Anti-Semitism.* New Haven, CT: Yale University Press, 1943. Reprint, Philadelphia: Jewish Publication Society, 1983.

Treue, Wolfgang. *Der Trienter Judenprozess: Voraussetzungen, Abläufe, Auswirkungen 1475–1588.* Forschungen zur Geschichte der Juden A 4. Hannover: Hahn, 1996.

Turniansky, Chava. "The Events in Frankfurt am Main 1612–1616 in Megillas Vints and in an Unknown Yiddish 'Historical' Song." In *Schöpferische Momente des europäischen Judentums in der frühen Neuzeit,* edited by Michael Graetz, 121–37. Heidelberg: Winter, 2000.

Turniansky, Chava, and Erika Timm. *Yiddish in Italia: Yiddish Manuscripts and Printed Books from the 15th to the 17th Century.* Milan: Associazione Italiana Amici dell' Universita di Gerusalemme, 2003.

Uhland, Friedwart. "Täufertum und Obrigkeit in Augsburg im 16. Jahrhundert." Ph.D. diss., Universität Tübingen, 1972.

Vaughan, Dorothy M. *Europe and the Turk: A Pattern of Alliances, 1350–1700.* Liverpool: Liverpool University Press, 1954. Reprint, New York: AMS Press, 1976.

Vogelstein, Hermann, and Paul Rieger. *Geschichte der Juden in Rom.* 2 vols. Berlin: Mayer & Müller, 1895/1896.

Voos, Julius. *David Reubeni und Salomo Molcho: Ein Beitrag zur Geschichte der messianischen Bewegung im Judentum in der 1. Hälfte des 1. Jahrhunderts.* Berlin, 1933.

Voß, Rebekka. "Charles V as Last World Emperor and Jewish Hero." *Jewish History* 30.1–2 (2016): 81–106.

———. "Entangled Stories: The Red Jews in Premodern Yiddish and German Apocalyptic Lore." *AJS Review* 36.1 (2012): 1–41.

———. "Habe die Mission treu erfüllt und begehre meinen Lohn darum: Frühneuzeitliche Definitionen von Amt, Funktion und Titel des Schtadlan in subjektiver Wahrnehmung." In *Selbstzeugnisse und Ego-Dokumente frühneuzeitlicher Juden in Aschkenas: Beispiele, Methoden und Konzepte,* edited by Birgit E. Klein and Rotraud Ries, 139–66. Minima judaica 10. Berlin: Metropol, 2011.

———. "A Jewish-Pietist Network: Dialogues between Protestant Missionaries and Yiddish Writers in Eighteenth-Century Germany." *Jewish Quarterly Review* (forthcoming).

———. "'Jüdische Irrlehre' oder exegetisches Experiment? Die Restitution Israels im 16. Jahrhundert." *Frühneuzeit-Info* (2011): 5–22.

———. "Love Your Fellow as Yourself: Early Haskalah Reform as Pietist Renewal." *Transversal: Journal for Jewish Studies* 13.1 (2015): 4–11.

———. "Rom am Rhein: Die SchUM-Gemeinden im jüdischen Messianischen Denken." In *Die SchUM-Gemeinden Speyer—Worms—Mainz: Auf dem Weg zum Welterbe,* edited by Pia Heberer and Ursula Reuter, 149–66. Regensburg: Schnell und Steiner, 2013.

Waddington, Raymond P. "Graven Images: Sixteenth-Century Portrait Medals of Jews." *The Medal* 23 (1993): 13–21.

Walde, Bernhard. *Christliche Hebraisten Deutschlands am Ausgang des Mittelalters*. Alttesta-mentliche Abhandlungen 6.2/3. Münster: Aschendorff, 1916.

Wall, Ernestine G. E. van der. "Petrus Serrarius and Menasseh ben Israel: Christian Mil-lenarianism and Jewish Messianism in Seventeenth-Century Amsterdam." In *Menasseh ben Israel and His World*, edited by Yosef Kaplan, Henry Méchoulan, and Richard H. Popkin, 164–90. Leiden: Brill, 1989.

———. "A Precursor of Christ, or a Jewish Imposter? Peter Serrarius and Jean de Labadie on the Jewish Messianic Movement around Sabbatai Sebi." *Pietismus und Neuzeit* 14 (1988): 109–24.

Walton, Michael T. "Anthonius Margaritha: Honest Reporter?" *Sixteenth Century Journal* 36.1 (2005): 129–41.

———. *Anthonius Margaritha and the Jewish Faith: Jewish Life and Conversion in Sixteenth-Century Germany*. Detroit, MI: Wayne State University Press, 2012.

Wasserstein, David J. "Eldad ha-Dani and Prester John." In *Prester John, the Mongols and the Ten Lost Tribes*, edited by Charles F. Beckingham and Bernard Hamilton, 213–36. Aldershot: Variorum, 1996.

Wasserstrom, Steven M. *Between Muslim and Jew: The Problem of Symbiosis under Early Islam*. Princeton, NJ: Princeton University Press, 1995.

Weber, Annette. "Das Antichristfenster der Marienkirche in Frankfurt (Oder) im kulturhis-torischen Kontext." In *Der Antichrist: Die Glasmalereien in der Marienkirche in Frank-furt (Oder)*, edited by Ulrich Knefelkamp and Frank Martin, 80–101. Leipzig: Edition Leipzig, 2008.

Weil, Gérard E. *Elie Levita, humaniste et massorète 1469–1549*. Leiden: Brill, 1963.

Weinreich, Max. "Internal Bilingualism in Ashkenaz up to the Enlightenment Period." *Di goldene keyt* 35 (1959): 80–88. [Hebrew]

Weinreich, Uriel. *Modern English-Yiddish, Yiddish-English Dictionary*. New York: YIVO Insti-tute for Jewish Research, 1986.

Weinstein, Donald. *Savonarola and Florence: Prophecy and Patriotism in the Renaissance*. Princeton, NJ: Princeton University Press, 1970.

Weinstein, Roni. *Kabbalah and Jewish Modernity*. Oxford: Littman Library of Jewish Civi-lization, 2016.

Weiser, Artur. *Das Buch Hiob*. Das Alte Testament Deutsch 13. 8th ed. Göttingen: Vanden-hoeck & Ruprecht, 1988.

Wengert, Timothy J. "Philip Melanchthon and the Jews: A Reappraisal." In *Jews, Judaism, and the Reformation in Sixteenth-Century Germany*, edited by Dean P. Bell and Stephen G. Burnett, 105–35. Studies in Central European Histories 37. Leiden: Brill, 2006.

Wenninger, Marcus. *Man bedarf keiner Juden mehr: Ursachen und Hintergründe ihrer Ver-treibung aus den deutschen Reichsstädten im 15. Jahrhundert*. Vienna: Böhlau, 1981.

———. "Von jüdischen Rittern und anderen waffentragenden Juden im mittelalterlichen Deutschland." *Aschkenas: Zeitschrift für Geschichte und Kultur der Juden* 13.1 (2003): 35–82.

Wenz, Gunther. *Theologie der Bekenntnisschriften der evangelisch-lutherischen Kirche*. Vol. 1, *Eine historische und systematische Einführung in das Konkordienbuch*. Berlin: De Gruyter, 1996.

Wenzel, Edith. *Do worden die Juden alle geschant: Rolle und Funktion der Juden in spätmit-telalterlichen Spielen.* Munich: Fink, 1992.

———. "The Representation of Jews and Judaism in Sixteenth-Century German Litera-ture." In *Jews, Judaism, and the Reformation in Sixteenth-Century Germany,* edited by Dean P. Bell and Stephen G. Burnett, 393–417. Studies in Central European Histories 37. Leiden: Brill, 2006.

———. "Zur Judenproblematik bei Hans Folz." *Zeitschrift für deutsche Philologie* 101 (1982): 79–104.

Werblowsky, Rafael Y. Z. *Joseph Karo: Lawyer and Mystic.* 2nd ed. Philadelphia: Jewish Pub-lication Society of America, 1977.

Werner, Michael, and Bénédicte Zimmermann. "Beyond Comparison: Histoire Croisée and the Challenge of Reflexivity." *History and Theory* 45 (2006): 30–50.

———. "Vergleich, Transfer, Verflechtung: Der Ansatz der Histoire croisée und die Heraus-forderung des Transnationalen." *Geschichte und Gesellschaft* 28 (2002): 607–36.

Wieder, Naphtali. "Regarding an Anti-Christian and Anti-Muslim Gematria." *Sinai: A Jour-nal for Torah and Jewish Studies* 76 (1975): 1–14. [Hebrew]

Wies, Ernst W. *Friedrich II. von Hohenstaufen: Messias oder Antichrist.* Munich: Bechtle, 1994.

Wijk, Jetteke van. "The Rise and Fall of Shabbatai Zevi as Reflected in Contemporary Press Reports." *Studia Rosenthaliana* 33 (1999): 7–27.

Wilken, Robert L. "The Restoration of Israel in Biblical Prophecy: Christian and Jewish Responses in the Early Byzantine Period." In *To See Ourselves as Others See Us: Chris-tians, Jews, "Others" in Late Antiquity,* 443–71. Chico, CA: Scholars Press, 1986.

Williams, Arthur L. *Adversus Judaeos: A Bird's-Eye View of Christian Apologiae until the Renaissance.* Cambridge: Cambridge University Press, 1935.

Williams, George H. *The Radical Reformation.* Sixteenth-Century Essays and Studies 15. 3rd ed. Kirksville, MO: Thomas Jefferson University Press, 2000.

Williams, R. L. "Martin Cellarius and the Reformation in Strasburg." *Journal of Ecclesiastical History* 32 (1981): 477–97.

Wisplinghoff, Erich. *Geschichte der Stadt Neuss von den mittelalterlichen Anfängen bis zum Jahre 1794.* Neuss: Stadtarchiv, 1975.

Wohlfeil, Rainer. "Bauernkrieg: Symbole der Endzeit?" *Rottenburger Jahrbuch für Kirchenge-schichte* 20 (2001): 53–71.

Worms, A. A. "Date certaine de la médaille trouvée à Lyon, vers le milieu du XVIIe siècle." *Archives israélites de France* 2 (1841): 280–82.

Wunderli, Richard. *Peasant Fires: The Drummer of Niklashausen.* Bloomington: Indiana Uni-versity Press, 1992.

Yaari, Abraham. *Toldot ḥag simḥat torah: Hishtalshelut minhagav be-tefuẓot Yisra'el le-doroteihen.* Jerusalem: Mossad Harav Kook, 1964.

Yadin, Yigal. *Bar-Kokhba: The Rediscovery of the Legendary Hero of the Second Jewish Revolt against Rome.* New York: Random House, 1971.

Yaniv, Shlomo. "'Ha-ḥevrah ha-utopit' me-ever le-Sambatyon." *Karmelit* 21/22 (1977): 277–91.

———. "Ha-moshi'a me-ereẓ aseret ha-shevatim." *Alei-siaḥ* 7/8 (1980): 125–31.

Yerushalmi, Yosef H. *Diener von Königen und nicht Diener von Dienern: Einige Aspekte der politischen Geschichte der Juden, Vortrag gehalten in der Carl Friedrich von Siemens Stiftung am 19, Oktober 1993.* Munich: Carl Friedrich von Siemens-Stiftung, 1995.

———. *From Spanish Court to Italian Ghetto: Isaac Cardoso: A Study in Seventeenth-Century Marranism and Jewish Apologetics.* New York: Columbia University Press, 1971.

———. "Messianic Impulses in Joseph ha-Kohen." In *Jewish Thought in the Sixteenth Century*, edited by Bernard D. Cooperman, 460–87. Harvard Judaica Texts and Studies 2. Cambridge, MA: Harvard University Press, 1983.

———. "'Servants of Kings, Not Servants of Servants': Some Aspects of the Jewish Political History." *Raisons politiques* 7.3 (2002): 19–52.

———. *Zakhor: Jewish History and Jewish Memory.* 2nd paperback ed. Seattle: University of Washington Press, 1999.

Yuval, Israel J. "Jewish Messianic Expectations towards 1240 and Christian Reactions." In *Toward the Millennium: Messianic Expectations from the Bible to Waco*, edited by Peter Schäfer and Marc Cohen, 105–21. Leiden: Brill, 1998.

———. *Moses redivivus: Maimonides—Helfer des Messias: 9. Arye Maimon-Vortrag an der Universität Treier, 9. November 2006.* Kleine Schriften des Arye Maimon-Instituts 9. Trier: Kliomedia, 2007.

———. *Two Nations in Your Womb: Perceptions of Jews and Christians in Late Antiquity and the Middle Ages.* Translated by Barbara Harshav and Jonathan Chipman. Berkeley: University of California Press, 2006.

Zambelli, Paola, ed. *Astrologi hallucinati: Stars and the End of the World in Luther's Time.* Berlin: De Gruyter, 1983.

Zeldes, Nadia. "A Magical Event in Sicily: Notes and Clarifications in the Messianic Movement in Sicily." *Zion* 58.3 (1993): 347–63. [Hebrew]

Zeeden, Ernst Walter. ". . . denn Daniel lügt nicht: Daniels Prophetie über den Gang der Geschichte in der Exegese des Kirchenvaters Hieronymus und Martin Luthers, Von der Dominanz der Tradition über das Bibelwort." In *Recht und Reich im Zeitalter der Reformation: Festschrift für Horst Rabe*, edited by Christine Roll et al. 2nd ed. Frankfurt am Main: Peter Lang, 1997.

Zeitlin, Solomon. "The Origin of the Term Edom for Rome and the Roman Church." *Jewish Quarterly Review* 60 (1969/70): 262f.

Zfatman, Sara. *The Marriage of a Mortal Man and a She-Demon: The Transformations of a Motif in the Folk Narrative of Ashkenazi Jewry in the Sixteenth–Nineteenth Centuries.* Yiddish: Texts and Studies. Jerusalem: Akademon, 1987. [Hebrew]

———. "The Mayse-Bukh: An Old Yiddish Literary Genre." *Ha-sifrut* 28 (1979): 126–52. [Hebrew]

———. *Yiddish Narrative Prose from Ist Beginnings to "Shivhei ha-Besht" (1504–1814): An Annotated Bibliography.* Research Projects of the Institute of Jewish Studies Monograph Series 6. Jerusalem: University Press, 1985. [Hebrew]

Zika, Charles. *Reuchlin und die okkulte Tradition der Renaissance.* Pforzheimer Reuchlin-schriften 6. Sigmaringen: Thorbecke, 1998.

Zimmels, Hirsch Jakob. *Ashkenazim and Sephardim: Their Relations, Differences, and Problems as Reflected in the Rabbinical Responsa*. Library of Sephardic History and Thought 3. London: Oxford University Press, 1958. Reprint, Hoboken, NJ: Ktav, 1996.

Zimmer, Eric. "Jewish and Christian Hebraist Collaboration in Sixteenth Century Germany." *Jewish Quarterly Review* 71 (1980): 69–88.

———. "The Persecutions of 1096 as Reflected in Medieval and Modern Minhag Books." In *Facing the Cross: The Persecutions of 1096 in History and Historiography*, edited by Yom Tov Assis et al., 157–70. Jerusalem: Magnes Press, 2000. [Hebrew]

Zinberg, Israel. *A History of Jewish Literature*. Vol. 7, *Old Yiddish Literature from Its Origins to the Haskalah Period*. Cleveland, OH: Press of Case Western Reserve University, 1975.

Zobel, Moritz. *Gottes Gesalbter: Der Messias und die messianische Zeit in Talmud und Midrasch*. Berlin: Schocken, 1938.

Zöller, Sonja. "Judenfeindschaft in den Schwänken des 16. Jahrhunderts." *Daphnis* 23 (1994): 345–69.

Zunz, Leopold. *Literaturgeschichte der synagogalen Poesie*. Berlin: Gerschel, 1865. Reprint, Hildesheim: Olms, 1966.

———. "Eine merkwürdige Medaille." *Israelitische Annalen: Ein Centralblatt für Geschichte, Literatur und Cultur der Israeliten aller Zeiten und Länder* 2.17 (1840): 148–49; 2.18 (1840), 156–57.

———. *Die Ritus des synagogalen Gottesdienste: Geschichtlich entwickelt*. 2nd ed. Berlin: Lamm, 1919.

INDEX

CPSIA information can be obtained
at www.ICGtesting.com
Printed in the USA
LVHW030946101121
702890LV00004B/117